CLYMER®

YAMAHA

XT350 & TT350 • 1985-2000

The world's finest publisher of mechanical how-to manuals

PRIMEDIA
Business Directories & Books

P.O. Box 12901, Overland Park, Kansas 66282-2901

629.28775
YAMAHA
D

Copyright ©2002 PRIMEDIA Business Magazines & Media Inc.

FIRST EDITION
First Printing March, 1991
Second Printing November, 1993
Third Printing January, 1996

SECOND EDITION
First Printing September, 1997

THIRD EDITION
First Printing August, 2002

Printed in U.S.A.

CLYMER and colophon are registered trademarks of PRIMEDIA Business Magazines & Media Inc.

ISBN: 0-89287-835-5

Library of Congress: 2002109523

MEMBER
MOTORCYCLE INDUSTRY COUNCIL, INC.

TECHNICAL PHOTOGRAPHY: Ron Wright, with assistance by Jordan Engineering, Santa Ana, California.

TECHNICAL ILLUSTRATIONS: Steve Amos.

COVER: Mark Clifford Photography, Los Angeles, California.

TOOLS AND EQUIPMENT: K&L Supply Co. (www.klsupply.com)

CONTENTS

QUICK REFERENCE DATA

TIRE INFLATION PRESSURE

	Front tire	Rear tire
XT350		
Size	3.00-21-4PR	110/80-18-58P
Tire pressure		
0-198 lb. (0-90 kg)	18 psi (1.3 kg/cm^2)	22 psi (1.5 kg/cm^2)
Maximum load	22 psi (1.5 kg/cm^2)	26 psi (1.8 kg/cm^2)
High speed riding	22 psi (1.5 kg/cm^2)	26 psi (1.8 kg/cm^2)
TT350		
Size	80/100-21	100/100-18
Tire pressure	14 psi (1.0 kg/cm^2)	14 psi (1.0 kg/cm^2)

RECOMMENDED LUBRICANTS AND FUEL

Engine oil	Yamalube 4-cycle oil, SAE 20W40 or 10W30 SG motor oil
Front fork oil	10 weight fork oil
Air filter	Foam air filter oil
Drive chain	Chain lube recommended for O-ring drive chains
Control cables	Cable lube
Control lever pivots	10W/30 motor oil
Swing arm pivot shaft	Lithium base waterproof wheel bearing grease
Suspension pivot shaft	Molybdenum disulfide grease
Steering head bearings	Lithium base waterproof wheel bearing grease
Fuel	Regular grade—research octane 87 or higher
Brake fluid	DOT 3/DOT 4

APPROXIMATE REFILL CAPACITIES

Engine oil	
Periodic oil change	1,300 cc (1.37 qt.)
With filter change	1,400 cc (1.48 qt.)
Engine rebuild	1,600 cc (1.7 qt.)
Front fork (each)	
TT350	533 cc (18.76 oz.)
XT350	319 cc (10.8 oz.)
Front fork oil level	
XT350	*
TT350	125 mm (4.92 in.)
Fuel tank	
TT350	
Total	2.5 gal. (9.5 l)
Reserve	0.26 gal. (1.0 l)
XT350	
Total	3.2 gal. (12.0 l)
Reserve	0.5 gal. (2.0 l)

* Not specified by Yamaha.

CHAPTER ONE

GENERAL INFORMATION

This Clymer shop manual covers Yamaha XT350 models from 1985-on and Yamaha TT350 models from 1986-1987.

Troubleshooting, tune-up, maintenance and repair are not difficult, if you know what tools and equipment to use and what to do. Step-by-step instructions guide you through jobs ranging from simple maintenance to complete engine and suspension overhaul.

This manual can be used by anyone from a first time do-it-yourselfer to a professional mechanic. Detailed drawings and clear photographs give you all the information you need to do the work right.

Some of the procedures in this manual require the use of special tools. The resourceful mechanic can, in many cases, think of acceptable substitutes for special tools—there is always another way. This can be as simple as using a few pieces of threaded rod, washers and nuts to remove or install a bearing or fabricating a tool from scrap material. However, using a substitute for a special tool is not recommended as it can be dangerous to and may damage the part. If you find that a tool can be designed and safely made, but will require some type of machine work, you may want to search out a local community college or high school that has a machine shop curriculum. Shop teachers sometimes welcome outside work that can be used as practical shop applications for advanced students.

Table 1 lists model coverage with engine and chassis serial numbers.

Metric and U.S. standards are used throughout this manual. U.S. to metric conversion is given in **Table 2**. General torque specifications are given in **Table 3**.

Tables 1-3 are found at the end of the chapter.

MANUAL ORGANIZATION

This chapter provides general information and discusses equipment and tools useful both for preventive maintenance and troubleshooting.

Chapter Two provides methods and suggestions for quick and accurate diagnosis and repair of problems. Troubleshooting procedures discuss typical symptoms and logical methods to pinpoint the trouble.

Chapter Three explains all periodic lubrication and routine maintenance necessary to keep your Yamaha operating properly. Chapter Three also includes recommended tune-up procedures, eliminating the need to constantly consult other chapters on the various assemblies.

Subsequent chapters describe specific systems such as the engine top end, engine bottom end, clutch, transmission, fuel, exhaust, electrical, suspension, steering and brakes. Each chapter provides disassembly, repair, and assembly procedures in simple step-by-step form. If a repair is impractical for a home mechanic, it is so indicated. It is usually faster and less expensive to take such repairs to a dealer or competent repair shop. Specifications concerning a particular system are included at the end of the appropriate chapter.

NOTES, CAUTIONS AND WARNINGS

The terms NOTE, CAUTION and WARNING have specific meanings in this manual. A NOTE provides additional information to make a step or procedure easier or clearer. Disregarding a NOTE could cause inconvenience, but would not cause damage or personal injury.

A CAUTION emphasizes areas where equipment damage could occur. Disregarding a CAUTION could cause permanent mechanical damage; however, personal injury is unlikely.

A WARNING emphasizes areas where personal injury or even death could result from negligence. Mechanical damage may also occur. WARNINGS *are to be taken seriously*. In some cases, serious injury and death has resulted from disregarding similar warnings.

SAFETY FIRST

Professional mechanics can work for years and never sustain a serious injury. If you observe a few rules of common sense and safety, you can enjoy many safe hours servicing your own machine. If you ignore these rules you can hurt yourself or damage the equipment.
1. Never use gasoline as a cleaning solvent.
2. Never smoke or use a torch in the vicinity of flammable liquids, such as cleaning solvent, in open containers.
3. If welding or brazing is required on the machine, remove the fuel tank and rear shock to a safe distance, at least 50 feet away.
4. Use the proper sized wrenches to avoid damage to fasteners and injury to yourself.
5. When loosening a tight or stuck nut, be guided by what would happen if the wrench should slip. Be careful; protect yourself accordingly.

6. When replacing a fastener, make sure to use one with the same measurements and strength as the old one. Incorrect or mismatched fasteners can result in damage to the vehicle and possible personal injury. Beware of fastener kits that are filled with cheap and poorly made nuts, bolts, washers and cotter pins. Refer to *Fasteners* in this chapter for additional information.

7. Keep all hand and power tools in good condition. Wipe greasy and oily tools after using them. They are difficult to hold and can cause injury. Replace or repair worn or damaged tools.

8. Keep your work area clean and uncluttered.

9. Wear safety goggles during all operations involving drilling, grinding, the use of a cold chisel or anytime you feel unsure about the safety of your eyes. Safety goggles should also be worn anytime solvent and compressed air is used to clean a part.

10. Keep an approved fire extinguisher (**Figure 1**) nearby. Be sure it is rated for gasoline (Class B) and electrical (Class C) fires.

11. When drying bearings or other rotating parts with compressed air, never allow the air jet to rotate the bearing or part. The air jet is capable of rotating them at speeds far in excess of those for which they were designed. The bearing or rotating part is very likely to disintegrate and cause serious injury and damage. To prevent bearing damage when using compressed air, hold the inner bearing race by hand (**Figure 2**).

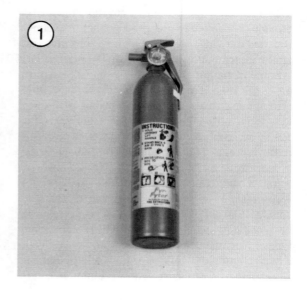

SERVICE HINTS

Most of the service procedures covered are straightforward and can be performed by anyone reasonably handy with tools. It is suggested, however, that you consider your own capabilities carefully before attempting any operation involving major disassembly of the engine or transmission.

1. "Front," as used in this manual, refers to the front of the motorcycle; the front of any component is the end closest to the front of the motorcycle. The "left-" and "right-hand" sides refer to the position of the parts as viewed by a rider sitting on the seat facing forward. For example, the throttle control is on the right-hand side. These rules are simple, but confusion can cause a major inconvenience during service.

2. Whenever servicing the engine or clutch, or when removing a suspension component, the bike should be secured in a safe manner. An excellent support for your Yamaha is a wooden box or stand. A sturdy box can be made with 3/4 in. plywood that will last a long time.

3. When disassembling any engine or suspension component, mark the parts for location and mark all parts which mate together. Small parts, such as bolts, can be identified by placing them in plastic sandwich bags. Seal the bags and label them with masking tape and a marking pen. When reassembly will take place immediately, an accepted practice is to place nuts and bolts in a cupcake tin or egg carton in the order of disassembly.

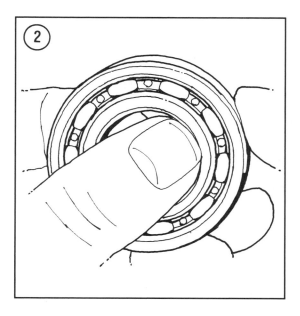

4. Finished surfaces should be protected from physical damage or corrosion. Keep gasoline and brake fluid off painted surfaces.

5. Use penetrating oil on frozen or tight bolts, then strike the bolt head a few times with a hammer and punch (use a screwdriver on screws). Avoid the use of heat where possible, as it can warp, melt or affect the temper of parts. Heat also ruins finishes, especially paint and plastics.

6. No parts removed or installed (other than bushings and bearings) in the procedures given in this manual should require unusual force during disassembly or assembly. If a part is difficult to remove or install, find out why before proceeding.

7. Cover all openings after removing parts or components to prevent dirt, small tools, etc. from falling in.

8. Read each procedure *completely* while looking at the actual parts before starting a job. Make sure you *thoroughly* understand what is to be done and then carefully follow the procedure, step-by-step.

9. Recommendations are occasionally made to refer service or maintenance to a Yamaha dealer or a specialist in a particular field. In these cases, the work will be done more quickly and economically than if you performed the job yourself.

10. In procedural steps, the term "replace" means to discard a defective part and replace it with a new or exchange unit. "Overhaul" means to remove, disassemble, inspect, measure, repair or replace defective parts, reassemble and install major systems or parts.

11. Some operations require the use of a hydraulic press. It would be wiser to have these operations performed by a shop equipped for such work, rather than to try to do the job yourself with makeshift equipment that may damage your machine.

12. Repairs go much faster and easier if your machine is clean before you begin work. There are many special cleaners on the market, like Bel-Ray Degreaser, for washing the engine and related parts. Follow the manufacturer's directions on the container for the best results. Clean all oily or greasy parts with cleaning solvent as you remove them. See *Washing the Bike* in this chapter.

WARNING
Never use gasoline as a cleaning agent.
It presents an extreme fire hazard. Be

sure to work in a well-ventilated area when using cleaning solvent. Keep a fire extinguisher, rated for gasoline fires, handy in any case.

CAUTION
If you use a car wash to clean your bike, don't direct the high pressure water hose at fork seals, steering bearings, carburetor hoses, suspension linkage components or wheel bearings. The water will flush grease out of the bearings or damage the seals. After washing your bike, remove the wheels and clean the wheel drums (if so equipped) of all water and dirt.

13. Much of the labor charges for repairs made by dealers are for the time involved during in the removal, disassembly, assembly, and reinstallation of other parts in order to reach the defective part. It is frequently possible to perform the preliminary operations yourself and then take the defective unit to the dealer for repair at considerable savings.
14. If special tools are required, make arrangements to get them before you start. It is frustrating and time-consuming to get partly into a job and then be unable to complete it.
15. Make diagrams (or take a Polaroid picture) wherever similar-appearing parts are found. For instance, crankcase bolts are often not the same length. You may think you can remember where everything came from—but mistakes are costly. There is also the possibility that you may be sidetracked and not return to work for days or even weeks—in which the time carefully laid out parts may have become disturbed.
16. When assembling parts, be sure all shims and washers are replaced exactly as they came out.
17. Whenever a rotating part butts against a stationary part, look for a shim or washer. Use new gaskets if there is any doubt about the condition of the old ones. A thin coat of oil on non-pressure type gaskets may help them seal more effectively.
18. If it is necessary to make a clutch cover or ignition cover gasket and you do not have a suitable old gasket to use as a guide, you can use the outline of the cover and gasket material to make a new gasket. Apply engine oil to the cover gasket

surface. Then place the cover on the new gasket material and apply pressure with your hands. The oil will leave a very accurate outline on the gasket material that can be cut around.

CAUTION
When purchasing gasket material to make a gasket, measure the thickness of the old gasket and purchase gasket material with the same approximate thickness.

19. Heavy grease can be used to hold small parts in place if they tend to fall out during assembly. However, keep grease and oil away from electrical and brake components.
20. A carburetor is best cleaned by disassembling it and soaking the parts in a commercial carburetor cleaner. Never soak gaskets and rubber parts in these cleaners. Never use wire to clean out jets and air passages. They are easily damaged. Use compressed air to blow out the carburetor only if the float has been removed first.
21. Take your time and do the job right. Do not forget that a newly rebuilt engine must be broken in just like a new one.

WASHING THE BIKE

The Yamaha TT350 is an off-road motorcycle and if you are riding it often and maintaining it properly, you will spend a good deal of time cleaning it. The same goes for the dual purpose XT350. After riding your Yamaha off-road, wash the bike. It will make maintenance and service procedures quick and easy. More important, proper cleaning will prevent dirt from falling into critical areas undetected. Failing to clean the bike or cleaning it incorrectly will add to your maintenance costs and shop time because dirty parts wear out prematurely. It's unthinkable that your bike could break because of improper cleaning, but it can happen.

When cleaning your Yamaha, you will need a few tools, shop rags, scrub brush, bucket, liquid cleaner and access to water. Many riders use a coin-operated car wash. Coin-operated car washes are convenient and quick, but with improper use, the high water pressures can do your bike more damage than good.

NOTE
A safe biodegradable, non-toxic and non-flammable liquid cleaner that works well for washing your bike as well as for removing grease and oil from engine and suspension parts is Simple Green. Simple Green can be purchased through some hardware, garden and discount supply houses. Follow the directions on the container for recommended dilution ratios.

When cleaning your bike, and especially when using a spray type degreaser, remember that what goes on the bike will rinse off and drip onto your driveway or into your yard. If you can, use a degreaser at a coin-operated car wash. If you are cleaning your bike at home, place thick cardboard or newspapers underneath the bike to catch the oil and grease deposits that are rinsed off.

CAUTION
The factory installed drive chain on all XT350 and TT350 models has O-rings installed between the chain plates. Lubrication for the chain pins is sealed by the O-rings (Figure 3). However, the chain rollers require external oiling. For the O-ring chain to work properly, it requires proper cleaning

and lubrication practices. Do not clean the O-ring drive chain with a high-pressure water hose, such as those found in coin-operated car washes. The high pressure can damage the O-rings and cause pre-mature chain failure.

If you are using a degreaser to clean your bike, note that the degreaser may damage the chain's rubber or neoprene O-rings. Always check that the degreaser is specified for use on O-ring type chains. See *Chain Cleaning* in Chapter Three for additional information on drive chain cleaning and lubrication. If possible, remove the drive chain before cleaning the bike.

1. Place the bike on a stand.
2. Check the following before washing the bike:
   a. Make sure the gas cap is screwed on tightly.
   b. Make sure the oil fill cap is tight.
   c. Plug the silencer opening with a large cork or rag.
3. Wash the bike from top to bottom with soapy water. Use the scrub brush to get excess dirt out of the wheel rims and engine crannies. Concentrate on the upper controls, engine, side panels and gas tank during this wash cycle. Don't forget to wash dirt and mud from underneath the fenders.
4. Remove the gas tank, side panels and seat. Wrap a plastic bag around the ignition coil and CDI unit.

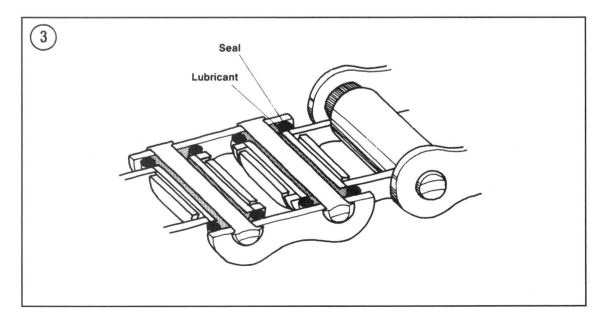

③

Seal

Lubricant

Concentrate the second wash cycle on the frame tube members, outer airbox areas, suspension linkage, rear shock and swing arm.

5. Direct the hose underneath the engine and swing arm. Wash this area thoroughly. If this area is extremely dirty, you may want to lay the bike on its side.

6. The final wash is the rinse. Use cold water without soap and spray the whole motorcycle again. Use as much time and care when rinsing the bike as when washing it. Built up soap deposits will quickly corrode electrical connections and remove the natural oils from tires, causing premature cracks and wear. Make sure you thoroughly rinse the bike off.

7. If you are washing the bike at home, start the engine. Idle the engine to burn off any internal moisture. Idle the bike long enough to use the gas remaining in the float bowl. This will prevent fuel leakage problems when cleaning the carburetor later.

8. Before taking the bike into the garage, wipe it dry with a shop rag. Inspect the machine as you dry it for further signs of dirt and grime. Make a quick visual inspection of the frame and other painted pieces. Spray any worn-down spots with WD-40 or Bel-Ray 6-in-1 to prevent rust from building on the bare metal. When the bike is back at your work area you can repaint the bare areas with touch-up paint. A quick shot from a paint can each time you work on the bike will keep it looking sharp and stop rust from building and weakening parts.

9. Lubricate the drive chain with a specially approved drive chain lubricant specified for O-ring use. See Chapter Three.

TORQUE SPECIFICATIONS

Torque specifications throughout this manual are given in Newton-meters (N·m) and foot-pounds (ft.-lb.).

Table 3 lists general torque specifications for nuts and bolts that are not listed in the respective chapters. To use the table, first determine the size of the nut or bolt by measuring it with a vernier caliper. **Figure 4** and **Figure 5** show how to do this.

FASTENERS

The materials and designs of the various fasteners used on your Yamaha are not arrived at

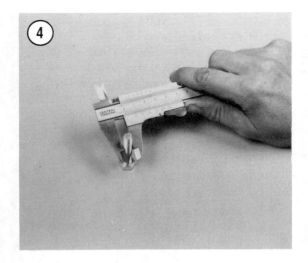

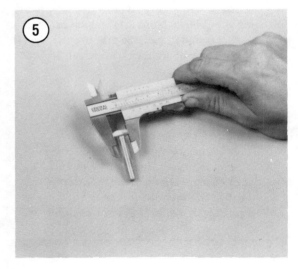

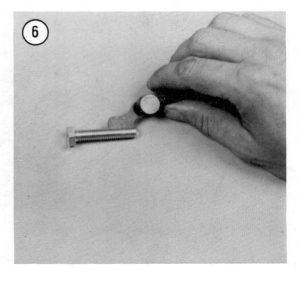

by chance or accident. Fastener design determines the type of tool required to work the fastener. Fastener material is carefully selected to decrease the possibility of physical failure.

Nuts, bolts and screws are manufactured in a wide range of thread patterns. To join a nut and bolt, the diameter of the bolt and the diameter of the hole in the nut must be the same. It is just as important that the threads on both be properly matched.

The best way to tell if the threads on 2 fasteners are matched is to turn the nut on the bolt (or the bolt into the threaded hole in a piece of equipment)

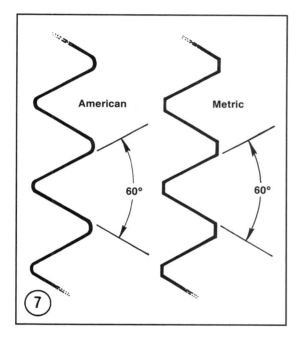

(7)

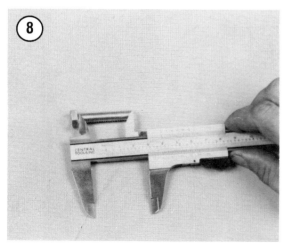

(8)

with fingers only. Be sure both pieces are clean. If much force is required, check the thread condition on each fastener. If the thread condition is good but the fasteners jam, the threads are not compatible. A thread pitch gauge (**Figure 6**) can also be used to determine pitch. Yamaha motorcycles are manufactured with ISO (International Organization for Standardization) metric fasteners. The threads are cut differently than that of American fasteners (**Figure 7**). Most threads are cut so that the fastener must be turned clockwise to tighten it. These are called right-hand threads. Some fasteners have left-hand threads; they must be turned counterclockwise to be tightened. Left-hand threads are used in locations where normal rotation of the equipment would tend to loosen a right-hand threaded fastener.

ISO Metric Screw Threads

ISO (International Organization for Standardization) metric threads come in 3 standard thread sizes: coarse, fine and constant pitch. The ISO coarse pitch is used for most all common fastener applications. The fine pitch thread is used on certain precision tools and instruments. The constant pitch thread is used mainly on machine parts and not for fasteners. The constant pitch thread, however, is used on all metric thread spark plugs. ISO metric threads are specified by the capital letter M followed by the diameter in millimeters and the pitch (or the distance between each thread) in millimeters separated by the sign $\times$. For example a M8 $\times$ 1.25 bolt is one that has a diameter of 8 millimeters with a distance of 1.25 millimeters between each thread. The measurement across 2 flats on the head of the bolt indicates the proper wrench size to be used. **Figure 4** shows how to determine bolt diameter.

NOTE
*When purchasing a bolt from a dealer or parts store, it is important to know how to specify bolt length. The correct way to measure bolt length is by measuring the length starting from underneath the bolt head to the end of the bolt (**Figure 8**). Always measure bolt length in this manner to prevent from purchasing bolts that are too long.*

Machine Screws

There are many different types of machine screws. **Figure 9** shows a number of screw heads requiring different types of turning tools. Heads are also designed to protrude above the metal (round) or to be slightly recessed in the metal (flat). See **Figure 10**.

Bolts

Commonly called bolts, the technical name for these fasteners is cap screw. Metric bolts are described by the diameter and pitch (or the distance between each thread).

Nuts

Nuts are manufactured in a variety of types and sizes. Most are hexagonal (6-sided) and fit on bolts, screws and studs with the same diameter and pitch. **Figure 11** shows several types of nuts. The common nut is generally used with a lockwasher.

Self-locking nuts have a nylon insert which prevents the nut from loosening; no lockwasher is required. Wing nuts are designed for fast removal by hand. Wing nuts are used for convenience in non-critical locations.

To indicate the size of a metric nut, manufacturers specify the diameter of the opening and the thread pitch. This is similar to bolt specifications, but without the length dimension. The measurement across 2 flats on the nut indicates the proper wrench size to be used.

Self-Locking Fasteners

Several types of bolts, screws and nuts incorporate a system that develops an interference between the bolt, screw, nut or tapped hole threads. Interference is achieved in various ways: by distorting threads, coating threads with dry adhesive or nylon, distorting the top of an all-metal nut, using a nylon insert in the center or at the top of a nut, etc.

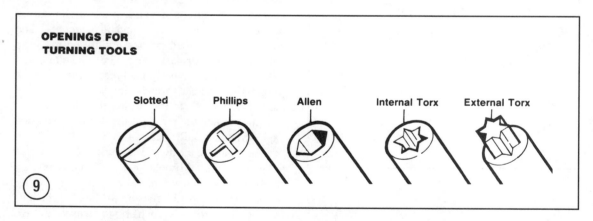

OPENINGS FOR TURNING TOOLS

Slotted   Phillips   Allen   Internal Torx   External Torx

⑨

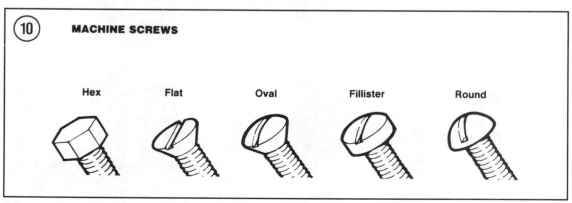

⑩   **MACHINE SCREWS**

Hex   Flat   Oval   Fillister   Round

Self-locking fasteners offer greater holding strength and better vibration resistance. Some self-locking fasteners can be reused if in good condition. Others, like the nylon insert nut, form an initial locking condition when the nut is first installed; the nylon forms closely to the bolt thread pattern, thus reducing any tendency for the nut to loosen. When the nut is removed, its locking efficiency is greatly reduced. For greatest safety, it is recommended that you install new self-locking fasteners whenever they are removed.

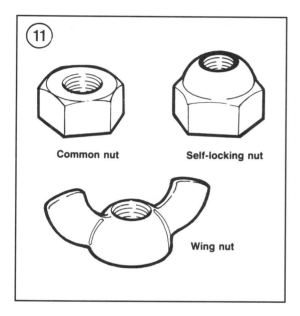

Common nut   Self-locking nut

Wing nut

Washers

There are 2 basic types of washers: flat washers and lockwashers. Flat washers are simple discs with a hole to fit a screw or bolt. Lockwashers are designed to prevent a fastener from working loose due to vibration, expansion and contraction. **Figure 12** shows several types of washers. Washers are also used in the following functions:

  a. As spacers.
  b. To prevent galling or damage of the equipment by the fastener.
  c. To help distribute fastener load during torquing.
  d. As seals.

Note that flat washers are often used between a lockwasher and a fastener to provide a smooth bearing surface. This allows the fastener to be turned easily with a tool.

Cotter Pins

Cotter pins (**Figure 13**) are used to secure special kinds of fasteners. The threaded stud must have a hole in it; the nut or nut lock piece has castellations around which the cotter pin ends wrap. Cotter pins should not be reused after removal.

Circlips

Circlips can be internal or external design. They are used to retain items on shafts (external type)

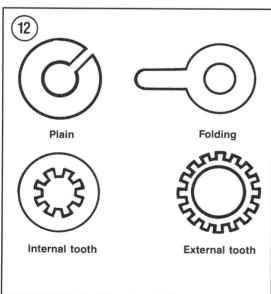

Plain   Folding

Internal tooth   External tooth

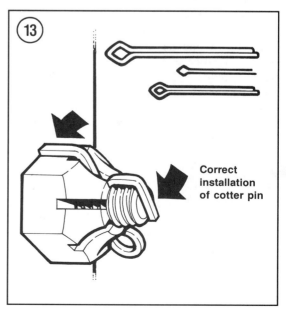

Correct installation of cotter pin

or within tubes (internal type). In some applications, circlips of varying thicknesses are used to control the end play of parts assemblies. These are often called selective circlips. Circlips should be replaced during installation, as removal weakens and deforms them.

Two basic styles of circlips are available: machined and stamped circlips. Machined circlips (**Figure 14**) can be installed in either direction (shaft or housing) because both faces are machined, thus creating two sharp edges. Stamped circlips (**Figure 15**) are manufactured with one sharp edge and one rounded edge. When installing stamped circlips in a thrust situation (transmission shafts, fork tubes, etc.), the sharp edge must face away from the part producing the thrust. When installing circlips, observe the following:

    a. Compress or expand circlips only enough to install them.

    b. After the circlip is installed, make sure it is completely seated in its groove.

LUBRICANTS

Periodic lubrication assures long life for any type of equipment. The *type* of lubricant used is just as important as the lubrication service itself, although in an emergency the wrong type of lubricant is better than none at all. The following paragraphs describe the types of lubricants most often used on motorcycle equipment. Be sure to follow the manufacturer's recommendations for lubricant types.

Generally all liquid lubricants are called "oil." They may be mineral-based (including petroleum bases), natural-based (vegetable and animal bases), synthetic-based or emulsions (mixtures). "Grease" is an oil to which a thickening base has been added so that the end product is semi-solid. Grease is often classified by the type of thickener added; lithium soap is commonly used.

Engine Oil

Four-stroke oil for motorcycle and automotive engines is graded by the American Petroleum Institute (API) and the Society of Automotive Engineers (SAE) in several categories. Oil containers display these ratings on the top or label.

API oil grade is indicated by letters; oils for gasoline engines are identified by an "S." Yamaha

models described in this manual require SG graded oil.

Viscosity is an indicator of the oil's thickness. The SAE uses numbers to indicate viscosity; thin oils have low numbers while thick oils have high numbers. A "W" after the number indicates that

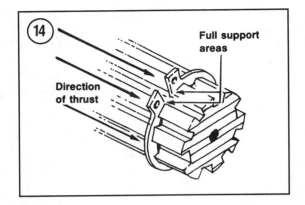

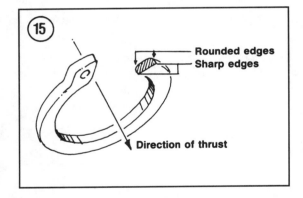

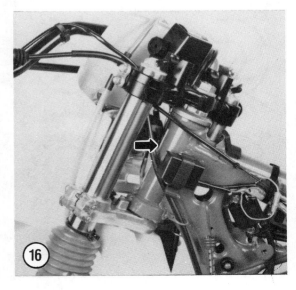

the viscosity testing was done at a low temperature to simulate cold-weather operation. Engine oils fall into the 5W-30 and 20W-50 range.

Multi-grade oils (for example 10W-40) are less viscous (thinner) at low temperatures and more viscous (thicker) at high temperatures. This allows the oil to perform efficiently across a wide range of engine operating conditions. The lower the number, the better the engine will start in cold climates. Higher numbers are usually recommended for engine running in hot weather conditions.

Grease

Greases are graded by the National Lubricating Grease Institute (NLGI). Greases are graded by

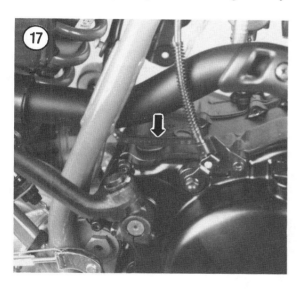

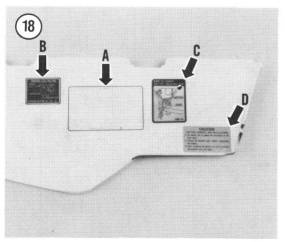

number according to the consistency of the grease; these range from No. 000 to No. 6, with No. 6 being the most solid. A typical multipurpose grease is NLGI No. 2. For specific applications, equipment manufacturers may require grease with an additive such as molybdenum disulfide (MOS2).

PARTS REPLACEMENT

Yamaha makes frequent changes during a model year, some minor, some relatively major. When you order parts from the dealer or other parts distributor, always order by frame and engine numbers. The frame number and the vehicle identification number are stamped on the steering head pipe (**Figure 16**). The engine number is stamped on a raised boss on the right-hand crankcase (**Figure 17**). Write the numbers down and carry them with you. Compare new parts to old before purchasing them. If they are not alike, have the parts manager explain the difference to you. **Table 1** lists engine and frame serial numbers for XT350 and TT350 models covered in this manual.

NOTE
*If your Yamaha was purchased second-hand and you are not sure of its model year, use the bike's engine serial number and the information listed in **Table 1**. Read your bike's engine serial number. Then compare the number with the engine and serial numbers listed in **Table 1**. If your bike's serial number is listed in **Table 1**, cross-reference the number with the adjacent model number and year.*

EMISSION CONTROL AND BATTERY DECALS (XT350)

A vehicle emission control information decal (A, **Figure 18**) is fixed to the backside of the right-hand side cover. This decal lists all emission control related tune-up information.

On California models, an emission hose routing label (B, **Figure 18**) is also fixed to the back of the side cover.

A battery breather hose diagram (C, **Figure 18**) and a battery caution label (D, **Figure 18**) are fixed to the back of the side cover. Refer to these whenever servicing or removing the battery for service.

BASIC HAND TOOLS

Many of the procedures in this manual can be carried out with simple hand tools and test equipment familiar to the average home mechanic. Keep your tools clean and in a tool box. Keep them organized with the sockets and related drives together, the open-end combination wrenches together, etc. After using a tool, wipe off dirt and grease with a clean cloth and return the tool to its correct place.

Top-quality tools are essential; they are also more economical in the long run. If you are now starting to build your tool collection, stay away from the "advertised specials" featured at some parts houses, discount stores and chain drug stores. These are usually a poor grade tool that can be sold cheaply and that is exactly what they are—*cheap*. They are usually made of inferior material, and are thick, heavy and clumsy. Their rough finish makes them difficult to clean and they usually don't last very long. If it is ever your misfortune to use such tools, you will probably find out that the wrenches do not fit the heads of bolts and nuts correctly and damage the fastener.

Quality tools are made of alloy steel and are heat treated for greater strength. They are lighter and better balanced than cheap ones. Their surface is smooth, making them a pleasure to work with and easy to clean. The initial cost of good-quality tools may be more but they are cheaper in the long run. Don't try to buy everything in all sizes in the beginning; do it a little at a time until you have the necessary tools.

The following tools are required to perform virtually any repair job. Each tool is described and the recommended size given for starting a tool collection. Additional tools and some duplicates may be added as you become familiar with the vehicle. Yamaha motorcycles are built with metric standard fasteners—so if you are starting your collection now, buy metric sizes.

Screwdrivers

The screwdriver is a very basic tool, but if used improperly it will do more damage than good. The slot on a screw has a definite dimension and shape. A screwdriver must be selected to conform with that shape. Use a small screwdriver for small screws and a large one for large screws or the screw head will be damaged.

Two basic types of screwdriver are required: common (flat-blade) screwdrivers (**Figure 19**) and Phillips screwdrivers (**Figure 20**).

Screwdrivers are available in sets which often include an assortment of common and Phillips blades. If you buy them individually, buy at least the following:

a. Common screwdriver—5/16 × 6 in. blade.
b. Common screwdriver—3/8 × 12 in. blade.
c. Phillips screwdriver—size 2 tip, 6 in. blade.

Use screwdrivers only for driving screws. Never use a screwdriver for prying or chiseling metal. Do not try to remove a Phillips or Allen head screw with a common screwdriver (unless the screw has

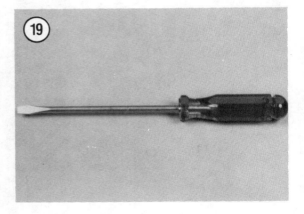

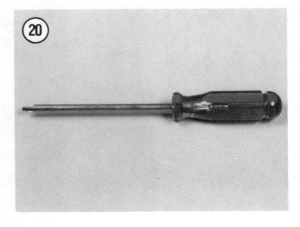

a combination head that will accept either type); you can damage the head so that the proper tool will be unable to remove it.

Keep screwdrivers in the proper condition and they will last longer and perform better. Always keep the tip of a common screwdriver in good condition. **Figure 21** shows how to grind the tip to the proper shape if it becomes damaged. Note the symmetrical sides of the tip.

Pliers

Pliers come in a wide range of types and sizes. Pliers are useful for cutting, bending and crimping. They should never be used to cut hardened objects or to turn bolts or nuts. **Figure 22** shows several pliers useful in motorcycle repairs.

Each type of pliers has a specialized function. Gas pliers are general purpose pliers and are used mainly for holding things and for bending. Needlenose pliers are used to hold or bend small objects. Waterpump pliers (commonly referred to as channel locks) can be adjusted to hold various sizes of objects; the jaws remain parallel to grip around objects such as pipe or tubing. There are many more types of pliers.

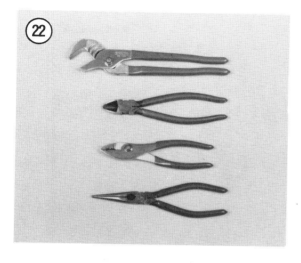

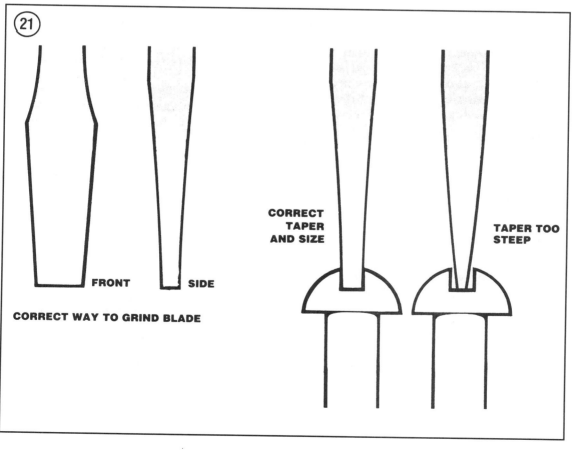

Vise-Grip Pliers

Vise-grip pliers (**Figure 23**) are used as pliers or to hold objects very tightly while another task is performed on the object. Vise-grips are available in many types for more specific tasks.

Circlip Pliers

Circlip pliers (**Figure 24**) are special in that they are only used to remove circlips from shafts or within engine or suspension housings. When purchasing circlip pliers, there are two kinds to distinguish from. External pliers (spreading) are used to remove circlips that fit on the outside of a shaft. Internal pliers (squeezing) are used to remove circlips which fit inside a gear or housing.

Box-end and Open-end Wrenches

Box-end and open-end wrenches (**Figure 25**) are available in sets or separately in a variety of sizes. The size number stamped near the end refers to the distance between 2 parallel flats on the hex head bolt or nut.

Box-end wrenches are usually superior to open-end wrenches. Open-end wrenches grip the nut on only 2 flats. Unless a wrench fits well, it may slip and round off the points on the nut. The box-end wrench grips on all 6 flats. Both 6-point and 12-point openings on box wrenches are available. The 6-point gives superior holding power; the 12-point allows a shorter swing.

Combination wrenches which are open on one side and boxed on the other are also available. Both ends are the same size. See **Figure 26**.

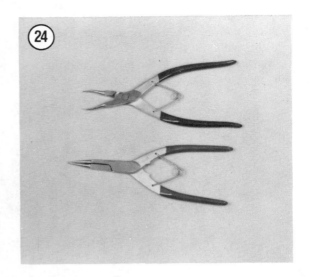

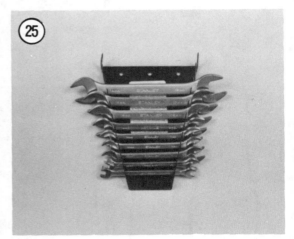

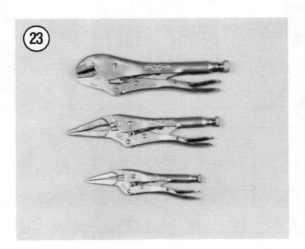

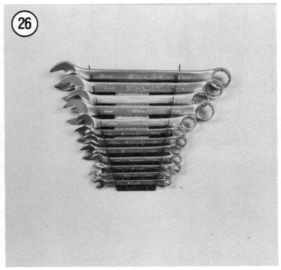

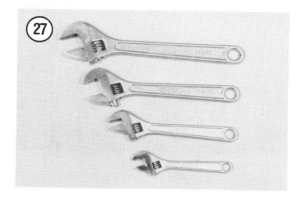

Adjustable Wrenches

An adjustable wrench can be adjusted to fit a variety of nuts or bolt heads (**Figure 27**). However, it can loosen and slip, causing damage to the nut and perhaps to your knuckles. Use an adjustable wrench only when other wrenches are not available.

Adjustable wrenches come in various sizes.

Socket Wrenches

This type is undoubtedly the fastest, safest and most convenient to use. Sockets which attach to a ratchet handle (**Figure 28**) are available with 6-point or 12-point openings and 1/4, 3/8, 1/2 and 3/4 in. drives (**Figure 29**). The drive size indicates the size of the square hole which mates with the ratchet handle.

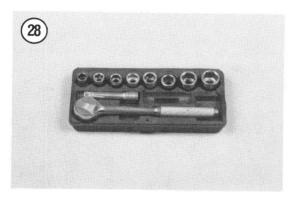

Torque Wrench

A torque wrench (**Figure 30**) is used with a socket to measure how tightly a nut or bolt is installed. They come in a wide price range and with either 3/8 or 1/2 in. square drive. The drive size indicates the size of the square drive which mates with the socket.

Impact Driver

This tool makes removal of tight fasteners easy and eliminates damage to bolts and screw slots. Impact drivers and interchangeable bits (**Figure 31**) are available at most large hardware and motorcycle dealers. Sockets can also be used with a hand impact driver. However, make sure the socket is designed for impact use. Do not use regular hand type sockets, as they may shatter.

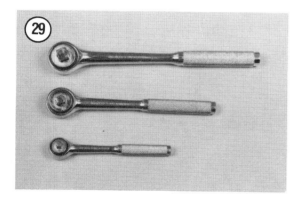

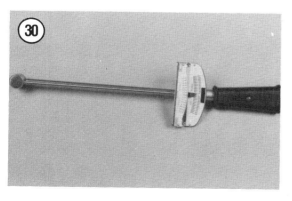

Hammers

The correct hammer (**Figure 32**) is necessary for repairs. Use only a hammer with a face (or head) of rubber or plastic or the soft-faced type that is filled with buckshot. These are sometimes necessary in engine teardowns. *Never* use a metal-faced hammer on engine or suspension parts, as severe damage will result in most cases. You can always produce the same amount of force with a soft-faced hammer. A metal-faced hammer, however, will be required when using a hand impact driver.

PRECISION MEASURING TOOLS

Precision measuring is an important part of motorcycle service. When performing many of the service procedures in this manual, you will be required to make a number of measurements. These include basic checks such as valve clearance, engine compression and spark plug gap. As you get deeper into engine disassembly and service, measurements will be required to determine the condition of the piston and cylinder bore, valve and guide wear, camshaft wear, crankshaft runout and so on. When making these measurements, the degree of accuracy will dictate which tool is required. Precision measuring tools are expensive. If this is your first experience at engine or suspension service, it may be more worthwhile to have the checks made at a dealer. However, as your skills and enthusiasm increase for doing your own service work, you may want to begin purchasing some of these specialized tools. The following is a description of the measuring tools required during engine and suspension overhaul.

Feeler Gauge

The feeler gauge (**Figure 33**) is made of either a piece of a flat or round hardened steel of a specified thickness. Wire gauges (A) are used to measure spark plug gap. Flat gauges (B) are used for all other measurements. Feeler gauges are also designed for specialized uses, such as for measuring valve clearances (C). On these gauges, the gauge end is usually small enough and angled so as to make checking valve clearances easier.

Vernier Caliper

This tool is invaluable when reading inside, outside and depth measurements to within close precision. It can be used to measure clutch spring length and the thickness of clutch plates, shims and thrust washers. See **Figure 34**.

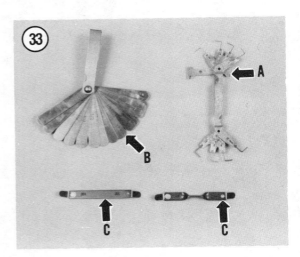

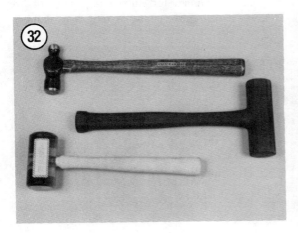

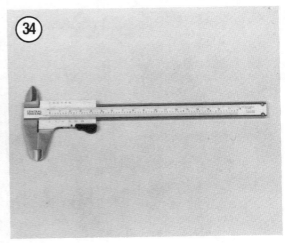

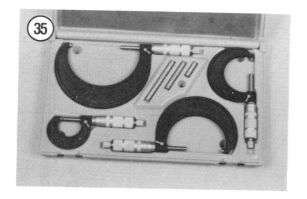

Outside Micrometers

One of the most reliable tools used for precision measurement is the outside micrometer (**Figure 35**). Outside micrometers will be required to measure valve shim thickness, piston diameter and valve stem diameter. Outside micrometers are also used with other tools to measure the cylinder bore and the valve guide inside diameters. Micrometers can be purchased individually or as a set.

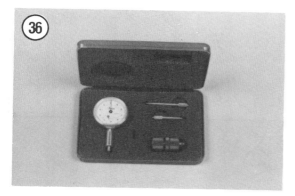

Dial Indicator

Dial indicators (**Figure 36**) are precision tools used to check dimension variations on machined parts such as transmission shafts and axles and to check crankshaft and axle shaft end play. Dial indicators are available with various dial types for different measuring requirements. For motorcycle repair, select a dial indicator with a continuous dial.

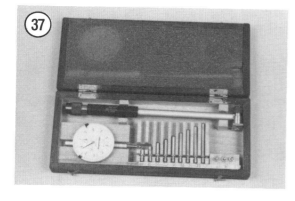

Cylinder Bore Gauge

The cylinder bore gauge is a very specialized precision tool. The gauge set shown in **Figure 37** is comprised of a dial indicator, handle and a number of length adapters to adapt the gauge to different bore sizes. The bore gauge can be used to make cylinder bore measurements such as bore size, taper and out-of-round. Depending on the bore gauge, it can sometimes be used to measure brake caliper and master cylinder bore sizes. An outside micrometer must be used together with the bore gauge to determine bore dimensions.

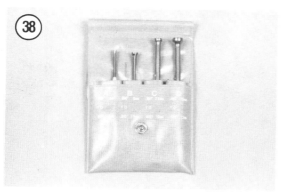

Small Hole Gauges

A set of small hole gauges (**Figure 38**) allow you to measure a hole, groove or slot ranging in size up to 13 mm (0.500 in.). A small hole gauge will be required to measure valve guide, brake caliper and brake master cylinder bore diameters. An outside micrometer must be used together with the small hole gauge to determine bore dimensions.

Compression Gauge

An engine with low compression cannot be properly tuned and will not develop full power. A compression gauge (**Figure 39**) measures engine compression. The one shown has a flexible stem with an extension that can allow you to hold it while kicking the engine over. Open the throttle all the way when checking engine compression. See Chapter Three.

Strobe Timing Light

This instrument is useful for checking ignition timing. By flashing a light at the precise instant the spark plug fires, the position of the timing mark can be seen. The flashing light makes a moving mark appear to stand still opposite a stationary mark.

Suitable lights range from inexpensive neon bulb types to powerful xenon strobe lights. See **Figure 40**. A light with an inductive pickup is recommended to eliminate any possible damage to ignition wiring.

When using a strobe timing light to check the ignition timing on TT350 models, you will also need a 6-volt battery to connect to the timing light.

Multimeter or VOM

This instrument (**Figure 41**) is invaluable for electrical system troubleshooting. See *Electrical Troubleshooting* in Chapter Nine for its use.

Battery Hydrometer

A hydrometer (**Figure 42**) is the best way to check a battery's state of charge. A hydrometer measures the weight or density of the sulfuric acid in the battery's electrolyte in specific gravity.

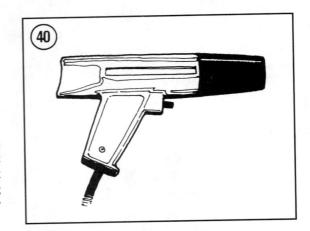

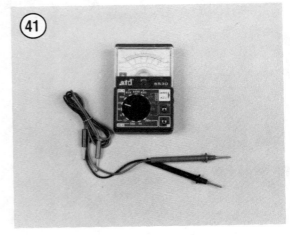

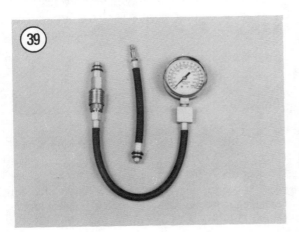

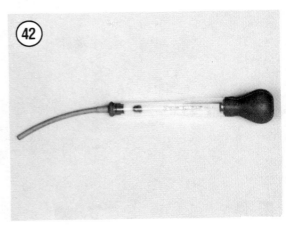

Screw Pitch Gauge

A screw pitch gauge (**Figure 43**) determines the thread pitch of bolts, screws, studs, etc. The gauge is made up of a number of thin plates. Each plate has a thread shape cut on one edge to match one thread pitch. When using a screw pitch gauge to determine a thread pitch size, try to fit different blade sizes onto the bolt thread until both threads match (**Figure 44**).

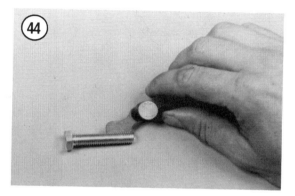

Plastigage

Plastigage (**Figure 45**) is a wax-like material sold in a flat color-coded envelope. The outside of the envelope is marked in both millimeters and thousandths of an inch. The color of the envelope specifies the specific clearance range of the Plastigage. Plastigage is used to measure camshaft, crankshaft and connecting rod bearing clearances.

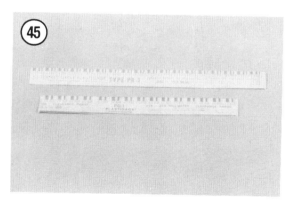

Magnetic Stand

A magnetic stand (**Figure 46**) is used to securely hold a dial indicator when checking the runout of a round object or when checking the end play of a shaft.

V-Blocks

V-blocks (**Figure 47**) are precision ground blocks used to hold a round object when checking its runout or condition. In motorcycle repair, V-blocks can be used when checking the runout of such items as valve stems, camshaft, balancer shaft, crankshaft, wheel axles and fork tubes.

SPECIAL TOOLS

This section describes special tools unique to motorcycle service and repair.

A few special tools may be required for major service. These are described in the appropriate chapters and are available either from Yamaha dealers or other manufacturers as indicated.

Spoke Wrench

This special wrench is used to tighten wheel spokes (**Figure 48**). Always use the correct size wrench to prevent from rounding out and damaging the spoke nipple.

The Grabbit

The Grabbit (**Figure 49**) is a special tool used to hold the clutch boss when removing the clutch nut and to secure the drive sprocket when removing the sprocket nut.

Tire Levers

When riding and maintaining an off-road or dual purpose motorcycle, get use to changing tires. To prevent from pinching tubes during tire changing, purchase a good set of tire levers (**Figure 50**). Never use a screwdriver in place of a tire lever; refer to Chapter Ten for its use. Before using a tire lever, check the working end of the tool and remove any burrs. Don't use a tire lever for prying anything but tires.

Flywheel Puller

A flywheel puller will be required whenever it is necessary to remove the rotor and service the stator plate assembly or when adjusting the ignition timing. In addition, when disassembling the engine, the rotor must be removed before the crankcases can be split. There is no satisfactory substitute for this tool. Because the rotor is a taper fit on the crankshaft, makeshift removal often results in crankshaft and rotor damage. Don't think about removing the rotor without this tool.

Chain Breaker

A chain breaker (**Figure 51**) is a useful tool for cutting a drive chain to size. Attempting to cut a drive chain using improper methods or tools may cause chain damage.

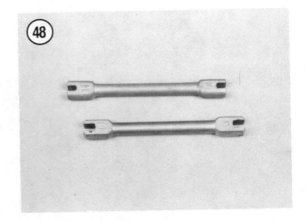

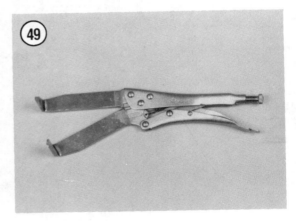

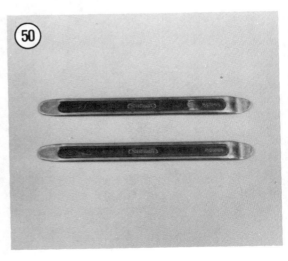

Fork Oil Level Gauge

When changing your Yamaha's front fork oil (TT350), you will find 2 different oil specifications: front fork oil capacity in cubic centimeters and front fork oil level in millimeters. To obtain maximum performance from your front forks, a fork oil level gauge (**Figure 52**) should be used to measure the fork oil level after pouring in the premeasured amount of fork oil. The oil level gauge allows excess oil to be removed without having to remove the drain screw and attempting to remove a small quantity of oil.

Expendable Supplies

Certain expendable supplies are also required. These include grease, oil, gasket cement, shop rags and cleaning solvent. Ask your dealer for the special locking compounds, silicone lubricants and lube products which make vehicle maintenance simpler and easier. Cleaning solvent is available at some service stations.

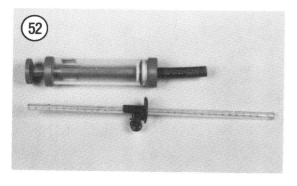

WARNING
Having a stack of clean shop rags on hand is important when performing engine and suspension service work. However, to prevent the possibility of fire damage from spontaneous combustion from a pile of solvent soaked rags, store them in a lid sealed metal container until they can be washed or discarded.

NOTE
To prevent from absorbing solvent and other chemicals into your skin while cleaning parts, wear a pair of petroleum-resistant rubber gloves. These can be purchased through industrial supply houses or well-equipped hardware stores.

MECHANIC'S TIPS

Removing Frozen Nuts and Screws

When a fastener rusts and cannot be removed, several methods may be used to loosen it. First, apply penetrating oil such as Liquid Wrench or WD-40 (available at hardware or auto supply stores). Apply it liberally and let it penetrate for 10-15 minutes. Rap the fastener several times with a small hammer; do not hit it hard enough to cause damage. Reapply the penetrating oil if necessary.

For frozen screws, apply penetrating oil as described, then insert a screwdriver in the slot and rap the top of the screwdriver with a hammer. This loosens the rust so the screw can be removed in the normal way. If the screw head is too chewed up to use this method, grip the head with Vise-grip pliers and twist the screw out.

Avoid applying heat unless specifically instructed, as it may melt, warp or remove the temper from parts.

Removing Broken Screws or Bolts

When the head breaks off a screw or bolt, several methods are available for removing the remaining portion.

If a large portion of the remainder projects out, try gripping it with Vise-grip pliers. If the projecting portion is too small, file it to fit a wrench or cut a slot in it to fit a screwdriver. See **Figure 53**.

If the head breaks off flush, use a screw extractor. To do this, centerpunch the exact center of the remaining portion of the screw or bolt. Drill a small hole in the screw and tap the extractor into the hole. Back the screw out with a wrench on the extractor. See **Figure 54**.

Remedying Stripped Threads

Occasionally, threads are stripped through carelessness or impact damage. Often the threads can be cleaned up by running a tap (for internal threads on nuts) or die (for external threads on bolts) through the threads. See **Figure 55**. To clean or repair spark plug threads, a spark plug tap can be used (**Figure 56**).

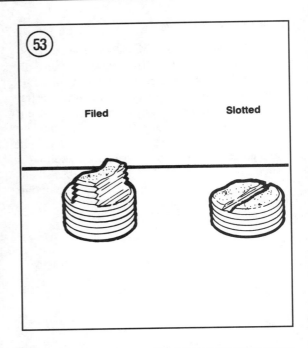

Filed   Slotted

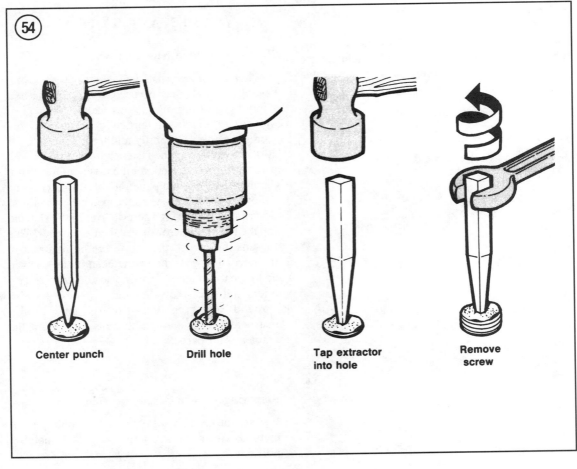

Center punch   Drill hole   Tap extractor into hole   Remove screw

NOTE
Tap and dies can be purchased individually or in a set as shown in **Figure 57**.

If an internal thread is damaged, it may be necessary to install a helicoil (**Figure 58**) or some other type of thread insert. Follow the manufacturer's instructions when installing the insert.

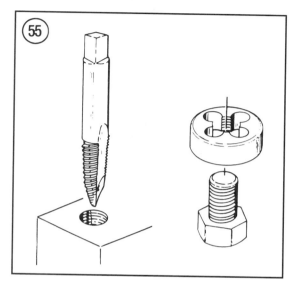

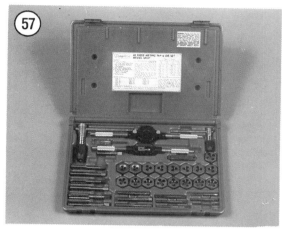

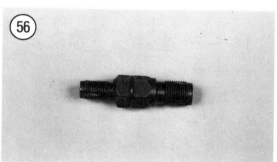

Table 1 ENGINE AND CHASSIS NUMBERS

Model number	Year	Engine/frame serial No.
TT350S	1986	1RG-000101-015100
TT350T	1987	1RG-015101-on
XT350N	1985	57T-000101-007100
XT350NC	1985	56R-000101-on
XT350S	1986	57T-007101-on
XT350SC	1986	56R-000101-001100
XT350T	1987	2KJ-000101-008100
XT350TC	1987	2GK-000101-002100
XT350U	1988	2KJ-008101-on
XT350UC	1988	2GK-002101-on
XT350W	1989	3NV-000101-on
XT350WC	1989	3NV-004101-on
XT350A	1990	3NV-005101-on
XT350AC	1990	3NV-008101-on
XT350B	1991	3NV-010101-on
	(continued)	

Table 1 ENGINE AND CHASSIS NUMBERS (continued)

Model number	Year	Engine/frame serial No.
XT350BC	1991	3NV-014101-on
XT350D	1992	3NV-013101-on
XT350DC	1992	3NV-018101-on
XT350E	1993	3NV-021101-on
XT350EC	1993	3NV-023101-on
XT350F	1994	3NV-026101-on
XT350FC	1994	3NV-029101-on
XT350G	1995	3NV-031101-on
XT350GC	1995	3NV-033101-on
XT350H	1996	3NV-035101-on
XT350HC	1996	3NV-038101-on
XT350J	1997	3NV-041271-on
XT350JC	1997	3NV-041271-on
XT350K	1998	3NV-041271-on
XT350KC	1998	3NV-041271-on
XT350L	1999	Not available
XT350LC	1999	Not available
XT350M	2000	JYA3NVEO-YA048150
XT350MC	2000	JYA3NVCO-YA048494

Table 2 DECIMAL AND METRIC EQUIVALENTS

Fractions	Decimal in.	Metric mm	Fractions	Decimal in.	Metric mm
1/64	0.015625	0.39688	33/64	0.515625	13.09687
1/32	0.03125	0.79375	17/32	0.53125	13.49375
3/64	0.046875	1.19062	35/64	0.546875	13.89062
1/16	0.0625	1.58750	9/16	0.5625	14.28750
5/64	0.078125	1.98437	37/64	0.578125	14.68437
3/32	0.09375	2.38125	19/32	0.59375	15.08125
7/64	0.109375	2.77812	39/64	0.609375	15.47812
1/8	0.125	3.1750	5/8	0.625	15.87500
9/64	0.140625	3.57187	41/64	0.640625	16.27187
5/32	0.15625	3.96875	21/32	0.65625	16.66875
11/64	0.171875	4.36562	43/64	0.671875	17.06562
3/16	0.1875	4.76250	11/16	0.6875	17.46250
13/64	0.203125	5.15937	45/64	0.703125	17.85937
7/32	0.21875	5.55625	23/32	0.71875	18.25625
15/64	0.234375	5.95312	47/64	0.734375	18.65312
1/4	0.250	6.35000	3/4	0.750	19.05000
17/64	0.265625	6.74687	49/64	0.765625	19.44687
9/32	0.28125	7.14375	25/32	0.78125	19.84375
19/64	0.296875	7.54062	51/64	0.796875	20.24062
5/16	0.3125	7.93750	13/16	0.8125	20.63750
21/64	0.328125	8.33437	53/64	0.828125	21.03437
11/32	0.34375	8.73125	27/32	0.84375	21.43125
23/64	0.359375	9.12812	55/64	0.859375	22.82812
3/8	0.375	9.52500	7/8	0.875	22.22500
25/64	0.390625	9.92187	57/64	0.890625	22.62187
13/32	0.40625	10.31875	29/32	0.90625	23.01875
27/64	0.421875	10.71562	59/64	0.921875	23.41562
7/16	0.4375	11.11250	15/16	0.9375	23.81250
29/64	0.453125	11.50937	61/64	0.953125	24.20937
15/32	0.46875	11.90625	31/32	0.96875	24.60625
31/64	0.484375	12.30312	63/64	0.984375	25.00312
1/2	0.500	12.70000	1	1.00	25.40000

Table 3 GENERAL TORQUE SPECIFICATIONS*

Thread size	N·m	ft.-lb.
Bolt		
6 mm	6	4.5
8 mm	15	11
10 mm	30	22
12 mm	55	40
14 mm	85	61
16 mm	130	94
Nut		
10 mm	6	4.5
12 mm	15	11
14 mm	30	22
17 mm	55	40
19 mm	85	61
22 mm	130	94

* Use these torque figures for all fasteners not individually listed.

1

CHAPTER TWO

TROUBLESHOOTING

Diagnosing mechanical problems is relatively simple if you use orderly procedures and keep a few basic principles in mind. The first step in any troubleshooting procedure is to define the symptoms as closely as possible and then localize the problem. Subsequent steps involve testing and analyzing those areas which could cause the symptoms. A haphazard approach may eventually solve the problem, but it can be very costly in terms of wasted time and unnecessary parts replacement.

Proper lubrication, maintenance and periodic tune-ups as described in Chapter Three will reduce the necessity for troubleshooting. Even with the best of care, however, an off-road or dual-purpose motorcycle is prone to problems which will require troubleshooting.

Never assume anything. Do not overlook the obvious. If you are riding along and the engine suddenly quits, check the easiest, most accessible problem spots first. Is there gasoline in the tank? Is the fuel shutoff valve in the ON position? Has the spark plug wire fallen off?

If nothing obvious turns up in a quick check, look a little further. Learning to recognize and describe symptoms will make repairs easier for you or a mechanic at the shop. Describe problems accurately and fully. Saying that "it won't run" isn't

the same thing as saying "it quit climbing a hill and won't start," or that "it sat in my garage for 3 months and then wouldn't start."

Gather as many symptoms as possible to aid in diagnosis. Note whether the engine lost power gradually or all at once, what color smoke came from the exhaust and so on. Remember that the more complicated a machine is, the easier it is to troubleshoot because symptoms point to specific problems.

After the symptoms are defined, areas which could cause problems are tested and analyzed. Guessing at the cause of a problem may provide the solution, but it can easily lead to frustration, wasted time and a series of expensive, unnecessary parts replacements.

You do not need fancy equipment or complicated test gear to determine whether repairs can be attempted at home. A few simple checks could save a large repair bill and lost time while the bike sits in a dealer's service department. On the other hand, be realistic and do not attempt repairs beyond your abilities. Service departments tend to charge heavily for putting together a disassembled engine that may have been abused. Some won't even take on such a job—so use common sense, don't get in over your head.

OPERATING REQUIREMENTS

An engine needs 3 basics to run properly: correct fuel:air mixture, compression and a spark at the right time. If one basic requirement is missing, the engine will not run. Four-stroke engine operating principles are described in Chapter Four under *Engine Principles*. The ignition system is the weakest link of the 3 basics. More problems result from ignition breakdowns than from any other source. Keep that in mind before you begin tampering with carburetor adjustments and the like.

If a bike has been sitting for any length of time and refuses to start, check and clean the spark plug. On XT350 models, check the condition of the battery to make sure it has an adequate charge. If these are okay, then look to the gasoline delivery system. This includes the tank, fuel shutoff valve, in-line fuel filter and fuel line to the carburetor. If your bike has a steel tank, rust may have formed in the tank, obstructing fuel flow. Gasoline deposits may have gummed up carburetor jets and air passages. Gasoline tends to lose its potency after standing for long periods. Condensation may contaminate it with water. Drain the old gas and try starting with a fresh tankful.

TROUBLESHOOTING INSTRUMENTS

Chapter One lists the instruments needed and detailed instruction on their use.

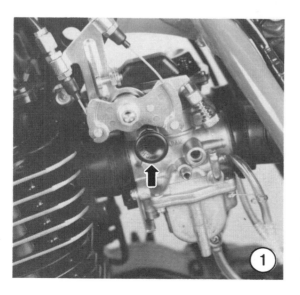

STARTING THE ENGINE

When your engine refuses to start, frustration can cause you to forget basic starting principles and procedures. The following outline will guide you through basic starting procedures.

An ignition control system is installed on all XT350 models that consists of an ignition control unit, neutral indicator light, neutral switch and a sidestand switch. When the ignition switch and the engine stop switch are ON, the ignition will produce a spark for starting only if the following conditions exist:

a. The sidestand is up (the sidestand switch is ON). The engine will start if the transmission is in gear and the clutch lever is pulled in.

b. The transmission is in neutral (the neutral switch is ON). Always allow the engine to sufficiently warm up before riding off. Do not rev or accelerate hard with a cold engine as this may cause premature engine wear.

Starting a Cold Engine

1. Shift the transmission into NEUTRAL.
2. Turn the fuel valve to ON.
3. Open the choke. Pull the choke knob out (**Figure 1**).
4. *XT350*: Turn the ignition key to ON and the engine stop switch to RUN. Position the sidestand up.
5. With the throttle completely *closed*, kick the engine over.
6. When the engine starts, work the throttle slightly to keep it running.
7. Idle the engine approximately for a minute or until the throttle responds cleanly and the choke can be closed.

Starting a Warm or Hot Engine

1. Shift the transmission into NEUTRAL.
2. Turn the fuel valve to ON.
3. Make sure the choke is closed. The choke knob should be pushed in (**Figure 1**).
4. *XT350*: Turn the ignition key to ON and the engine stop switch to RUN. Position the sidestand up.
5. Open the throttle slightly and kick the engine over. If the engine does not start, try again with the throttle opened approximately 1/4 to 1/2.

Starting a Flooded Engine

If the engine is flooded, open the throttle all the way and kick the engine over until it starts.

> *NOTE*
> *If the engine refuses to start, check the carburetor overflow hose attached to the fitting at the bottom of the float bowl (A, Figure 2). If fuel is running out of the hose, the floats may be stuck open.*

STARTING DIFFICULTIES

When the bike is difficult to start, or won't start at all, it does not help to kick away at the kickstarter. Check for obvious problems even before getting out your tools. Go down the following list step-by-step. Do each one. If the bike still will not start, refer to the appropriate troubleshooting procedures which follow in this chapter.

1. Is there fuel in the tank? Remove the filler cap and rock the bike from side-to-side. Listen for fuel sloshing around.

> *WARNING*
> *Do not use an open flame to check in the tank. A serious explosion is certain to result.*

2. If there is fuel in the tank, pull off the fuel line at the carburetor. Turn the fuel valve (B, **Figure 2**) to RES and see if fuel flows freely. If none comes out and there is a fuel filter installed in the fuel line, remove the filter and turn the fuel valve to RES again. If fuel flows, the filter is clogged and should be replaced. If no fuel comes out, the fuel valve may be shut off, blocked by foreign matter, or the fuel cap vent may be plugged. If the carburetor is getting usable fuel, turn to the compression next.

> *NOTE*
> *All XT350 models sold in California are equipped with an evaporative emission control system. On these models, the fuel cap is unvented. Instead of checking the fuel cap, check the carbon canister hoses for bending,*

kinks or other damage. Refer to ***Emission Control*** *in Chapter Eight.*

3. If the engine is getting fuel, kick the kickstarter normally and observe its operation. If the kickstarter feels normal (adequate engine compression), proceed to Step 4. However, if the kickstarter operation feels unusually light or heavy, perform the *Compression Test* under *Tune-Up* in Chapter Three.

4A. *XT350*: Check that the engine stop switch (**Figure 3**) is in the RUN position. If necessary, test the switch as described under *Switches* in Chapter Nine.

4B. *TT350*: Make sure the kill switch (**Figure 4**) is not stuck or working improperly or that the wire

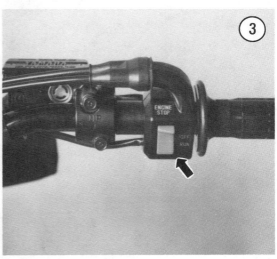

is broken and shorting out. If necessary, test the kill switch as described under *Switches* in Chapter Nine.

5. Is the spark plug wire on tight (**Figure 5**)? Push it on and slightly rotate it to clean the electrical connection between the plug and the connector.

6. Is the choke knob in the right position? Refer to *Starting the Engine* in this chapter.

ENGINE STARTING TROUBLES

An engine that refuses to start or is difficult to start is very frustrating. More often than not, the problem is very minor and can be found with a simple and logical troubleshooting approach.

The following items show a beginning point from which to isolate engine starting problems.

Engine Fails to Start

Perform the following spark test to determine if the ignition system is operating properly.

CAUTION
Before removing the spark plug in Step 1, clean all dirt and debris from the plug base. Dirt that falls into the cylinder will cause rapid piston, piston ring and cylinder wear.

NOTE
If you are checking the spark plug while on the trail, more than likely there is dirt clogged underneath the fuel tank. When the spark plug is removed, dirt could fall from the tank and into the cylinder. If you do not have time to remove the fuel tank, wrap a large clean cloth or riding jacket around the fuel tank. Then remove the spark plug and check or replace it as required. Remove the cloth after reinstalling the spark plug.

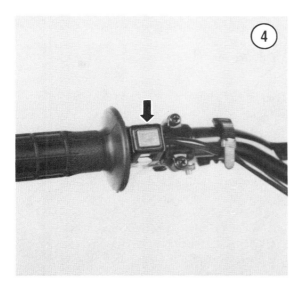

1. Remove the spark plug.
2. Connect the spark plug wire and connector to the spark plug and touch the spark plug base to the cylinder head to ground it. Position the spark plug so you can see the electrode.
3. *XT350*: Turn the ignition key to ON and the engine stop switch to RUN. Shift the transmission into neutral.
4. Kick the engine over with the kickstarter. A fat blue spark should be evident across the spark plug electrode.

WARNING
Do not hold the spark plug, wire or connector or a serious electrical shock may result.

5. If the spark is good, check for one or more of the following possible malfunctions:
   a. Obstructed fuel line or fuel filter.
   b. Leaking head or cylinder base gasket.
6. If spark is weak or nonexistent, check for one or more of the following:
   a. Weak ignition coil.
   b. Weak CDI unit.
   c. Loose electrical connections.
   d. Dirty electrical connections.
   e. Loose or broken ignition coil ground wire.

Engine is Difficult to Start

Check for one or more of the following possible malfunctions:
   a. Fouled spark plug.
   b. Improperly operating choke.
   c. Contaminated fuel system.
   d. Improperly adjusted carburetor.
   e. Loose electrical connections.
   f. Dirty electrical connections.
   g. Weak CDI unit.
   h. Weak ignition coil.
   i. Poor compression

Engine Will Not Crank

If the engine will not crank because of a mechanical problem, check for one or more of the following possible malfunctions:
   a. Defective kickstarter and/or gear.
   b. Seized piston.
   c. Seized crankshaft bearings.
   d. Broken connecting rod.

ENGINE PERFORMANCE

In the following check list, it is assumed that the engine runs, but is not operating at peak performance. This will serve as a starting point from which to isolate a performance malfunction.

The possible causes for each malfunction are listed in a logical sequence and in order of probability.

Engine Will Not Idle

   a. Carburetor incorrectly adjusted.
   b. Pilot jet clogged.
   c. Obstructed fuel line or fuel shutoff valve.
   d. Fouled or improperly gapped spark plug.

Engine Misses at High Speed

   a. Fouled or improperly gapped spark plug.
   b. Improper carburetor main jet selection.
   c. Carburetor main jet and/or needle jet clogged.
   d. Obstructed fuel line or fuel shutoff valve.
   e. Ignition timing incorrect due to ignition system malfunction.

Engine Overheating

   a. Incorrect carburetor jetting or fuel/oil ratio mixture.
   b. Ignition timing incorrect due to ignition system malfunction.
   c. Improper spark plug heat range.
   d. Intake system air leak.
   e. Damaged or blocked cooling fins.
   f. Dragging brake(s).

Excessive Exhaust Smoke and Engine Runs Roughly

   a. Clogged air filter element.
   b. Carburetor adjustment incorrect—mixture too rich.
   c. Carburetor floats damaged or incorrectly adjusted.
   d. Choke not operating correctly.
   e. Water or other contaminants in fuel.
   f. Clogged fuel line.
   g. Excessive piston-to-cylinder clearance.
   h. Valve component wear.

Engine Loses Power

   a. Carburetor incorrectly adjusted.
   b. Engine overheating.
   c. Ignition timing incorrect due to ignition system malfunction.
   d. Incorrectly gapped spark plug.
   e. Obstructed silencer.
   f. Dragging brake(s).

Engine Lacks Acceleration

   a. Carburetor adjustment incorrect.
   b. Clogged fuel line.
   c. Ignition timing incorrect due to ignition system malfunction.
   d. Dragging brake(s).

ENGINE NOISES

1. *Knocking or pinging during acceleration—* Caused by using a lower octane fuel than recommended. May also be caused by poor fuel available at some "discount" gasoline stations. Pinging can also be caused by a spark plug of the wrong heat range and incorrect carburetor jetting. Refer to *Correct Spark Plug Heat Range* in Chapter Three.

2. *Slapping or rattling noises at low speed or during acceleration—* May be caused by piston slap, i.e., excessive piston-to-cylinder wall clearance.

3. *Knocking or rapping while decelerating—* Usually caused by excessive rod bearing clearance.

4. *Persistent knocking and vibration—* Usually caused by worn main bearings.

5. *Rapid on-off squeal—* Compression leak around cylinder head gasket or spark plug.

EXCESSIVE VIBRATION

This can be difficult to find without disassembling the engine. Usually this is caused by loose engine or suspension mounting hardware.

CLUTCH

The three basic clutch troubles are:
a. Clutch noise.
b. Clutch slipping.
c. Improper clutch disengagement.

All clutch troubles, except adjustments, require partial engine disassembly to identify and cure the problem. Refer to Chapter Six for procedures.

The troubleshooting procedures outlined in **Figure 6** will help you solve the majority of clutch troubles in a systematic manner.

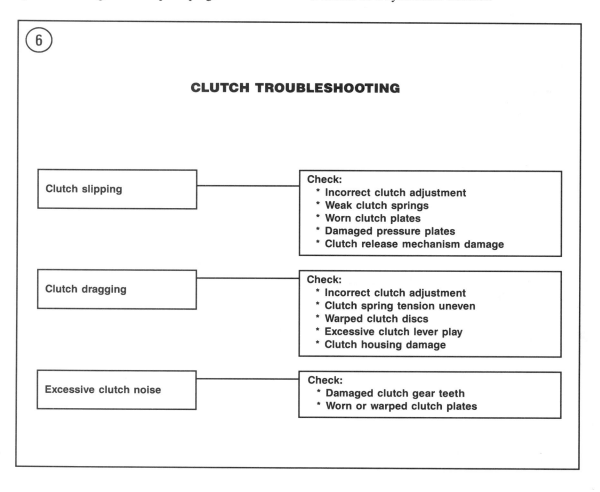

(6)

CLUTCH TROUBLESHOOTING

Clutch slipping

Check:
* **Incorrect clutch adjustment**
* **Weak clutch springs**
* **Worn clutch plates**
* **Damaged pressure plates**
* **Clutch release mechanism damage**

Clutch dragging

Check:
* **Incorrect clutch adjustment**
* **Clutch spring tension uneven**
* **Warped clutch discs**
* **Excessive clutch lever play**
* **Clutch housing damage**

Excessive clutch noise

Check:
* **Damaged clutch gear teeth**
* **Worn or warped clutch plates**

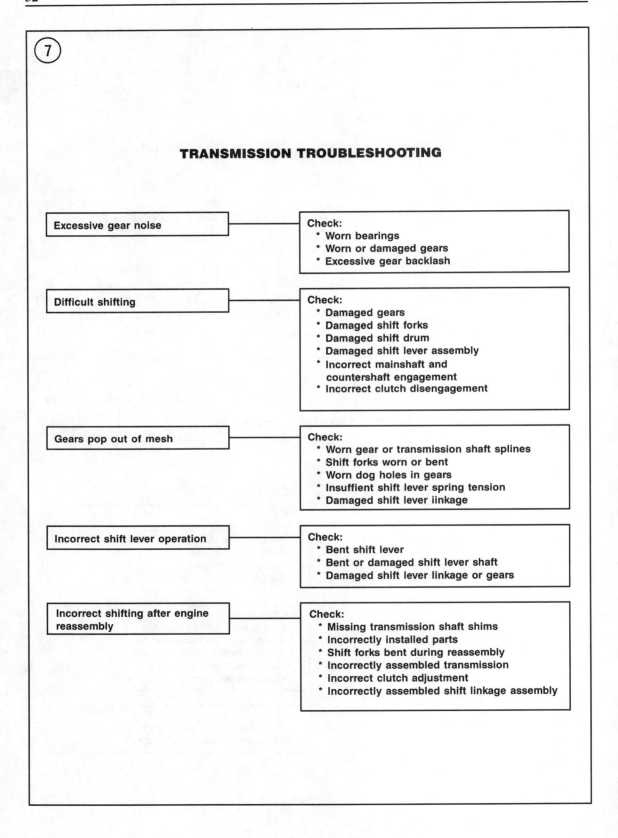

⑦

TRANSMISSION TROUBLESHOOTING

Excessive gear noise

Check:
* Worn bearings
* Worn or damaged gears
* Excessive gear backlash

Difficult shifting

Check:
* Damaged gears
* Damaged shift forks
* Damaged shift drum
* Damaged shift lever assembly
* Incorrect mainshaft and
  countershaft engagement
* Incorrect clutch disengagement

Gears pop out of mesh

Check:
* Worn gear or transmission shaft splines
* Shift forks worn or bent
* Worn dog holes in gears
* Insuffient shift lever spring tension
* Damaged shift lever iinkage

Incorrect shift lever operation

Check:
* Bent shift lever
* Bent or damaged shift lever shaft
* Damaged shift lever linkage or gears

Incorrect shifting after engine reassembly

Check:
* Missing transmission shaft shims
* Incorrectly installed parts
* Shift forks bent during reassembly
* Incorrectly assembled transmission
* Incorrect clutch adjustment
* Incorrectly assembled shift linkage assembly

TRANSMISSION

The basic transmission troubles are:

a. Excessive gear noise.
b. Difficult shifting.
c. Gears pop out of mesh.
d. Incorrect shift lever operation.

Transmission symptoms are sometimes hard to distinguish from clutch symptoms. Be sure that the clutch is not causing the trouble before working on the transmission.

The troubleshooting procedures outlined in **Figure 7** will help you solve the majority of transmission troubles.

IGNITION SYSTEM

All XT350 and TT350 models are equipped with a capacitor discharge ignition (CDI) system. This solid state system uses no contact breaker point or other moving parts. Because of the solid state design, problems with the capacitor discharge system are relatively few. However, when problems arise they stem from one of the following:

a. Weak spark.
b. No spark.

It is possible to check CDI systems that:

a. Do not spark.
b. Have broken or damaged wires.
c. Have a weak spark.

It is difficult to check CDI systems that malfunction due to:

a. Vibration problems.
b. Components that malfunction only when the engine is hot or under a load.

1. Disconnect the engine stop switch (XT350) or the kill switch (TT350) and see if the problem still exists.
2. Make sure that the stator plate screws are tight. If the screws are loose, recheck the ignition timing as described in Chapter Three.
3. Remove the fuel tank and untape all electrical connectors. Make sure the connectors are connected properly. If necessary, clean the connectors with electrical contact cleaner.
4. Check the stator plate for cracks or damage that would cause the coils to be out of alignment.
5. If you cannot locate the problem, refer to *Ignition System Troubleshooting* for your model in Chapter Nine.

FRONT SUSPENSION AND STEERING

Poor handling may be caused by improper front or rear tire pressure, a damaged or bent frame or front steering components, worn swing arm bushings, worn wheel bearings or dragging brakes.

BRAKES

Front Disc Brake

The front disc brake is critical to riding performance and safety. It should be inspected frequently and any problems located and repaired immediately. When replacing or refilling the brake fluid, use only DOT3/DOT4 brake fluid from a closed and sealed container. See Chapter Twelve for additional information on brake fluid and disc brake service. The troubleshooting procedures in **Figure 8** will help you isolate the majority of front disc brake troubles.

Drum Brakes

The rear drum brake is relatively simple in design and operation. Yet, many riders do not get full stopping power because the shoes and drum are covered with residue. This residue buildup is due mainly from lack of maintenance. To work properly, the drum brakes must be cleaned and serviced weekly. Periodic maintenance will also allow inspection of parts so that they can be replaced before a part fails.

Refer to the troubleshooting chart in **Figure 9** for drum brake problems and checks to make.

Figures 8 and 9 are on the following pages.

DISC BRAKE TROUBLESHOOTING   ⑧

Disc brake fluid leakage

Check:
* Loose or damaged line fittings
* Worn caliper piston seals
* Scored caliper piston or bore
* Loose banjo bolts
* Damaged oil line washers
* Leaking master cylinder diaphragm
* Leaking master cylinder secondary seal
* Cracked master cylinder housing
* Too high brake fluid level
* Loose or damaged master cylinder cover

Brake overheating

Check:
* Warped brake disc
* Incorrect brake fluid
* Caliper piston and/or brake pads hanging up
* Riding brakes during riding

Brake chatter

Check:
* Warped brake disc
* Incorrect caliper alignment
* Loose caliper mounting bolt
* Loose front axle nut and/or clamps
* Worn wheel bearings
* Damaged hub
* Restricted brake hydraulic line
* Contaminated brake pads

Brake locking

Check:
* Incorrect brake fluid
* Plugged passages in master cylinder
* Caliper piston and/or brake pads hanging up
* Warped brake disc

Insufficient brakes

Check:
* Air in brake lines
* Worn brake pads
* Low brake fluid
* Incorrect brake fluid
* Worn brake disc
* Worn caliper piston seals
* Glazed brake pads
* Leaking primary cup seal in master cylinder
* Contaminated brake pads and/or disc

Brake squeal

Check:
* Contaminated brake pads and/or disc
* Dust or dirt collected behind brake pads
* Loose parts

(9)

2

DRUM BRAKE TROUBLESHOOTING

Brakes do not hold

Check:
* Worn brake linings
* Glazed brake linings
* Worn brake drum
* Glazed brake drum
* Incorrect brake adjustment
* Worn or damaged brake cable
* Worn or defective brake return springs

Brakes grab

Check:
* Worn or damaged brake return springs
* Incorrect brake adjustment
* Brake drum out-of-round
* Warped brake lining web
* Loose or worn wheel bearings

Brakes squeal or scrape

Check:
* Worn brake linings
* Brake drum out-of-round or scored
* Contaminated brake linings and/or drum
* Broken, loose or damaged brake component
* Loose or worn wheel bearing
* Loose brake drum

Brake chatter

Check:
* Brake drum out-of-round
* Brake linings worn unevenly
* Warped brake lining web
* Incorrect brake adjustment
* Loose or worn wheel bearing
* Worn or damaged brake return springs

CHAPTER THREE

LUBRICATION, MAINTENANCE, AND TUNE-UP

Your bike can be cared for by two methods: preventive and corrective maintenance. Because a motorcycle is subjected to tremendous heat, stress and vibration—even in normal use—preventive maintenance prevents costly and unexpected corrective maintenance. When neglected, any bike becomes unreliable and actually dangerous to ride. When properly maintained, your Yamaha is one of the most reliable bikes available and will give many miles and years of dependable and safe riding. By maintaining a routine service schedule as described in this chapter, costly mechanical problems and unexpected breakdowns can be prevented.

The procedures presented in this chapter can be easily performed by anyone with average mechanical skills. **Table 1** is a suggested factory maintenance schedule. **Tables 1-11** are located at the end of this chapter.

PRE-CHECKS

The following checks should be performed prior to the first ride of the day.
1. Inspect the fuel line and fittings for wetness.
2. Make sure the fuel tank is full.
3. Make sure the air cleaner is clean and that the cover is securely in place.
4. Check the engine oil level.
5. Check the operation of the clutch and adjust if necessary.
6. Check that the clutch and brake levers operate properly with no binding.
7. Inspect the condition of the front and rear suspension. Make sure it has a good solid feel with no looseness.
8. Check the drive chain for wear and correct tension.
9. Check tire pressure (**Table 2**).

NOTE
*While checking tire pressure, also check the position of the valve stem. If the valve stem is cocked sideways like that shown in **Figure 1**, your riding time could end quickly because of a flat tire. Refer to **Valve Stem Alignment** in this chapter.*

10. Check the exhaust system for damage.
11. Check the tightness of all fasteners, especially engine and suspension mounting hardware.

12. Check the rear sprocket and bolts as follows:

a. Check the sprocket holes for signs of egg-shaping. If the sprocket is found in this condition, the sprocket bolts have loosened during riding. If wear is severe, it may be best to replace the sprocket before the hub is destroyed.

b. Check the sprocket bolts for tightness. If Allen head bolts (**Figure 2**) are used on your model, always tighten the nut rather than the bolt. Also, check the surface between the countersunk bolt head and the machined countersunk area in the hub. The bolt should sit flush in the countersunk area.

c. Replace nuts that have started to round at their corners.

13. *XT350*: Perform the following checks.

a. Pull the front brake lever and check that the brake light comes on.

b. Push the rear brake pedal and check that the brake light comes on soon after you have begun depressing the pedal.

c. With the engine running, check to see that the headlight and taillight are on.

d. Move the dimmer switch up and down between the high and low positions, and check to see that both headlight elements are working.

e. Push the turn signal switch to the left position and then to the right position and check that all 4 turn signal lights work properly.

f. Push the horn button and note if the horn blows loudly.

g. If the horn or any light failed to work properly, refer to Chapter Nine.

14. *TT350*: Start the engine and pull the engine light switch up. The headlight and taillight should be on. Now push the light switch down. The lights should go off. Refer to Chapter Nine if the lights failed to work properly.

TIRES AND WHEELS

Tire Pressure

Tire pressure should be checked and adjusted to maintain good traction and handling. An accurate gauge should be carried in your tool box. The approximate tire inflation pressure specification for all models is listed in **Table 2**.

Tire Inspection

The tires take a lot of punishment due to the variety of terrain they are subject to. Inspect them periodically for excessive wear, cuts, abrasions, etc. Sidewall tears are the most common cause of tire failure. This type of damage is usually caused by sharp rocks or other trail conditions. Often times, sidewall tears cannot be seen from the outside. If necessary, remove the tire from the rim as described in Chapter Ten. Run your hand around the inside tire casing to feel for tears or sharp objects imbedded in the casing. The outside of the tire can be inspected visually.

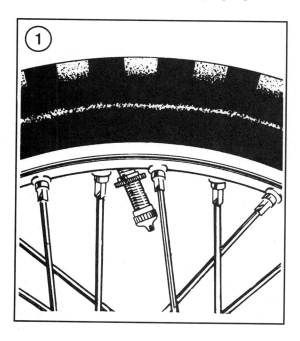

While checking the tires, also check the position of the valve stem. If the valve stem is cocked sideways like that shown in **Figure 1**, your riding day could end because of a flat tire. Refer to *Valve Stem Alignment* in this chapter.

Wheel Spoke Tension

Tap each spoke with a wrench. The higher the pitch of sound it makes, the tighter the spoke. The lower the sound frequency, the looser the spoke. A "ping" is good, a "klunk" says the spoke is too loose.

If one or more spokes are loose, tighten them as described in Chapter Ten.

> *NOTE*
> *Most spokes loosen as a group rather than individually. Extra-loose spokes should be tightened carefully. Burying just a few spokes tight into the rim will put improper pressure across the wheel. Refer to Chapter Ten.*

Rim Inspection

Frequently inspect the condition of the wheel rims. If a rim has been damaged, it may be enough to cause excessive side-to-side play. Refer to Chapter Ten.

Valve Stem Alignment

Before each riding day, check each valve stem for alignment. **Figure 1** shows a valve stem that has slipped. If the tube is not repositioned, the valve stem will eventually pull away from the tube, causing a flat. However, don't get your tire irons out yet. The tube can be aligned without removing the tire.

1. Wash the tire (especially the sides) if it is dirty or caked with mud.
2. Remove the valve stem core and release all air pressure from the tube.
3. Loosen the rim lock nut (**Figure 3**) if so equipped.
4. With an assistant steadying the bike and holding the brake on, squeeze the tire and break the tire-to-wheel seal all the way around the wheel. If the tire seal is very tight, it may be necessary to lay the bike on its side and break the tire seal with your foot or a rubber hammer. Use care though; have an assistant steady the bike so that it doesn't rock and damage the handlebars or a control lever.
5. After the tire seal is broken, put the bike on a stand so that the wheel clears the ground.
6. Apply a mixture of soap and water from a spray container (like that used when changing a tire) along the tire bead on both sides of the tire.
7. Have an assistant apply the brake "hard." If necessary, tighten the front or rear brake adjuster.
8. Using both of your hands, grab hold of the tire and turn it and the tube until the valve stem is straight up (90°). See **Figure 4**.
9. When the valve stem is straight up, install the valve stem core and inflate the tire. If the soap and water solution has dried, reapply it to help the tire seat on the rim. Check the tire to make sure it seats all the way around the rim.

3

WARNING
Do not overinflate the tire and tube. If the tire will not seat properly, remove the valve stem core and re-lubricate the tire.

10. Tighten the rim locknut (**Figure 3**) securely.
11. Adjust the tire pressure (**Table 2**). When installing the valve stem nut, do not tighten it against the rim. If the tire and tube slip again, the valve stem will pull away from the tube and cause a flat. Instead, tighten the nut against the valve cap as shown in **Figure 4**. This will allow the valve stem to slip without damage until you can reposition the tire and tube.

LUBRICANTS

Engine Oil

Oil is graded according to its viscosity, which is an indication of how thick it is. The Society of Automotive Engineers (SAE) system distinguishes oil viscosity by numbers, called "weights." Thick (heavy) oils have higher viscosity numbers than thin (light) oils. For example, a 5 weight (SAE 5) oil is a light oil while a 90 weight (SAE 90) oil is relatively heavy. The viscosity of the oil has nothing to do with its lubricating properties.

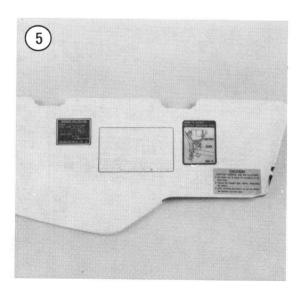

Grease

A good-quality grease—preferably waterproof—should be used for many of the parts on your Yamaha. Water does not wash grease off parts as easily as it washes off oil. In addition, grease maintains its lubricating qualities better than oil on long and strenuous events.

BATTERY
(XT350)

The battery is an important component in your Yamaha's electrical system. It is also the one most frequently neglected. In addition to checking and correcting the battery electrolyte level on a weekly basis, the battery should be cleaned and inspected at periodic intervals.

The battery used on your Yamaha should be checked periodically for electrolyte level, state of charge and corrosion. During hot weather periods, frequent checks are recommended. If the electrolyte level is below the fill line, add distilled water as required. To assure proper mixing of the water and acid, operate the engine immediately after adding water. *Never* add battery acid instead of water; this will shorten the battery's life.

CAUTION
If it becomes necessary to remove the battery vent tube when performing any of the following procedures, make sure to route the tube correctly during installation to prevent acid from spilling on parts. A battery vent tube routing diagram is located behind the right-hand side cover **Figure 5.**

Removal/Installation and
Electrolyte Level Check

The battery is the heart of the electrical system. It should be checked and serviced as indicated in **Table 1**. Most electrical system troubles can be attributed to neglect of this vital component.

In order to correctly service the electrolyte level, it is necessary to remove the battery from the frame. The electrolyte level should be maintained between the two marks on the battery case (**Figure 6**). If the electrolyte level is low, it's a good idea to completely remove the battery so that it can be thoroughly cleaned, serviced and checked.

1. Make sure the ignition switch is turned OFF.
2. Remove the seat.
3. Remove the left-hand side cover.
4. Disconnect the negative battery cable electrical connector (A, **Figure 7**).
5. Disconnect the positive battery cable (B, **Figure 7**).
6. Disconnect the battery hold-down strap (C, **Figure 7**).
7. Pull the battery out slightly and disconnect the battery vent tube from the right-hand side of the battery.
8. Slide the battery out of the battery box and remove it.

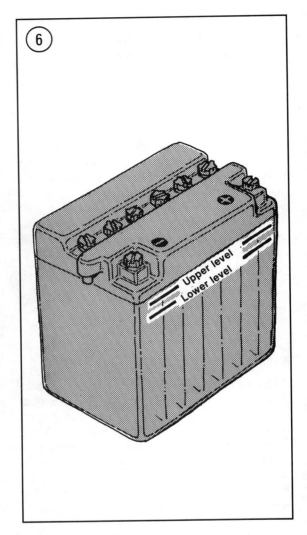

> *WARNING*
> *Protect your eyes, skin and clothing. If electrolyte gets into your eyes, flush your eyes thoroughly with clean water and get prompt medical attention.*

> *CAUTION*
> *Be careful not to spill battery electrolyte on painted or polished surfaces. The liquid is highly corrosive and will damage the finish. If it is spilled, wash it off immediately with soapy water and thoroughly rinse with clean water.*

9. If the electrolyte level is low, remove the caps (**Figure 6**) from the battery cells and add distilled water. Never add electrolyte (acid) to correct the level. Fill only to the upper battery level mark (**Figure 6**).
10. After the level has been corrected and the battery allowed to stand for a few minutes, check the specific gravity of the electrolyte in each cell with a hydrometer (**Figure 8**). Follow the manufacturer's instructions for reading the instrument. See *Testing* in this chapter.
11. After the battery has been refilled, recharged or replaced, install it by reversing these removal steps.

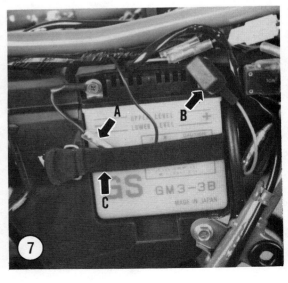

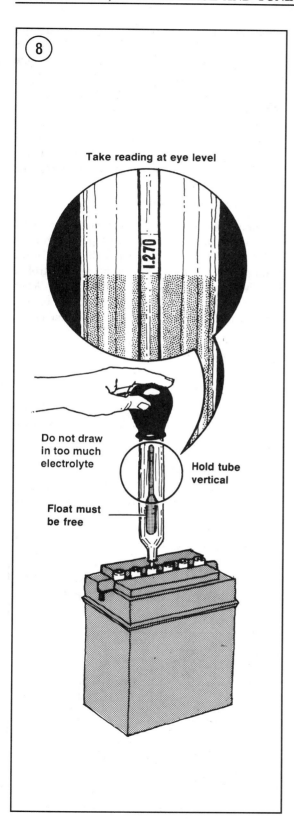

Take reading at eye level

1.270

Do not draw in too much electrolyte

Hold tube vertical

Float must be free

NOTE
When reconnecting the battery leads, always reconnect the positive lead first (B, Figure 7), then reconnect the negative lead or connector (A, Figure 7).

CAUTION
Make sure to reconnect the battery breather tube to the battery. If the tube was removed with the battery, make sure to route it in its correct position.

CAUTION
Make sure to reconnect the battery hold down strap (C, Figure 7) to prevent the battery from vibrating during service. Vibration can damage the battery plates and short out the battery.

Testing

Hydrometer testing is the best way to check battery condition. Use a hydrometer with numbered graduations from 1.100 to 1.300 rather than one with just color-coded bands. To use the hydrometer, squeeze the rubber ball, insert the tip into the cell and release the ball. Draw enough electrolyte to float the weighted float inside the hydrometer. Note the number in line with surface of the electrolyte; this is the specific gravity for this cell. Return the electrolyte to the cell from which it came. See **Figure 8**.

The specific gravity of the electrolyte in each battery cell is an excellent indication of that cell's condition (**Table 3**). A fully charged cell will read 1.260-1.280, while a cell in acceptable condition reads from 1.230-1.250 and anything below 1.160 is discharged.

NOTE
It is important to note that specific gravity varies with temperature. If a temperature-compensated hydrometer is not used, add 0.004 to the specific gravity reading for every 10° above 80° F (25° C). For every 10° below 80° F (25° C), subtract 0.004.

If the cells test in the poor range, the battery requires recharging. The hydrometer is useful for checking the progress of the charging operation. **Table 3** shows approximate state of charge.

Charging

> *CAUTION*
> *Always remove the battery from the motorcycle before connecting charging equipment.*

> *WARNING*
> *During charging, highly explosive hydrogen gas is released from the battery. The battery should be charged only in a well-ventilated area, and open flames and cigarettes should be kept away. Never check the charge of the battery by arcing across the terminals; the resulting spark can ignite the hydrogen gas.*

1. Remove the battery from the motorcycle as described in this chapter.
2. Connect the positive (+) charger lead to the positive battery terminal and the negative (−) charger lead to the negative battery terminal.
3. Remove all vent caps from the battery, set the charger at 12 volts, and switch it on. Normally, a battery should be charged at a slow charge rate of 1/10 its given capacity. The recommended charging rate for batteries in models covered in this manual is 0.3 amps.

> *CAUTION*
> *The electrolyte level must be maintained at the upper level during the charging cycle; check and refill as necessary.*

4. The charging time depends on the discharged condition of the battery. The chart in **Figure 9** can be used to determine approximate charging times at different specific gravity readings. For example, if the specific gravity of your battery is 1.180, the approximate charging time would be 6 hours.
5. To ensure good electrical contact, cables must be clean and tight on the battery's terminals. If the cable terminals are badly corroded, even after performing the above cleaning procedures, the cables should be disconnected, removed from the bike and cleaned separately with a wire brush and a baking soda solution. After cleaning, apply a very thin coating of petroleum jelly such as Vaseline or a light mineral grease to the battery terminals before reattaching the cables. After connecting the cables, apply a light coating to the connections also—this will delay future corrosion.

New Battery Installation

When replacing the old battery with a new one, be sure to charge it completely (specific gravity, 1.260-1.280) before installing it in the bike. Failure to do so, or using the battery with a low electrolyte level will permanently damage the battery. When purchasing a new battery, the correct battery capacity for XT350 models is 12 volts/3 amp hours.

PERIODIC LUBRICATION

Engine Oil Level Check

Engine oil level is checked through the inspection window located at the bottom of the clutch cover (**Figure 10**).
1. Start the engine and let it reach normal operating temperature.
2. Stop the engine and allow the oil to settle.
3. Park the bike so that it is off the sidestand and level.

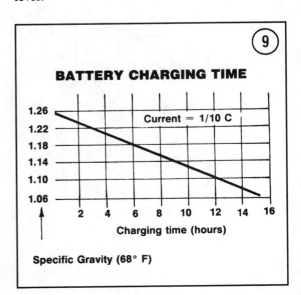

(9)

BATTERY CHARGING TIME

Current = 1/10 C

Charging time (hours)

Specific Gravity (68° F)

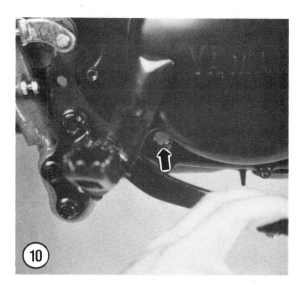

4. The oil level should be between the maximum and minimum window marks (**Figure 10**). If necessary, remove the oil fill cap (**Figure 11**) and add the recommended oil (**Table 4**) to raise the oil to the proper level. Do not overfill.

Engine Oil and Filter Change

The factory-recommended oil and filter change interval is specified in **Table 1**. This assumes that the motorcycle is operated in moderate climates. The time interval is more important than the mileage interval because combustion acids, formed by gasoline and water vapor, will contaminate the oil even if the motorcycle is not run for several months. If a motorcycle is operated under dusty conditions, the oil will get dirty more quickly and should be changed more frequently than recommended. Use only a detergent oil with an API rating of SG. The quality rating is stamped on top of the can (**Figure 12**). Try always to use the same brand of oil. Use of oil additives is not recommended. Refer to **Table 4** for correct weight of oil to use under different temperatures.

To change the engine oil and filter you will need the following:

   a. Drain pan.
   b. Funnel.
   c. Can opener or pour spout.
   d. Allen wrench.
   e. Wrench or socket to remove drain plug.
   f. Oil (see **Table 5**).
   g. New oil filter element.

There are a number of ways to discard the used oil safely. The easiest way is to pour it from the drain pan into a gallon plastic bleach, juice or milk container for disposal.

> *NOTE*
> *Some service stations and oil retailers will accept your used oil for recycling. Do not discard oil in your household trash or pour it onto the ground.*

1. Start the engine and run it until it is at normal operating temperature, then turn it off.

2. Remove the skid plate (**Figure 13**) from underneath the engine.

> *WARNING*
> *The oil will be hot when draining it in*
> *the following steps. Protect your hands*
> *accordingly.*

3. Place a drip pan under the crankcase and remove the engine drain bolt from the left-hand side (**Figure 14**).

4. From underneath the engine, loosen and remove the oil strainer plug assembly (**Figure 15**).

5. Remove the oil filter cover (**Figure 16**) and remove the oil filter (**Figure 17**).

6. Check the O-ring in the oil filter cover (A, **Figure 18**) and on the oil strainer plug (A, **Figure 19**). Also check the O-ring in the clutch cover (**Figure 20**). Replace all worn or damaged O-rings.

7. Replace the oil filter element (B, **Figure 18**) if contaminated or if the bike has reached the oil change mileage interval specified in **Table 1**.

8. Clean the oil strainer screen, spring (B, **Figure 19**) and plug in solvent and thoroughly dry with compressed air. Inspect the filter screen for holes or defects; replace as necessary. Thoroughly clean out the drain plug area in the crankcase with a shop rag and solvent.

9. Install the oil strainer assembly (B, **Figure 19**) as follows:

   a. Make sure the O-ring is installed on the plug (A, **Figure 19**).

   b. Insert the spring into the end of the plug. Then insert the strainer into the end of the spring as shown in **Figure 15**.

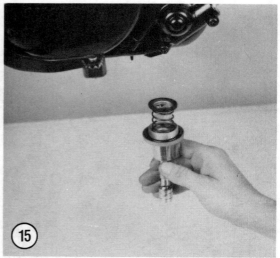

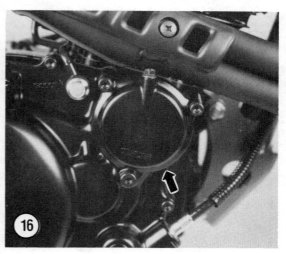

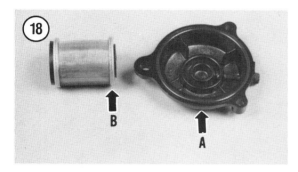

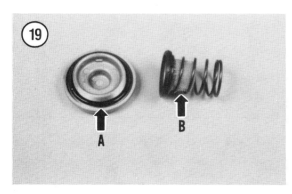

c. Install the strainer assembly so that the portion of the strainer with the rubber end goes into the crankcase cavity first (**Figure 15**).

d. Carefully align the plug threads with the crankcase and install the plug.

e. Tighten the oil strainer plug to the tightening torque in **Table 6**.

10. Install the oil filter as follows:

a. Make sure an O-ring is installed in the oil filter cover (A, **Figure 18**).

b. Make sure an O-ring is installed in the clutch cover as shown in **Figure 20**.

c. Insert the oil filter (**Figure 17**) into the oil filter cavity.

d. Install the oil filter cover (**Figure 16**). Tighten the cover screws securely.

11. Install the engine drain bolt (**Figure 14**) and washer. Tighten the bolt to the torque specification in **Table 6**.

12. Insert a funnel into the oil fill hole and fill the engine with the correct type (**Table 4**) and quantity (**Table 5**) of oil.

13. Screw in the oil filler cap securely.

14. Check the engine oil pressure as follows:

a. Loosen the oil pipe banjo bolt in the cylinder head (**Figure 21**).

b. Start the engine and allow it to idle; do not increase engine rpm

c. Oil should seep out of the banjo bolt fitting within one minute. If not, immediately stop the engine and locate the problem.

d. Tighten the banjo bolt to the torque specification in **Table 6**.

15. Recheck the engine oil level after the oil has settled and fill as required until the correct level is obtained.

16. Install the skid plate underneath the engine.

Front Fork Oil Change (XT350)

The fork oil should be changed at the interval listed in **Table 1**.

1. Support the motorcycle so that the front wheel clears the ground.

2. For 1985-1995 models, remove the fork tube air valve cap. Use a small screwdriver or punch and release all air pressure in the fork (**Figure 22**).

> *CAUTION*
> *Release the air pressure gradually. If released too fast, oil may spurt out with the air. Protect your eyes accordingly.*

3. Place a drip pan underneath the drain screw. Remove the drain screw and allow the oil to drain. Never reuse the oil. See **Figure 23**.

> *CAUTION*
> *Do not allow the fork oil to contact any of the brake components or to run onto the front tire.*

4. Remove the stand or blocks from underneath the bike. With both of the bike's wheels on the ground, grab the front brake lever and push down on the handlebar. Repeat this action until all the oil is released from the fork tube.

5. Check the drain screw seal. Replace it if worn or damaged.

6. Apply Loctite 242 (blue) onto the screw threads and reinstall the drain screw. Tighten it securely.

7. Repeat Steps 2-6 for the opposite fork.

8. Place the motorcycle on a stand so that the front wheel clears the ground.

9. Loosen the top fork tube pinch bolts (A, **Figure 24**).

10. Loosen and remove the fork cap (B, **Figure 24**).

11. Remove the spacer (**Figure 25**).

12. Remove the spring seat (**Figure 26**).

13. Remove the fork spring (**Figure 27**).

14. Fill the fork with the specified weight and quantity of fork oil. See **Table 4** and **Table 5**.

15. Repeat Steps 9-14 for the opposite fork.

16. Place the bike onto the stand so that the front wheel clears the ground. Push down on the front wheel so that the forks are completely extended.

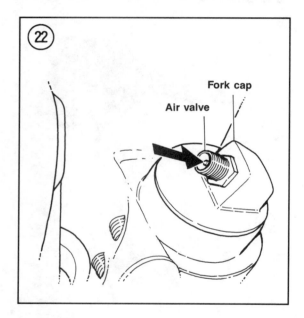

Fork cap

Air valve

17. Check the O-ring in the fork cap. Replace it if worn or damaged.

18. Install the fork spring (**Figure 27**), spring seat (**Figure 26**) and spacer (**Figure 25**).

19. Place the fork cap on the spring seat and push it down. Install the fork cap by carefully threading it into the fork. Don't cross thread it. Tighten the fork cap to the tightening torque in **Table 6**.

20. Tighten the fork tube pinch bolts (A, **Figure 24**) to the torque specification in **Table 6**.

21. Inflate each fork tube to the correct amount of air pressure as described in this chapter.

Front Fork Oil Change
(TT350)

The fork oil should be changed at the interval described in **Table 1**.

1. Support the motorcycle so that the front wheel clears the ground.

2. Remove the fork tube air valve cap. Use a small screwdriver or punch and release all air pressure in the fork (**Figure 22**).

CAUTION
Release the air pressure gradually. If
released too fast, oil may spurt out with
the air. Protect your eyes accordingly.

3. Place a drip pan underneath the drain screw. Remove the drain screw and allow the oil to drain. Never reuse the oil. See **Figure 28**.

CAUTION
Do not allow the fork oil to contact any
of the brake components or to run onto
the front tire.

4. Remove the stand or blocks from underneath the bike. With both of the bike's wheels on the ground, grab the front brake lever and push down on the handlebar. Repeat this action until all the oil is released from the fork tube.
5. Check the drain screw seal. Replace it if worn or damaged.
6. Apply Loctite 242 (blue) onto the screw threads and reinstall the drain screw. Tighten it securely.
7. Repeat Steps 2-6 for the opposite fork.
8. Place the motorcycle on a stand so that the front wheel clears the ground.
9. Remove the handlebar clamp bolts and remove the clamps. Then lift the handlebar assembly forward and move it away from the upper fork bracket. It is not necessary to disconnect any control cable at the handlebar when performing this procedure; however, do not allow any of the cables to become kinked or damaged.

10. Loosen the top fork tube pinch bolts (A, **Figure 29**).
11. Loosen and remove the fork cap (B, **Figure 29**).
12. Remove the spacer (**Figure 30**).
13. Remove the spring seat (**Figure 31**).
14. Remove the fork spring (**Figure 32**).
15. Fill the fork with the specified weight and quantity fork oil. See **Table 4** and **Table 5**.
16. Repeat Steps 10-15 for the opposite fork.
17. Allow the oil to settle for a few minutes. Then with an assistants help, push the front wheel up and down to remove all air bubbles from the fork oil.

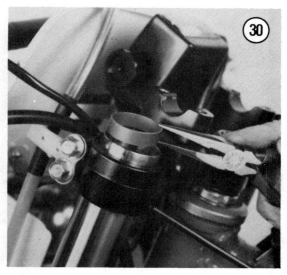

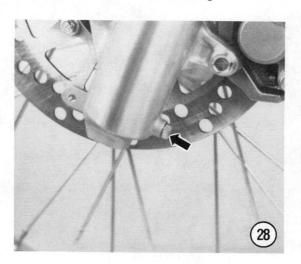

18. Measure the fork oil level as follows.

19. With an assistant's help, roll the bike off of the stand so that the forks are placed in a vertical position.

20. Using a fork oil level gauge (see Chapter One), measure the distance from the top of the fork tube to the top of the oil (**Figure 33**). Refer to **Table 5** for the correct specifications. Repeat for the opposite fork. If the oil level is too high, use the gauge to siphon some of the oil out of the fork tube. If the oil level is too low, pour some fork oil into the fork tube. Remeasure the fork oil level.

NOTE
A tape measure or ruler can be used to perform Step 20. However, to assure a precise oil level, you may want to invest in a fork oil level gauge sold through Yamaha or a motorcycle accessory dealer.

21. Place the bike onto the stand so that the front wheel clears the ground. Push down on the front wheel so that the forks are completely extended.

22. Check the O-ring in the fork cap. Replace it if worn or damaged.

23. Install the fork spring (**Figure 32**), spring seat (**Figure 31**) and spacer (**Figure 30**).

24. Place the fork cap on the spring seat and push it down against the fork tube. Install the fork cap by carefully threading it into the fork. Don't cross thread it. Tighten the fork cap securely.

25. Tighten the fork tube pinch bolts (A, **Figure 29**) to the torque specification in **Table 6**.

26. Inflate each fork tube to the correct amount of air pressure as described in this chapter.

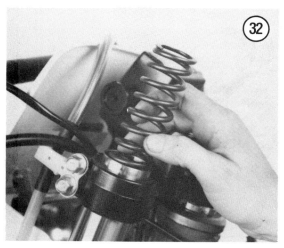

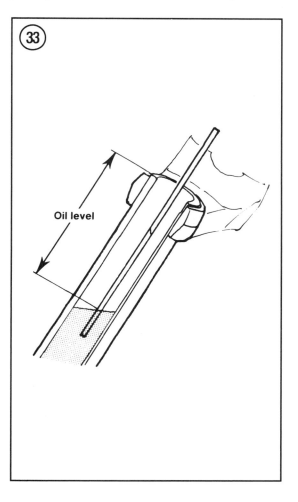

Oil level

Drive Chain

The factory installed drive chain on all XT350 and TT350 models has O-rings installed between the chain plates. Lubrication for the chain pins is permanently sealed by the O-rings (**Figure 34**). However, the chain rollers require external oiling. For the O-ring chain to work properly, it requires proper cleaning and lubrication practices. Do not clean the O-ring drive chain with a high-pressure water hose, such as those found in coin-operated car washes. The high pressure can damage the chain's O-rings and cause pre-mature chain failure.

A properly maintained drive chain will provide maximum service life and reliability. The drive chain should be lubricated before each ride and during the day as required. Models that are ridden off-road will require more frequent drive chain lubrication and cleaning.

Periodic lubrication

1. Place a milk crate or wood block(s) under the engine to support the bike securely.
2. Shift the transmission to NEUTRAL.
3. Oil the bottom run of the chain with a commercial chain lubricant specified for use on O-ring drive chains.
4. Rotate the wheel until all of the chain is lubricated.

5. Moisten a shop cloth in solvent or with soap and water and wipe off any chain lubrication residue from the rear tire and rim.

Chain cleaning

1. Disconnect the master link (**Figure 35**) and remove the chain from the motorcycle.

> *CAUTION*
> *Only kerosene should be used to clean an O-ring equipped drive chain. Do not use gasoline or other solvents that will cause the O-rings to swell or deteriorate.*

2. Immerse the chain in a pan of kerosene and allow it to soak for about a half hour. Move it around and flex it during this period so that the dirt around the rollers may work its way out.
3. Hang up the drive chain and allow it to thoroughly dry. Place an empty container underneath the chain to catch all runoff.
4. While the drive chain is still hanging up, lubricate it with a good grade of chain lubricant, carefully following the manufacturer's instructions.
5. Reinstall the chain on the motorcycle. Use a new master link clip and install it so that the closed end of the clip is facing the direction of chain travel (**Figure 35**). Store the old master link in your bike's tool bag so that it can be used in case of an emergency.

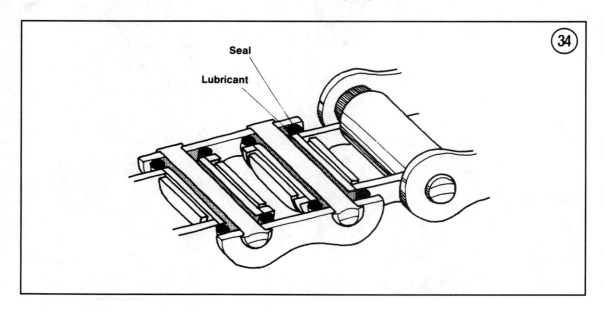

Seal

Lubricant

(34)

WARNING
Always check the master link clip after the bike has been rolled backwards such as unloading from a truck or trailer. The master link clip may have snagged on the chain guide or tensioner and become disengaged. Obviously, losing a chain while riding can cause a serious spill not to mention the chain and engine damage which may occur.

Control Cables

The control cables should be lubricated at intervals as described in **Table 1**. Also, they should be inspected at this time for fraying, and the cable sheath should be checked for chafing. The cables are relatively inexpensive and should be replaced when found to be faulty.

A can of cable lube and a cable lubricator will be required for this procedure.

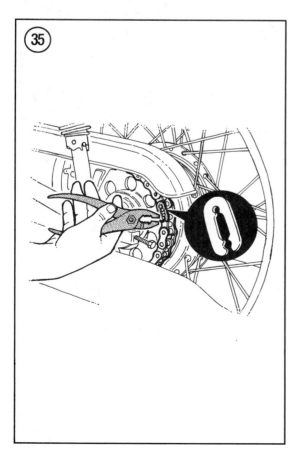

NOTE
If you are having trouble with the stock cables, you may want to install Teflon-lined cables. These cables are smoother than the stock cables and can be washed in warm soapy water. They don't require any oiling and will last longer than steel lined cables.

This procedure should be performed on steel lined cables only. *Do not* oil Teflon-lined cables.
1. Disconnect the cables from the clutch lever and the throttle grip assembly and from where they attach to the carburetor and clutch mechanism.
2. Attach a cable lubricator following the manufacturer's instructions (**Figure 36**).
3. Insert the nozzle of the lubricant can into the lubricator, press the button on the can and hold down until the lubricant begins to flow out of the other end of the cable.

NOTE
Place a shop cloth at the end of the cable to catch the oil as it runs out the end or place the end in an empty container. Discard this oil as it is dirty.

4. Remove the lubricator, reconnect the cable(s) and adjust the cable(s) as described in this chapter.

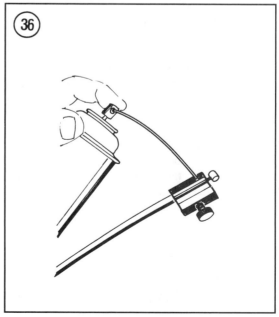

Swing Arm and Relay Arm Lubrication

The swing arm and relay arm pivot shafts are equipped with grease nipples (**Figure 37**) for periodic lubrication. At the intervals specified in **Table 1**, use a grease gun filled with a lithium soap base grease and lubricate each of the pivot shafts.

> *CAUTION*
> *Make sure to wipe off the grease nipple with a shop cloth before using the grease gun. This prevents dirt from being mixed with the grease and contaminating the pivot shaft and bearing area.*

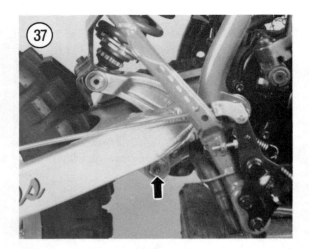

Speedometer/Tachometer Cable Lubrication

Lubricate the speedometer and tachometer cables every year or whenever needle operation become erratic.
1. Unscrew the retaining collar and remove the cables from the instrument panel (**Figure 38**) or at the front wheel.
2. Pull the cable(s) from the cable sheath.
3. If the grease on the cable is contaminated, thoroughly clean off all old grease.
4. Thoroughly coat the cable with a good grade of multipurpose grease and reinstall into the sheath.
5. Make sure the cable is correctly seated into the drive unit. If the cable is hard to seat, perform the following:
   a. *Speedometer cable*: Unscrew the cable collar at the front wheel (**Figure 39**) and disconnect the cable from the speedometer drive unit.
   b. *Tachometer cable (XT350)*: Remove the small Phillips screw at the clutch cover and pull the tachometer cable (**Figure 40**) out of the drive unit in the cover.
   c. Reassemble the cable into the drive unit and attach the cable at the instrument panel. Tighten all cable collars or screw securely.

Miscellaneous Lubrication Points

Lubricate the clutch lever, front brake lever, rear brake pedal pivot point and the sidestand pivot point.

PERIODIC MAINTENANCE

Drive Chain Free Play Inspection

The drive chain (A, **Figure 41**) must have adequate free play so that the chain is not strung tight when the swing arm is horizontal. On the other hand, too much play may cause the chain to jump off the sprockets with potentially disastrous results. When riding in mud and sand, dirt buildup will make the chain tighter. Recheck chain play and readjust as required. Set free play within the specifications listed in **Table 7**.

1. Place the bike on a crate so that the rear wheel clears the ground. Spin the wheel and check the chain for tightness at several spots. Check and adjust the chain at its tightest point.

2. Lower the bike so that both wheels are on the ground and the bike is in a vertical position. There should not be a rider on the seat when performing the following step.

3. Push the middle of the lower chain run up and down (**Figure 42**). The play should be within the specifications in **Table 7**.

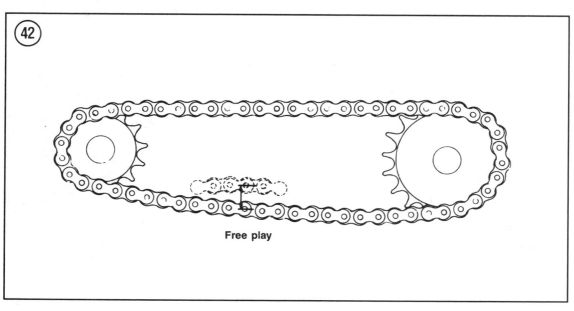

Free play

Drive Chain Adjustment

When adjusting the drive chain, you must also maintain rear wheel alignment. A misaligned rear wheel can cause poor handling and pulling to one side, as well as increased sprocket and chain wear.

On all models, cam type chain adjusters (**Figure 43**) are used. Slots (A) are cut into the outside of the adjuster that align with a series of numbers and index marks. The slots engage a hardened pin (B) installed in each side of the swing arm. When both adjusters are set at the same mark, the rear wheel should be aligned correctly.

1. Loosen the rear brake adjuster wing nut (**Figure 44**).

2A. *XT350*: Remove the cotter pin and loosen the rear axle nut (**Figure 45**). Discard the cotter pin.

2B. *TT350*: Loosen the rear axle nut (**Figure 46**).

3. Turn each chain adjuster back and equal amount until the chain play is within specification. The left- and right-hand adjusters should be set to the same alignment mark. Do not overtighten the drive chain.

4. When the chain play is correct, check wheel alignment. Sight along the top of the drive chain from the rear sprocket to see that it is correctly aligned. It should leave the top of the rear sprocket in a straight line (A, **Figure 47**). If it is cocked to one side or the other (B and C, **Figure 47**) the wheel is incorrectly aligned and must be corrected.

> *NOTE*
> *If the chain alignment is incorrect, check the chain adjusters (A, Figure 43) for damage. If the adjusters are okay, check the hardened pin (B, Figure 43) installed in each side of the swing arm.*

> *NOTE*
> *To prevent a spongy-feeling brake, **partially** tighten the axle nut, spin the wheel, stop it forcefully with the brake pedal, then tighten the axle nut. This centers the brake backing plate in the brake drum.*

5. Tighten the axle nut to the torque specification in **Table 6**.

> *NOTE*
> *When tightening the axle nut, check the position of the chain adjusters. Typically, one adjuster will slip or rotate out of its adjustment slot (usually the one on the opposite side of the axle nut) as the axle nut is tightened. If an adjuster moves, check the hardened pin(s) and adjuster(s) for damage. Because the adjuster engagement area is small, any damage to the adjuster or pin will allow the adjuster to slip when the axle nut is tightened. When tightening the axle nut, make sure the adjuster slots engage the hardened pin completely. If an adjuster does not register with the hardened pin*

correctly, it will become damaged. This is something you will have to check whenever the rear axle nut is tightened.

6. Recheck chain play and alignment.

7. *XT350*: When the chain play and alignment is correct, install a new cotter pin through the end of the axle. Bend the pin over to lock the nut.

3

45

46

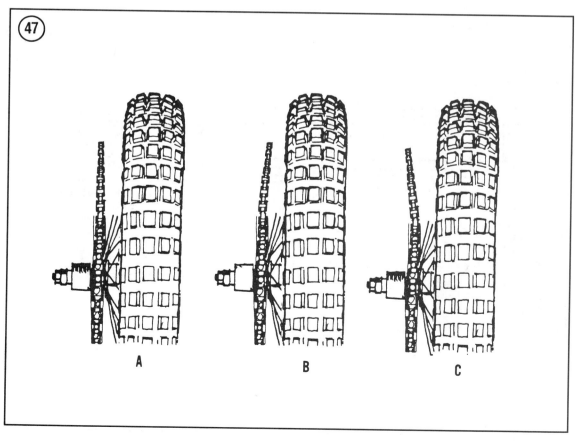

47

A   B   C

WARNING
The rear axle on TT350 models does not use a cotter pin to lock the rear nut. Instead, a prevailing torque nut is used. The end of this particular nut is designed to develop an interference between the nut and axle threads as the nut is threaded and tightened on the axle. Prevailing torque fasteners offer greater holding strength and this particular type of nut can be reused if in good condition. However, the locking efficiency of any prevailing torque nut is reduced each time it is loosened and tightened. For greatest safety, replace the nut whenever you feel its locking strength has been reduced.

8. Adjust the rear brake. *See Rear Brake Adjustment* in this chapter.

Drive Chain Inspection

Even with proper lubrication, cleaning and periodic adjustment, the drive chain and sprockets will wear out. Wear to the pins and bushings (**Figure 48**) results in chain stretch or lengthening of the chain.

To get an indication of chain stretch, pull one of the links away from the rear sprocket (**Figure 49**). If the link pulls away more than 1/2 the height of a sprocket tooth, the chain may be severely worn.

To accurately measure chain stretch, perform the following:

1. Loosen the axle nut and turn the chain adjusters to move the wheel rearward until the chain is taut.

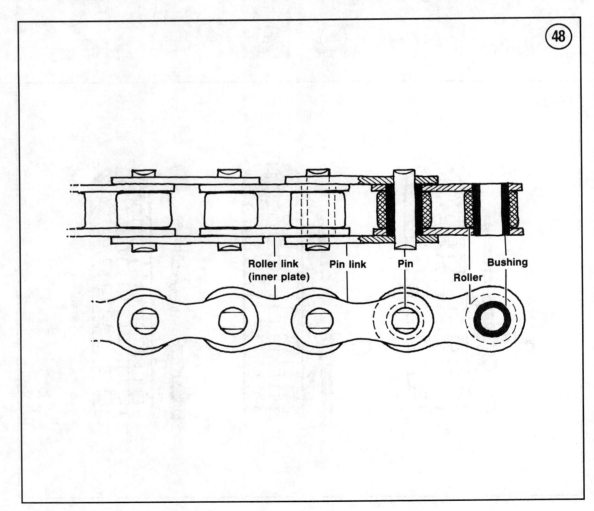

(48)

Roller link (inner plate)　　Pin link　　Pin　　Bushing　　Roller

NOTE
This procedure can be performed with the drive chain removed. If the chain is removed, pull it as tight as possible when performing the following.

2. Lay a scale along the top chain run (**Figure 50**), and measure the length of any 21 links in the chain, from the center of the first pin you select to the 21st pin. If the link length is more than the limit given in **Table 7**, install a new drive chain.

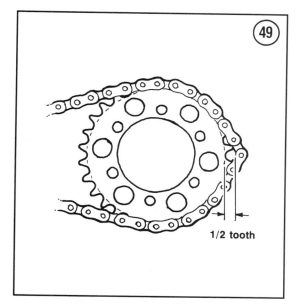

1/2 tooth

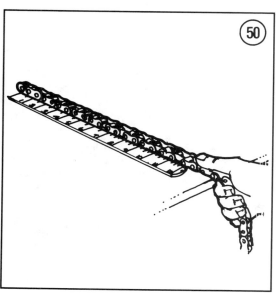

3. If the drive chain is worn, inspect the rear wheel and engine drive sprockets for undercutting or sharp teeth (**Figure 51**). If wear is evident, replace the sprockets too, or you'll soon wear out a new drive chain.

NOTE
*Check the inner faces of the inner plates (**Figure 48**). They should be lightly polished on both sides. If they show considerable wear on both sides, the sprockets are not aligned. Adjust alignment as described under **Drive Chain Adjustment** in this chapter.*

4. Readjust the drive chain, if necessary, as described in this chapter.

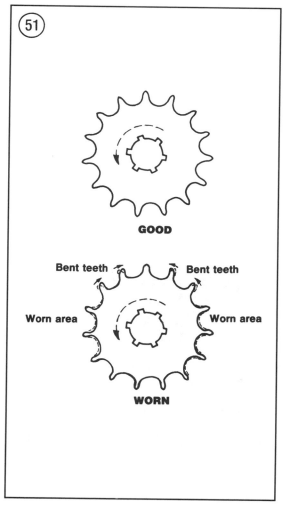

GOOD

Bent teeth   Bent teeth

Worn area   Worn area

WORN

3

Drive Chain Guard and Rollers Replacement

The drive chain rollers (**Figure 52** or **Figure 53**) and swing arm chain guide (B, **Figure 41**) should be inspected and replaced as necessary. A worn or damaged chain roller or guard will allow the drive chain to damage the rear swing arm.

To replace a chain roller, loosen and remove the drive chain if necessary. Then remove the roller bolt (**Figure 52** or **Figure 53**) and replace the roller. Also check the bushings, bolts and nuts for wear. Reverse to install.

To replace a swing arm chain guide (B, **Figure 41**), it is necessary to first remove the rear swing arm. Refer to Chapter Eleven.

Front Brake Lever Adjustment

Brake pad wear in the caliper is automatically adjusted as the piston moves forward in the caliper. However, the front brake lever free play must be maintained to prevent excessive brake drag. This would cause premature brake pad wear. Set the brake lever to have approximately 5-8 mm (3/16-5/16 in.) free play.

1. Slide the rubber cover away from the front brake lever.
2. Loosen the adjust screw locknut (**Figure 54**) and turn the adjust screw in or out to obtain the correct amount of brake lever free play.
3. Tighten the locknut and recheck the free play.
4. Reposition the rubber cover over the brake lever.
5. Operate the brake lever and make sure it moves freely.

Rear Brake Pedal Adjustment

Two adjustments are required for proper rear brake adjustment:
  a. Rear brake pedal height.
  b. Rear brake free play.

Rear brake pedal height

1. Measure the height position from the top of the right-hand footpeg to the top of the rear brake pedal and compare to the specifications in **Table 8**. See **Figure 55** (XT350) or **Figure 56** (TT350).
2. To adjust the pedal height, loosen the pedal adjust screw locknut and turn the adjust screw (**Figure 57**) as required.
3. Tighten the locknut and recheck the pedal height position.

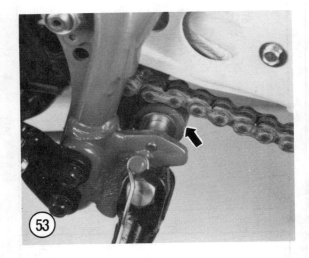

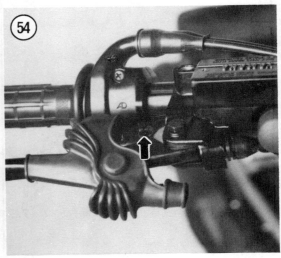

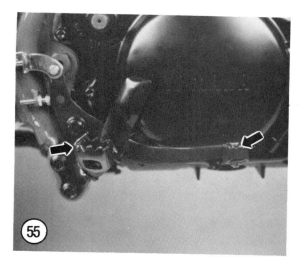

55

56

57

Rear brake free play

Rear brake pedal free play must be checked and maintained due to brake shoe wear. With your hand, move the rear brake pedal from its at-rest position to the point where the shoes contact the brake drum. This distance is rear brake pedal free play. Refer to **Table 8** for specifications. Adjust as follows.

1. Check the rear brake pedal height position as described in this chapter and adjust if necessary.
2. Turn the rear brake adjuster wingnut (**Figure 58**) as required to obtain the correct amount of free play.
3. Rotate the rear wheel and check for brake drag. Also operate the pedal several times to make sure it returns to the at-rest position immediately after release.

NOTE
Brake drag can sometimes be difficult to check because of the drag induced by the drive chain. If you are having brake problems and you want to be sure you have removed all brake drag, remove the master link and slip the drive chain off of the rear sprocket. Spin the rear wheel and check the rear brake. Adjust the rear brake as required then reinstall the drive chain.

WARNING
Do not ride your bike until you are sure the rear brake is operating correctly.

58

Rear Brake Light Switch Adjustment (XT350)

1. Turn the ignition switch to ON.

2. Depress the brake pedal. The light should come on just as the brake begins to work.

3. To make the light come earlier, hold the switch body and turn the adjusting nut as required.

Front Brake Fluid Level Check

The front brake reservoir should always be kept above the lower level line marked on the master cylinder window with brake fluid. See **Figure 59** (XT350) or **Figure 60** (TT350).

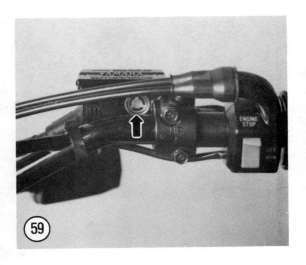

NOTE
If the brake fluid level lowers rapidly, check the disc brake line and fittings.

1. Place the bike on level ground and position the handlebar so the master cylinder reservoir is level.

2. Clean any dirt from the top cover prior to removing the cover.

3. Remove the 2 top cover screws and remove the cover (A, **Figure 61**) and diaphragm.

4. Add fresh brake fluid from a sealed container.

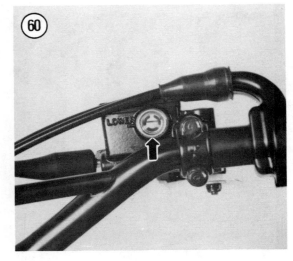

WARNING
Use brake fluid clearly marked DOT 3/DOT 4 and specified for disc brakes. Others may vaporize and cause brake failure. Do not intermix different brands or types of brake fluid as they may not be compatible. Do not intermix a silicone based (DOT 5) brake fluid as it can cause brake component damage leading to brake system failure.

CAUTION
Be careful when handling brake fluid. Do not spill it on painted or plastic surfaces as it will destroy the surface. Wash the area immediately with soap and water and thoroughly rinse it off.

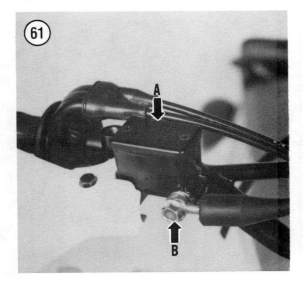

5. Reinstall the diaphragm and top cover. Install the screws and tighten securely.

Disc Brake Lines

Check the brake line between the master cylinder and the brake caliper. If there is any leakage, tighten the connections and bleed the brake as described in Chapter Twelve. See B, **Figure 61** and **Figure 62**. If this does not stop the leak or if a brake line is obviously damaged, cracked or chafed, replace the brake line and bleed the system.

Disc Brake Pad Wear

Both the XT350 and TT350 have a rubber inspection plug installed in the rear of the brake caliper. **Figure 63** shows the plug on XT350 models. Remove the plug and inspect the brake pads for excessive or uneven wear, scoring and oil or grease on the friction surface. Replace the brake pads if their thickness is 0.8 mm (0.031 in.) or less. Reinstall the plug. Refer to Chapter Twelve for brake pad replacement.

Disc Brake Fluid Change

Every time the reservoir cap is removed, a small amount of dirt and moisture enters the brake fluid. The same thing happens if a leak occurs or any part of the hydraulic system is loosened or disconnected. Dirt can clog the system and cause unnecessary wear. Water in the brake fluid vaporizes at high temperature, impairing the hydraulic action and reducing the brake's stopping ability.

To maintain peak performance, change the brake fluid once a year. To change brake fluid, follow the *Brake Bleeding* procedures in Chapter Twelve.

WARNING
Use brake fluid clearly marked DOT 3/DOT 4 only. Others may vaporize and cause brake failure.

Rear Brake Shoe Wear Check (XT350)

The XT350 has a rubber inspection plug installed in the rear brake panel (**Figure 64**). Remove the plug and inspect the brake shoes for excessive wear, scoring and oil or grease on the friction surface. Replace the brake shoes if their thickness is 2.0 mm (0.08 in.) or less. Reinstall the plug. Refer to Chapter Twelve for brake shoe replacements.

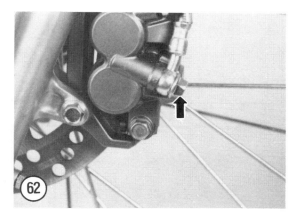

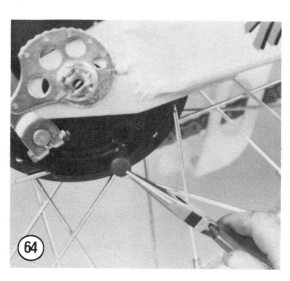

Rear Brake Shoe Wear Check (TT350)

To check rear brake shoe wear on TT350 models, depress the rear brake pedal. Then check the pointed wear indicator fixed to the brake arm (**Figure 65**). If the indicator points to the wear limit line cast into the brake panel plate, replace the brake shoes. Refer to Chapter Twelve for brake shoe replacement.

Clutch Adjustment

Continuous use of the clutch lever causes the clutch cable to stretch. For the clutch to operate correctly, the clutch cable free play must be maintained at 2-3 mm (3/32-1/8 in.). See **Figure 66** (XT350) or **Figure 67** (TT350). If there is no clutch cable free play, the clutch cannot disengage completely. This would cause clutch slippage and rapid clutch plate wear.

> *NOTE*
> *Clutch lever free play on TT350 models is measured at the end of the clutch lever because the handlebar hand protector prevents accurate measurement at the adjuster.*

> *NOTE*
> *When rebuilding or reassembling the clutch assembly, perform the **Clutch Mechanism Adjustment** in Chapter Six before adjusting the clutch cable.*

1. Pull the clutch lever toward the handlebar. When cable resistance is felt, hold the lever and measure the gap shown in **Figure 66** (XT350) or **Figure 67** (TT350); this is clutch cable free play. If resistance was felt as soon as you pulled the clutch lever, there is no cable free play.

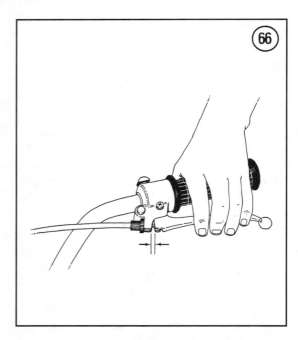

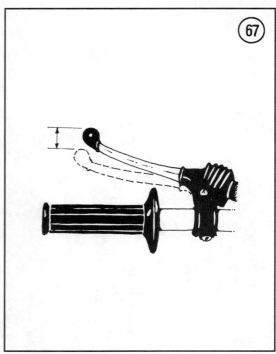

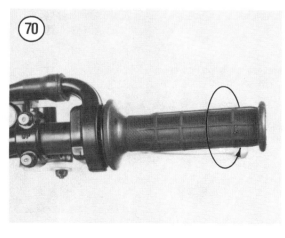

2. See **Figure 68**. At the hand lever, loosen the locknut (A) and turn the adjusting barrel (B) in or out to obtain the correct amount of free play. Tighten the locknut.

3. If the proper amount of free play cannot be achieved at the handlebar adjuster, perform the following:

    a. Loosen the locknut (A, **Figure 68**) and turn the adjuster (B, **Figure 68**) all the way in toward the clutch lever.

    b. Loosen the clutch cable adjuster locknuts at the engine (**Figure 69**). Then move the cable to take up as much clutch cable slack as possible. Tighten the locknuts (**Figure 69**).

    c. At the hand lever, loosen the locknut (A, **Figure 68**) and turn the adjusting barrel (B, **Figure 68**) in or out to obtain the correct amount of free play. Tighten the locknut.

4. If the clutch cable free play cannot be achieved using these adjustment points, the clutch cable has stretched excessively and must be replaced.

Throttle Cable Adjustment and Operation

All models use a dual throttle cable setup. For correct operation, the throttle should have 2-5 mm (3/32-3/16 in.) free play. In time, the throttle cable free play will become excessive from cable stretch. This will delay throttle response and affect low speed operation. On the other hand, if there is no throttle cable free play, an excessively high idle can result.

1. Start the engine and allow it to idle.

2. Adjust the engine idle speed as described in this chapter.

3. With the engine at idle, twist the throttle (**Figure 70**) to raise engine speed.

4. Determine the amount of movement (free play) required to raise the engine speed from idle. If the free play is incorrect, perform the following.

5. Remove the fuel tank as described under *Fuel Tank Removal/Installation* in Chapter Eight.

6. Locate the 2 throttle cables at the point where they attach to the carburetors. The throttle cables are labeled 1 and 2. See **Figure 71** for cable identification.

7. Loosen the No. 1 throttle cable adjuster locknuts and turn the adjuster a maximum of 5 mm (3/16 in.) until the free play is correct. Tighten the locknuts. If the free play cannot be corrected by turning the No. 1 cable, adjust the No. 2 throttle cable. Loosen the No. 2 throttle cable adjuster locknuts and turn the adjuster until the free play is correct. Tighten the locknuts and recheck the free play adjustment.

NOTE
If the throttle cable free play cannot be adjusted correctly, the throttle cables have stretched excessively and must be replaced as a set.

8. Make sure the throttle grip rotates freely from a fully closed to fully open position.
9. Reinstall the fuel tank.
10. Start the engine and allow it to idle. Turn the handlebar from side-to-side. If the idle increases, the throttle cable is routed incorrectly or there is not enough cable free play.

Throttle Grip

Periodically, the throttle grip and throttle housing should be cleaned and serviced.

1. Remove the Phillips screws securing the throttle housing (A, **Figure 72**).
2. Separate the throttle housings (B, **Figure 72**).
3. Disconnect the throttle cables at the twist grip.
4. Clean the inner twist grip bore with electrical contact cleaner.
5. Clean the throttle housings thoroughly.
6. Check the end of the handlebar for burrs or other damage that would cause the twist grip to stick or operate sluggishly. If necessary, smooth the end of the handlebar with a file.
7. Install by reversing these steps. Make sure the throttle grip rotates freely from a fully closed to fully open position.

Decompression Cable Adjustment

The decompression cable should always be checked and adjusted after adjusting the valves or when the cable is removed or replaced.
1. Park the bike on its sidestand.
2. Remove the spark plug. This will make it easier to rotate the engine by hand.
3. Remove the pinch bolt securing the gearshift lever and remove the lever. If the lever is tight, insert a screwdriver into the slot in the back of the lever and pull it off.

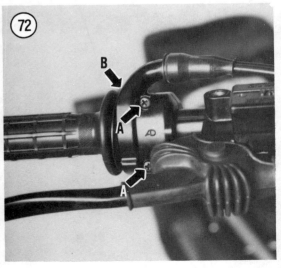

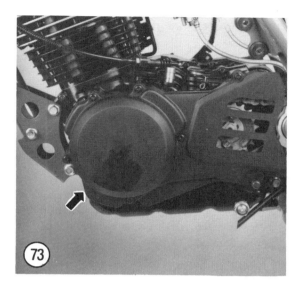

73

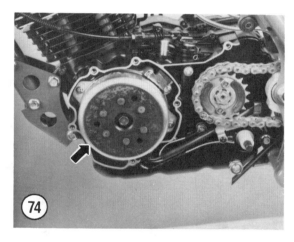

74

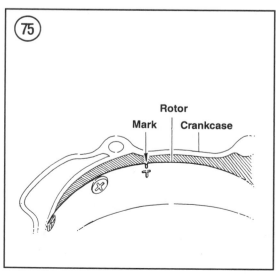

75

4. Remove the alternator cover screws and remove the cover (**Figure 73**).

5. Turn the rotor (**Figure 74**) and align the "T" mark on the rotor with the crankcase timing mark (**Figure 75**) to bring the piston to top dead center (TDC) as described under *Valve Clearance Measurement*.

6. Measure the free play at the end of the decompression cam lever as shown in **Figure 76**. The correct amount of free play is listed in **Table 9**.

7. To adjust the free play, locate the decompression cable adjuster on the right-hand side of the engine (**Figure 77**). Loosen the cable adjuster locknut (A) and turn the adjuster (B) until the correct amount of free play at the cam lever is achieved (**Figure 75**). Tighten the locknut (A, **Figure 77**).

3

CAUTION
If the free play is not adjusted correctly, it will result in hard starting (excessive free play) or cause erratic engine idle and possibly a burned exhaust valve (insufficient free play).

8. Reinstall the spark plug, alternator cover and shift lever.

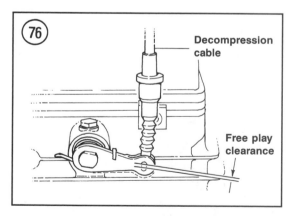

76 Decompression cable

Free play clearance

77

Air Filter

The air filter element should be removed, cleaned, and re-oiled at intervals indicated in **Table 1**.

The air filter removes dust and abrasive particles from the air before it enters the carburetor and engine. Very fine particles that enter into the engine will cause rapid wear to the piston rings, cylinder and bearings and may clog small passages in the carburetor. Never run your Yamaha without the air filter element installed.

Proper air filter servicing can do more to ensure long service from your engine than any other single item.

All models are equipped with a foam air filter element. To work properly, the filter element must be properly cleaned and oiled with a *foam* air filter oil.

1A. *XT350*: Remove the air filter element as follows:

a. Remove the right-hand side cover.

b. Remove the screws securing the air filter cover and remove the cover (**Figure 78**).

c. Grasp the air filter guide plastic tab (**Figure 79**) and pull the air filter element out of the housing.

d. Pull the plastic guide out of the filter element (**Figure 80**).

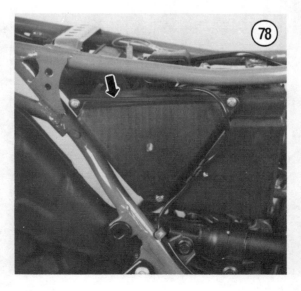

1B. *TT350*: Remove the air filter element as follows:

a. Remove the left-hand side cover.

b. Disconnect the rubber cover band (A, **Figure 81**) and remove the air filter cover (B, **Figure 81**).

c. Disconnect the filter element wire hook (A, **Figure 82**) and remove the air filter element (B, **Figure 82**).

d. Pull the filter support out of the air filter element.

2. Examine the inside of the air box. There should be no signs of dust or dirt on the inside of the air box cover or sides. If dirt is noticeable, the air filter may be damaged or it was improperly serviced. On XT350 models, check the air box screen (**Figure 83**) for damage.

3. Clean the inside of the air box with a clean shop rag soaked in solvent or soap and water.

4. After the air box has dried, coat the inside of the air box with a layer of wheel bearing grease.

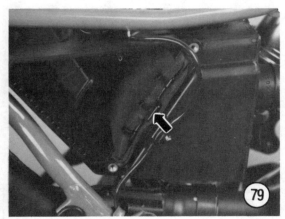

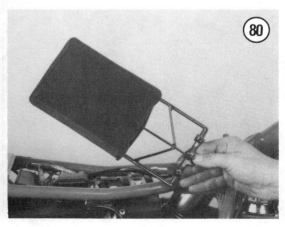

Apply the grease with your hands so that it covers all of the air box inside surfaces. The grease works like an additional filter and will help to absorb dirt in the air box. On XT350 models, do not apply grease to the air box screen (**Figure 83**).

> *CAUTION*
> *Do not clean the air filter element with gasoline. Besides being an extreme fire hazard, gasoline will break down the seam glue used to hold the filter together. This will cause filter damage and allow unfiltered air to enter the engine.*

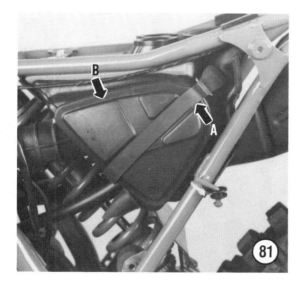

5. Fill a clean pan with liquid cleaner and warm water. If you are using an accessory air filter, the manufacturer may also sell a special air filter cleaner. Check with your dealer.

6. Submerge the filter into the cleaning solution and gently work the cleaner into the filter pores. Soak and squeeze (gently) the filter to clean it.

> *CAUTION*
> *Do not wring or twist the filter when cleaning it. This harsh action could damage a filter pore or tear the filter loose at a seam. This would allow unfiltered air to enter the engine and cause severe and rapid engine wear.*

7. Rinse the filter under warm water while soaking and gently squeezing it.

8. Repeat Step 6 and Step 7 two or three times or until there are no signs of dirt being rinsed from the filter.

9. After cleaning the filter, inspect it. If it is torn or broken in any area it should be replaced. Do not run the engine with a damaged filter as it may allow dirt to enter the engine and cause severe engine wear.

10. Set the filter aside and allow it to dry thoroughly.

> *CAUTION*
> *A damp filter will not trap fine dust. Make sure the filter is completely dry before oiling it.*

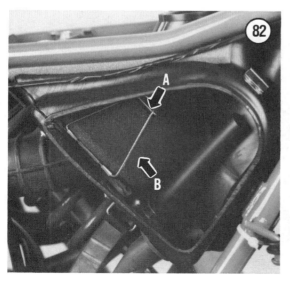

11. Properly oiling an air filter element is a messy job. You may want to wear a pair of disposable rubber gloves when performing this procedure. Oil the filter as follows:

a. Purchase a box of gallon size reclosable storage bags. These bags can be used when cleaning the filter as well as for storing engine and carburetor parts during disassembly.

b. Place the cleaned filter into a storage bag.

c. Pour foam air filter oil onto the filter to soak it.

d. Gently squeeze and release the outside of the bag to soak filter oil into the filter's pores. Repeat until all of the filter's pores are discolored with the oil.

e. Remove the filter from the bag and check the pores for uneven oiling. This is indicated by light or dark areas. If necessary, soak the filter and squeeze it again.

f. When the filter oiling is even, squeeze the filter a final time.

12. Remove the filter from the bag. Install the filter support inside the filter.

13. *TT350*: Apply a coat of thick wheel bearing grease to the filter's sealing surface (**Figure 84**).

14. Check the seal on the air filter cover (**Figure 85**) for wear or damage. The seal is a weak area as it is easily deformed and damaged. Replace the seal if necessary.

15A. *XT350*: Install the air filter element as follows:

a. Align the filter assembly with the slots in the air filter housing and install the air filter assembly. The filter support should face out when the filter is installed as shown in **Figure 79**.

b. Install the air filter cover and its mounting screws.

c. Install the right-hand side cover.

15B. *TT350*: Install the air filter element as follows:

a. Insert the air filter element (B, **Figure 82**) into the air box.

b. Secure the air filter element with the metal hook (A, **Figure 82**). Make sure the hook is firmly connected.

c. Install the air filter cover (B, **Figure 81**) and secure it with the rubber strap (A, **Figure 81**). Make sure the strap connects firmly to the hook on the air box housing.

16. Pour the left-over filter oil from the bag back into the bottle for reuse.

17. Dispose of the plastic bag.

Fuel Line Inspection

Inspect the fuel line from the fuel tank to the carburetor (**Figure 86**). If it is cracked or starting to deteriorate, it must be replaced. Make sure the small hose clamps are in place and holding securely. Also make sure that the overflow and vent tubes are in place.

WARNING
A damaged or deteriorated fuel line presents a very dangerous fire hazard to both the rider and the machine if fuel should spill onto a hot engine or exhaust pipe.

NOTE
If you have been experiencing fuel contamination that is plugging up carburetor jets (especially the pilot jet), install a fuel filter in the fuel line between the fuel tank and the carburetor. Use the stock Yamaha fasteners to hold the line to the filter. If the contamination problem is severe, you may want to flush the fuel tank before installing the filter.

Emission Control Hoses (XT350 California Models)

All XT350 models originally sold in California are equipped with an evaporative emission control system. Refer to *Emission Control* in Chapter Eight for inspection procedures and additional information.

Wheel Bearings

The wheel bearings should be periodically checked for roughness or other damage. Factory

equipped sealed bearings do not require periodic lubrication. However, if non-sealed bearings have been installed by a previous owner, they should be cleaned and repacked every six month or more often if the vehicle is operated often in water (especially salt water). Service procedures are covered in Chapter Ten (front) and Chapter Eleven (rear).

Steering Head Adjustment Check

Tapered roller bearings are installed in the upper and lower bearing mounting areas. A loose bearing adjustment will hamper steering and cause premature bearing and race wear. In severe conditions, a loose bearing adjustment can cause loss of control. Steering head play should be checked often, especially after riding the bike off-road.

1. Place the bike on a stand so that the front wheel clears the ground.

2. Center the front wheel. Push lightly against the left handlebar grip to start the wheel turning to the right, then let go. The wheel should continue turning under its own momentum until the forks hit their stop. Try the same in the other direction.

3. If, with a light push in either direction, the front wheel will turn all the way to the top, the steering adjustment is not too tight.

4. Center the front wheel and kneel in front of it. Grasp the bottoms of the fork legs. Try to pull the forks toward you, and then try to push them toward the engine. If no play is felt, the steering adjustment is not too loose.

5. If the steering adjustment is too tight or too loose, readjust it as described under *Steering Adjustment* in Chapter Ten.

Handlebars

Inspect the handlebars weekly for any signs of damage. A bent or damaged handlebar should be replaced. The knurled section of your bars should be kept very rough. Keep the clamps clean with a wire brush. Any time that the bars slip in the clamps (like when you land flat and they move forward slightly) they should be removed and wire brushed clean to prevent small balls of aluminum from gathering in the clamps and reducing the grip surface area.

Spark Arrester Cleaning

Periodically remove the screw holding the spark arrester (**Figure 87**) and pull it out of the end of the muffler housing. Clean the pipe of all exhaust residue with a wire brush and solvent. Reverse to install.

Nuts, Bolts and Other Fasteners

Constant vibration can loosen many of the fasteners on the motorcycle. Check the tightness of all fasteners, especially those on:

   a. Engine mounting hardware.
   b. Engine crankcase covers.
   c. Handlebar and front forks.
   d. Gearshift lever.
   e. Kickstarter lever.
   f. Brake pedal and lever.
   g. Exhaust system.

FRONT FORK AIR PRESSURE

For models with a pressurized fork, the air pressure must be maintained at the correct pressure and both legs must have the same pressure.

1. Support the bike so that the front wheel clears the ground.

2. Remove the air valve caps.

3. Attach a small manual air pump to the air valve fitting on one of the fork tubes. Inflate to the desired inflation pressure, making sure to keep within the following pressure range:

   a. Standard: 0 psi (0 kg/cm^2).
   b. Maximum: 17 psi (1.2 kg/cm^2).

> *CAUTION*
> *Never use a high pressure air supply to pressurize the legs. Never exceed the maximum allowable air pressure listed or the oil seal will be damaged. The air pressure difference between*

the 2 legs should not be more than 1.4 psi (0.1 kg/cm^2).

> *WARNING*
> *Use only compressed air—**do not** use any other type of compressed gas as an explosion may result. Never heat the front fork with a torch or place them near an open flame or extreme heat.*

4. Repeat for the opposite leg.

5. Reinstall the air valve cap.

ENGINE TUNE-UP

A tune-up consists of a series of inspections, adjustments and parts replacement to compensate for normal wear and deterioration of engine components. Regular tune-ups are especially important to off-road and dual-purpose motorcycles.

Since proper engine operation depends upon a number of interrelated system functions, a tune-up consisting of only one or two corrections will seldom give lasting results. For improved power, performance and operating economy, a thorough and systematic procedure of analysis and correction is necessary.

The following paragraphs discuss each facet of a proper tune-up which should be performed in the order given. Unless otherwise specified, the engine

should be thoroughly cool before starting any tune-up procedure.

A tune-up consists of the following:

a. Valve clearance check and adjustment.
b. Engine compression check.
c. Ignition system inspection.
d. Carburetor check and adjustment.

To perform a tune-up on your Yamaha, you will need the following tools and equipment:

a. Spark plug wrench.
b. Ratchet and assorted sockets.
c. Flat feeler gauge.
d. Special tool for changing valve lifter shims (Yamaha valve adjusting tool, part No. YM-4106).
e. Compression gauge.
f. Spark plug wire feeler gauge and gapper tool.
g. Ignition timing light.
h. Tachometer.

Valve Clearance Measurement

Valve clearance measurement must be made with the engine cool, at room temperature.

1. Remove the valve cover as described under *Valve Cover Removal/Installation* in Chapter Four.

CAUTION
*To prevent expensive engine damage, refer to **CAUTION** under **Spark Plug Removal** in this chapter.*

2. Remove the spark plug. This will make it easier to rotate the engine with a wrench.
3. Remove the pinch bolt securing the gearshift lever and remove the lever. If the lever is tight, insert a screwdriver into the slot in the back of the lever and pull it off.
4. Remove the alternator cover screws and remove the cover (**Figure 73**).
5. Turn the rotor (**Figure 74**) counterclockwise by hand and align the "T" mark on the rotor with the crankcase timing mark (**Figure 75**). This positions the piston at top dead center (TDC) on the compression stroke.

NOTE
*The cylinder position can be verified by observing the position of the camshaft lobes. When the piston is at TDC on the compression stroke, the camshaft lobes will be facing away from their respective lifter surface. See **Figure 88** and **Figure 89**.*

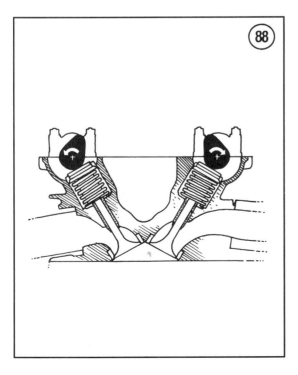

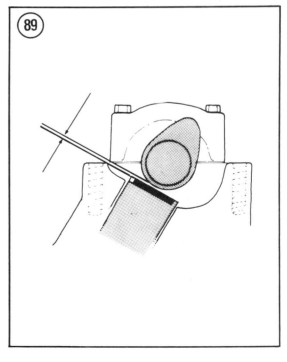

6. Insert a flat feeler gauge between the bottom of the cam and the top of the valve shim (**Figure 90**). Record the measurement and repeat for each valve. The valve clearance must be measured very accurately. If the clearance of any valve is incorrect, perform the *Valve Clearance Adjustment* procedure.

Valve Clearance Adjustment

To correct the clearance, the shim on top of the valve lifter must be replaced with one of the correct thickness. These shims are available in 25 different thicknesses from No. 200 (2.00 mm) to No. 320 (3.20 mm) in increments of 0.05 mm. These shims are available from Yamaha dealers. The thickness is marked on the face that contacts the lifter body (**Figure 91**).

A special tool, the Yamaha tappet adjusting tool (part No. YM-4106), is necessary for this procedure (**Figure 92**). The tappet adjusting tool holds the valve lifter down so the adjusting shim can be removed and replaced.

There is no set order to follow when replacing the valve shims as each valve can be serviced on the same rotor mark.

1. Turn the rotor (**Figure 74**) counterclockwise by hand and align the "T" mark on the rotor with the crankcase timing mark (**Figure 75**). This positions the piston at top dead center (TDC) on the compression stroke.

NOTE
The cylinder position can be verified by observing the position of the camshaft lobes. When the piston is at

TDC on the compression stroke, the camshaft lobes will be facing away from their respective lifter surface. See ***Figure 88*** *and* ***Figure 89***.

2. The top of each valve lifter has 2 slots (**Figure 93**) facing 180 degrees apart. The slot in each of the valve lifters must face toward the front and rear of the bike. With the rotor mark at "T" and no pressure is placed on the valve shims, rotate the valve lifters so that their lifter slots face forward and rearward.

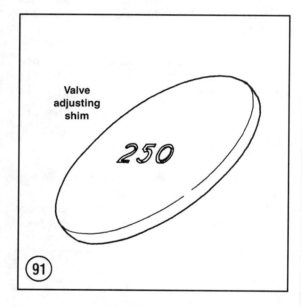

Valve adjusting shim

250

(91)

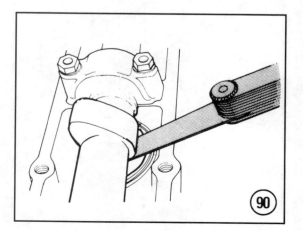

(90)

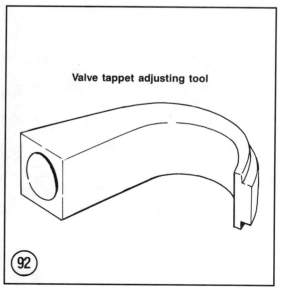

Valve tappet adjusting tool

(92)

3. Determine the valve to be adjusted.
4. Install the tappet adjusting tool into the cylinder head next to the valve lifter (**Figure 94**).
5. Turn the cam by rotating the crankshaft until the cam lobe fully depresses the valve lifter (valve is now completely open).

CAUTION
Do not allow the cam lobe to come in contact with the valve adjusting tool as it may fracture the cylinder head. To avoid cam contact with the tool, rotate the intake cam clockwise and the exhaust cam counterclockwise, as viewed from the left-hand side of the bike. See Figure 88.

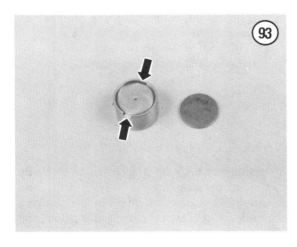

6. Carefully rotate the cam lobe off of the shim so it can be removed. Remove the shim from the lifter with a small screwdriver and needlenose pliers. Turn the shim over and note the number (**Figure 91**). Confirm the marking with a micrometer.
7. For correct shim selection proceed as follows:

NOTE
The following numbers are examples only. Use the actual measured clearance, correct clearance specification and existing shim number from your engine.

Actual measured clearance . . . . 0.50 mm
Minus specified clearance . . . . −0.19 mm
Equals excess clearance . . . . =0.31 mm

Existing shim number 220
Plus excess clearance . . . . +031
(0.31 mm)
Equals new shim number . . . . =251
Round off to the nearest
shim number 250

8. Install the new shim into the lifter with the number facing down. Make sure the shim is positioned correctly into the lifter.
9. Carefully rotate the cam until the lobe comes in contact with the new shim and lifter (see CAUTION following Step 5). Remove the adjusting tool.
10. Rotate the cam a couple of times to make sure the shim has properly seated into the lifter.
11. Recheck valve clearance as described under *Valve Clearance Measurement*. If clearance is incorrect, repeat these steps until proper clearance is obtained.
12. Repeat Steps 1-11 for remaining valves as necessary.

Compression Test

An engine with low compression cannot be properly tuned. A compression test measures the compression built up in the cylinder. At every tune-up, check cylinder compression. Record the results and compare them at the next check. A running record will show trends in deterioration so that corrective action can be taken before complete failure. The results, when properly interpreted, can indicate general cylinder, piston ring and valve condition.

NOTE
The valves must be properly adjusted to correctly interpret the results of this test.

1. Ensure that the choke valve is completely open. On XT350 models, make sure the engine stop switch is in the OFF position. On TT350 models, depress the engine kill switch while kicking the engine over.

CAUTION
To prevent expensive engine damage, refer to CAUTION under Spark Plug Removal in this chapter.

2. Remove the spark plug.

NOTE
A screw-in type compression gauge with a flexible adapter will be required for this procedure. See Compression Gauge in Chapter One. Before using the gauge, check that the rubber gasket on the end of the adapter is not cracked or damaged; the gasket seals the cylinder to ensure accurate compression readings.

3. Connect the compression gauge to the cylinder following manufacturer's instructions. Lubricate the adapter threads with engine oil to prevent damaging the spark plug threads.
4. *Open the throttle completely* and using the kickstarter, kick the engine over until there is no further rise in pressure. Maximum pressure is usually reached with 4-7 kicks.
5. Record the reading and then release the gauge pressure valve. Remove the compression gauge.

6. Standard compression pressure is specified in **Table 11**. Greater differences indicate worn or broken rings, leaky or sticky valves, blown head gasket or a combination of all.

If a low reading (10% or more) is obtained, it indicates valve or ring trouble. To determine which, pour about a teaspoon of engine oil through the spark plug hole onto the top of the piston. Turn the engine over once to clear some of the excess oil, then take another compression test and record the reading. If the compression returns to normal, the valves are good but the rings are defective. If compression does not increase, the valves require servicing. A valve could be hanging open but not burned or a piece of carbon could be on a valve seat.

NOTE
If the compression is low, the engine cannot be tuned to maximum performance. The worn parts must be replaced and the engine rebuilt.

Correct Spark Plug Heat Range

The proper spark plug is important in obtaining maximum performance and reliability. The condition of a used spark plug can tell a trained mechanic a lot about engine condition and carburetion.

Select a plug of the heat range designed for the loads and conditions under which the bike will be run. Use of incorrect heat ranges can cause a seized piston, scored cylinder wall, or damaged piston crown.

In general, use a hot plug for low speeds and low temperatures. Use a cold plug for high speeds, high engine loads and high temperatures. The plug should operate hot enough to burn off unwanted deposits, but not so hot that they burn themselves or cause preignition. A spark plug of the correct heat range will show a light tan color on the portion of the insulator within the cylinder after the plug has been in service. See **Figure 95**.

The reach (length) of a plug is also important. A longer than normal plug could interfere with the piston, causing permanent and severe damage. Refer to **Figure 96**.

SPARK PLUG CONDITION

(95)

3

NORMAL

- Identified by light tan or gray deposits on the firing tip.
- Can be cleaned.

GAP BRIDGED

- Identified by deposit buildup closing gap between electrodes.
- Caused by oil or carbon fouling. If deposits are not excessive, the plug can be cleaned.

OIL FOULED

- Identified by wet black deposits on the insulator shell bore and electrodes.
- Caused by excessive oil entering combustion chamber through worn rings and pistons, excessive clearance between valve guides and stems, or worn or loose bearings. Can be cleaned. If engine is not repaired, use a hotter plug.

CARBON FOULED

- Identified by black, dry fluffy carbon deposits on insulator tips, exposed shell surfaces and electrodes.
- Caused by too cold a plug, weak ignition, dirty air cleaner, too rich a fuel mixture, or excessive idling. Can be cleaned.

LEAD FOULED

- Identified by dark gray, black, yellow, or tan deposits or a fused glazed coating on the insulator tip.
- Caused by highly leaded gasoline. Can be cleaned.

WORN

- Identified by severely eroded or worn electrodes.
- Caused by normal wear. Should be replaced.

FUSED SPOT DEPOSIT

- Identified by melted or spotty deposits resembling bubbles or blisters.
- Caused by sudden acceleration. Can be cleaned.

OVERHEATING

- Identified by a white or light gray insulator with small black or gray brown spots and with bluish-burnt appearance of electrodes.
- Caused by engine overheating, wrong type of fuel, loose spark plugs, too hot a plug, or incorrect ignition timing. Replace the plug.

PREIGNITION

- Identified by melted electrodes and possibly blistered insulator. Metallic deposits on insulator indicate engine damage.
- Caused by wrong type of fuel, incorrect ignition timing or advance, too hot a plug, burned valves, or engine overheating. Replace the plug.

The standard heat range spark plug for the various models is listed in **Table 11**.

Spark Plug Removal

1. Grasp the spark plug lead (**Figure 97**) as near the plug as possible and pull it off the plug. If it is stuck to the plug, twist it slightly to break it loose.

> *CAUTION*
> *When the spark plug is removed, dirt around the plug can fall into the spark plug hole. This can cause expensive engine damage. In addition, dirt built-up underneath the fuel tank can also break loose and fall into the spark plug hole. If necessary, wrap a large cloth around the fuel tank before removing the spark plug.*

2. Blow away any dirt that has accumulated next to the spark plug base with compressed air. Use a compressor if you have one. Cans of compressed inert gas are available from photo stores.
3. Remove the spark plug with a 14 mm spark plug wrench.

> *NOTE*
> *If the plug is difficult to remove, apply penetrating oil, like WD-40 or Liquid Wrench, around the base of the plug and let it soak in about 10-20 minutes.*

4. Inspect the plug carefully. Look for broken center porcelain, excessively eroded electrodes and excessive carbon or oil fouling. See **Figure 95**.

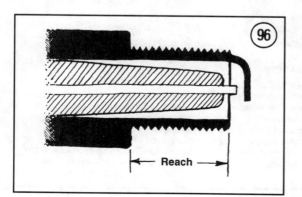

Reach

Gapping and Installing the Plug

A new spark plug should be carefully gapped to ensure a reliable, consistent spark. You must use a special spark plug tool with a wire gauge.
1. Remove the new spark plug from the box. Screw in the small piece that is loose in the box (**Figure 98**).

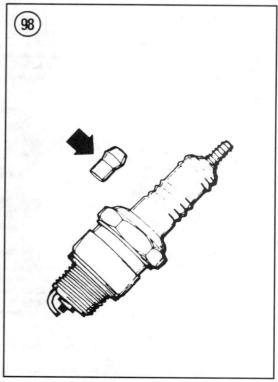

2. Insert a wire feeler gauge between the center and side electrode (**Figure 99**). The correct gap is listed in **Table 11**. If the gap is correct, you will feel a slight drag as you pull the wire through. If there is no drag, or the gauge won't pass through, bend the side electrode with the gapping tool (**Figure 100**) to set the proper gap. Remeasure with the wire gauge.

CAUTION
Never try to close the electrode gap by tapping the spark plug on a solid surface. This can damage the plug internally. Always use the special tool to open or close the gap.

3. Check the spark plug hole threads and clean with an appropriate size spark plug chaser, if necessary, before installing the plug. This will remove any corrosion, carbon build-up or minor flaws from the threads. Coat the chaser threads with grease to catch chips or foreign matter. Use care to avoid cross-threading.

4. Apply a thin film of anti-seize compound to the spark plug threads and screw the plug in by hand until it seats. Very little effort is required. If force is necessary, you have the plug cross-threaded. Unscrew it and try again.

5. Use a spark plug wrench and tighten the plug an additional 1/4 to 1/2 turn after the gasket has made contact with the head or tighten it to the torque specification in **Table 6**. If you are installing an old, regapped plug and reusing the old gasket, only tighten an additional 1/4 turn.

NOTE
Do not overtighten. This will only squash the gasket and destroy its sealing ability.

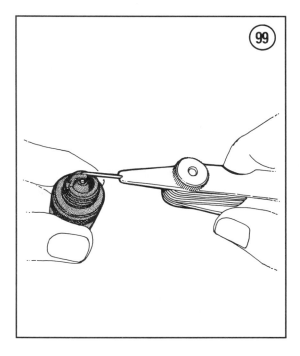

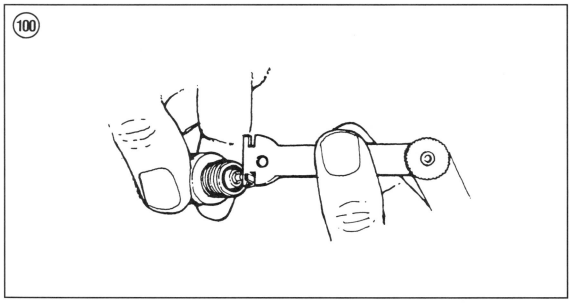

6. Install the spark plug lead. Make sure it is on tight.

CAUTION
Make sure the spark plug lead is pulled away from the exhaust pipe.

Reading Spark Plugs

Much information about engine and spark plug performance can be determined by careful examination of the spark plug. This information is only valid after performing the following steps.
1. Ride the bike a short distance at full throttle in any gear.
2. Push the engine stop switch to OFF (XT350) or push on the kill switch (TT350) before closing the throttle and simultaneously pull in the clutch or shift to neutral; coast and brake to a stop.
3. Remove the spark plug and examine it. Compare it to **Figure 95**.

If the insulator is white or burned, the engine is running hot. If you changed the spark plug, make sure the new plug has the correct heat range.

A too-cold plug will have sooty or oily deposits.

If the plug has a light tan or gray colored deposit and no abnormal gap wear or electrode erosion is evident, the plug and the engine are running properly.

If the plug exhibits a black insulator tip, damp oily film over the firing end, and a carbon layer over the entire nose, it is oil fouled. An oil fouled plug can be cleaned, but it is better to replace it.

NOTE
A too-hot or too-cold plug reading is also an indication that the engine is not operating correctly. If the correct spark plug is installed for the altitude that you are riding in, one of the engine systems is malfunctioning or the system is tuned incorrectly. Refer to Chapter Two.

Ignition Timing

The models covered in this manual are equipped with a capacitor discharge ignition (CDI) system. This system uses no breaker points and is non-adjustable. The timing should be checked to make

sure all ignition components are operating correctly.

Incorrect ignition timing can cause a drastic loss of engine performance and efficiency. It may also cause overheating.

Before starting on this procedure, check all electrical connections related to the ignition system. Make sure all connections are tight and free of corrosion and that all ground connections are tight. Refer to *Ignition System* in Chapter Nine.
1. Place the bike on the sidestand.
2. Remove the pinch bolt securing the gearshift lever and remove the lever. If the lever is tight, insert a screwdriver into the slot in the back of the lever and pull it off.
3. Remove the alternator cover screws and remove the cover (**Figure 73**).
4. Connect a portable tachometer following the manufacturer's instructions. The bike's tachometer is not accurate enough in the low rpm range for this adjustment.
5. Connect a timing light to the spark plug following the manufacturer's instructions.
6. Start the engine and let it idle at the idle speed listed in **Table 11**.
7. Aim the timing light at the crankcase timing mark next to the rotor. If the "F" timing mark aligns with the timing mark on the crankcase (**Figure 101**), the timing is correct.
8. Shut off the engine and disconnect the timing light and portable tachometer.
9. If the timing is incorrect, refer to *Ignition System Troubleshooting* in Chapter Nine. There is no method of adjusting ignition timing.
10. Install the alternator cover and the gear shift lever.

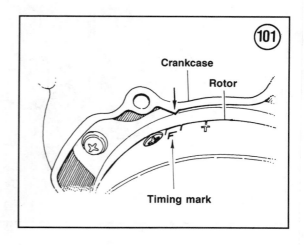
Crankcase
Rotor
Timing mark

Carburetor Idle Speed Adjustment

Proper idle speed is a balance between a low enough idle to give adequate compression braking and a high enough idle to prevent engine stalling (if desired). The idle air/fuel mixture affects transition from idle to part throttle openings.
1. Make sure that the throttle cable free play is correct as described in this chapter.
2. Start the engine and allow it to warm up for 2-3 minutes.
3. Turn the throttle stop screw (**Figure 102**) to set the idle speed.

> *WARNING*
> *With the engine idling, move the handlebar from side-to-side. If idle speed increases during this movement, the throttle cable needs adjusting or it may be incorrectly routed through the frame. Correct this problem immediately. Do not ride the bike in this unsafe condition.*

STORAGE

Several months of inactivity can cause serious problems and a general deterioration of your Yamaha. This is especially true in areas of weather extremes. During the winter months it is advisable to specially prepare the bike for lay-up.

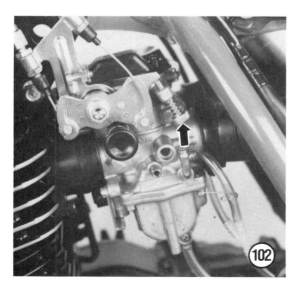

Selecting a Storage Area

Most riders store their bikes in their home garages. If you do not have a home garage, facilities suitable for long-term motorcycle storage are readily available for rent or lease in most areas. In selecting a building, consider the following points.
1. The storage area must be dry, free from dampness and excessive humidity. Heating is not necessary, but the building should be well insulated to minimize extreme temperature variations.
2. Buildings with large window areas should be avoided, or such windows should be masked (also a good security measure) if direct sunlight can fall on the bike.
3. Buildings in industrial areas, where factories are liable to emit corrosive fumes, are not desirable, nor are facilities near bodies of salt water.
4. The area should be selected to minimize the possibility of loss from fire, theft, or vandalism. The area should be fully insured, perhaps with a package covering fire, theft, vandalism, weather, and liability. Talk this over with your insurance agent and get approval on these matters. The building should be fireproof and items such as the security of doors and windows, alarm facility, and proximity of police should be considered.

Preparing Bike for Storage

Careful preparation will minimize deterioration and make it easier to restore the bike to service later. Use the following procedure.
1. Wash the bike completely. Make certain to remove all dirt in all the hard to reach parts like the cooling fins on the head and cylinder. Completely dry all parts of the bike to remove all moisture. Wax all painted and polished surfaces.
2. Run the bike for about 20-30 minutes to warm up the oil. Drain the oil, regardless of the time since the last oil change. Refill with the normal quantity and type of oil.
3. Drain all gasoline from the fuel tank, interconnecting hose, and the carburetor. Leave the fuel shutoff valve in the ON position.
4. Lubricate the drive chain and control cables; refer to specific procedures in this chapter.

5. Remove the spark plug and add about one teaspoon of engine oil into the cylinder. Reinstall the spark plug and turn the engine over to distribute the oil to the cylinder walls and piston. Depress the engine kill switch while doing this to prevent it from starting.

6. Tape or tie a plastic bag over the end of the silencer to prevent the entry of moisture.

7. Check the tire pressure, inflate to the correct pressure and move the bike to the storage area. Place it securely on a milk crate or wood blocks with both wheels off the ground.

8. *XT350*: Remove the battery as described in this chapter. Coat the battery cables with a petroleum jelly such as Vaseline or a light mineral grease. Store the battery in a cool and accessible area so that it can be checked monthly.

9. Cover the bike with a tarp, blanket or heavy plastic drop cloth. Place this cover over the bike mainly as a dust cover—do not wrap it tightly, especially any plastic material, as it may trap moisture causing condensation. Leave room for air to circulate around the bike.

Inspection During Storage

Try to inspect the bike weekly while in storage. Any deterioration should be corrected as soon as possible. For example, if corrosion of bright metal parts is observed, cover them with a light coat of grease or silicone spray after a thorough polishing.

Turn the engine over a couple of times. Don't start it; use the kickstarter and hold the kill switch on. Pump the front forks to keep the seals lubricated.

Once a month, check the battery as described in this chapter. Service as required.

Restoring Bike to Service

A bike that has been properly prepared and stored in a suitable area requires only light maintenance to restore to service. It is advisable, however, to perform a spring tune-up.

1. Before removing the bike from the storage area, reinflate the tires to the correct pressures. Air loss during storage may have nearly flattened the tires, and moving the bike can cause damage to tires, tubes and rims.

2. When the bike is brought to the work area, turn the fuel shutoff valve to the OFF position, and refill the fuel tank with the correct fuel/oil mixture. Remove the main jet cover on the base of the carburetor, turn the fuel shutoff valve to the ON position, and allow several cups of fuel to pass through the fuel system. Turn the fuel shutoff valve to the OFF position and install the main jet cover.

WARNING
Place a metal container under the carburetor to catch all expelled fuel— this presents a real fire danger if allowed to drain onto the bike and the floor. Dispose of the fuel properly.

3. Remove the spark plug and squirt a small amount of fuel into the cylinder to help remove the oil coating.

4. Reinstall the battery as described in this chapter. Service or charge battery as required.

5. Install a fresh spark plug and start up the engine.

6. Perform the standard tune-up as described earlier in this chapter.

7. Check the operation of the engine stop switch (XT350) or the engine kill switch (TT350). Oxidation of the switch contacts during storage may make it inoperative.

8. Clean and test ride the motorcycle.

Table 1 MAINTENANCE SCHEDULE*

3

Every 300 miles (500 km)
• Lubricate drive chain.
• Check and adjust drive chain slack.
• Check chain for excessive wear.
Initial 600 miles (1,000 km)
• Check and adjust valve clearance.
• Change engine oil and filter. Clean oil strainer.
• Check and adjust rear brake pedal free play.
• Check and adjust clutch cable free play.
• Lubricate control cables.
• Check sidestand switch operation.
Every 3,800 miles (6,000 km) or 7 months
• Check and adjust valve clearance.
• Check fuel line. Replace if necessary.
• Check exhaust system and gaskets.
• Check and adjust carburetor idle speed.
• Check and adjust carburetor throttle cable.
• Check and adjust decompression cable free play.
• Change engine oil and filter. Clean oil strainer.
• Clean and reoil air filter element.
• Check and adjust rear brake pedal free play.
• Check front brake pad wear.
• Check rear brake shoe wear.
• Check and adjust clutch cable free play.
• Lubricate control cables.
• Lubricate swing arm pivot shaft.
• Lubricate suspension link pivot shafts.
• Lubricate brake and clutch lever pivot bolts.
• Lubricate sidestand pivot shaft.
• Lubricate kickstarter crank boss.
• Change front fork oil.
• Check front steering bearing play.
• Check wheel bearing condition.
• Check battery specific gravity and fluid level.
• Check sidestand switch operation.
Every 4,400 miles (7,000 km) or 7 months
• Check spark plug gap and condition.
• Check crankcase ventilation system.
Every year
• Replace the spark plugs.
Every 15,500 miles (25,000 km) or 25 months.
• Repack front steering bearings.
* This Yamaha factory maintenance schedule should be considered as a guide to general maintenance and lubrication intervals. Harder than normal use and exposure to mud, water, sand, high humidity, etc. will dictate more frequent attention to most maintenance items.

Table 2 TIRE INFLATION PRESSURE

	Front tire	Rear tire
XT350		
Size	3.00-21-4PR	110/80-18-58P
Tire pressure		
0-198 lb. (0-90 kg)	18 psi (1.3 kg/cm^2)	22 psi (1.5 kg/cm^2)
Maximum load	22 psi (1.5 kg/cm^2)	26 psi (1.8 kg/cm^2)
High speed riding	22 psi (1.5 kg/cm^2)	26 psi (1.8 kg/cm^2)
TT350		
Size	80/100-21	100/100-18
Tire pressure	14 psi (1.0 kg/cm^2)	14 psi (1.0 kg/cm^2)

Table 3 BATTERY STATE OF CHARGE

Specific gravity	State of charge
1.110-1.130	Discharged
1.140-1.160	Almost discharged
1.170-1.190	One-quarter charged
1.200-1.220	One-half charged
1.230-1.250	Three-quarters charged
1.260-1.280	Fully charged

Table 4 RECOMMENDED LUBRICANTS AND FUEL

Engine oil	Yamahube 4-cycle oil, SAE 20W40 or 10W30 SG motor oil
Front fork oil	10 weight fork oil
Air filter	Foam air filter oil
Drive chain	Chain lube recommended for O-ring drive chains
Control cables	Cable lube
Control lever pivots	10W/30 motor oil
Swing arm pivot shaft	Lithium base waterproof wheel bearing grease
Suspension pivot shaft	Molybdenum disulfide grease
Steering head bearings	Lithium base waterproof wheel bearing grease
Fuel	Regular grade—research octane 87 or higher
Brake fluid	DOT 3/DOT 4

Table 5 APPROXIMATE REFILL CAPACITIES

Engine oil	
Periodic oil change	1,300 cc (1.37 qt.)
With filter change	1,400 cc (1.48 qt.)
Engine rebuild	1,600 cc (1.7 qt.)
Front fork (each)	
TT350	533 cc (18.76 oz.)
XT350	319 cc (10.8 oz.)
Front fork oil level	
XT350	*
TT350	125 mm (4.92 in.)
Fuel tank	
TT350	
Total	2.5 gal. (9.5 l)
Reserve	0.26 gal. (1.0 l)
XT350	
Total	3.2 gal. (12.0 l)
Reserve	0.5 gal. (2.0 l)

*Not specified by Yamaha.

Table 6 MAINTENANCE TORQUE SPECIFICATIONS

Item	N·m	ft.-lb.
Oil pipe banjo bolt	20	14
Oil strainer plug	32	23
Oil filter cover bolt	10	7.2
Oil filter cover screw	7	5.1
Oil filter cover bleed screw	5	3.6
Engine drain bolt	43	31
Spark plug	17.5	12.5
Front axle nut		
TT350	58	42
XT350	107	77.4
Rear axle nut		
TT350	100	72
XT350	107	77.4
Front fork cap	23	17
Front fork pinch bolts	23	17
Handlebar clamp bolts		
TT350	23	17
XT350	20	14

Table 7 DRIVE CHAIN SERVICE SPECIFICATIONS

Model	Specifications
XT350	
Type	428VS/DAIDO
Number of links	130
Free play	30-40 mm (1.18-1.57 in.)
Chain stretch	
Nominal	254 mm (10 in.)
Stretch limit	261 mm (10 5/16 in.)
TT350	
Type	520VS/DAIDO
Number of links	108
Free play	40-45 mm (1.6-1.8 in.)
Chain stretch	
Nominal	318 mm (12 1/2 in.)
Wear limit	327 mm (12 3/4 in.)

Table 8 BRAKE LEVER AND PEDAL ADJUSTMENT SPECIFICATIONS

	mm	in.
Front brake lever free play	5-8	3/16-5/16
Rear brake pedal free play	20-30	25/32-1 3/16
Rear brake pedal height position		
XT350	15	19/32
TT350	0	0

Table 9 DECOMPRESSION CABLE ADJUSTMENT

Model	Specification
XT350	3-5 mm (1/8-3/16 in.)
TT350	2-3 mm (3/32-1/8 in.)

Table 10 CLUTCH LEVER FREE PLAY ADJUSTMENT

Model	Specification
XT350	2-3 mm (3/32-1/8 in.)
TT350	8-13 mm (5/16-1/2 in.)

Table 11 TUNE-UP SPECIFICATIONS

Valve clearance	
Intake	0.08-0.12 mm (0.003-0.005 in.)
Exhaust	0.13-0.17 mm (0.005-0.007 in.)
Engine compression pressure	
Standard	11 kg/cm^2 (156 psi)
Minimum	9 kg/cm^2 (128 psi)
Maximum	12 kg/cm^2 (171 psi)
Spark plugs	
Type	NGK D8EA or ND X24ES-U
Gap	
XT350	0.7-0.8 mm (0.028-0.032 in.)
TT350	0.6-0.7 mm (0.024-0.028 in.)
Ignition timing	Fixed at:
	12° ± 2° BTDC at 1200 rpm
	34° ± 2° BTDC at 5000 rpm
Idle speed	
XT350	1,350-1,450 rpm
TT350	1,400-1,500 rpm

CHAPTER FOUR

ENGINE TOP END

The engine is an air-cooled, double-overhead cam, four-valve, single. Valves are operated by two chain-driven camshafts.

This chapter provides complete service and overhaul procedures, including information for disassembly, removal, inspection, service and reassembly of the engine top end components. These include the camshafts, valves, cylinder head, piston, piston rings and cylinder subassemblies.

Before starting any work, read the service hints in Chapter One. You will do a better job with this information fresh in your mind.

Table 1 lists general engine specifications and **Table 2** lists engine service specifications. **Tables 1-3** are at the end of the chapter.

ENGINE PRINCIPLES

Figure 1 explains basic four-stroke engine operation. This will be helpful when troubleshooting or repairing your engine.

SERVICING ENGINE IN FRAME

Many components can be serviced while the engine is mounted in the frame:

a. Cylinder head.
b. Cylinder and piston.
c. Gearshift mechanism.
d. Clutch.
e. Kickstarter.
f. Oil pump
g. Carburetor.
h. Rotor and electrical systems.

CYLINDER HEAD COVER

Removal/Installation

1. Support the bike and raise the rear wheel off the ground with a suitable wheel stand.
2. Remove the left- and right-hand side covers.
3. Remove the seat.
4. *XT350*: Disconnect the negative battery terminal connector (**Figure 2**).
5. Remove the fuel tank as described under *Fuel Tank Removal/Installation* in Chapter Eight.
6. Remove the left- and right-hand air scoops.
7. Remove the nuts, washers and bolts and remove the upper engine brace (**Figure 3**).
8. Remove the cylinder head cover mounting screws.

① **4-STROKE PRINCIPLES**

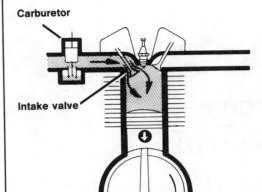

Carburetor

Intake valve

A

As the piston travels downward, the exhaust valve is closed and the intake valve opens, allowing the new air-fuel mixture from the carburetor to be drawn into the cylinder. When the piston reaches the bottom of its travel (BDC), the intake valve closes and remains closed for the next 1 1/2 revolutions of the crankshaft.

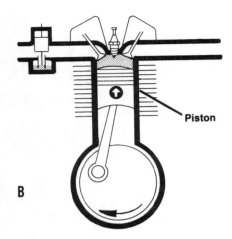

Piston

B

While the crankshaft continues to rotate, the piston moves upward, compressing the air-fuel mixture.

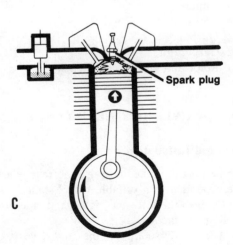

Spark plug

C

As the piston almost reaches the top of its travel, the spark plug fires, igniting the compressed air-fuel mixture. The piston continues to top dead center (TDC) and is pushed downward by the expanding gases.

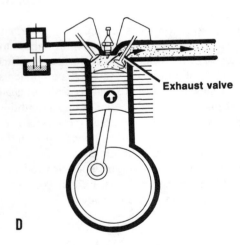

Exhaust valve

D

When the piston almost reaches BDC, the exhaust valve opens and remains open until the piston is near TDC. The upward travel of the piston forces the exhaust gases out of the cylinder. After the piston has reached TDC, the exhaust valve closes and the cycle starts all over again.

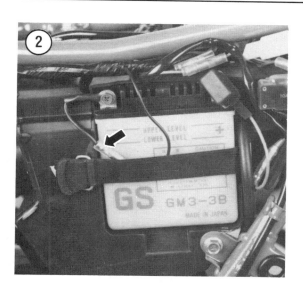

9. Remove the air scoop (**Figure 4**).

10. Lift the cylinder head cover up and remove it (**Figure 5**).

11. Installation is the reverse of these steps. Note the following.

12. Before installing the cylinder head cover, check that all 4 rubber oil plugs (**Figure 6**) are installed in each of the camshaft cap holes.

CAUTION
*The rubber oil plugs (**Figure 6**) ensure that a full supply of oil will be routed to the camshafts. Failing to install the rubber plugs will cause engine damage.*

4

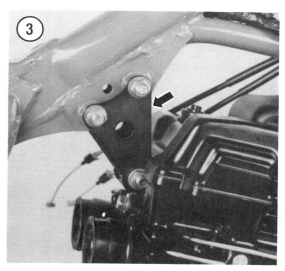

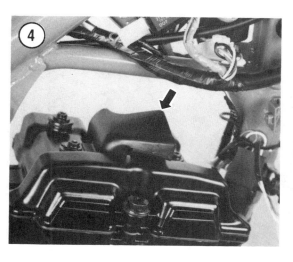

13. Replace the cylinder head cover gasket (**Figure 7**), if necessary.
14. Tighten the cylinder head cover bolts to the torque specification in **Table 3**.

CAMSHAFTS

This section describes removal, inspection and installation procedures for the camshaft components.

Removal

1. Remove the cylinder head cover as described in this chapter.

> *CAUTION*
> *To prevent expensive engine damage, refer to CAUTION under Spark Plug Removal in Chapter Three.*

2. Remove the spark plug. This will make it easier to turn the engine by hand.
3. Remove the 4 camshaft cap oil plugs (**Figure 6**).
4. Remove the shift lever (**Figure 8**). Remove the pinch bolt and pull the shift lever off. If the splined boss is tight on the shaft, spread the slot open with a screwdriver.
5. Remove the left-hand side cover (**Figure 9**).
6. Turn the rotor counterclockwise and align the "T" mark on the rotor with the crankcase index mark (**Figure 10**). This places the engine at top dead center (TDC) on the compression stroke.

> *NOTE*
> *Confirm engine positioning by observing the position of the camshafts. When the piston is at TDC on the compression stroke, the camshaft lobes will be facing away from the valve shims and lifters.*

7. Remove the 2 Allen screws securing the cam chain tensioner (**Figure 11**) and remove the tensioner assembly from the cylinder housing.

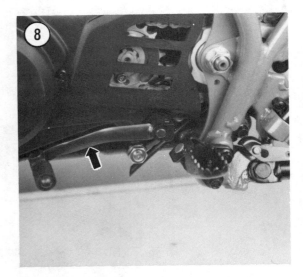

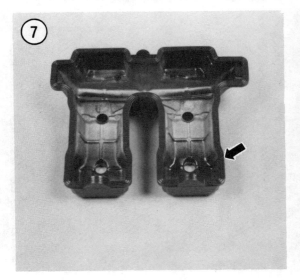

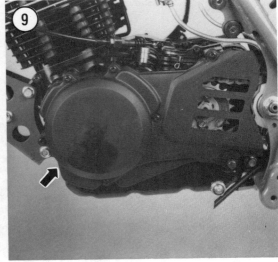

8. Remove the bolt securing the upper chain guide (**Figure 12**) and remove it.

9. Lift the front chain guide (**Figure 13**) out of the chain tunnel.

10. Loosen the camshaft cap bolts (**Figure 14**) in a crisscross pattern in 2-3 steps.

NOTE
The camshaft caps are marked for alignment and must be reinstalled in their original positions. Check the caps for their alignment marks, and if the marks are not visible, make your own.

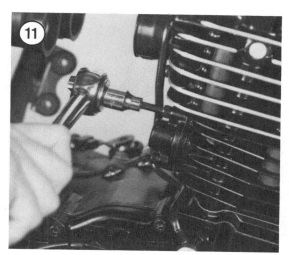

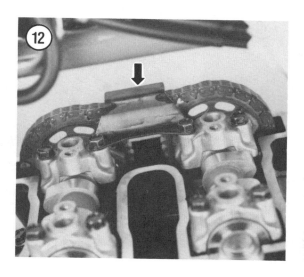

11. Carefully work the camshaft caps (**Figure 15**) loose from their dowel pins and lift them off of the camshaft.

12. Remove the camshaft cap dowel pins (**Figure 16**).

13. Secure the camshaft chain with wire.

14. Remove both camshafts with their sprockets (**Figure 17**). Remove the camshafts slowly to prevent damaging any cam lobe or bearing surface.

CAUTION
The crankshaft can be turned with the camshafts removed. However, pull the camshaft chain tight to prevent it from binding at the crankshaft sprocket.

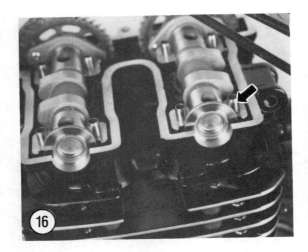

Camshaft Inspection

1. Check cam lobes (A, **Figure 18**) for wear. The lobes should not be scored and the edges should be square.

2. Even though the cam lobe surface appears to be satisfactory, with no visible signs of wear, each lobe must be measured with a micrometer. Measure the lobe height (**Figure 19**) and the base circle diameter (**Figure 20**). Replace the shaft(s) if worn beyond the service specifications (measurements less than those given in **Table 2**).

3. Check the camshaft bearing journals (B, **Figure 18**) for wear and scoring.

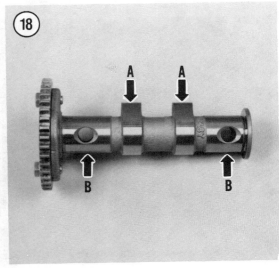

4. Even though the camshaft bearing journal surface appears satisfactory, with no visible signs of wear, the camshaft bearing journal outside diameter must be measured with a micrometer (**Figure 21**). Replace the shaft(s) if worn beyond the service specifications (measurements less than those given in **Table 2**).

5. Place the camshaft on a set of V-blocks and check its runout with a dial indicator. Replace the camshaft if runout exceeds the service limit in **Table 2**. Repeat for the opposite camshaft.

6. Inspect the camshaft sprockets (**Figure 22**). Check each sprocket for worn or damaged gear teeth. Also check the teeth for cracking or rounding. If one sprocket is worn severely, the other sprocket should also be replaced. When installing the camshaft sprockets, tighten the sprocket bolts to the torque specification in **Table 3**.

NOTE
If the camshaft sprockets are worn, also check the camshaft chain, chain guides and chain tensioner.

CAUTION
The camshaft sprocket bolts are made of a hardened material. When replacing these bolts, use only Yamaha replacement bolts. Do not substitute with another type of bolt as severe engine damage could result from bolt damage.

4

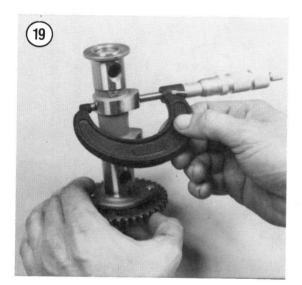

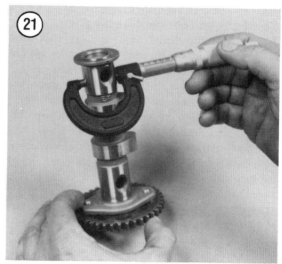

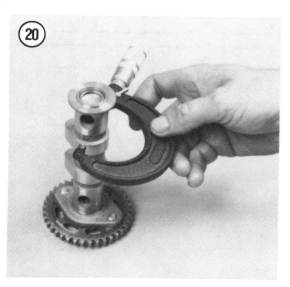

7. Check the camshaft bearing journals in the cylinder head (**Figure 23**) and camshaft caps for wear and scoring. They should not be scored or excessively worn. If necessary, replace the cylinder head and camshaft caps as a matched pair.

8. Check the cam chain guides as described in this chapter.

Camshaft Bearing Clearance Measurement

This procedure requires the use of a Plastigage set (**Figure 24**). The camshaft must be installed into the head. Prior to installation, wipe all oil residue from each cam bearing journal and bearing surface in the head and all camshaft caps.

1. Each camshaft is identified for correct placement in the cylinder head (**Figure 25**). They are identified as follows:

   a. "IN"—intake camshaft.

   b. "EX"—exhaust camshaft.

2. Install each camshaft into its correct location in the head. Position the cam lobes so they are not depressing the valve shims and lifters.

3. Install all camshaft cap locating dowels into position in the camshaft caps (**Figure 16**).

4. Wipe all oil from the cam bearing journals before using the Plastigage material.

5. Place a strip of Plastigage material on top of each cam bearing journal (**Figure 26**), parallel to the cam.

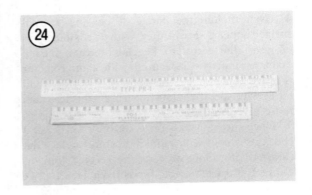

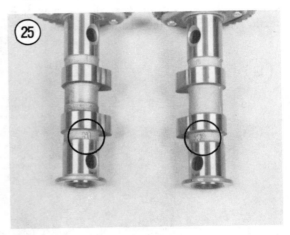

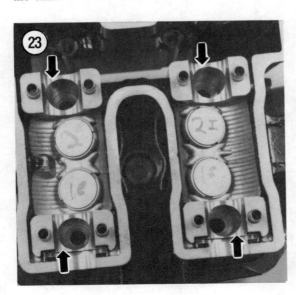

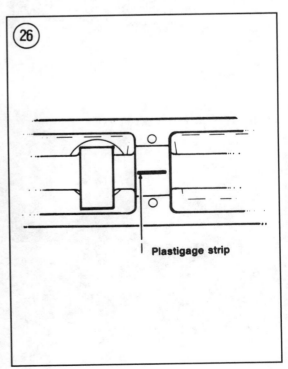

Plastigage strip

6. Each camshaft cap is identified for correct placement in the cylinder head (**Figure 27**).

7. Place the camshaft caps into their correct position.

8. Install all camshaft cap bolts and the bolts that hold the cam chain guide in place. Install finger-tight at first, then tighten in a crisscross pattern to the final torque specification listed in **Table 3**.

CAUTION
Do not rotate the camshaft with the Plastigage material in place.

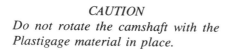
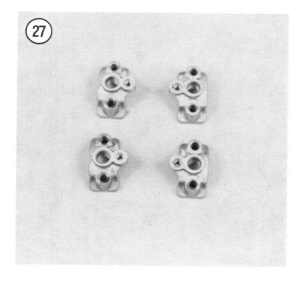

9. Gradually remove the camshaft cap bolts in a crisscross pattern. Remove the camshaft caps carefully.

10. Measure the width of the flattened Plastigage according to manufacturer's instructions (**Figure 28**).

11. If the clearance exceeds the wear limit in **Table 2**, measure the camshaft bearing journal outside diameter (**Figure 21**) with a micrometer and compare to the limits in **Table 2**. If the camshaft bearing journal is less than dimension specified, replace the cam. If the cam is within specifications, the cylinder head and camshaft caps must be replaced as a matched set.

CAUTION
Remove all particles of Plastigage from all camshaft bearing journals and the camshaft caps. Be sure to clean the camshaft cap groove. This material must not be left in the engine as it can plug up an oil control orifice and cause severe engine damage.

Camshaft Installation

1. If camshaft bearing clearance was checked, make sure all Plastigage material has been removed from the camshaft and camshaft cap surfaces.

CAUTION
When rotating the crankshaft in Step 2, lift the cam chain tightly on the exhaust side (front) to prevent it from binding on the crankshaft sprocket.

2. Turn the rotor counterclockwise and align the "T" mark on the rotor with the crankcase index mark (**Figure 10**). This places the engine at top dead center (TDC) on the compression stroke.

3. Coat all camshaft lobes and bearing journals with molybdenum disulfide grease or assembly oil.

4. Also coat the bearing surfaces in the cylinder head and the camshaft caps.

5. Each camshaft is identified for correct placement in the cylinder head (**Figure 25**). They are identified as follows:

    a. "IN"—intake camshaft.

    b. "EX"—exhaust camshaft.

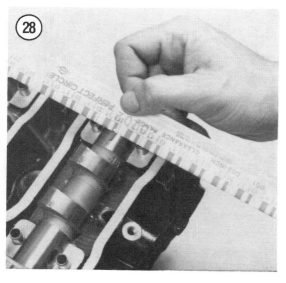

NOTE
*The end of each camshaft (opposite the sprocket side) has a timing mark (**Figure 29**). When installing the camshafts in Step 6, the timing mark on both camshafts must face **up**.*

6. See **Figure 30**. Install the exhaust camshaft (A) toward the front and the intake camshaft (B) toward the rear of the cylinder head. Make sure the timing mark on the end of each camshaft faces up (**Figure 31**).
7. Install the camshaft cap dowel pins (**Figure 16**).
8. Each camshaft cap is identified for correct placement in the cylinder head (**Figure 27**).
9. Place the camshaft caps into their correct position.

NOTE
*The 2 left-hand camshaft caps have timing marks cast into the side of the cap (**Figure 32**). These timing marks are used to check camshaft timing in the following procedure.*

NOTE
*When turning the crankshaft in the following steps, turn it **counter-clockwise**.*

10. Check camshaft timing as follows:
  a. Check that the timing mark on each camshaft aligns with the camshaft cap timing mark as shown in **Figure 32**.

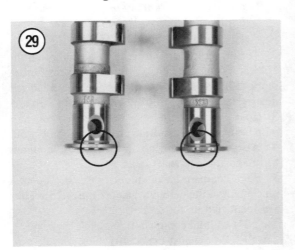

b. Then check that the "T" mark on the rotor aligns with the crankcase index mark (**Figure 33**).

c. When the timing marks in sub-step a and b are correct (**Figure 34**), proceed to Step 11. If the timing marks are incorrect, reposition the camshafts or rotor as required.

11. Install the camshaft cap bolts (except the 2 bolts that hold the cam chain guide) in place. Install finger-tight at first, then tighten in a crisscross pattern to the final torque specification listed in **Table 3**.

CAUTION
If there is any binding while turning the crankshaft in Step 12, "stop." Recheck the camshaft timing marks. Improper timing can cause valve and piston damage.

12. Rotate the engine *counterclockwise* 360° (1 turn).

13. Check that the "T" mark on the rotor aligns with the crankcase index mark (**Figure 33**) and that the timing marks on the camshafts align with the timing mark on the camshaft caps (**Figure 32**).

14. If the alignment is incorrect, correct by removing the cam sprocket bolts and repositioning the sprockets. If the alignment is correct, proceed to Step 15.

NOTE
*If it is necessary to reposition the camshaft sprockets, apply Loctite 242 (blue) to the sprocket bolt threads and tighten the bolts to the torque specification in **Table 3**.*

15. Recheck camshaft timing by performing Step 12 and Step 13 again.

CAUTION
Very expensive damage could result from improper camshaft and chain alignment. Make this final check to be sure alignment is correct. If alignment is incorrect, it must be corrected at this time.

16. When the camshaft timing is correct, proceed to Step 17.

17. Install the upper chain guide (**Figure 35**). Tighten the bolts securely.

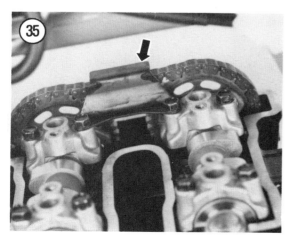

18. Install the front chain guide (**Figure 36**) into the chain tunnel. Make sure the guide seats all the way into the cylinder head cavity (**Figure 37**).

19. Install the cam chain tensioner as follows:

a. Install a new gasket onto the back of the tensioner housing.

b. Unscrew and remove the blind plug from the end of the tensioner body (**Figure 38**).

c. Insert a small straight-tipped screwdriver into the end of the tensioner body and turn the tensioner rod clockwise until it stops (**Figure 39**). Hold the tensioner rod in this position.

d. While still holding the tensioner rod with the screwdriver, install the tensioner assembly onto the cylinder (**Figure 40**). Have an assistant install the 2 tensioner housing bolts. Tighten the bolts securely.

e. When the tensioner assembly is mounted securely against the cylinder, remove the screwdriver from the tensioner. This releases the tension rod to apply pressure against the cam chain.

f. Install the blind plug (**Figure 41**). Tighten the bolt securely.

20. Install the 4 camshaft cap oil plugs (**Figure 42**).

21. Check valve adjustment as described in Chapter Three.

22. Install the cylinder head cover as described in this chapter.

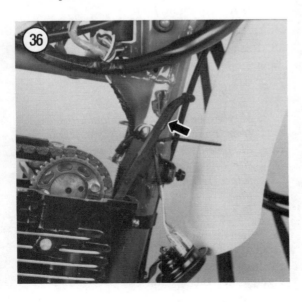

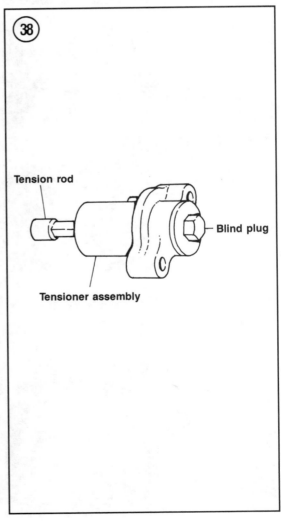

Tension rod

Blind plug

Tensioner assembly

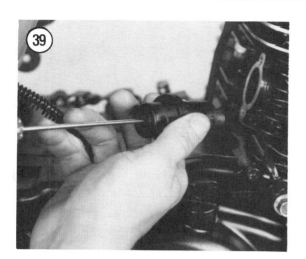

CYLINDER HEAD

The cylinder head can be removed with the engine mounted in the frame.

Removal

1. Remove the camshafts as described in this chapter.
2. Remove the carburetors as described under *Carburetor Removal/Installation* in Chapter Eight.
3. Remove the 2 oil pipe banjo bolts and washers (A, **Figure 43**) and remove the oil pipe (B, **Figure 43**).

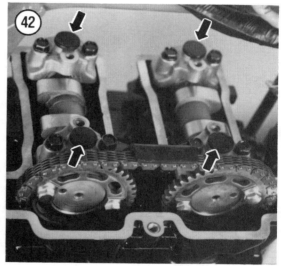

4. Remove the front cylinder head-to-cylinder Acorn nut and washer (**Figure 44**).

5. Remove the rear cylinder head-to-cylinder Acorn nut and washer (**Figure 45**).

6. Remove the two 6 mm bolts labeled 5 and 6 in **Figure 46**.

7. Using an 8 mm Allen wrench (**Figure 47**), loosen the 4 cylinder head mounting bolts in a crisscross pattern. See **Figure 46**.

8. Remove the long cylinder head mounting bolts and washers (**Figure 48**).

9. Loosen the cylinder head by tapping around the perimeter with a rubber or plastic mallet.

10. Lift the cylinder head (**Figure 49**) off of the cylinder. Place the head on a soft surface upside

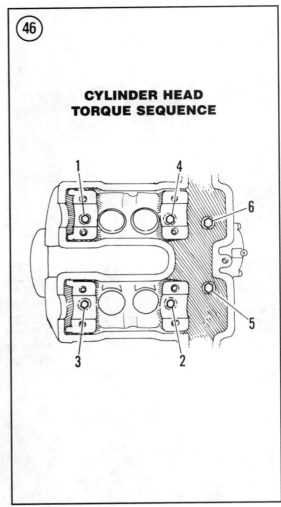

CYLINDER HEAD TORQUE SEQUENCE

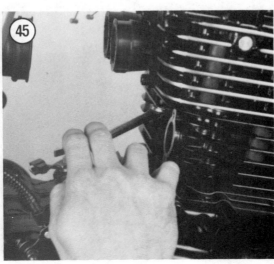

down to prevent scratching or otherwise damaging the head-to-block mating surface. Remove and discard the cylinder head gasket.

11. Place a clean shop rag into the cam chain tunnel in the cylinder to prevent the entry of foreign matter.

12. Remove the 2 dowel pins (**Figure 50**).

13. Label the 4 valve shims and lifters (**Figure 51**) and remove them. See **Figure 52**.

14. Remove the decompression lever as follows:

a. Remove the bolt and washer (**Figure 53**) securing the decompression lever.

b. Pull the decompression lever and spring (**Figure 54**) out of the cylinder head. See **Figure 55**.

NOTE
After removing the cylinder head, check the top and bottom mating surfaces for any indications of leakage. Also check the head and base gaskets for signs of leakage. A blown gasket could indicate possible cylinder head warpage or other damage.

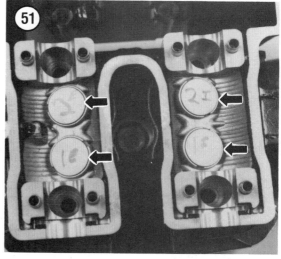

Cylinder Head Inspection

1. Remove all traces of gasket residue from the head and cylinder mating surfaces. Do not scratch the gasket surface.

2. Without removing the valves, remove all carbon deposits from the combustion chamber (A, **Figure 56**). Use a fine wire brush dipped in solvent or make a scraper from hardwood. Take care not to damage the head, valves or spark plug threads.

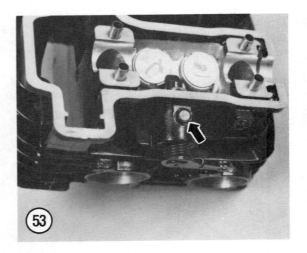

> *CAUTION*
> *If the combustion chamber is cleaned while the valves are removed, you will damage the valve seat surfaces. A damaged or even slightly scratched valve seat will cause poor valve seating.*

3. Examine the spark plug threads (B, **Figure 56**) in the cylinder head for damage. If damage is minor or if the threads are dirty or clogged with carbon, use a spark plug thread tap to clean the threads following the manufacturer's instructions. If thread damage is severe, the threads can be restored by installing a steel thread insert. Thread insert kits can be purchased at automotive supply stores or you can have the inserts installed by a Yamaha dealer or machine shop.

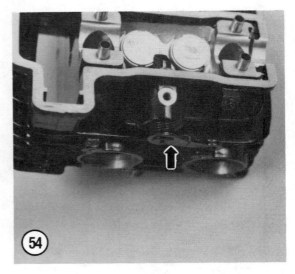

> *NOTE*
> *When using a tap to clean spark plug threads, coat the tap with an aluminum tap cutting fluid or kerosene.*

> *NOTE*
> *Aluminum spark plug threads are commonly damaged due to galling, cross-threading and overtightening. To prevent galling, apply an anti-seize compound on the plug threads before installation and do not overtighten.*

4. After all carbon is removed from combustion chambers and valve ports, and the spark plug thread holes are repaired, clean the entire head in solvent.

NOTE
If the cylinder head was bead-blasted, make sure to clean the head thoroughly with solvent and then with hot soapy water. Residue grit seats in small crevices and other areas and can be hard to get out. Also chase each exposed thread with a tap to remove grit between the threads or you may damage a thread later. Residue grit left in the engine will wind up in the oil and cause premature piston, ring and bearing wear.

5. Examine the piston crown (**Figure 50**). The crown should show no signs of wear or damage.

If the crown appears pecked or spongy-looking, also check the spark plug, valves and combustion chamber for aluminum deposits. If these deposits are found, the cylinder is suffering from excessive heat caused by a lean fuel mixture or preignition.

CAUTION
Do not clean the piston crown with the cylinder assembled on the crankcase. Carbon scraped from the top of the piston could fall between the cylinder wall and piston and onto the piston rings. Because carbon grit is very abrasive, premature cylinder, piston and ring wear will occur. If the piston crown is heavily carboned, remove the piston as described in this chapter and clean it. Excessive carbon build-up on the piston crown reduces piston cooling which raises engine compression and causes overheating.

6. Inspect the carburetor boots (**Figure 57**) for cracks or other damage that would allow unfiltered air to enter the engine. Also check the hose clamps for breakage or fatigue. When installing boots, make sure to reinstall them with the boot marked "L" on the left-hand side and the boot marked "R" on the right-hand side.

7. Check for cracks in the combustion chamber and exhaust ports (**Figure 58**). A cracked head must be replaced if it cannot be repaired by welding.

8. After the head has been thoroughly cleaned, place a straightedge across the gasket surface at several points (**Figure 59**). Measure warp by attempting to insert a feeler gauge between the straightedge and cylinder head at each location. Maximum allowable warpage is listed in **Table 2**. Warpage or nicks in the cylinder head surface could cause an air leak and result in overheating. If warpage exceeds this limit, the cylinder head must be resurfaced or replaced. Consult a Yamaha dealer or machine shop experienced in this type of work.

9. Check the 2 cylinder head studs (**Figure 60**) for looseness or thread damage. Slight thread damage can be repaired with a thread file or die. If thread damage is severe, replace the damaged stud(s) as follows:

> *NOTE*
> *Stud replacement will require two 10 mm wrenches, two 6 mm nuts, a new stud and a tube of Loctite 271 (red) (Figure 61).*

a. Screw two 6 mm nuts onto the end of the damaged stud as shown in **Figure 62**. If the stud threads are too severely damaged, you may have to remove the stud with a pair of Vise-grip pliers.
b. With 2 wrenches, tighten the nuts against each other (**Figure 63**).
c. Unscrew the stud with a wrench on the lower nut (**Figure 64**).

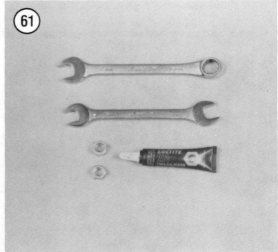

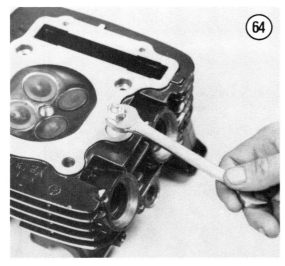

d. Clean the tapped hole with solvent and check for thread damage and carbon build-up. If necessary, clean the threads with a metric tap.

e. Remove the nuts from the old stud and install them on the end of a new stud.

f. Tighten the nuts against each other.

g. Apply Loctite 271 (red) to the threads of the new stud.

h. Screw the stud into the cylinder head with a wrench on the upper nut (**Figure 65**). Tighten the stud securely.

i. Remove the nuts from the new stud.

10. Check the valves and valve guides as described under *Valves and Valve Components* in this chapter.

11. Check the decompression lever oil seal (**Figure 66**) for wear, damage or signs of oil leakage. Replace the seal as follows:

a. Carefully pry the oil seal out of the cylinder head with a straight-tipped screwdriver. Place a rag underneath the screwdriver to prevent from damaging the cylinder head. See **Figure 67**.

b. Clean the oil seal mounting area with solvent and dry thoroughly. Check the mounting area for cracks or other damage before installing the new seal.

c. Tap the new seal into position with a suitable size socket placed on the outside of the seal (**Figure 68**). Tap the seal until it is flush with the bore surface.

12. Check the decompression lever (**Figure 55**) for excessive wear or damage.

13. Check the oil pipe (A, **Figure 69**) and the banjo bolts (B, **Figure 69**) for damage. Check the washers for cracks and other damage.

14. Check the cylinder head bolts (**Figure 70**) for thread damage, cracks and twisting. Also check the washers for cracks and other damage.

Installation

1. Install the decompression lever assembly as follows:

a. Slide the spring onto the lever (**Figure 71**).

b. Lightly oil the lever shaft and install it into the cylinder head. Engage the spring with the cylinder head as shown in **Figure 72**.

c. A groove is machined in the middle of the decompression lever (A, **Figure 71**). Install the lever bolt (B, **Figure 71**) so that the end of the bolt engages the lever groove. Tighten the bolt securely.

2. Clean the cylinder head and cylinder mating surfaces of all gasket residue.

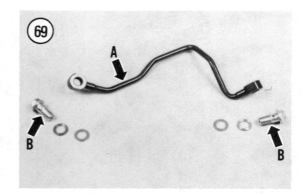

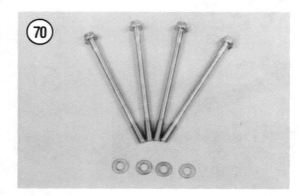

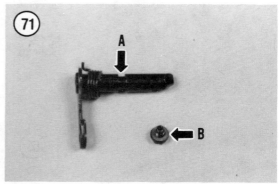

3. Install the valve shims and lifters (**Figure 51**) into their original positions. Follow the marks made during removal for correct installation.

4. See **Figure 73**. Install the 2 dowel pins (A) and a new head gasket (B).

5. Guide the cam chain through the cylinder head tunnel and install the cylinder head (**Figure 74**). Make sure the cylinder head seats squarely against the cylinder.

6. Lubricate the cylinder head bolt threads with engine oil.

7. Install the cylinder head bolts and washers finger-tight. See **Figure 75**.

8. Install the front (**Figure 76**) and rear (**Figure 77**) Acorn nuts and washers finger-tight.

9. Tighten the cylinder head bolts in 2-3 steps to the torque specifications in **Table 3**. Tighten the bolts in the torque sequence shown in **Figure 75**.

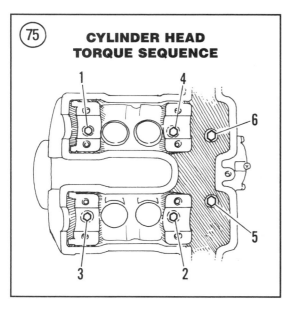

CYLINDER HEAD TORQUE SEQUENCE

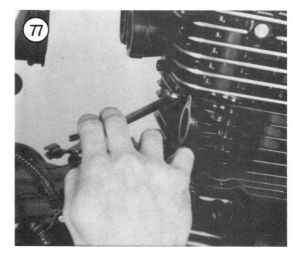

NOTE
Bolts 1, 2, 3, 4, 5 and 6 are shown in
Figure 75. *Bolt number 8 is the front*
*Acorn nut (**Figure 76**). Bolt number 7*
*is the rear Acorn nut (**Figure 77**).*

10. Install the oil pipe (**Figure 78**) and the 2 banjo bolts and washers.
11. Install the camshafts as described in this chapter.
12. Install the carburetors. See Chapter Eight.

CAM CHAIN GUIDES

See **Figure 79**. Check the top (A), rear (B) and front (C) cam chain guides for wear, damage or cracks. The top and front cam chain guides can be removed after removing the valve cover. Rear cam chain guide removal is described in Chapter Five. If the chain guides are worn or damaged, also check the cam chain tensioner and the cam chain.

VALVES AND VALVE COMPONENTS

Correct valve service requires a number of special tools. The following procedures describe how to check for valve component wear and to determine what type of service is required. In most cases, valve troubles are caused by poor valve seating, worn valve guides and burned valves. A valve spring compressor (**Figure 80**) will be required to remove the valves.

Refer to **Figure 81** for this procedure.

1. Remove the cylinder head as described in this chapter.
2. Label the 4 valve shims and lifters (**Figure 82**) and remove them from the cylinder head.
3. Install a valve spring compressor squarely over the valve retainer with the other end of tool placed against valve head (**Figure 83**).

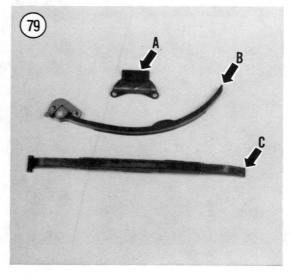

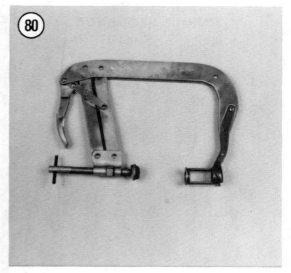

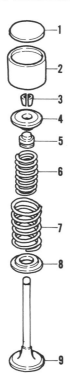

VALVE ASSEMBLY

81

1
2
3
4
5
6
7
8
9

1. Shim
2. Bucket
3. Valve keepers
4. Upper spring seat
5. Oil seal
6. Inner valve spring
7. Outer valve spring
8. Lower spring seat
9. Valve

4. Tighten valve spring compressor until the valve keepers separates. Lift valve keepers out through the valve spring compressor (**Figure 84**) with needle nose pliers.

5. Gradually loosen the valve spring compressor and remove it from the head. Remove the upper spring seat (**Figure 85**).

4

6. Remove the outer (**Figure 86**) and inner valve springs (**Figure 87**).

7. Remove the lower valve seat (**Figure 88**).

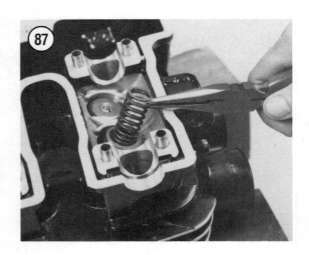

> *CAUTION*
> *Remove any burrs from the valve stem grooves before removing the valve (**Figure 89**); otherwise the valve guides will be damaged.*

8. Turn the cylinder head over and remove the valve (**Figure 90**).

9. Turn the cylinder head over and pull the oil seal (**Figure 91**) off of the valve guide.

> *CAUTION*
> *All component parts of each valve assembly (**Figure 92**) must be kept together. Do not mix with like components from other valves or excessive wear may result.*

10. Repeat Steps 3-9 and remove remaining valve(s).

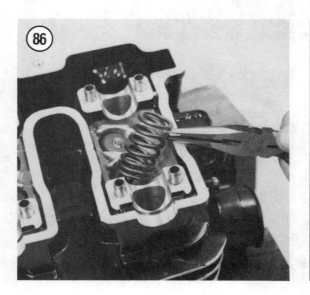

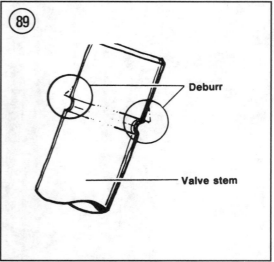

Deburr

Valve stem

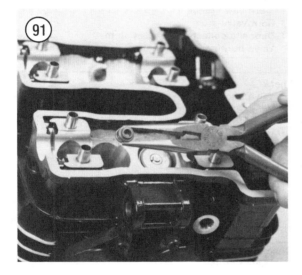

Inspection

Refer to the troubleshooting chart in **Figure 93** when performing valve inspection procedures in this section.

1. Clean valves in solvent. Do not gouge or damage the valve seating surface.

2. Inspect the contact surface of each valve for burning. Minor roughness and pitting can be removed by lapping the valve as described in this chapter. Excessive unevenness to the contact surface is an indication that the valve is not serviceable.

3. Inspect the valve stems for wear and roughness. Then measure the valve stem outside diameter for wear using a micrometer (**Figure 94**). Compare with specifications in **Table 2**.

4. Remove all carbon and varnish from the valve guides with a stiff spiral wire brush before checking wear.

NOTE
If you do not have the required measuring devices, proceed to Step 7.

5. Measure each valve guide at top, center and bottom inside diameter with a small hole gauge (**Figure 95**). Then measure the small hole gauge with a micrometer (**Figure 96**) to determine the valve guide inside diameter. Compare measurements with specification in **Table 2**.

6. Subtract the measurement made in Step 3 from the measurement made in Step 5. The difference is the valve guide-to-valve stem clearance. See **Table 2** for correct clearance. Replace any guide or valve that is not within tolerance. Valve guide replacement is described later in this chapter.

7. If a small hole gauge is not available, insert each valve in its guide. Hold the valve just slightly off its seat and rock it sideways. If the valve rocks more than slightly, the guide is probably worn and should be replaced. As a final check, take the cylinder head to a dealer or machine shop and have the valve guides measured.

8. Check the inner and outer valve springs (**Figure 97**) as follows:

   a. Check each of the valve springs for visual damage.

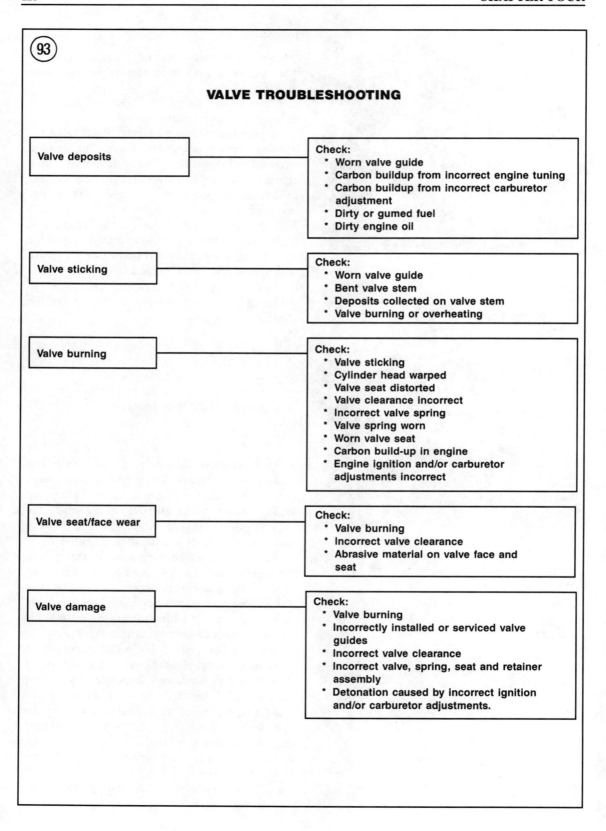

93

VALVE TROUBLESHOOTING

Valve deposits

Check:
* Worn valve guide
* Carbon buildup from incorrect engine tuning
* Carbon buildup from incorrect carburetor adjustment
* Dirty or gumed fuel
* Dirty engine oil

Valve sticking

Check:
* Worn valve guide
* Bent valve stem
* Deposits collected on valve stem
* Valve burning or overheating

Valve burning

Check:
* Valve sticking
* Cylinder head warped
* Valve seat distorted
* Valve clearance incorrect
* Incorrect valve spring
* Valve spring worn
* Worn valve seat
* Carbon build-up in engine
* Engine ignition and/or carburetor adjustments incorrect

Valve seat/face wear

Check:
* Valve burning
* Incorrect valve clearance
* Abrasive material on valve face and seat

Valve damage

Check:
* Valve burning
* Incorrectly installed or serviced valve guides
* Incorrect valve clearance
* Incorrect valve, spring, seat and retainer assembly
* Detonation caused by incorrect ignition and/or carburetor adjustments.

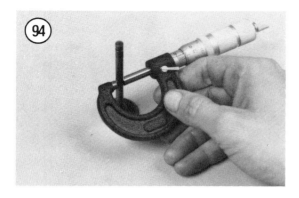

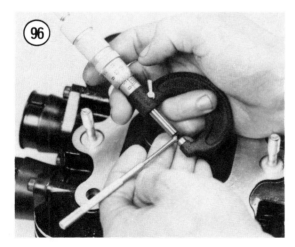

b. Use a square and check each spring for distortion or tilt (**Figure 98**). Compare to specifications in **Table 2**.

c. Measure the valve spring length with a vernier caliper (**Figure 99**). All should be of length specified in **Table 2** with no bends or other distortion.

d. Replace defective springs as a set.

9. Check the valve spring retainer and valve keepers. If they are in good condition, they may be reused.

10. Inspect valve seats (**Figure 100**). If worn or burned, they may be reconditioned as described in this chapter. Seats and valves in near-perfect condition can be reconditioned by lapping with fine carborundum paste. Lapping, however, is always

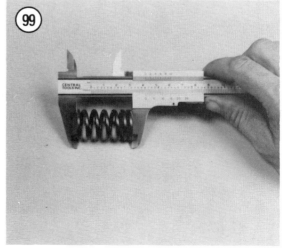

inferior to precision grinding. Check as follows:

a. Clean the valve seat and valve mating areas with contact cleaner.

b. Coat the valve seat with machinist's blue.

c. Install the valve into its guide (**Figure 90**) and rotate it against its seat with a valve lapping tool (**Figure 101**). See *Valve Lapping* in this chapter.

d. Lift the valve out of the guide and measure the seat width with vernier calipers.

e. The seat width for intake and exhaust valves should measure within the specifications listed in **Table 2** all the way around the seat. If the seat width exceeds the service limit (**Table 2**), regrind the seats as described in this chapter.

f. Remove all machinist's blue residue from the seats and valves.

11. Check the valve stem runout with a V-block and dial indicator as shown in **Figure 102**. Compare runout to specifications in **Table 2**.

12. Measure the head diameter of each valve with a vernier caliper or micrometer (**Figure 103**). Compare to specifications in **Table 2**.

Valve Guide Replacement

The valve guides must be removed and installed with special tools that can be ordered from a Yamaha dealer or motorcycle accessory store. The required special tools are listed as follows:

a. 5.5 mm valve guide remover, Yamaha part No. YM-01122.

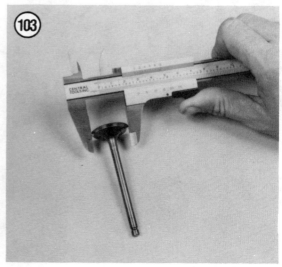

b. Valve guide installer, Yamaha part No. YM-01129.
c. 5.5 mm valve guide reamer, Yamaha part No. YM-01196.

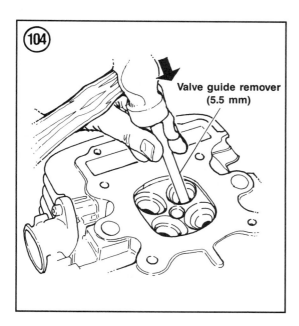

Valve guide remover (5.5 mm)

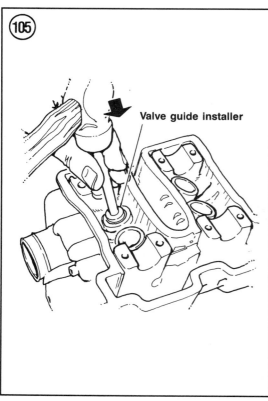

Valve guide installer

NOTE
Before driving the valve guides out of the cylinder head, place the new valve guides in the freezer. The freezing temperature will shrink the new guides slightly and ease installation.

1. Measure the distance from the top of the valve guide to the cylinder head. Record this distance so that the new guide can be installed to the correct height.
2. The valve guides are installed with a slight interference fit. The cylinder head must be heated to a temperature of approximately 212-300° F (100-150° C) in a shop oven or on a hot plate.

CAUTION
Do not heat the cylinder head with a torch (propane or acetylene)—never bring a flame into contact with the cylinder head. The direct heat may cause warpage of the cylinder head.

WARNING
Heavy gloves must be worn when performing this procedure—the cylinder head will be very hot.

3. Remove the cylinder head from the oven or hot plate and place onto wood blocks with the combustion chamber facing *up*.
4. Drive the old valve guide out from the combustion chamber side of the cylinder head (**Figure 104**) with the valve guide remover.
5. After the cylinder head cools, check the guide bores for carbon or other contamination. Clean the bores thoroughly.
6. Reheat the cylinder head to approximately 212-300° F (100-150° C).
7. Remove the cylinder head from the oven or hot plate and place it on wood blocks with the combustion chamber facing *down*.
8. Using the valve guide installer, install the new valve guide (**Figure 105**) so that distance from the cylinder head to the top of the valve guide is the same as that recorded in Step 1.
9. After the cylinder head has cooled to room temperature, ream the new valve guides as follows:
   a. Coat the valve guide and valve guide reamer with cutting oil.

b. See **Figure 106**. Ream the valve guide by rotating the reamer *clockwise* only. Do not turn the reamer counterclockwise.

c. Measure the valve guide inside diameter with a small hole gauge (**Figure 95**). Then measure the small hole gauge with a micrometer (**Figure 96**) to determine the valve guide inside diameter. The valve guide should be within the service specifications listed in **Table 2**.

10. The valve seats must be refaced with a 45° cutter after replacing valve guides. Reface the valve seats as described under *Valve Seat Reconditioning* in this chapter.

11. Clean the cylinder head thoroughly in solvent. Lightly oil the valve guides to prevent rust.

Valve Seat Reconditioning

The valve seats must be cut with special tools that are available from a Yamaha dealer or motorcycle accessory dealer. The following tools will be required:

a. Valve seat cutters (see Yamaha dealer for part numbers).

NOTE
*The valve seat cutters listed in **Figure 107** are required for this procedure.*

b. Vernier caliper.
c. Machinist's blue.
d. Valve lapping tool.

NOTE
Follow the manufacturer's instructions with using valve facing equipment.

1. Inspect valve seats (**Figure 100**). If worn or burned, they should be reconditioned. Seats and valves in near-perfect condition can be reconditioned by lapping with fine carborundum paste. Lapping, however, is always inferior to precision grinding. Check as follows:

a. Clean the valve seat and valve mating areas with contact cleaner.
b. Coat the valve seat with machinist's blue.
c. Install the valve into its guide and rotate it against its seat with a valve lapping tool (**Figure 101**). See *Valve Lapping* in this chapter.

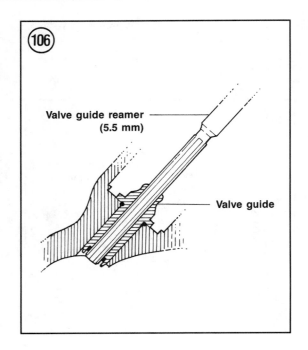
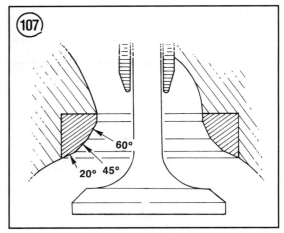
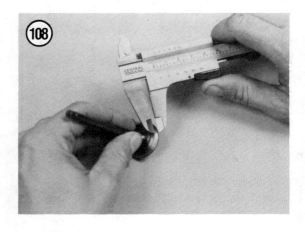

d. Lift the valve out of the guide and measure the seat width with vernier calipers (**Figure 108**). See **Figure 109**.

e. The seat width for intake and exhaust valves should measure within the specifications listed in **Table 2** all the way around the seat. If the seat width exceeds the service limit (**Table 2**), regrind the seats as follows.

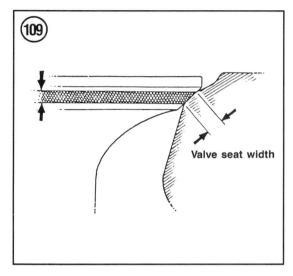

Valve seat width

CAUTION
*When grinding valve seats, work **slowly** to prevent from grinding the seats too much. Overgrinding the valve seats will sink the valves too far into the cylinder head. Sinking the valves too far may reduce valve clearance and make it impossible to adjust valve clearance. In this condition, the cylinder head would have to be replaced.*

2. Install a 45° cutter onto the valve tool and lightly cut the seat to remove roughness.

3. Measure the valve seat with a vernier caliper (**Figure 108**). Record the measurement to use as a reference point when performing the following.

CAUTION
The 20° cutter removes material quickly. Work carefully and check your progress often.

4. Install a 20° cutter onto the valve tool and lightly cut the seat to remove 1/4 of the existing valve seat (**Figure 110**).

5. Install a 60° cutter onto the valve tool and lightly cut the seat to remove the lower 1/4 of the existing valve seat (**Figure 111**).

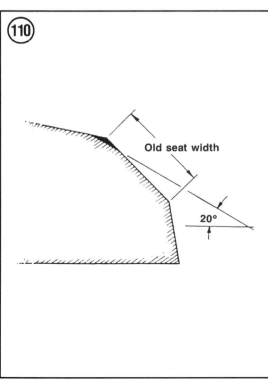

Old seat width

20°

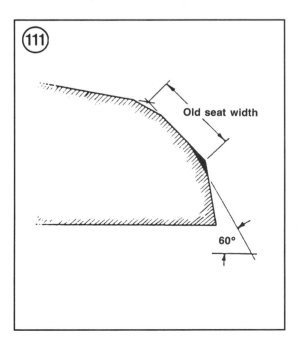

Old seat width

60°

6. Measure the valve seat with a vernier caliper. Then fit a 45° cutter onto the valve tool and cut the valve seat to the specified seat width listed in **Table 2**. See **Figure 112**.
7. When the valve seat width is correct, check valve seating as follows.
8. Clean the valve seat and valve mating areas with solvent.
9. Coat the valve seat with machinist's blue.
10. Install the valve into its guide and rotate it against its seat with a valve lapping tool (**Figure 101**). See *Valve Lapping* in this chapter.
11. Remove the valve and check the contact area on the valve (**Figure 113**). Interpret results as follows:
   a. The valve contact area should be approximately in the center of the valve seat area.
   b. If the contact area is too high on the valve, lower the seat with a 20° flat cutter.
   c. If the contact area is too low on the valve, raise the seat with a 60° interior cutter.
   d. Refinish the seat using a 45° cutter.
12. When the contact area is correct, lap the valve as described in this chapter.

Valve Lapping

Valve lapping is a simple operation which can restore the valve seal without machining—if the amount of wear or distortion is not too great.

This procedure should only be performed after determining that valve seat width and outside diameter are within specifications.
1. Smear a light coating of fine grade valve lapping compound on seating surface of valve.
2. Insert the valve into the head.
3. See **Figure 101**. Wet the suction cup of the lapping stick and stick it onto the head of the valve. Lap the valve to the seat by spinning the lapping stick in both directions. Every 5 to 10 seconds, rotate the valve 180° in the valve seat. Continue this action until the mating surfaces on the valve and seat are smooth and equal in size.
4. Closely examine valve seat in cylinder head. It should be smooth and even with a smooth, polished seating "ring."
5. Thoroughly clean the valves and cylinder head in solvent and then in hot soapy water to remove all grinding compound. Any compound left on the valves or the cylinder head will end up in the engine

and cause excessive wear and damage. Rinse with plain water and blow dry.
6. After the lapping has been completed and the valve assemblies have been reinstalled into the head, the valve seal should be tested. Check the seal of each valve by pouring solvent into each of the intake and exhaust ports. There should be no leakage past the seat. If leakage occurs, combustion chamber will appear wet (**Figure 114**). If fluid leaks past any of the seats, disassemble that valve assembly and repeat the lapping procedure until there is no leakage.

Installation

1. Coat a valve stem with molybdenum disulfide paste and install into its correct guide.
2. Carefully slide a new oil seal (**Figure 115**) over the valve and seat it onto the end of the valve guide.

NOTE
Oil seals should be replaced whenever a valve is removed.

3. Install the lower spring seat (**Figure 116**).

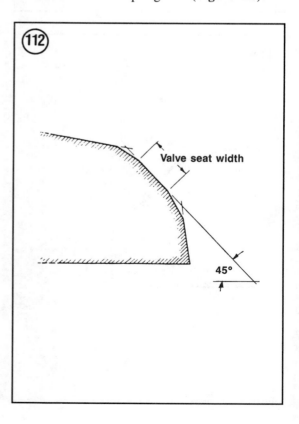
Valve seat width
45°

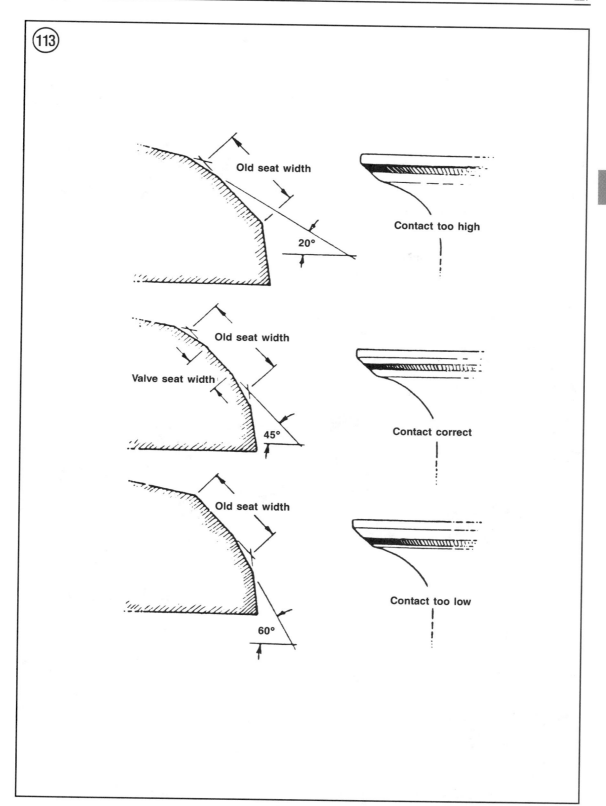

(113)

Old seat width

20°

Contact too high

Old seat width

Valve seat width

45°

Contact correct

Old seat width

60°

Contact too low

4

NOTE
Install valve springs with the narrow pitch end (end with coils closest together) facing the cylinder head. See Figure 117.

4. Install the inner and outer valve springs (**Figure 118**).

5. Install the upper valve spring seat (**Figure 119**).

6. Push down on the upper valve seat with the valve spring compressor and install the valve keepers (**Figure 120**). After releasing tension from the compressor, examine valve keepers and make sure they are seated correctly (**Figure 121**).

7. Repeat Steps 1-6 for remaining valve(s).

8. Install the valve lifters and shims (**Figure 122**) into their correct positions.

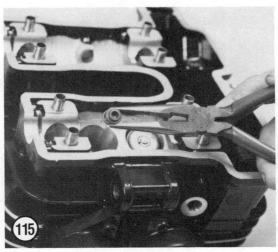

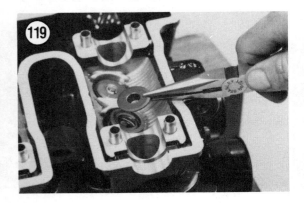

9. After installing the cylinder head onto the engine, check valve clearance and adjust as necessary as described in Chapter Three.

CYLINDER

The alloy cylinder block has a pressed-in cast iron cylinder sleeve, which can be bored to 0.25 mm (0.010 in.) oversize and again to 0.5 mm (0.020 in.) oversize.

The cylinder can be removed with the engine mounted in the frame.

Removal

1. Remove the cylinder head as described under *Cylinder Head Removal/Installation* in this chapter.
2. Loosen the cylinder by tapping around the perimeter with a rubber or plastic mallet.
3. Pull the cylinder (**Figure 123**) straight up and off the crankcase.
4. If necessary, remove the piston as described under *Piston Removal/Installation* in this chapter.
5. Remove the 2 dowel pins (**Figure 124**) and base gasket.
6. Stuff clean shop rags into the crankcase opening to prevent objects from falling into the crankcase.

Inspection

1. Wash the cylinder block in solvent to remove any oil and carbon particles. The cylinder bore must be cleaned thoroughly before attempting any measurement as incorrect readings may be obtained.

2. Remove all gasket residue from the top (A, **Figure 125**) and bottom (A, **Figure 126**) gasket surfaces.

3. Check the dowel pin holes (B, **Figure 125** and B, **Figure 126**) for cracks or other damage.

4. Check the cylinder O-ring (C, **Figure 126**) for wear or deterioration; replace if necessary.

5. Measure the cylinder bores with a bore gauge or inside micrometer (**Figure 127**). Then measure the bore gauge with a micrometer to determine the bore diameter (**Figure 128**). Measure the cylinder bore at the points shown in **Figure 129**. Measure in 3 axes—in line with the piston pin and at 90° to the pin. If the taper or out-of-round is greater than specifications (**Table 2**), the cylinder must be rebored to the next oversize and new piston and rings installed.

NOTE
The new piston should be obtained first before the cylinder is bored so that the piston can be measured. The cylinder must be bored to match the piston. Piston-to-cylinder clearance is specified in Table 2.

6. If the cylinder is not worn past the service limit, check the bore carefully for scratches or gouges. The bore still may require boring and reconditioning.

7. If the cylinder requires boring, remove all dowel pins from the cylinder before dropping it off with the dealer or machine shop.

8. After the cylinder has been serviced, wash the bore in hot soapy water. This is the only way to clean the cylinder wall of the fine grit material left

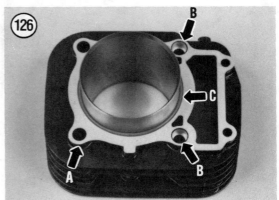

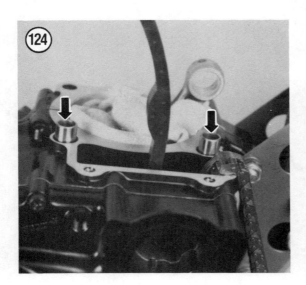

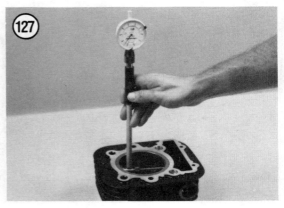

from the bore or honing job. After washing the cylinder wall, run a clean white cloth through it. The cylinder wall should show no traces of grit or other debris. If the rag is dirty, the cylinder wall is not clean and must be rewashed. After the cylinder is cleaned, lubricate the cylinder wall with clean engine oil to prevent the cylinder liner from rusting.

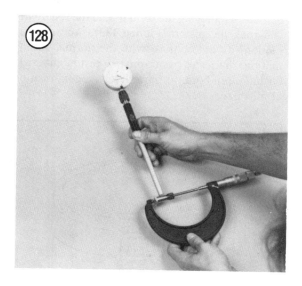

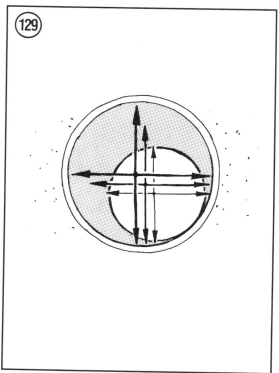

CAUTION
A combination of soap and water is the only solution that will completely clean the cylinder wall. Solvent and kerosene cannot wash fine grit out of cylinder crevices. Grit left in the cylinder will act as a grinding compound and cause premature wear to the new rings.

Installation

1. Check that the top and bottom cylinder surfaces are clean of all gasket residue.
2. Install the 2 dowel pins into the crankcase (**Figure 124**).

NOTE
*The Yamaha base gasket has a bead of gasket sealer on one side of the gasket. Install the base gasket so that the sealer side faces **up**. See **Figure 130**.*

3. Install a new base gasket (**Figure 130**). Make sure all holes align.
4. Install the piston, as described in this chapter.

CAUTION
Make sure the piston pin circlips are installed and seated correctly.

5. Install a piston holding fixture under the piston.

NOTE

A piston holding fixture can be made out of a scrap piece of wood. See Figure 131.

6. Lubricate the cylinder wall and piston liberally with engine oil prior to installation.

7. Carefully align the cylinder with the piston and install the cylinder. Compress each ring as it enters the cylinder with your fingers or by using an aircraft type hose clamp (**Figure 132**).

NOTE

Once the cylinder is installed, run the chain and wire up through the cylinder.

CAUTION

Don't tighten the clamp any more than necessary to compress the rings. If the rings can't slip through easily, the clamp may gouge the rings.

8. Remove the piston holding fixture and push the cylinder (**Figure 123**) all the way down.

9. While holding the cylinder down with one hand, operate the kickstarter lever with your other hand. The piston should move smoothly and quietly up and down in the bore.

10. Install the cylinder head as described in this chapter.

PISTONS AND PISTON RINGS

Piston
Removal/Installation

1. Remove the cylinder as described in this chapter.

2. Stuff the crankcase with clean shop rags to prevent objects from falling into the crankcase.

3. Before removing the piston, hold the rod tightly and rock the piston (**Figure 133**). Any rocking motion (do not confuse with the normal sliding motion) indicates wear on the piston pin, rod bushing, pin bore, or more likely, a combination of all three.

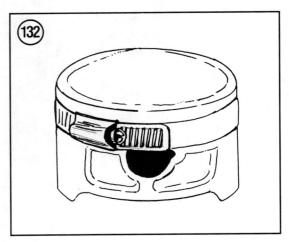

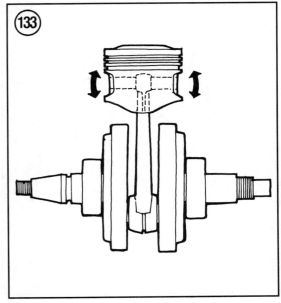

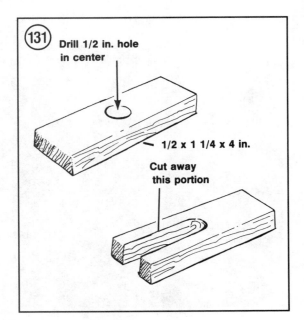

Drill 1/2 in. hole in center

1/2 x 1 1/4 x 4 in.

Cut away this portion

4. Remove the circlips from the piston pin bores (A, **Figure 134**).

NOTE
Discard the piston circlips. New circlips must be installed during reassembly.

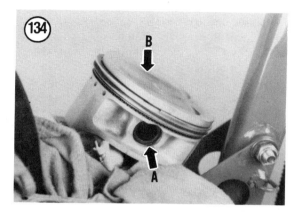

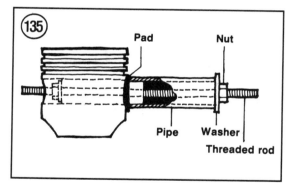

5. Push the piston pin out of the piston by hand. If the pin is tight, use a homemade tool (**Figure 135**) to remove it. Do not drive the piston pin out as this action may damage the piston pin, connecting rod or piston.

6. Lift the piston (B, **Figure 134**) off the connecting rod.

7. Inspect the piston as described in this chapter.

4

NOTE
New piston circlips should be installed.

8. Coat the connecting rod bushing, piston pin and piston with assembly oil.

9. Place the piston over the connecting rod so that the arrow on the piston crown (**Figure 136**) faces forward.

10. Insert the piston pin through one side of the piston (**Figure 137**) until it starts to enter the connecting rod. Then it may be necessary to move the piston around until the pin enters the connecting rod. Do not force installation or damage may occur. If the pin does not slide easily, use the homemade tool (**Figure 135**) but eliminate the piece of pipe. Push the pin in until it is centered in the piston.

11. Install the 2 piston circlips in the circlip grooves. Make sure the circlips seat all the way in the circlip grooves.

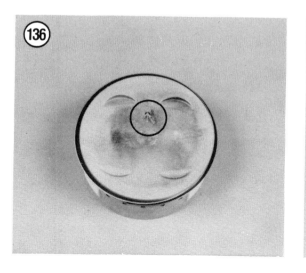

Piston Inspection

1. Remove the piston rings as described in this chapter.

2. Carefully clean the carbon from the piston crown (**Figure 138**) with a soft scraper or wire wheel. Large carbon accumulations reduce piston cooling and results in detonation and piston damage. Do not remove or damage the carbon ridge around the circumference of the piston above the top ring. If the piston, rings and cylinder are found to be dimensionally correct and can be reused, removal of the carbon ring from the top of the piston or the carbon ridges from the cylinders will promote excessive oil consumption.

CAUTION
Do not wire brush the sides of the piston as the brush will leave scratches on the ring grooves and piston skirt.

3. After cleaning the piston, examine the crown. The crown should show no signs of wear or damage. If the crown appears pecked or spongy-looking, also check the spark plug, valves and combustion chamber for aluminum deposits. If these deposits are found, the cylinder is suffering from excessive heat caused by a lean fuel mixture or preignition.

4. Examine each ring groove (**Figure 139**) for burrs, dented edges and wide wear. Pay particular attention to the top compression ring groove, as it usually wears more than the others. Because the oil rings are constantly bathed in oil, these rings and grooves wear little compared to compression rings and their grooves. If there is evidence of oil ring groove wear or if the oil ring assembly is tight and difficult to remove, the piston skirt may have collapsed due to excessive heat and is permanently deformed. Replace the piston.

5. Check the oil control holes in the piston for carbon or oil sludge buildup. Clean the holes with a small diameter drill bit. See **Figure 140**.

6. Check the piston skirt for cracks or other damage. If a piston shows signs of partial seizure (bits of aluminum build-up on the piston skirt), the piston should be replaced and the cylinder bored (if necessary) to reduce the possibility of engine noise and further piston seizure.

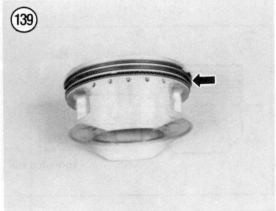

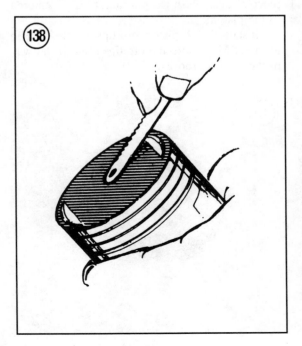

NOTE
If the piston skirt is worn or scuffed unevenly from side-to-side, the connecting rod may be bent or twisted.

7. Inspect the piston pin (**Figure 141**) for chrome flaking or cracks. Replace if necessary.
8. Install a new piston pin circlip in each piston circlip groove and check the groove for wear or circlip looseness by pulling the circlip from side-to-side. If the circlip has any side play, the groove is worn and the piston must be replaced.
9. Measure piston-to-cylinder clearance as described under *Piston Clearance* in this chapter.
10. If damage or wear indicate piston replacement, select a new piston as described under *Piston Clearance* in this chapter.

Piston Clearance

1. Make sure the piston and cylinder walls are clean and dry.
2. Measure the cylinder bores with a bore gauge or inside micrometer (**Figure 127**). Then measure the bore gauge with a micrometer to determine the bore diameter (**Figure 128**). Measure the cylinder bore at the points shown in **Figure 129**. Measure in 3 axes—in line with the piston pin and at 90° to the pin.

NOTE
*When measuring the piston diameter in Step 3, measure the piston diameter at a point 1 mm (1/32 in.) (XT350) or 2 mm (3/32 in.) (TT350) from the lower edge of the piston skirt. See **Figure 142**.*

3. Measure the piston diameter with a micrometer at a right angle to the piston pin bore (**Figure 143**).
4. Subtract the piston diameter from the largest bore diameter; the difference is piston-to-cylinder clearance. If clearance exceeds specifications, the piston should be replaced and the cylinder bored oversize. Purchase the new piston first. Measure its diameter and add the specified clearance to determine the proper cylinder bore diameter.

Piston Ring
Inspection/Removal/Installation

1. Measure the side clearance of each ring in its groove with a flat feeler gauge (**Figure 144**) and compare with the specifications in **Table 2**. If the

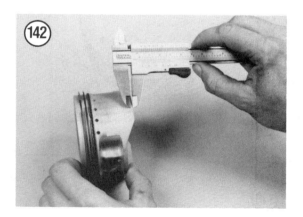

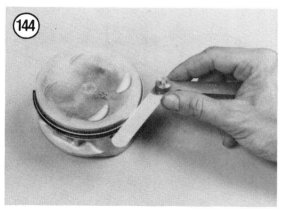

clearance is greater than specified, the rings must be replaced. If the clearance is still excessive with the new rings, the piston must be replaced.

WARNING
The edges of all piston rings are very sharp. Be careful when handling them to avoid cut fingers.

NOTE
Store the rings in order of removal.

2. Remove the old rings with a ring expander tool (**Figure 145**) or by spreading the ring ends with your thumbs and lifting the rings up evenly (**Figure 146**).
3. Using a broken piston ring, remove all carbon from the piston ring grooves (**Figure 147**).
4. Inspect grooves carefully for burrs, nicks or broken or cracked lands. Replace piston if necessary.
5. Check end gap of each ring. To check, insert the ring into the top of the cylinder bore approximately 20 mm (25/32 in.) and square it with the cylinder wall by tapping it with the piston (**Figure 148**). Measure the end gap with a feeler gauge (**Figure 149**). Compare gap with **Table 2**. Replace ring if gap is too large. If the gap on the new ring is smaller than specified, hold a small file in a vise, grip the ends of the ring with your fingers and enlarge the gap.
6. Roll each ring around its piston groove as shown in **Figure 150** to check for binding. Minor binding may be cleaned up with a fine-cut file.

NOTE
*Install the piston rings in the order shown in (**Figure 151**).*

NOTE
Install all rings with the manufacturer's markings facing up.

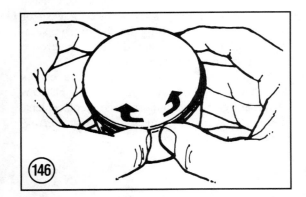

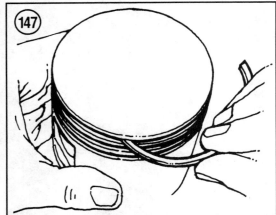

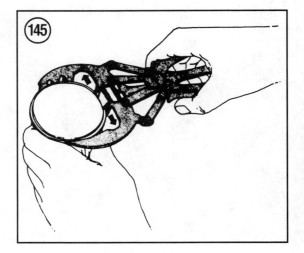

7. Install the piston rings—first the bottom, then the middle, then the top ring—by carefully spreading the ends with your thumbs and slipping the rings over the top of the piston. Remember that the piston rings must be installed with the marks on them facing up toward the top of the piston or there is the possibility of oil pumping past the rings.

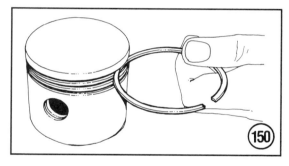

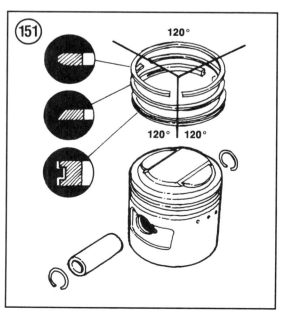

a. Install the oil ring assembly into the bottom ring groove. The assembly is comprised of 2 steel rails and 1 expander. The expander is installed in the middle of the steel rails.

b. The top and middle piston rings are different. The middle ring is slightly tapered and must be installed as shown in **Figure 151**. The top ring is symmetrical and must be installed as shown in **Figure 151**.

8. Make sure the rings are seated completely in their grooves all the way around the piston and that the end gaps are distributed around the piston as shown in **Figure 152**. It is important that the ring gaps are not aligned with each other when installed to prevent compression pressures from escaping past them.

9. If installing oversize compression rings, check the number to make sure the correct rings are being installed. The ring numbers should be the same as the piston oversize number.

10. If new rings are installed, the cylinders must be deglazed or honed. This will help to seat the new rings. If necessary, refer honing service to a Yamaha dealer or motorcycle repair shop. After honing, measure the end gap of each ring and compare to dimensions in **Table 2**.

NOTE
*If the cylinders were deglazed or honed, clean the cylinders as described under **Cylinder Block Inspection** in this chapter.*

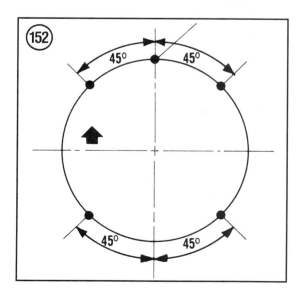

Table 1 GENERAL ENGINE SPECIFICATIONS

Engine type	4-stroke, DOHC, 4-valve single cylinder
Bore × stroke	86.0 × 59.6 mm (3.39 × 2.35 in.)
Compression ratio	9.0:1
Displacement	346 cc (21.1 cu. in.)
Lubrication system	Wet sump

Table 2 ENGINE TOP END SERVICE SPECIFICATIONS

Item	Specifications mm (in.)	Wear limit mm (in.)
Cylinder head		
Warp limit	—	0.03
	—	(0.0012)
Cylinder		
Bore	85.97-86.02	—
	(3.385-3.387)	
Taper limit	—	0.08
	—	(0.003)
Out of round	—	0.08
	—	(0.003)
Piston		
Diameter		
Standard	85.92-85.97	86.1
	(3.383-3.385)	(3.390)
2nd over	86.50	—
	(3.406)	—
4th over	87.00	—
	(3.425)	—
Clearance	0.040-0.060	0.1
	(0.00157-0.00246)	(0.004)
Piston rings		
End gap		
Top and 2nd	0.25-0.40	0.8
	(0.0098-0.0157)	(0.032)
Oil	0.20-0.70	—
	(0.0079-0.0276)	—
Side clearance		
Top	0.04-0.08	0.15
	(0.002-0.003)	(0.006)
2nd	0.03-0.07	0.15
	(0.001-0.003)	(0.006)
Oil	0.02-0.06	—
	(0.0008-0.0024)	—
Camshaft		
Outside diameter	24.967-24.980	—
	(0.9830-0.9835)	—
Cam cap ID	25.000-25.021	—
	(0.984-0.985)	—
Clearance	0.020-0.054	—
	(0.0008-0.0020)	—

(continued)

Table 2 ENGINE TOP END SERVICE SPECIFICATIONS (continued)

Item	Specifications mm (in.)	Wear limit mm (in.)
Camshaft (continued)		
Cam dimensions		
Outside diameter	27.998-28.098	—
	(1.102-1.106)	—
Lobe height	35.75-35.85	—
	(1.407-1.411)	—
Base diameter	27.998-28.098	—
	(1.102-1.106)	—
Runout limit	—	0.03
	—	(0.001)
Valve		
Stem runout limit	—	0.01
	—	(0.0004)
Head diameter		
Intake		
XT350	27.90-28.10	—
	(1.098-1.106)	—
TT350	28.90-29.11	—
	(1.138-1.146)	—
Exhaust	24.90-25.10	—
	(0.980-0.988)	—
Face width	2.26	—
	(0.089)	—
Seat width	0.9-1.1	1.8
	(0.035-0.043)	(0.07)
Margin thickness		
Intake		
XT350	0.6-1.0	—
	(0.024-0.039)	—
TT350	0.8-1.2	—
	(0.031-0.047)	—
Exhaust	0.8-1.2	—
	(0.031-0.047)	—
Valve stem outside diameter		
Intake	5.475-5.490	—
	(0.2156-0.2161)	—
Exhaust	5.460-5.475	—
	(0.2150-0.2156)	—
Valve guide inside diameter		
Intake & Exhaust	5.500-5.512	5.6
	(0.2165-0.2170)	(0.22)
Valve stem-to-guide clearance		
Intake	0.010-0.037	0.1
	(0.0004-0.0015)	(0.004)
Exhaust	0.025-0.040	0.1
	(0.00098-0.0016)	(0.004)
Valve springs		
Inner (all)	38.1	36.1
	(1.500)	(1.421)
Outer (all)	41.2	39.2
	(1.622)	(1.543)
Spring tilt limit	—	1.7
	—	(0.067)

Table 3 ENGINE TOP END TIGHTENING TORQUES

	N·m	ft.-lb.
Cylinder head		
10 mm flange bolt	40	29
8 mm nut	20	14
6 mm bolt	10	7.2
Spark plug	17.5	12.5
Camshaft cap	10	7.2
Cylinder head cover	10	7.2
Primary drive gear nut	80	58
Balancer shaft drive gear nut	60	43
Magneto bolt	60	43
Camshaft sprocket bolt	20	14
Cam chain tensioner bolt	12	8.7
Rear cam chain guide bolt	8	5.8
Oil pump assembly screw	7	5.1
Oil pump cover screw	7	5.1
Oil strainer plug	32	23
Oil filter cover bolt	10	7.2
Oil filter cover screw	7	5.1
Oil filter cover air bleed screw	5	3.6
Engine drain plug	43	31
Exhaust pipe flange bolt	12	8.7
Muffler clamp flange bolt	20	14
Muffler mount bolt	27	19
Crankcase screws	7	5.1
Crankcase cover screws	7	5.1
Balancer shaft bearing retainer screw*	7	5.1
Kickstarter bolt	20	14
Oil pipe banjo bolt	20	14
Engine mounting bolts		
Rear mounting bolt	38	27
All other bolts	33	24

* Apply Loctite 242 (blue) before tightening screw.

CHAPTER FIVE

ENGINE LOWER END

This chapter describes service procedures for the following lower end components:

a. Crankcases.
b. Crankshaft.
c. Connecting rod.
d. Transmission (removal and installation).
e. Internal shift mechanism (removal and installation).

Prior to removing and disassembling the crankcase, clean the entire engine and frame with a good grade commercial degreaser, like Gunk or Bel-Ray engine degreaser or equivalent. It is easier to work on a clean engine and you will do a better job.

Make certain that you have all the necessary tools available, especially any special tool(s), and purchase replacement parts prior to disassembly. Also make sure you have a clean place to work.

One of the more important aspects of engine overhaul is preparation. Improper preparation before and failing to identify and store parts during removal will cause a headache when it comes time to reinstall and assemble the engine. Before removing the first bolt and to prevent frustration during installation, get a number of boxes, plastic bags and containers and store the parts as they are

removed (**Figure 1**). Also have on hand a roll of masking tape and a permanent, waterproof marking pen to label each part or assembly as required. If your bike was purchased second hand and it appears that some of the wiring may have been changed or replaced, it will be to your advantage to label each electrical connection before disconnecting it.

In the text there is frequent mention of the left-hand and right-hand side of the engine. This refers to the engine as it sits in the bike's frame, not as it sits on your workbench.

Crankshaft specifications are listed in **Table 1**. **Tables 1** and **2** are found at the end of the chapter.

SERVICING ENGINE IN FRAME

Some of the components can be serviced while the engine is mounted in the frame (the bike's frame is a great holding fixture—especially for breaking loose stubborn bolts and nuts):

a. Cylinder head.
b. Cylinder and piston.
c. Gearshift mechanism.
d. Clutch.
e. Kickstarter.
f. Oil pump

g. Carburetor.

h. Rotor and electrical systems.

ENGINE

Removal/Installation

This procedure describes engine removal and installation. If service work requires only the removal of a top end component, the engine can be left in the frame and the top end disassembled only as far as required to remove the desired sub-assembly. If the engine requires crankcase disassembly, it will be easier to remove as many sub-assemblies from the engine before removing the crankcase from the frame. By following this method, the frame can be used as a holding fixture as the engine is disassembled. Attempting to disassemble the complete engine while it is placed on a workbench is more time consuming and will require an assistant to help hold the engine while you loosen many of the larger nuts and bolts.

1. Support the bike and raise the rear wheel off the ground with a suitable wheel stand.

2. Remove the left- and right-hand side covers.

3. Remove the seat.

4. *XT350*: Disconnect the negative battery terminal connector (**Figure 2**).

5. Remove the fuel tank as described under *Fuel Tank Removal/Installation* in Chapter Eight.

6. Remove the left- and right-hand air scoops.

7. *XT350 California models*: Disconnect the carbon canister hose at the carburetor. Then remove the canister mounting bolts and remove the canister (A, **Figure 3**).

8. Disconnect the crankcase ventilation hose at the crankcase (B, **Figure 3**).

9. Remove the exhaust pipe and muffler assembly as described under *Exhaust System* in Chapter Eight.

10. *XT350*: Remove the Phillips screw and pull the tachometer cable (**Figure 4**) out of the drive unit in the clutch cover.

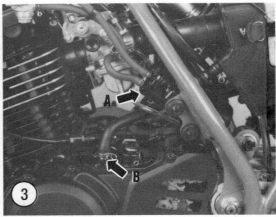

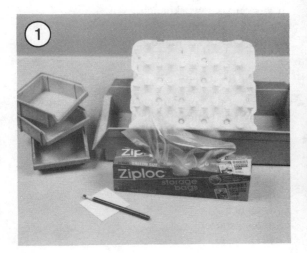

11. Loosen the clutch cable adjuster locknut (A, **Figure 5**) and turn the adjuster (B, **Figure 5**) toward the clutch lever. Then disconnect the clutch cable at the release lever at the crankcase (**Figure 6**).

12. Disconnect the decompression cable as follows:

   a. Locate the decompression cable mid-line adjuster on the right-hand side of the bike. Then loosen the adjuster locknut (A, **Figure 7**) and turn the adjuster clockwise (B, **Figure 7**) to obtain as much cable slack as possible.

   b. Remove the decompression cable bracket (**Figure 8**) at the cylinder head.

   c. See **Figure 9**. Loosen and remove the Acorn nut (A) and Allen screw (B). Then disconnect the decompression cable from the bracket. Reinstall the bracket and Acorn nut.

13. Remove the carburetor as described under *Carburetor Removal/Installation* in Chapter Eight.

14. Remove the shift lever (**Figure 10**). Remove the pinch bolt and pull the shift lever off the shaft. If the splined boss is tight on the shaft, spread the slot open with a screwdriver.

15. Remove the left-hand side cover (**Figure 11**).

16. Remove the drive sprocket as follows:

  a. Remove the 2 sprocket lockplate mounting bolts (A, **Figure 12**).

  b. Turn the sprocket lockplate (B, **Figure 12**) and slide it off of the countershaft.

  c. Slide the drive sprocket (**Figure 13**) off of the countershaft.

NOTE
If the drive chain is tight, loosen the rear axle nut and loosen the chain adjusters.

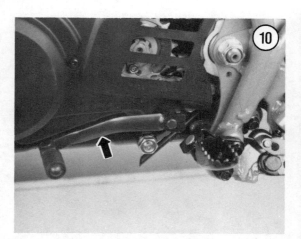

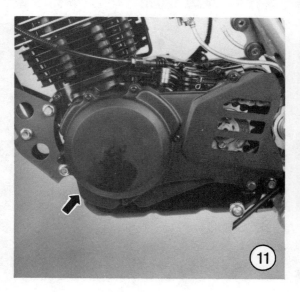

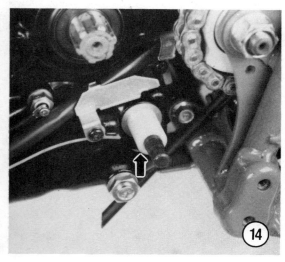

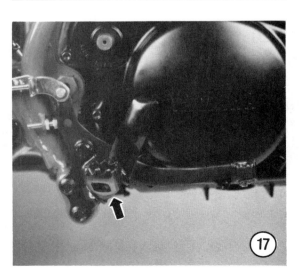

17. Slide the spacer (**Figure 14**) and washer (**Figure 15**) off of the external shift shaft.

18A. *XT350*: Disconnect the brake light return spring at the rear brake pedal (**Figure 16**). Then remove the right-hand footpeg/brake pedal bracket assembly bolts and remove the bracket (**Figure 17**).

18B. *TT350*: Remove the bolts securing the right-hand footpeg/brake pedal bracket assembly and remove the bracket (**Figure 18**).

19A. *XT350*: Disconnect the following electrical connectors:

   a. Spark plug lead (**Figure 19**).

5

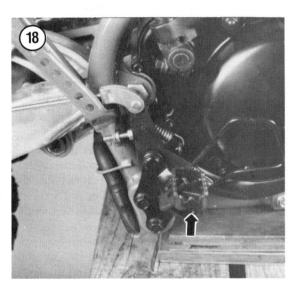

b. Charge coil/lighting coil connector (**Figure 20**).

c. Source coil/pickup coil connector (**Figure 21**).

19B. *TT350*: Disconnect the following electrical connectors:

a. Spark plug, lead (**Figure 19**).

b. CDI magneto leads (**Figure 22**).

20. Disconnect the electrical wire clamps from the wires disconnected in Step 19 and route the wiring harness away from the frame.

21. If the engine requires disassembly, remove the following sub-assemblies:

a. Cylinder Head (Chapter Four).

b. Cylinder and piston (Chapter Four).

c. Rotor assembly (Chapter Nine).

d. Clutch (Chapter Six).

e. Primary drive gear and balancer driven gear assemblies (this chapter).

f. Kickstarter (Chapter Six).

g. Oil pump (this chapter).

22. If the engine is being removed with the top end installed, remove the cylinder head-to-frame mount (**Figure 23**).

23. Remove the engine assembly as follows:

a. Place a hydraulic jack underneath the engine. Raise the jack so that the pad just rests against the bottom of the engine. If necessary, place a block of wood on the jack pad to protect the engine case. If you do not have access to a jack, place wood blocks underneath the engine. The idea is to have a support available when the engine mount bolts are loosened.

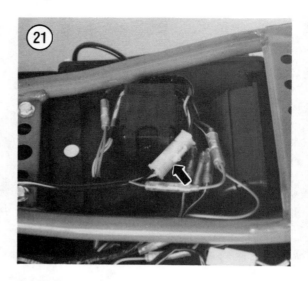

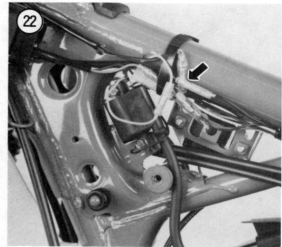

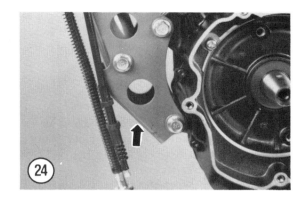

b. Remove the front engine mounting bolts and brackets (**Figure 24**).

c. Loosen the swing arm pivot shaft nut (**Figure 25**).

d. Remove the lower engine mount nut and bolt (**Figure 26**).

e. Remove the engine-to-swing arm pivot shaft nut (**Figure 25**) and withdraw the pivot shaft (**Figure 27**) from the right-hand side.

f. Lift the engine (**Figure 28**) out of the frame.

g. The swing arm is now loose from its mounting on the frame. If it is necessary to move the bike, align the swing arm with the frame and install the pivot shaft and nut (**Figure 29**).

24. While the engine is removed, check the engine frame mounts for cracks or other damage.

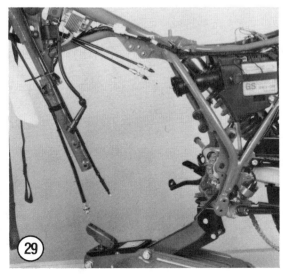

5

25. Install by reversing these removal steps.
26. Tighten the engine mounting bolts to the torque specifications in **Table 2**. Tighten the pivot shaft nut to the torque specification in **Table 2**.
27. If the engine oil was drained, refill it as described in Chapter Three.
28. Adjust the following as described in Chapter Three:
   a. Decompression cable.
   b. Clutch cable.
   c. Drive chain.
   d. Rear brake pedal.
29. Start the engine and check for leaks.

CRANKCASE AND CRANKSHAFT

Disassembly of the crankcase—splitting the cases—and removal of the crankshaft assembly requires engine removal from the frame. However, the cylinder head, cylinder and all other attached assemblies should be removed with the engine in the frame.

The crankcase is made in 2 halves of precision diecast aluminum alloy and is of the "thin-walled" type. To avoid damage to them, do not hammer or pry on any of the interior or exterior projected walls. These areas are easily damaged if stressed beyond what they are designed for. They are assembled without a gasket; only gasket sealer is used while dowel pins align the crankcase halves when they are bolted together. The crankcase halves are sold as a matched set only (**Figure 30**). If one crankcase half is severely damaged, both must be replaced.

The crankshaft assembly is made up of 2 full-circle flywheels pressed together on a hollow crankpin. The connecting rod big end bearing on the crankpin is a needle bearing assembly (**Figure 31**). The crankshaft assembly is supported by 2 ball bearings in the crankcase.

The procedure which follows is presented as a complete, step-by-step major lower end overhaul that should be followed if the engine is to be completely reconditioned.

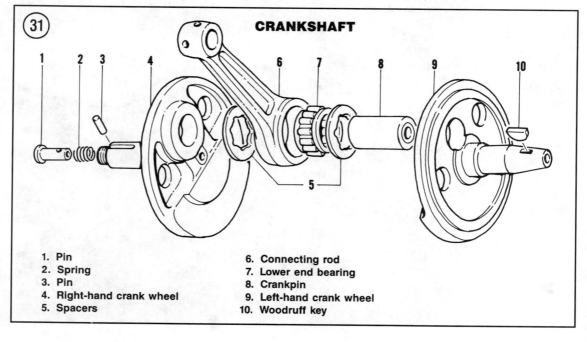

CRANKSHAFT

1. Pin
2. Spring
3. Pin
4. Right-hand crank wheel
5. Spacers
6. Connecting rod
7. Lower end bearing
8. Crankpin
9. Left-hand crank wheel
10. Woodruff key

Remember that the right- and left-hand side of the engine relates to the engine as it sits in the bike's frame, not as it sits on your workbench.

Special Tools

When splitting the crankcase assembly, a few special tools will be required. These tools allow easy disassembly and reassembly of the engine without prying or hammer use. Remember, the

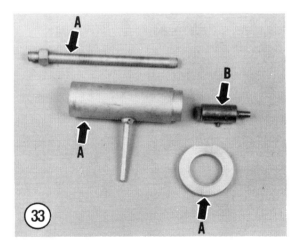

crankcase halves can be easily damaged by improper disassembly or reassembly techniques.

  a. Yamaha crankcase separating tool (part No. YU-01135) (**Figure 32**). This tool threads into the crankcase and is used to separate the crankcase halves and to press the crankshaft out of the crankcase. The tool is very simple in design and a similar type of tool, such as a steering wheel puller can be substituted.

  b. Yamaha crankshaft installing set (part No. YU-90050) (A, **Figure 33**) and the Yamaha adapter (part No. YU-1383) (B, **Figure 33**). These tools are used together to pull the crankshaft back into the crankcase assembly.

Crankcase Disassembly

This procedure describes disassembly of the crankcase halves and removal of the crankshaft, transmission and internal shift mechanism. Disassembly and reassembly of the transmission and the internal shift mechanism assembly is described in Chapter Seven.

NOTE
Drain the clutch/transmission oil as described in Chapter Three. To avoid misplacing the drain bolt, reinstall it after the oil is completely drained.

1. Remove all exterior engine assemblies as described in this chapter and other related chapters.
2. Note the position of all hose guides and clamps. See **Figure 34** and **Figure 35**.

3. Remove the circlip from the transmission countershaft (**Figure 36**) if it was not removed when the idler gear was removed.

4. To prevent from damaging the countershaft oil seal when the countershaft is removed, install an O-ring in the groove in the end of the countershaft (**Figure 37**).

5. Place the engine assembly on a couple of wood blocks with the left-hand side facing up (**Figure 38**).

NOTE
An impact driver with a Phillips bit (described in Chapter One) will be necessary to loosen the crankcase screws in Step 6. Attempting to loosen the screws with a screwdriver may ruin the screw heads.

6. Loosen all screws securing the crankcase halves together one-quarter turn. To prevent warpage, loosen them in a crisscross pattern.

7. Remove all screws loosened in Step 6. Be sure to remove all of them.

NOTE
To prevent loss and to ensure proper location during assembly, draw the crankcase outline on cardboard, then punch holes to correspond with screw locations. Insert the screws in their appropriate locations.

CAUTION
Perform this operation over and close down to the work bench as the crankcase halves may easily separate. Do not hammer on the crankcase halves as they will be damaged.

8. Turn the crankcase over so that the right-hand side faces up (**Figure 36**).

CAUTION
Pry points have been cast into the 2 crankcase halves. When prying the crankcase halves apart in Step 9, only pry between the pry points. Do not pry between the crankcase mating

surfaces. Doing so will result in oil leaks, requiring replacement of both case halves.

9. Use 2 large flat-tipped screwdrivers at the crankcase pry points as shown in **Figure 39** and carefully pry the crankcase halves apart. Use a

plastic or rubber mallet and tap the transmission shafts to help during separation.

10. Carefully lift the right-hand crankcase assembly off of the engine. The transmission, balancer shaft, crankshaft and internal shift mechanism will stay in the left-hand crankcase half (**Figure 40**).

NOTE
Check the crankshaft, balancer shaft, transmission shafts and the right-hand crankcase half for shims that may have been installed by a previous owner. There are no factory installed shims on the outer portion of the transmission shafts, balancer shaft or crankshaft.

11. Remove the 2 dowel pins (**Figure 40**) after removing the right-hand crankcase half.

12. Remove the transmission and internal shift mechanism assembly as follows:

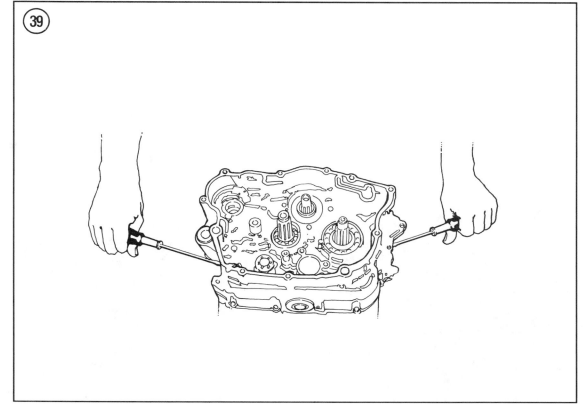

a. Remove the No. 2 shift fork shaft (**Figure 41**).
b. Remove the No. 1 shift fork shaft (**Figure 42**).
c. Remove the shift drum assembly (**Figure 43**).
d. Remove the No. 3 shift fork (**Figure 44**).
e. Remove the No. 1 shift fork (**Figure 45**).
f. Remove the No. 2 shift fork (**Figure 46**).
g. Remove the 2 transmission shafts (**Figure 47**).

13. Remove the balancer shaft (**Figure 48**).

14. Remove the crankshaft (**Figure 49**) as follows:
   a. Thread the rotor holding bolt into the end of the crankshaft (**Figure 50**).
   b. Install the crankcase separating tool (**Figure 51**) into the threaded holes on the left-hand crankcase. Center the pressure bolt on the end of the crankshaft. Tighten the long separating bolts into the crankcase, making sure the tool body is parallel with the crankcase. If necessary, back out one of the long bolts.
   c. Screw the puller *clockwise* and push the crankshaft out of the crankcase.
   d. When the crankshaft is free of the crankcase bearing, remove it.

Crankcase Inspection

1. Remove the crankcase oil seals as described under *Bearing and Oil Seal Replacement* in this chapter.

CAUTION
When drying the crankcase bearings in Step 2, do not allow the inner bearing race to spin. The bearing will be dry of all lubrication and damage will result. When drying the bearings, hold the inner race with your hand.

In addition, when drying bearings with compressed air, never allow the air jet to rotate the bearing. The jet is capable of rotating the bearing at speeds far in excess of those for which they were designed. The likelihood of a bearing disintegrating and causing serious injury and damage is very great.

2. Clean both crankcase halves inside and out and all crankcase bearings with cleaning solvent. Thoroughly dry with compressed air and wipe off with a clean shop cloth. Be sure to remove all traces of old gasket sealer from all mating surfaces.

3. Oil the crankshaft main bearings (**Figure 52**) with engine oil before checking the bearings in Steps 4 and 5.

4. Check the crankshaft main bearings (A, **Figure 52**) for roughness, pitting, galling, and play by rotating them slowly by hand. If any roughness or play can be felt in the bearing, it must be replaced.

NOTE
Always replace both crankcase main bearings as a set.

5. Inspect the other bearings as described in the previous step. See **Figure 53** and **Figure 54**.

6. Replace any worn or damaged bearings as described under *Bearing and Oil Seal Replacement* in this chapter.

7. Carefully inspect the cases for cracks and fractures, especially in the lower areas (**Figure 55**) where they are vulnerable to rock damage. Also, check the areas around the stiffening ribs, around bearing bosses and threaded holes. If any are found, have them repaired by a shop specializing in the repair of precision aluminum castings or replace them.

56

8. Check the threaded holes (**Figure 56**) in both crankcase halves for thread damage or dirt or oil buildup. If necessary, clean or repair the threads with a suitable size metric tap. Coat the tap threads with kerosene or an aluminum tap fluid before use.
9. Check the kickstarter stop (**Figure 57**) for damage. Also check the stop bolts for tightness.

Bearing and Oil Seal Replacement

1. Pry out the oil seals (**Figure 58**) with a screwdriver. Place a rag or wood block underneath the screwdriver to prevent from damaging the crankcase (**Figure 59**). If the seals are old and difficult to remove, heat the cases as described later and use an awl to punch a small hole in the steel backing of the seal. Install a small sheet metal screw into the seal and pull the seal out with a pair of pliers.

> *CAUTION*
> *Do not install the screw too deep or it may contact and damage the bearing behind it.*

> *NOTE*
> *An impact driver with a Phillips bit (described in Chapter One) will be required to loosen the bearing retainer plate screws described in Step 2. Attempting to loosen the screws with a Phillips screwdriver may ruin the screw heads.*

5

57

58

59

2. Some bearings are held in position by a retainer plate (**Figure 60**). Remove the retainers before removing the bearings. If it is not necessary to remove the bearings, check the retainer plate screws for tightness.

> *CAUTION*
> *Before heating the crankcases, in this procedure, to remove the bearings, wash the cases thoroughly with detergent and water. Rinse and rewash the cases as required to remove all traces of oil and other debris.*

> *NOTE*
> *The main bearings are installed in a steel sleeve that is part of the crankcase (**B, Figure 52**). When attempting to remove these bearings, the sleeve should also be supported with wood blocks on the opposite side to prevent it from being driven out with the bearing.*

3. The bearings are installed with a slight interference fit. The crankcase must be heated to a temperature of about 212° F (100° C) in a shop oven or on a hot plate. An easy way to check to see that it is at the proper temperature is to drop tiny drops of water on the case; if they sizzle and evaporate immediately, the temperature is correct. Heat only one case at a time.

> *CAUTION*
> *Do not heat the cases with a torch (propane or acetylene)—never bring a flame into contact with the bearing or case. The direct heat will destroy the case hardening of the bearing and will likely warp the case half.*

4. Remove the case from the oven or hot plate and hold onto the 2 crankcase studs with a kitchen pot holder, heavy gloves, or heavy shop cloths—*it is hot.*

5. Remove the oil seals if not already removed.

> *NOTE*
> *A suitable size socket and extension works well for removing and installing bearings.*

6. Hold the crankcase with the bearing side down and tap the bearing out. Repeat for all bearings in that case half.

7. While heating up the crankcase halves, place the new bearings in a freezer if possible. Chilling them will slightly reduce their overall diameter while the hot crankcase is slightly larger due to heat expansion. This will make installation much easier.

> *NOTE*
> *Prior to installing new bearing(s) or oil seal(s), apply a light coat of lithium based grease to the inside and outside to aid in installation. Be sure to apply the same grease to the lips of new oil seals.*

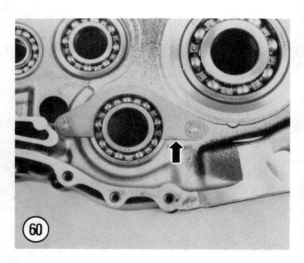

8. While the crankcase is still hot, press the new bearing(s) into place in the crankcase by hand until it seats completely. If necessary, tap the bearings into the case with a suitable size socket placed on the outer bearing race (**Figure 61**). Do not drive the bearing in by tapping on the inner bearing race.

NOTE
Always install bearings with the manufacturer's mark or number facing outward or so that after the crankcase is assembled you can still see these marks.

NOTE
Pack all crankcase oil seals with a heat durable grease before installation.

9. Oil seals can be installed with a suitable size socket and extension (**Figure 62**). When installing oil seals, it is important to drive the seal in squarely. Drive the seals in until they are flush with the case.

10. Align the bearing retainers with the crankcase. Apply Loctite 242 (blue) to the retainer screws and tighten them securely. See **Figure 60**.

Crankshaft Inspection

1. Clean the crankshaft thoroughly with solvent. Dry the crankshaft thoroughly. Then lubricate all bearing surfaces with a light coat of engine oil.
2. Check the crankshaft journals (A, **Figure 63**) and crankpin for scratches, heat discoloration or other defects.
3. Check flywheel taper, threads and keyway (B, **Figure 63**) for damage. If one crankshaft half is damaged, the crankshaft can be disassembled and the damaged part replaced as described in this chapter.
4. Check crankshaft oil seal surfaces for grooving, pitting or scratches.
5. Check crankshaft bearing surfaces for chatter marks and excessive or uneven wear. Minor cases of chatter mark may be cleaned up with 320 grit carborundum cloth. If 320 cloth is used, clean crankshaft in solvent and check surfaces. If they did not clean up properly, disassemble the crankshaft and replace the damaged part.
6. Check the crankshaft lower end area (**Figure 64**) for signs of seizure, bearing or thrust washer damage or connecting rod damage.

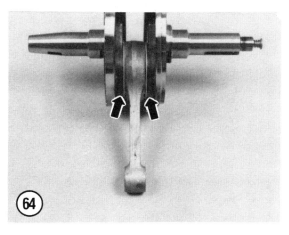

7. Check the connecting rod small end (**Figure 65**) for signs of excessive heat (blue coloration) or other damage.

8. Slide the connecting rod to one side and check the connecting rod-to-crankshaft side clearance with a flat feeler gauge (**Figure 66**). Compare to dimensions given in **Table 1**. If the clearance is greater than specified, the crankshaft assembly must be disassembled and the connecting rod replaced.

9. Check crankshaft runout with a dial indicator and V-blocks as shown in **Figure 67**. Retrue the crankshaft if the runout exceeds the service limit in **Table 1**.

10. If necessary, overhaul the crankshaft as described in this chapter.

Crankshaft Overhaul

Crankshaft overhaul requires a hydraulic press of 30 ton capacity, holding jigs, crankshaft alignment jig, dial indicators and a micrometer or vernier caliper. A typical crankshaft is shown in **Figure 68**.

1. Measure the crank wheel width with a micrometer or vernier caliper (**Figure 69**). Record the measurement so that it can be used during crankshaft reassembly.

2. Mark the side of the crank wheels with machinist blue. When the fluid has dried, scribe alignment marks across both crankwheels with a square and a scribe (**Figure 70**). These marks can be used to help align the crank wheels during its initial assembly.

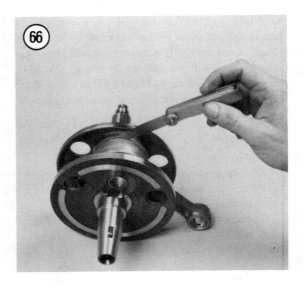

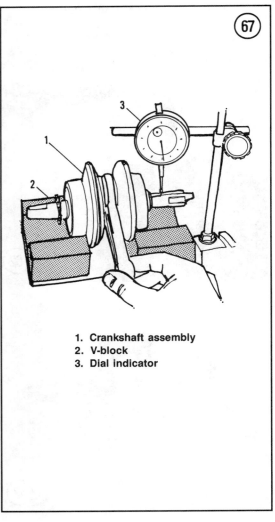

1. Crankshaft assembly
2. V-block
3. Dial indicator

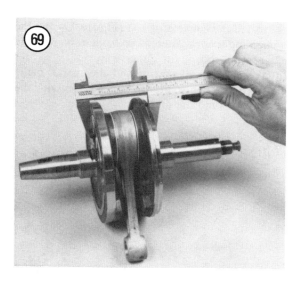

3. Place the crankshaft assembly in a suitable jig so that it is perfectly flat. Then press out the crankpin. Use an adapter between the press and crankpin. See **Figure 71**. Make sure to catch the lower crank half and crankpin assembly.

WARNING
When pressing the crankpin out, check that the crankshaft assembly remains flat. Because of the amount of force required to disassembly the crankshaft, the jig may bend slightly and side load the pin. This is dangerous and must be avoided. If the jig starts to bend, you will have to use stiffer material to support the crankshaft.

5

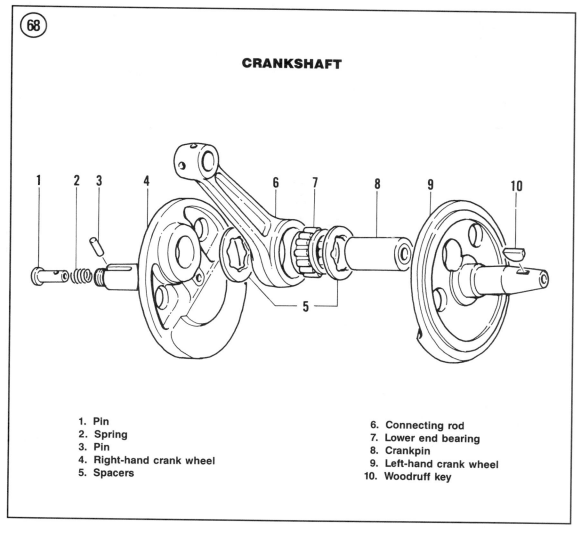

CRANKSHAFT

1. Pin
2. Spring
3. Pin
4. Right-hand crank wheel
5. Spacers
6. Connecting rod
7. Lower end bearing
8. Crankpin
9. Left-hand crank wheel
10. Woodruff key

4. Remove the spacers, connecting rod and lower end bearing (**Figure 72**).

5. Press out the crankpin (**Figure 73**).

6. Wash the crank halves thoroughly in solvent.

> *CAUTION*
> *When assembling the crankshaft assembly, the oil passages in the crank pin and the crank half must be aligned within 1 mm (0.04 in.). See **Figure 74**.*

> *NOTE*
> *When reassembling the crankshaft, apply white assembly grease to all bearing surfaces.*

7. Using a suitable alignment fixture, press the replacement crankpin into one crank half (**Figure 75**) until the crankpin is flush with the outside of the crank half.

8. Install a spacer and the needle bearing over the crankpin (**Figure 76**).

9. Install the connecting rod (**Figure 77**) and the remaining spacer. There is no front or back to the connecting rod; it fits either way.

10. Using a small square and the marks made during disassembly (**Figure 70**), start pressing the crank half onto the crankpin.

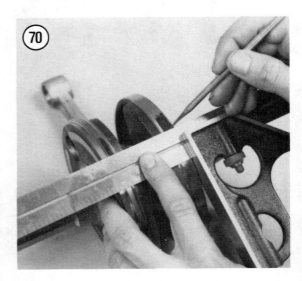

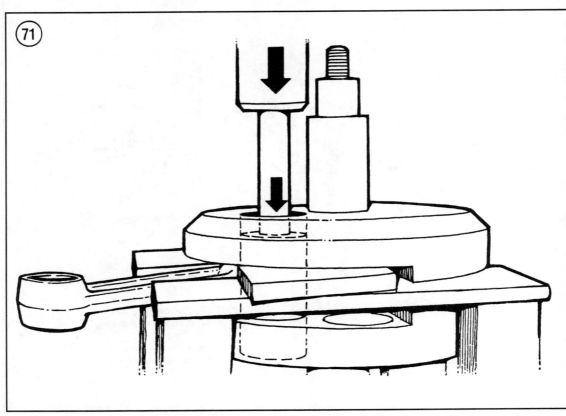

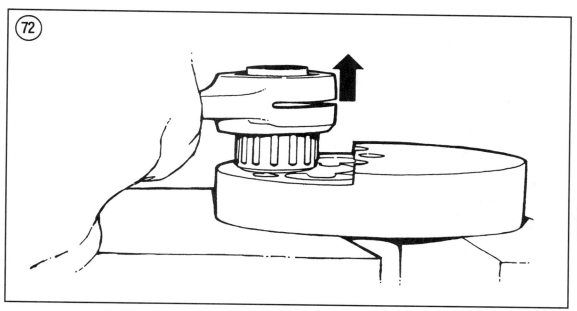

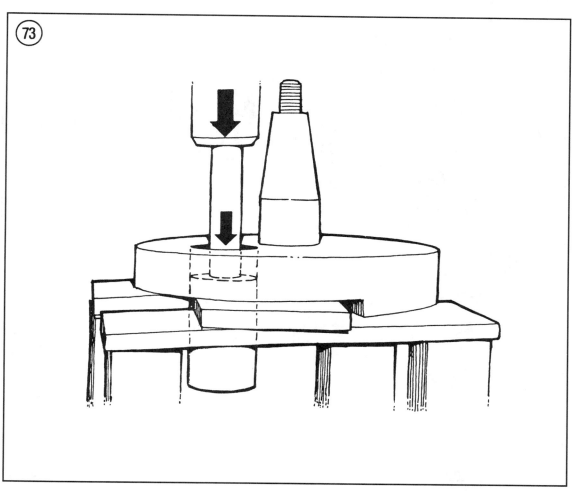

11. Insert a suitable size feeler gauge between the upper thrust washer and the crank half (**Figure 78**). Then continue pressing the crank half onto the crankpin until the feeler gauge fits tightly. Refer to connecting rod side clearance in **Table 1** for clearance.

12. Release all pressure from the press. The feeler gauge will then slip out easily.

13. Measure crank wheel width (**Figure 69**) and compare to the specifications recorded in Step 1. Use this measurement as a guide only. The connecting rod side clearance should be the determining factor when assembling the crankshaft assembly.

14. Check and adjust crankshaft alignment as described in this chapter.

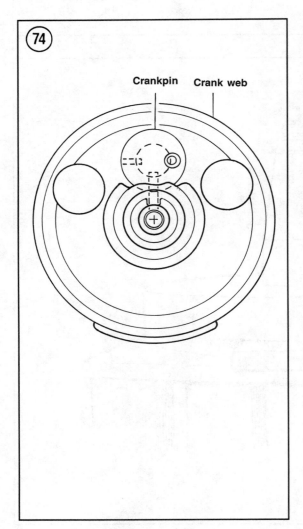

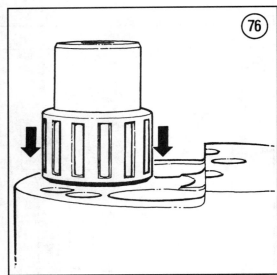

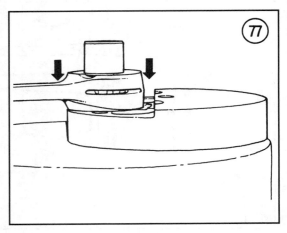

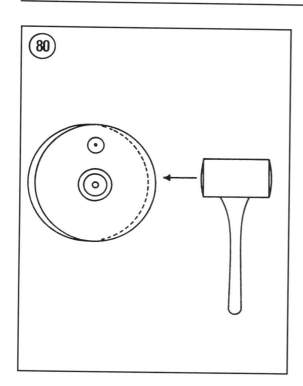

Crankshaft Alignment

After overhauling the crankshaft or when disassembling the engine, it is important to check crankshaft alignment and adjust as required so that both crank halves and the shafts extending from them all rotate on a common center. The crankshaft should be checked for runout and wheel deflection as follows.

Mount the assembled crankshaft in a suitable fixture or on V-blocks using 2 dial indicators (**Figure 79**). Slowly rotate the crankshaft through one or more complete turns and observe both dial indicators. One of several conditions will be observed:

1. *Runout*: Neither dial indicator needle begins its swing at the same time, and the needles will move in opposite directions during part of the crankshaft rotation cycle. Each needle will probably indicate a different amount of total travel. This condition is caused by eccentricity (both crank wheels not being on the same center), as shown in **Figure 79**. To correct, slowly rotate the crankshaft assembly

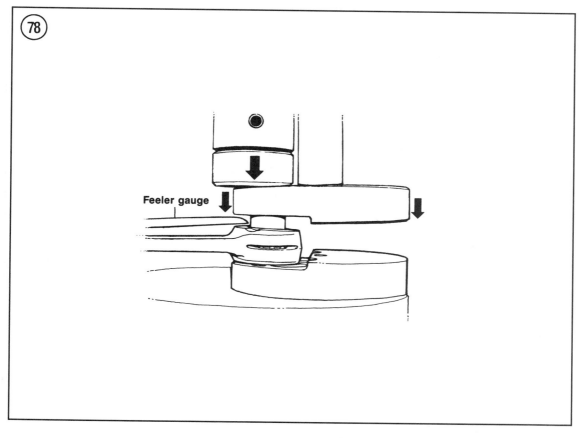

Feeler gauge

until the drive side dial gauge indicates its maximum. Mark the rim of the drive side crank wheel at the point in line with the plungers on both dial indicators. Remove the crankshaft assembly. Then, while holding one side of the crankshaft, strike the chalk mark a sharp blow with a brass hammer (**Figure 80**). Recheck alignment after each blow, and continue this procedure until both dial gauges begin and end their swings at the same time.

> *CAUTION*
> *Make sure that only a brass faced hammer is used to strike the crankshaft wheels. A lead hammer will damage the crankshaft wheels, requiring replacement.*

2. *Wheel deflection*: The crank wheels can become pinched or spread. This conditioned can be checked by measuring crank wheel width (**Figure 69**) at various spots or by checking runout with 2 dial indicators (**Figure 81** and **Figure 82**). When checking in an alignment jig, both dial indicators will indicate maximum travel when the crankpin is toward the dial gauges if the crank wheels are pinched. Correct the condition by removing the crankshaft assembly from the fixture. Then drive a wedge or chisel between the two crank wheels at a point opposite maximum dial gauge indication. Recheck alignment after each adjustment. Continue until the dial gauges indicate no more than 0.03 mm (0.0010 in.).

If the dial gauges indicated their maximum when the crankpin was on the side of the alignment jig away from the dial gauges, the crank wheels are spread. Correct this condition by tapping the outside of one of the wheels toward the other with a brass hammer. Recheck alignment after each blow. Continue adjustment until runout is within 0.03 mm (0.0010 in.) runout.

> *NOTE*
> *When adjusting wheel deflection, it will be necessary to check and adjust runout as required.*

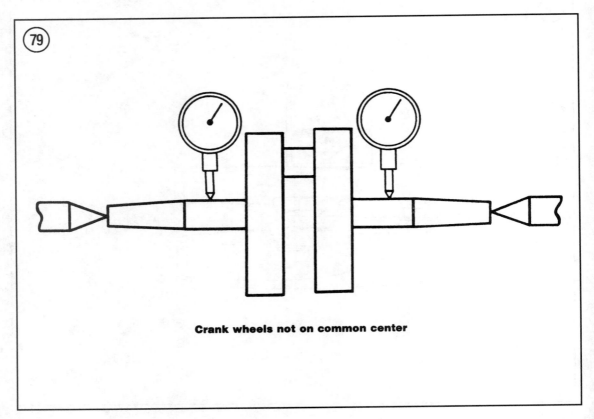

Crank wheels not on common center

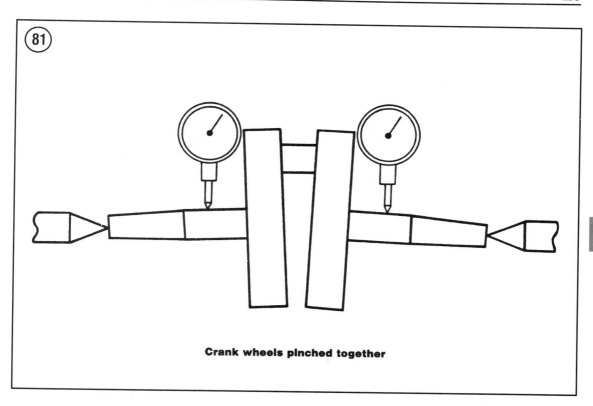

Crank wheels pinched together

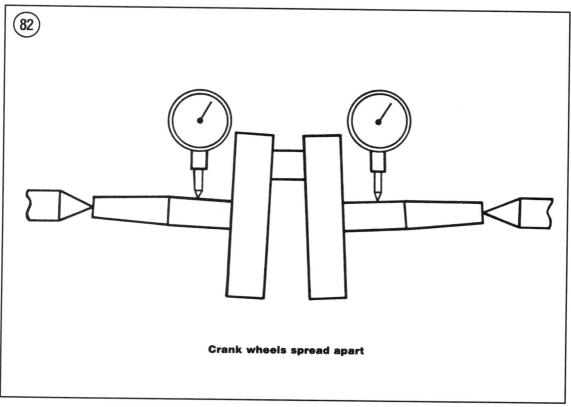

Crank wheels spread apart

Balancer Shaft
Inspection

1. Check the balancer shaft bearing journals (**Figure 83**) for deep scoring, excessive wear, heat discoloration or cracks.
2. Check the keyway in the end of the balancer shaft (**Figure 84**) for cracks or excessive wear.
3. Replace the balancer shaft if necessary.

Crankcase Assembly

1. Pack all of the crankcase oil seals with a heat durable grease.
2. Apply engine oil to both crankshaft main bearings.
3. Using the Yamaha crankshaft installing set (part No. YU-90050) (A, **Figure 85**) and the Yamaha adapter (part No. YU-1383) (B, **Figure 85**), install the crankshaft into the left-hand crankcase as follows:

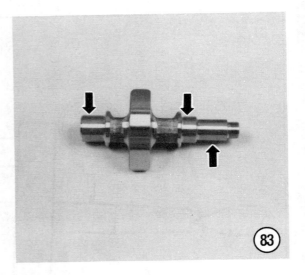

NOTE
If you do not have access to the Yamaha crankshaft installing set shown in Figure 85, a tool can be fabricated using the parts shown in Figure 86. It is important to note that the long threaded bolts must have a metric thread size of M10 × 1.25. If you cannot find a metric bolt of this size, purchase a 5/8 in. threaded rod and have one end rethreaded to the metric size M10 × 1.25. This can be done by a machine shop. The long nut used to connect the 2 bolts can be made by drilling and tapping a piece of hex stock.

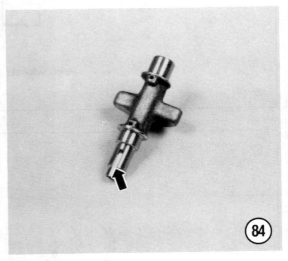

CAUTION
If you do not have access to a tool, have the crankshaft installed by a dealer or machine shop. Do not drive the crankshaft into the bearing. Do not drive the crankshaft into the crankcase with a hammer.

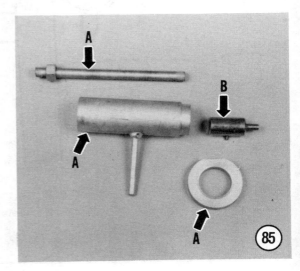

a. Apply a light coat of engine oil to the left-hand crankshaft bearing journal.

b. Place the left-hand crankcase assembly on wood blocks. Then insert the crankshaft into the main bearing so that the crankshaft assembly is square with the crankcase mating surface (**Figure 87**). Using hand pressure only, push the crankshaft into the bearing until it stops.

c. Tilt the crankcase assembly up and install the crankshaft installing set.

CAUTION
*When installing the crankshaft, make sure to position the connecting rod at top dead center (TDC) (**Figure 87**). If the connecting rod turns sideways, it could catch onto the side of the crankcase; this would damage the connecting rod and crankcase.*

5

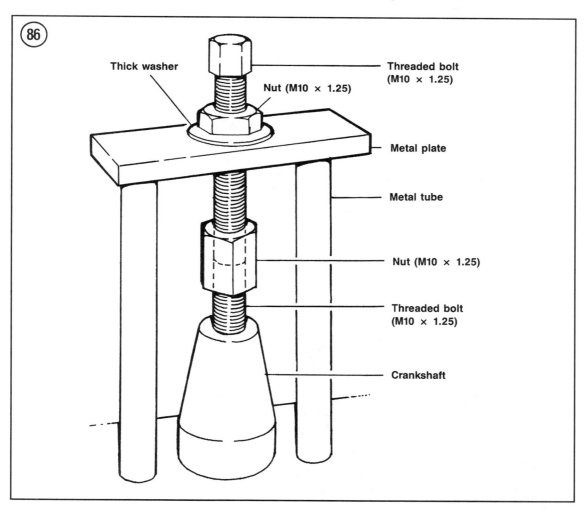

d. Using the crankshaft installing set, pull the crankshaft into the crankcase (**Figure 88**). Check the crankshaft often to make sure it is being pulled straight in with no side load. Pull the crankshaft until it is completely seated in the crankcase (**Figure 89**).

e. After installing the crankshaft, remove the crankshaft tool. Then spin the crankshaft. It should turn freely without any signs of roughness or noise.

4. Place the crankcase assembly onto wood blocks as shown in **Figure 89**.

5. Apply engine oil to the inner race of all bearings in the left-hand crankcase half.

6. Install the balancer shaft (**Figure 90**).

7. Install the transmission and internal shift mechanism as follows:

a. Install an O-ring onto the end of the countershaft as shown in **Figure 91**. The O-ring will prevent the possibility of damaging the countershaft oil seal when the shaft is installed.

NOTE
There are no factory installed shims on the outside of the gears that are not secured by a circlip. However, a previous owner may have reshimmed the transmission and there may be shims placed on the outside of the circlips or gear. If this is the case, make sure you do not drop a shim into the case when installing the transmission shafts.

b. Mesh the transmission shafts together (**Figure 92**) and install the transmission assembly into the left-hand crankcase bearings. See **Figure 93**.

> *NOTE*
> *The shift forks are labeled with an embossed number on one side. Install the shift forks so that the number faces down (facing toward the left-hand side).*

c. Engage the No. 2 shift fork with the mainshaft third/fourth gear (**Figure 94**).

d. Engage the No. 1 shift fork with the countershaft sixth gear (**Figure 95**).

e. Engage the No. 3 shift fork with the countershaft fifth gear (**Figure 96**).

5

f. Pivot each of the shift forks away from the center of the crankcase (**Figure 97**).

g. Insert the shift drum into the blind hole in the case (**Figure 98**).

h. Engage the pin on the No. 1 shift fork with the top shift drum groove (A, **Figure 99**).

i. Engage the pin on the No. 3 shift fork with the bottom shift drum groove (B, **Figure 99**).

j. Engage the pin on the No. 2 shift fork with the middle shift drum groove (**Figure 100**).

k. Install the No. 1 shift fork shaft through the No. 1 and No. 3 shift forks (**Figure 101**).

l. Install the No. 2 shift fork shaft through the No. 2 shift fork (**Figure 102**). Make sure the circlip on the shaft is installed securely.

m. Make sure both shift fork shafts are seated completely in the crankcase.

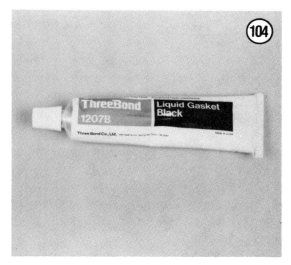

8. Spin the transmission shafts and shift through the gears using the shift drum. Make sure you can shift into all gears. This is the time to find that something may be installed incorrectly—not after the crankcase is completely assembled.

NOTE
Step 8 is best done with the aid of a helper as the assemblies are loose and don't want to spin very easily. Have the helper spin the transmission shaft while you turn the shift drum through all the gears.

9. After making sure the transmission shifts into all of the gears correctly, shift the transmission assembly into NEUTRAL.
10. Set the crankcase assembly on 2 wood blocks or a wood holding fixture shown in **Figure 103**.
11. Install the 2 locating dowels (**Figure 103**).
12. Apply a light coat of a black *non-hardening liquid gasket* such as Three Bond (**Figure 104**) or equivalent to the mating surfaces of both crankcase halves.

NOTE
Make sure the mating surfaces are clean and free of all old gasket material. This is to make sure you get a leak free seal.

13. See **Figure 105**. Set the upper crankcase half over the one on the blocks. Push it down squarely into place until it engages the dowel pins and then seats completely against the lower case half.

CAUTION
Crankcase halves should fit together without force. If the crankcase halves do not fit together completely, do not attempt to pull them together with the crankcase screws. Separate the crankcase halves and investigate the cause of the interference. If the transmission shafts were disassembled, recheck to make sure that a gear is not installed backwards. Crankcase halves are a matched set and are very expensive. Do not risk damage by trying to force the cases together.

14. Install all the crankcase screws (**Figure 106**) and tighten only finger-tight at first. Install the wire clamp with the No. 4 screw (**Figure 107**). Install the wire bracket with the No. 7 and No. 14 screw (**Figure 108**).

15. Securely tighten the screws in 2 stages in the order shown in **Figure 106**. Tighten the screws until they are tight.

16. After the crankcase halves are completely assembled, rotate the crankshaft and transmission shafts to make sure there is no binding. If any is present, disassemble the crankcase and correct the problem.

17. Remove the O-ring from the end of the countershaft (**Figure 109**).

18. Install all exterior engine assemblies as described in this chapter and other related chapters.

BREAK-IN PROCEDURE

If the rings were replaced, a new piston installed, the cylinder rebored or honed or major lower end work performed, the engine should be broken in just as though it were new. The performance and service life of the engine depends greatly on a careful and sensible break-in.

During break-in, oil consumption will be higher than normal. It is therefore important to frequently check and correct the oil level (Chapter Three). At no time during the break-in or later should the oil level be allowed to drop below the minimum level. If the oil level is low, the oil will become overheated resulting in insufficient lubrication and increased wear.

For the first 300 miles (500 km), do not operate the engine above 4,000 rpm. Yamaha recommends to stop the engine and allow it to cool for approximately 5 to 10 minutes after each one hour

of operation. Prolonged steady running at one speed, no matter how moderate, is to be avoided as well as hard acceleration.

Between 300-600 miles (500-1,000 km), do not operate the engine above 5,000 rpm or use full throttle at any time.

After 600 miles (1,000 km), change the engine oil and filter and clean the oil strainer as described in Chapter Three. It is essential to perform this service to ensure that all of the particles produced during break-in are removed from the lubrication system. The small added expense may be considered a smart investment that will pay off in increase engine life.

After 600 miles (1,000 km), the engine may be operated at full throttle.

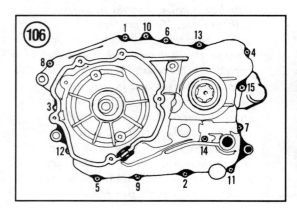

Table 1 CRANKSHAFT SERVICE SPECIFICATIONS

Item	Specifications mm (in.)	Wear limit mm (in.)
Crankshaft		
Width	58.95-59.00	—
	(2.321-2.323)	—
Runout limit	—	0.03
	—	(0.001)
Big end side clearance	0.35-0.85	—
	(0.014-0.033)	—
Small end free play limit	—	2.0
	—	(0.079)

Table 2 ENGINE LOWER END TIGHTENING TORQUES

	N•m	ft.-lb.
Primary drive gear nut	80	58
Balancer shaft drive gear nut	60	43
Magneto bolt	60	43
Oil pump assembly screw	7	5.1
Oil pump cover screw	7	5.1
Oil strainer plug	32	23
Oil filter cover bolt	10	7.2
Oil filter cover screw	7	5.1
Oil filter cover air bleed screw	5	3.6
Engine drain plug	43	31
Crankcase screws	7	5.1
Crankcase cover screws	7	5.1
Balancer shaft bearing retainer screw*	7	5.1
Kickstarter bolt	20	14
Oil pipe banjo bolt	20	14
Engine mounting bolts		
Rear mounting bolt	38	27
All other bolts	33	24
Swing arm pivot shaft nut	85	61

*Apply Loctite 242 (blue) before tightening screw.

5

CHAPTER SIX

CLUTCH, KICKSTARTER AND EXTERNAL SHIFT MECHANISM

This chapter describes service procedures for the following sub-assemblies:

  a. Clutch.
  b. Clutch release mechanism.
  c. Primary drive gear and balancer driven gear.
  d. Lower cam chain sprocket and chain.
  e. Kickstarter.
  f. Oil pump.
  g. External shift mechanism.

These sub-assemblies can be removed with the engine in the frame. General clutch specifications are listed in **Table 1**. **Tables 1-5** are found at the end of the chapter.

CLUTCH COVER

Removal/Installation

1. Drain the engine oil as described in Chapter Three.
2. Remove the oil filter as described in Chapter Three.
3. *XT350*: Perform the following:
  a. Remove the lower skid plate (**Figure 1**).
  b. Remove the Phillips screw and remove the tachometer cable (**Figure 2**) from the clutch cover drive unit.

4. Remove the rear brake pedal as follows. See **Figure 3** (XT350) or **Figure 4** (TT350).
  a. Loosen the rear brake rod wing nut (**Figure 5**).
  b. Remove the bolts securing the right-hand footpeg and rear brake pedal assembly and remove the assembly. On XT350 models, disconnect the rear brake light switch return spring.
5. Remove the kickstarter lever pinch bolt and remove the lever (**Figure 6**).

①

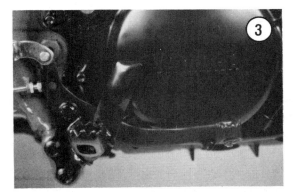

6. Usually it is unnecessary to disconnect the decompression cable (**Figure 7**) at the clutch cover when removing the cover. However, if service to the decompression lever in the clutch cover is required, perform the following:

   a. Loosen and remove the decompression cable mounting bracket on the cylinder head (**Figure 8**).

   b. See **Figure 7**. Loosen and remove the Acorn nut (A) and Allen screw (B) at the clutch cover. Then disconnect and remove the decompression cable (C).

7. Loosen the oil line banjo bolt at the clutch cover. Then remove the banjo bolt and the 2 special washers.

8. Remove the Allen bolts securing the clutch cover and remove the cover (**Figure 9**).

9. Remove the 2 dowel pins (**Figure 10**) and gasket. Discard the gasket.

10. Installation is the reverse of these steps. Note the following.

11. Make sure to install the 2 dowel pins and a new cover gasket.

12. Refill the engine oil as described in Chapter Three.

13. Adjust the decompression lever as described under *Decompression Cable Adjustment* in Chapter Three.

Clutch Cover Oil Seal Replacement

Replace the kickstarter shaft (A, **Figure 11**) and decompression lever (B, **Figure 11**) oil seals if worn or damaged.

1. Carefully pry the oil seal out of the cover with a flat-tipped screwdriver. Place a rag underneath the screwdriver to prevent from damaging the clutch cover.

2. Remove the clutch cover as described in this chapter.

3. Remove the decompression lever from the clutch cover as described in this chapter.

4. Remove all oil residue from the seal area and clean the cover thoroughly.

5. Check the seal mounting area for any signs of damage. Repair with sandpaper or a file.

6. Install the new seal by tapping it into the cover with a suitable size socket placed on the outer seal surface. Tap the seal in squarely until it is flush with the case.

Decompression Lever
Removal/Installation

1. Remove the clutch cover as described in this chapter.

2. Slide the decompression lever (**Figure 12**) out of the clutch cover.

3. Check the lever assembly (**Figure 13**) for worn or damaged parts.

4. Install by reversing these steps. Make sure to install the washer on the lever (**Figure 13**) before installing the lever. After installing the lever, engage the spring with the cover as shown in **Figure 12**.

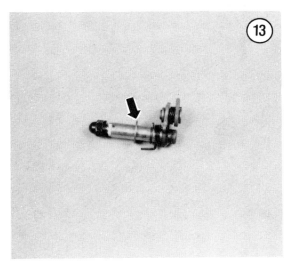

Tachometer Gear Assembly
Removal/Inspection/Installation
(XT350)

The tachometer gear assembly is installed inside the clutch cover.

1. Remove the clutch cover as described in this chapter.

2. Perform the following:
   a. Remove the circlip (**Figure 14**).
   b. Remove the washer (**Figure 15**).
   c. Remove the nylon gear (**Figure 16**).
   d. Remove the washer (**Figure 17**).

3. Check the driven gear for wear or damage. If necessary, pull the gear (**Figure 18**) out of the clutch cover and remove it.

4. When parts have been disassembled and cleaned, visually inspect them for any signs of wear, cracks, breakage or other damage. If there is any doubt as to the condition of any part, replace it with a new one.

5. Installation is the reverse of these steps. Make sure the nylon gear circlip seats completely in the gear shaft groove.

CLUTCH

The clutch is a wet multiplate type which operates immersed in the oil supply it shares with the transmission. The clutch boss is splined to the transmission mainshaft and the clutch housing can rotate freely on the mainshaft. The clutch housing is geared to the primary drive gear attached to the crankshaft.

The clutch release mechanism is mounted within the left-hand crankcase cover on the opposite side of the clutch mechanism. The clutch can be removed with the engine in the frame.

Removal

Refer to **Figure 19** for this procedure.

1. Remove the clutch cover as described in this chapter.

2. Loosen the clutch spring bolts in a crisscross pattern. Then remove the bolts (**Figure 20**).

3. Remove the clutch springs (**Figure 21**).

4. Remove the pressure plate (**Figure 22**).

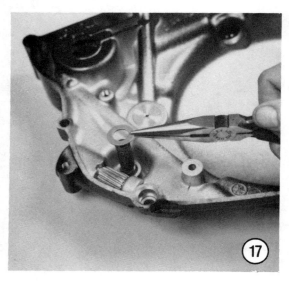

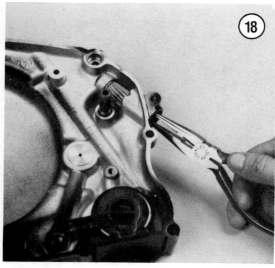

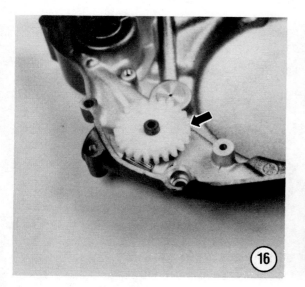

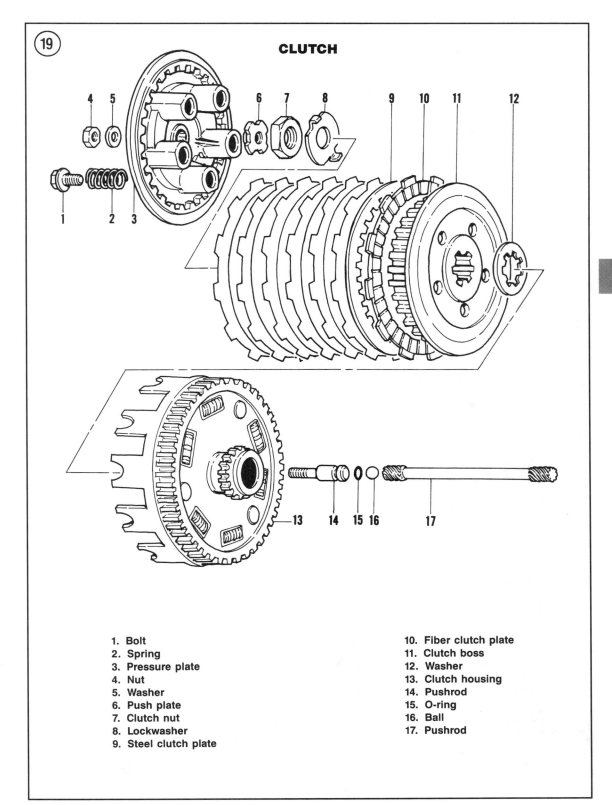

CLUTCH

1. Bolt
2. Spring
3. Pressure plate
4. Nut
5. Washer
6. Push plate
7. Clutch nut
8. Lockwasher
9. Steel clutch plate
10. Fiber clutch plate
11. Clutch boss
12. Washer
13. Clutch housing
14. Pushrod
15. O-ring
16. Ball
17. Pushrod

5. Remove the push plate (**Figure 23**) and remove the adjust screw and nut (**Figure 24**) from the pressure plate.

6. Remove a fiber plate (**Figure 25**) and a steel clutch plate (**Figure 26**). Continue and remove all plates in order.

7. Remove the clutch ball (**Figure 27**).

8. Remove the pushrod with a magnet (**Figure 28**).

9. Bend the clutch nut lockwasher tab away from the clutch nut.

10. Secure the clutch boss with a holding tool such as the "Grabbit" (**Figure 29**). Turn the clutch nut counterclockwise and remove it.

CAUTION
Do not insert a screwdriver or pry bar between the clutch housing and the clutch boss. The fingers on the clutch housing are fragile and can be broken very easily.

11. Remove the washer (**Figure 30**).

12. Remove the clutch boss (**Figure 31**).

13. Remove the washer (**Figure 32**).

14. Remove the clutch housing (**Figure 33**).

6

Inspection

Clutch service specifications and wear limits are listed in **Table 2**.

1. Clean all parts in solvent and thoroughly dry with compressed air.

2. Measure the free length of each clutch spring (**Figure 34**) with a vernier caliper. Replace the springs as a set if any one spring is too short.

3. **Table 1** lists the number of stock friction discs (**Figure 35**) used in each model. The friction material is made of cork that is bonded onto an aluminum plate for warp resistance and durability. Measure the thickness of each friction plate at several places around the disc (**Figure 36**) with a vernier caliper. Replace all friction plates if any one is found too thin. Do not replace only 1 or 2 plates.

4. **Table 1** lists the number of stock clutch metal plates (**Figure 37**) used in each model. Place each clutch metal plate on a surface plate or a thick piece of glass and check for warpage with a feeler gauge

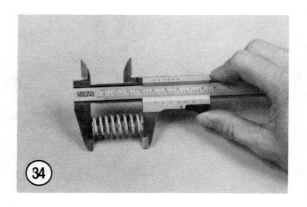

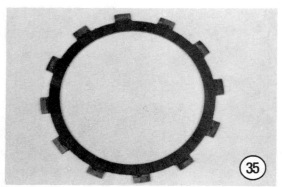

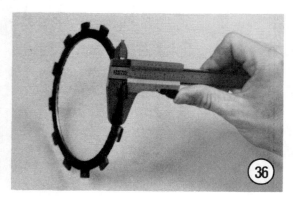

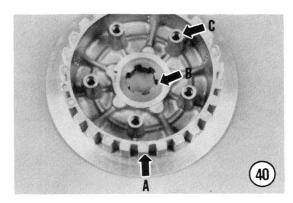

(**Figure 38**). If any plate is warped more than specified, replace the entire set of plates. Do not replace only 1 or 2 plates.

5. The clutch metal plate inner teeth mesh with the clutch boss splines (**Figure 39**). Check the splines for cracks or galling. They must be smooth for chatter-free clutch operation. If the clutch boss splines (A, **Figure 40**) are worn, check the clutch metal plate teeth for wear or damage.

6. Inspect the shaft splines (B, **Figure 40**) in the clutch boss assembly. If damage is only a slight amount, remove any small burrs with a fine cut file. If damage is severe, replace the assembly.

7. Inspect the clutch boss bolt studs (C, **Figure 40**) for thread damage or cracks at the base of the studs. Thread damage may be repaired with the correct size metric tap. Use kerosene on the tap threads. If a bolt stud is cracked, the clutch boss must be replaced.

8. The friction plates have tabs that slide in the clutch housing grooves (**Figure 41**). Inspect the tabs for cracks or galling in the grooves. The tabs (A, **Figure 42**) must be smooth for chatter-free clutch operation. Light damage can be repaired with an oilstone. Replace the clutch housing if damaged is severe.

9. Check the clutch housing bearing bore (B, **Figure 42**) for cracks, deep scoring, excessive wear or heat discoloration. If the bearing bore is damaged, also check the mainshaft for damage. Replace worn or damaged parts.

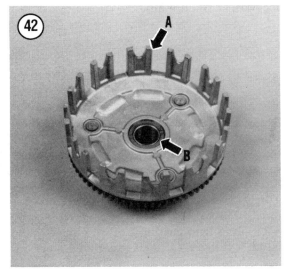

6

10. Check the clutch housing gear teeth (**Figure 43**) for tooth wear, damage or cracks. Replace the clutch housing if necessary.

NOTE
If the clutch housing gear teeth are damaged, the gear teeth on the primary drive gear and the kickstarter idler gear may also be damaged.

11. Check the pushrod for straightness with a set of V-blocks and a dial indicator (**Figure 44**) or roll the pushrod on a flat surface such as a surface plate or a piece of thick glass. Replace the pushrod if it exceeds the bend limit in **Table 2**.
12. Check the pressure plate spring towers (A, **Figure 45**) for cracks at the base of the tower. Check the adjust screw bore in the pressure plate (B, **Figure 45**) for cracks or damage.
13. If there is any doubt as to the condition of any part, replace it with a new one.

Assembly

1. Coat all clutch parts with transmission oil before reassembly.
2. Install the clutch housing (**Figure 33**).
3. Install the washer (**Figure 32**).
4. Install the clutch boss (**Figure 31**).
5. Align the 2 tabs on the lockwasher with the 2 flat notches in the clutch boss and install the lockwasher (**Figure 30**).

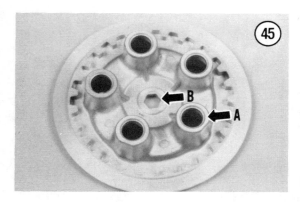

NOTE
Install a new lockwasher if the old one has been removed 2 times.

6. Install the clutch nut and secure the clutch boss with the same tool used during removal. Tighten the clutch nut (**Figure 46**) to the torque specification in **Table 5**.
7. Install the clutch pushrod (**Figure 28**). Apply a light coat of grease to the pushrod prior to installation.
8. Apply a light coat of grease to the ball and install it (**Figure 47**). Make sure it does not roll out.

9. Install a friction disc first (**Figure 48**) and then a steel clutch plate (**Figure 49**). Continue to install a friction disc, then a clutch plate until all are installed. The last plate installed will be a friction disc.

CAUTION
If either or both friction discs and/or clutch plates have been replaced with new ones or if they were cleaned, apply new clutch/transmission oil to all surfaces to avoid damaging the plates when the engine is started.

10. Install the pushrod and adjuster nut through the front of the pressure plate (**Figure 50**). Then install the push plate onto the pushrod on the back of the pressure plate (**Figure 51**).
11. Align the arrow on the pressure plate with the arrow on the clutch boss and install the pressure plate (**Figure 52**).
12. Install the clutch springs (**Figure 53**) and bolts (**Figure 54**). Tighten the bolts in a crisscross pattern.
13. Perform the *Clutch Mechanism Adjustment* as described in this chapter.
14. Install the clutch cover as described in this chapter.

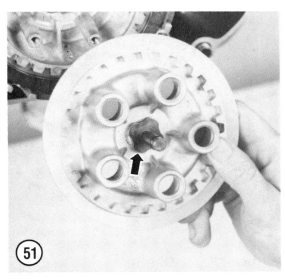

Clutch Mechanism Adjustment

This procedure should be performed whenever the clutch assembly is disassembled or when major clutch adjustment is required.

1. Remove the clutch cover as described in this chapter.

2. Loosen the clutch cable adjuster locknut (A, **Figure 55**) at the handlebar. Then turn the adjuster (B, **Figure 55**) counterclockwise to obtain as much clutch cable slack as possible. Then disconnect the clutch cable (A, **Figure 56**) at the push lever (B, **Figure 56**).

3. Loosen the clutch mechanism adjuster locknut (**Figure 57**).

4. Push the clutch push lever (B, **Figure 56**) toward the front of the engine until the end of the lever aligns with the embossed mark on the crankcase. See **Figure 58**. Hold the lever in this position.

5. Turn the adjuster screw (**Figure 57**) in or out until the end of the screw lightly touches the clutch pushrod ball. Tighten the adjuster screw locknut (**Figure 57**) and release the push lever.

6. Reconnect the clutch cable at the push lever (A, **Figure 56**).

7. Adjust the clutch as described under *Clutch Adjustment* in Chapter Three.

8. Reinstall the clutch cover as described in this chapter.

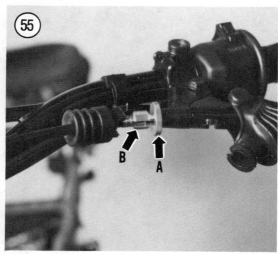

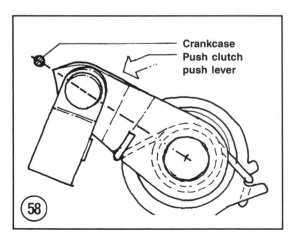

Crankcase
Push clutch
push lever

CLUTCH RELEASE MECHANISM

Removal/Installation

Refer to **Figure 59** for this procedure.

1. Remove the ball and pushrod as outlined under *Clutch Removal* in this chapter.

2. Remove the shift lever and remove the left-hand side cover (**Figure 60**).

3. Loosen the clutch cable adjuster locknut (A, **Figure 55**) at the handlebar. Then turn the adjuster (B, **Figure 55**) counterclockwise to obtain as much clutch cable slack as possible. Disconnect the clutch cable (A, **Figure 56**) at the push lever (B, **Figure 56**).

4. Remove the Phillips screw (C, **Figure 56**) and lift the push lever assembly (1, **Figure 59**) up and out of the crankcase.

5. Check the push lever for any signs of wear, cracks or breakage. Check the spring for wear or damage. Replace worn or damaged parts as required.

6. Install the push lever and spring into the crankcase. Install the Phillips screw (C, **Figure 56**) so that it engages the top push lever groove. Tighten the screw securely.

7. Perform the *Clutch Mechanism Adjustment* described in this chapter.

PRIMARY DRIVE GEAR AND BALANCER DRIVEN GEAR

This procedure describes service to the primary drive gear and the balancer driven gear assembly (**Figure 61**). Removal of the balancer shaft (8, **Figure 61**) requires crankcase disassembly (see Chapter Five).

Removal

1. Remove the clutch as described in this chapter.

2. Pry the lockwasher tabs away from the primary drive gear nut (A, **Figure 62**) and the balancer driven gear nut (B, **Figure 62**).

NOTE
*When loosening the primary drive gear and the balancer driven gear nuts in Step 3, it will be necessary to use an air gun and socket or to use a rotor holding tool and hold the rotor (**Figure 63**) while loosening the 2 nuts.*

CLUTCH RELEASE MECHANISM

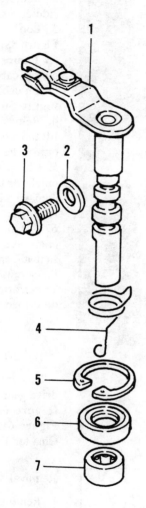

1. Push lever
2. Washer
3. Bolt
4. Spring
5. Circlip
6. Oil seal
7. Needle bearing

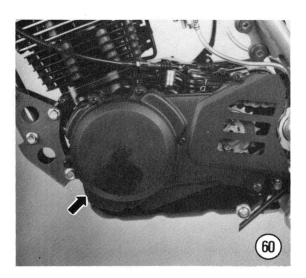

3. Loosen the primary drive gear nut (A, **Figure 62**) and the balancer driven gear nut (B, **Figure 62**).

4. Remove the following parts in order:

a. Primary drive gear nut (A, **Figure 62**).
b. Lockwasher (**Figure 64**).
c. Washer (**Figure 65**).
d. Primary drive gear (**Figure 66**).
e. Washer (**Figure 67**).
f. Balancer drive gear (**Figure 68**).
g. Washer (**Figure 69**).
h. Woodruff key (**Figure 70**).

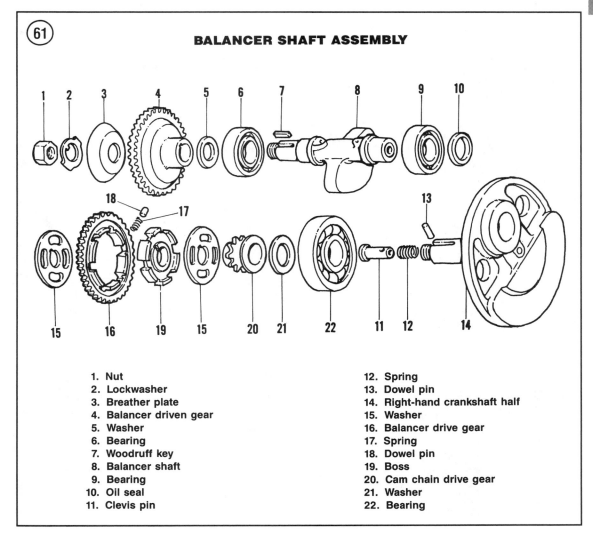

BALANCER SHAFT ASSEMBLY

1. Nut
2. Lockwasher
3. Breather plate
4. Balancer driven gear
5. Washer
6. Bearing
7. Woodruff key
8. Balancer shaft
9. Bearing
10. Oil seal
11. Clevis pin
12. Spring
13. Dowel pin
14. Right-hand crankshaft half
15. Washer
16. Balancer drive gear
17. Spring
18. Dowel pin
19. Boss
20. Cam chain drive gear
21. Washer
22. Bearing

5. Remove the following parts in order:
   a. Balancer driven gear nut (B, **Figure 62**).
   b. Lockwasher (**Figure 71**).
   c. Breather plate (**Figure 72**).
   d. Balancer driven gear (**Figure 73**).
   e. Woodruff key (**Figure 74**).
   f. Washer (**Figure 75**).

Inspection

1. Clean all of the parts in solvent and thoroughly dry.

2. When parts have been cleaned, visually inspect them for any signs of wear, cracks, breakage or other damage. If there is any doubt as to the condition of any part, replace it with a new one.

3. The balancer drive gear can be disassembled and worn or damaged parts replaced. See **Figure 61**.

4. When reassembling the balancer drive gear, align the mark on the gear with the mark on the inner boss (**Figure 76**).

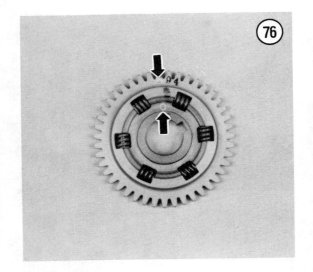

Installation

NOTE
Nearly all of the following components are machined with a keyway for alignment purposes. Make sure to install the parts correctly.

1. Install the following parts in order:
   a. Washer (**Figure 75**).
   b. Balancer driven gear (**Figure 73**).
   c. Align the keyway in the gear with the keyway in the balancer shaft and install the Woodruff key (**Figure 77**).
   d. Align the slot in the breather plate (**Figure 72**) with the keyway in the balancer shaft and install the breather plate.
   e. Align the tab in the lockwasher (**Figure 78**) with the balancer shaft keyway and install the lockwasher. See **Figure 71**.
   f. Install the balancer driven gear nut. Do not tighten it at this point.

2. Install the following parts in order:
   a. Woodruff key (**Figure 70**).
   b. Washer (**Figure 69**).
   c. Align the timing mark on the balancer driven and balancer drive gears and install the balancer drive gear. See **Figure 79**.
   d. Washer (**Figure 67**).
   e. Primary drive gear (**Figure 66**).
   f. Align the washer tab with the keyway in the primary drive gear and install the washer (**Figure 65**).

g. Align the tab on the lockwasher with the primary drive gear keyway and install the lockwasher (**Figure 64**).

h. Install the balancer drive gear nut. Do not tighten it at this point.

3. Use the same tool as during removal to tighten the primary drive (A, **Figure 62**) and driven (B, **Figure 62**) gear nuts. Refer to the torque specifications in **Table 5**.

4. Bend the lockwasher tabs over the nuts to lock them.

5. Install the clutch as described in this chapter.

CAM CHAIN, SPROCKET AND GUIDE

This procedure describes service to the cam chain, chain sprocket and the rear cam chain guide.

Removal

1. Remove the balancer drive gear as described under *Primary Drive Gear and Balancer Driven Gear* in this chapter.

2. If the camshafts are installed in the cylinder head, remove the camshaft sprockets as described in Chapter Four.

3. Remove the bolts securing the rear cam chain guide (**Figure 80**) and remove the guide. See **Figure 81**.

4. Remove the cam chain (**Figure 82**).

5. Remove the lower cam chain sprocket (**Figure 83**).

6. Remove the washer (**Figure 84**).

7. When parts have been disassembled and cleaned, visually inspect them for any signs of wear, cracks, breakage or other damage. If there is any doubt as to the condition of any part, replace it with a new one.

8. If the cam chain (**Figure 85**) is worn, the sprockets (upper and lower) as well as the cam chain guides are probably worn also. Inspect all parts closely. Running the engine with new and used parts will cause rapid wear to the new parts.

9. Installation is the reverse of these steps. Note the following:

   a. Align the keyway slot in the cam chain sprocket with the crankshaft when installing the sprocket (**Figure 86**).

   b. Apply Loctite 242 (blue) to the rear cam chain guide bolts (**Figure 80**). Tighten the bolts securely.

KICKSTARTER

Refer to **Figure 87** when servicing the kickstarter assembly.

Removal/Installation

1. Remove the clutch as described in this chapter.

2. Using a pair of needlenose pliers, remove the kickstarter return spring from its post position in

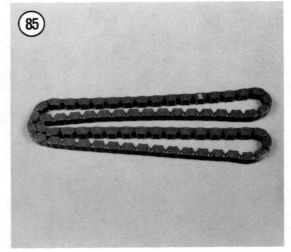

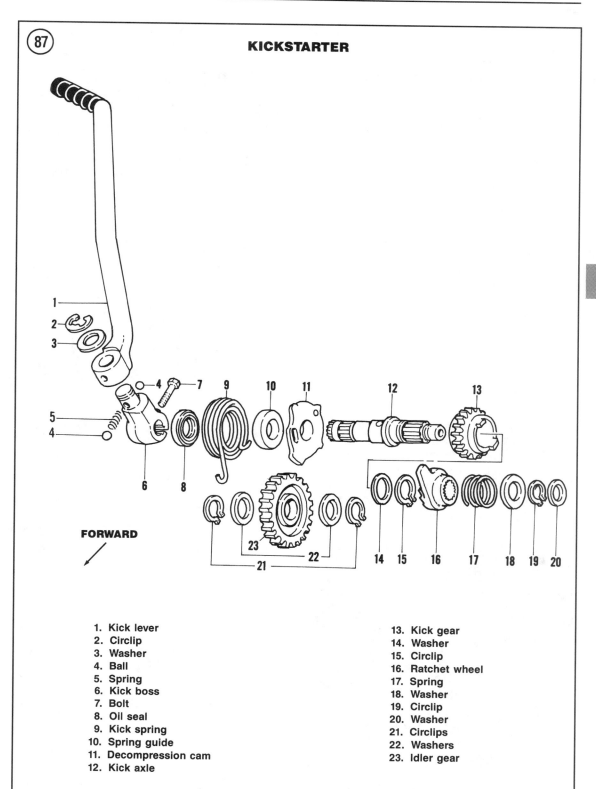

87 KICKSTARTER

FORWARD

1. Kick lever
2. Circlip
3. Washer
4. Ball
5. Spring
6. Kick boss
7. Bolt
8. Oil seal
9. Kick spring
10. Spring guide
11. Decompression cam
12. Kick axle
13. Kick gear
14. Washer
15. Circlip
16. Ratchet wheel
17. Spring
18. Washer
19. Circlip
20. Washer
21. Circlips
22. Washers
23. Idler gear

6

CHAPTER SIX

the crankcase (**Figure 88**). Release the spring and allow it to relax. Then rotate the kickstarter assembly counterclockwise by hand and remove it from the crankcase. See **Figure 89**.

NOTE
*A washer is installed on the end of the kickstarter shaft (**Figure 90**).*

3. Remove the idler gear as follows:

   a. Remove the circlip (**Figure 91**).
   b. Remove the washer (**Figure 92**).
   c. Remove the idler gear (**Figure 93**).
   d. Remove the washer (**Figure 94**).
   e. Remove the circlip (**Figure 95**).

4. If necessary, disassemble the kickstarter assembly and service it as described in this chapter.
5. Installation is the reverse of these steps. Note the following.
6. Install the kickstarter assembly as follows.

   a. Install the washer onto the end of the kickstarter shaft (**Figure 90**).
   b. With the kickstarter stopper positioned at the top, insert the kickstarter into the crankcase.
   c. Using needlenose pliers, hook the return spring (**Figure 88**) onto the spring post in the crankcase. See **Figure 96**.

Disassembly

Refer to **Figure 87**.

> *NOTE*
> *Before disassembling the kickstarter assembly, collect a number of small boxes or an egg carton to store the parts in order of removal (**Figure 97**).*

1. Remove the large washer (**Figure 98**).
2. Remove the return spring (**Figure 99**).
3. Remove the washer (**Figure 100**).

6

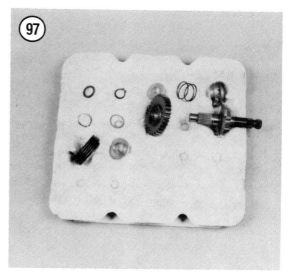

4. Remove the circlip (**Figure 101**).
5. Remove the washer (**Figure 102**).
6. Remove the ratchet wheel spring (**Figure 103**).
7. Remove the ratchet wheel (**Figure 104**).
8. Remove the circlip (**Figure 105**).
9. Remove the washer (**Figure 106**).
10. Remove the kick gear (**Figure 107**).

Inspection

1. Wash all parts thoroughly in solvent.
2. Check for broken, chipped, or missing teeth on the kick gear and ratchet (**Figure 108**). Replace the gear and ratchet as a set.

3. Check the kickstarter shaft (**Figure 109**) as follows:

  a. Check the kickstarter lever splines (A) for damage that would allow the lever to slip when the kickstarter is used.

  b. Check the shaft surface (B) for cracks, deep scoring or other damage.

  c. Check the return spring hole (C) in the shaft for cracks, wallowing or other conditions that would allow the spring to slip out when using the kickstarter.

  d. Install the kick gear onto the shaft and check that the gear operates smoothly on the shaft. Check the shaft splines (D) for cracks or other damage.

  e. Replace the kickstarter shaft if necessary.

6

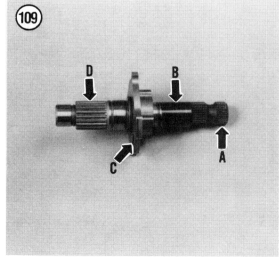

4. Check the return spring (**Figure 110**) for cracks, breakage or other damage. Replace if necessary.
5. Measure the ratchet spring free length with a vernier caliper (**Figure 111**). Replace the spring if the free length is too short (see **Table 3**).

Assembly

Refer to **Figure 87** for this procedure.

1. Apply assembly oil to the sliding surfaces of all parts.
2. Install the kick gear so that the splines face as shown in **Figure 107**.
2. Install the washer (**Figure 106**).
3. Install the circlip (**Figure 105**) into the groove next to the washer. After installing the circlip, spin the kick gear to make sure it turns smoothly.
4. Align the dot on the end of the kickstarter shaft (A, **Figure 112**) with the straight surface on the ratchet wheel (B, **Figure 112**) and install the ratchet wheel.
5. Install the ratchet wheel spring (**Figure 103**).
6. Install the washer (**Figure 102**).
7. Compress the washer and install the circlip (**Figure 101**). Make sure the circlip seats in the groove completely.
8. Install the washer (**Figure 100**).
9. Hook the end of the return spring (A, **Figure 113**) into the notch in the kickstarter shaft (B, **Figure 113**). See **Figure 114**.
10. Install the large washer (**Figure 98**).

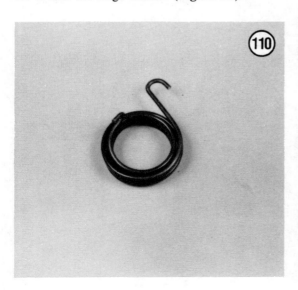

OIL PUMP

Removal/Installation

1. Remove the clutch as described in this chapter.
2. Remove the oil pump idle gear as follows:
   a. Remove the circlip (**Figure 115**).
   b. Remove the washer (**Figure 116**).
   c. Remove the idle gear (**Figure 117**).
   d. Remove the washer (**Figure 118**).
3. Remove the oil pump mounting screws and remove the oil pump (**Figure 119**).
4. Remove the O-ring from the crankcase cavity (**Figure 120**).
5. Installation is the reverse of these steps. Note the following.
6. Make sure to install a new O-ring into the crankcase cavity (**Figure 120**) before installing the oil pump.
7. Tighten the oil pump mounting screws securely.
8. Make sure the idle gear circlip seats in the shaft groove completely.

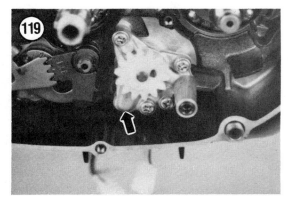

Disassembly/Inspection/Reassembly

1. Remove the Phillips screw (A, **Figure 121**) and separate the 2 oil pump halves. See **Figure 122**.
2. Remove the pin (**Figure 123**) and remove the oil pump driven gear (**Figure 124**).
3. Remove the 2 alignment pins (**Figure 125**).
4. Remove the inner (**Figure 126**) and outer (**Figure 127**) rotors.
5. Clean all parts (**Figure 128**) in solvent and dry thoroughly.
6. Inspect the inner and outer rotors (**Figure 129**) for scoring, cracks or other damage. Check the inner rotor pin slot for damage.
7. Check the 2 oil pump covers (**Figure 130**) for cracks or other damage. Check the rotor mounting area for damage.
8. Check both gears (**Figure 131**) for cracks, wear, breakage or other damage.
9. Check the pin hole in the oil pump driven gear shaft (**Figure 132**). Check the hole for cracks or other damage.

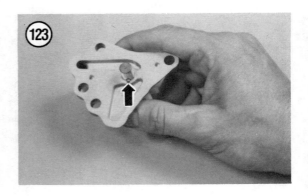

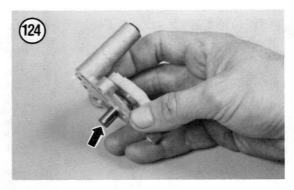

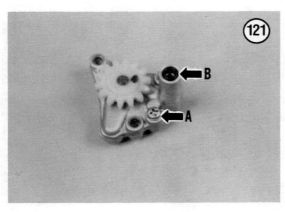

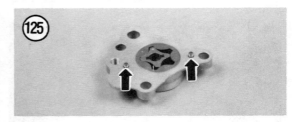

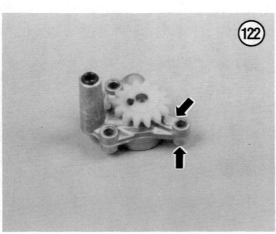

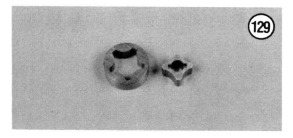

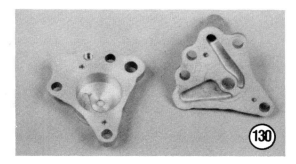

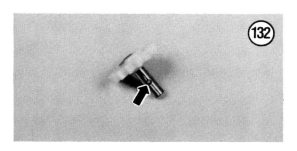

10. Inspect the rotors as follows:

a. Install the outer (**Figure 127**) and inner (**Figure 126**) rotors into the housing. Make sure the inner rotor pin slot faces up.

b. Check the clearance between the inner and outer rotors with a flat feeler gauge (**Figure 133**). If the clearance is greater than the service limit in **Table 4**, the oil pump must be replaced.

c. Check the clearance between the outer rotor and the housing (**Figure 134**) with a flat feeler gauge. If the clearance is greater than the service limit in **Table 4**, the oil pump must be replaced.

6

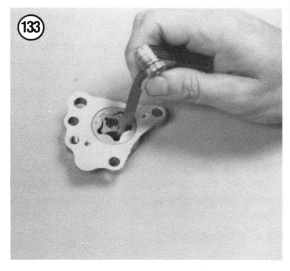

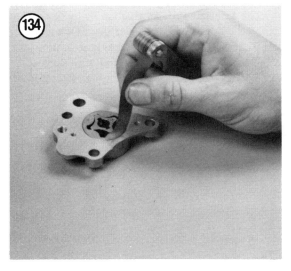

d. Check the side clearance with a straightedge and flat feeler gauge (**Figure 135**). If the clearance is greater than the service limit in **Table 4**, the oil pump must be replaced.

11. Remove the rotors after performing the tests in Step 10.

12. Oil all components with clean engine oil.

13. Install the outer rotor into the housing (**Figure 127**).

14. Install the inner rotor into the housing so that the pin slot faces up (**Figure 126**).

15. Install the 2 alignment pins into the housing (**Figure 125**).

16. Insert the oil pump driven gear through the housing as shown in **Figure 124**. Insert the pin through the shaft hole (**Figure 123**).

17. Align the pin (A, **Figure 136**) with the notch in the inner rotor (B, **Figure 136**) and assemble the oil pump housings. Make sure the pin engages the notch. The oil pump housings must fit together flush. See **Figure 122**.

18. Apply Loctite 242 (blue) to the Phillips screw (A, **Figure 121**) and tighten it securely.

19. Install a new O-ring (B, **Figure 121**).

20. Turn the pump shaft and make sure it turns smoothly. If the pump shaft is tight, something is wrong. Disassemble the pump and check the parts.

EXTERNAL SHIFT MECHANISM

The external shift mechanism is located on the same side of the crankcase as the clutch assembly and can be removed with the engine in the frame. To remove the shift drum and shift forks, it is necessary to remove the engine and split the crankcases (see Chapter Five).

NOTE
The gearshift lever is subject to a lot of abuse on an off-road bike. If the motorcycle has been in a hard spill, the gearshift lever may have been hit and the shaft may have been bent. If the shaft is bent, it is very hard to

straighten without subjecting the crankcase to abnormal stress where the shaft enters the case. If the shaft is bent enough to prevent it from being withdrawn from the crankcase, there is little recourse but to cut the shaft off with a hacksaw very close to the crankcase. It is much cheaper in the long run to replace the shaft than risk damaging a set of expensive crankcases. After cutting off the end of the shaft, use a file or rotary grinder to remove all burrs from the shaft before removing it.

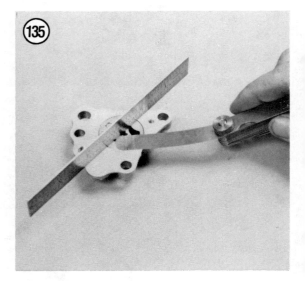

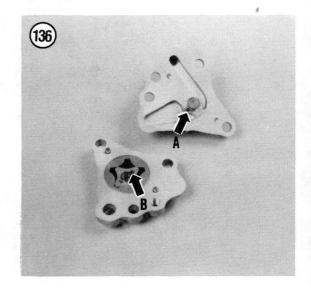

Removal/Installation

Refer to **Figure 137** for this procedure.
1. Remove the pinch bolt and remove the shift lever (A, **Figure 138**) from the left-hand side.
2. Remove the left-hand side cover (B, **Figure 138**).
3. Slide the spacer (**Figure 139**) and washer (**Figure 140**) off of the shift shaft.
4. Remove the clutch as described in this chapter.
5. Remove the oil pump idler gear as described under *Oil Pump Removal* in this chapter.
6. Remove the change lever circlip (**Figure 141**).
7. Lower the change lever arm and remove the change lever assembly (**Figure 142**).

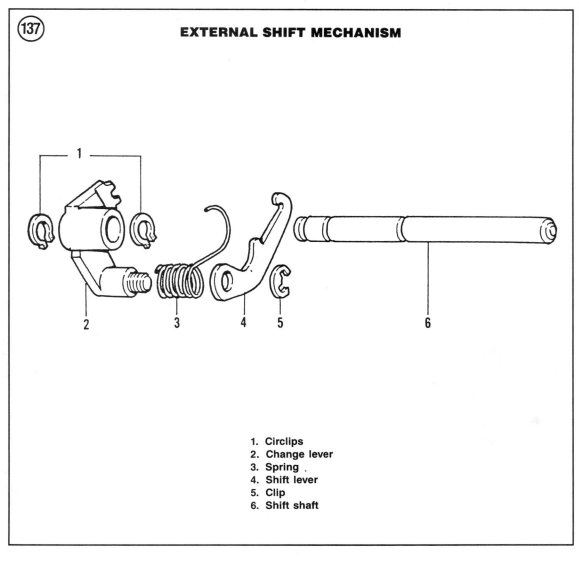

EXTERNAL SHIFT MECHANISM

1. Circlips
2. Change lever
3. Spring
4. Shift lever
5. Clip
6. Shift shaft

8. Lower the roller away from the shift drum
(**Figure 143**) and remove the shift shaft assembly
(**Figure 144**).

9. Inspect the external shift mechanism assembly
as follows. Replace worn or damaged parts.

a. Slide the roller assembly (**Figure 145**) off of
the shift shaft.
b. Check the shift shaft (**Figure 146**) for cracks
or bending. Check the splines on the end of
the shaft for damage.
c. Check the return spring on the shift shaft. The
return spring arms should be installed on the
shaft arm as shown in **Figure 147**. Replace the

return spring if it shows signs of fatigue or if it is cracked.

   d. Check the roller assembly (**Figure 148**) for any signs of wear, cracks or breakage.

   e. Check the change lever assembly (**Figure 149**). Check the engagement arms on the lever for wear or damage. Damage or severe wear with the engagements will cause shifting problems.

10. Slide the roller assembly onto the shift shaft (**Figure 145**).

11. Install the shift shaft assembly (**Figure 144**). Engage the roller with the shift drum (**Figure 143**). Make sure the return spring engages the pin in the crankcase (**Figure 144**).

12. Install the change lever assembly (**Figure 142**). Engage the lever arm with the shift drum pins (**Figure 150**).

13. Make sure the 2 marks on the shift shaft and the change lever align as shown in **Figure 151**.

14. Install the circlip (**Figure 141**).

15. Reverse Steps 1-5 to complete assembly.

CLUTCH CABLE

Replacement

In time, the clutch cable will stretch to the point that it is no longer useful and will have to be replaced.

1. Remove the fuel tank.

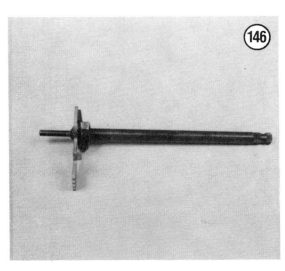

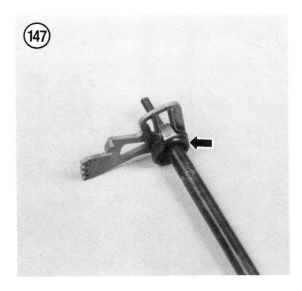

NOTE
One of the identified figures is shown with the engine partially disassembled for clarity. It is not necessary to remove these components for cable replacement.

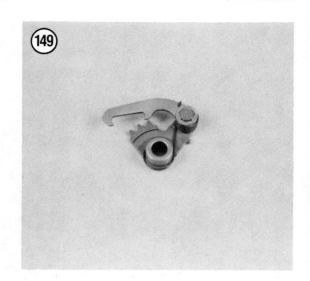

2. Pull the protective boot away from the clutch lever and loosen the locknut (A, **Figure 55**) and adjusting barrel (B, **Figure 55**).
3. Slip the cable end out of the hand lever.
4. Disconnect the clutch cable (A, **Figure 56**) at the clutch release mechanism on the left-hand side of the engine.

NOTE
Prior to removing the cable, make a drawing (or take a Polaroid picture) of the cable routing through the frame. It is very easy to forget its routing after it has been removed. Replace the cable exactly as it was, avoiding any sharp turns.

5. Pull the cable out of any retaining clips on the frame.
6. Remove the cable and replace it with a new one.
7. Install by reversing these removal steps. Make sure it is correctly routed with no sharp turns. Adjust the clutch cable as described in Chapter Three.

Table 1 GENERAL CLUTCH SPECIFICATIONS

Clutch type	Wet, multiple-disc
Clutch release method	Cam push type
Number of clutch plates	
Friction	7
Steel plates	5
Special steel plate	1

Table 2 CLUTCH SERVICE SPECIFICATIONS

Item	Specification mm (in.)	Wear limit mm (in.)
Friction plate thickness		
XT350 (1985-1995)	2.9-3.1 (0.114-0.122)	2.5 (0.098)
TT350, XT350 (1996-on)	2.7-2.9 (0.106-0.114)	2.5 (0.098)
Steel clutch plate thickness		
XT350		
Thick plate	2.0 (0.078)	—
Thin plates	1.6 (0.063)	—
Warp limit	—	0.05 (0.002)
TT350		
Thick plate	1.5-1.7 (0.059-0.067)	—
Thin plates	1.1-1.3 (0.043-0.051)	—
Warp limit	—	0.05 (0.002)
Clutch spring free length	41.2 (1.622)	40.3 (1.587)
Clutch housing thrust clearance	0.08-0.33 (0.003-0.013)	—
Push rod bend limit	—	0.5 (0.02)

Table 3 KICKSTARTER SERVICE SPECIFICATIONS

Item	Specification	Wear limit
Ratchet spring free length	17.2 mm (0.677 in.)	15.0 mm (0.59 in.)

Table 4 OIL PUMP SERVICE SPECIFICATIONS

Item	Specification mm (in.)	Wear limit mm (in.)
Oil pump		
Inner and outer rotor clearance	0.15 (0.006)	—
Housing and outer rotor clearance		
1985-1995	0.03-0.09 (0.001-0.004)	—
1996-on	0.10-0.15 (0.004-0.006)	—
Side clearance	0.03-0.09 (0.001-0.004)	—

Table 5 TIGHTENING TORQUES

Item	N•m	ft.-lb.
Clutch nut	60	43
Clutch spring screw	8	5.8
Balancer shaft driven gear nut	60	43
Primary drive gear nut	80	58

CHAPTER SEVEN

TRANSMISSION AND INTERNAL SHIFT MECHANISM

The transmission on all models is a 6-speed unit. To gain access to the transmission and internal shift mechanism, it is necessary to remove the engine and split the crankcase (Chapter Five). Once the crankcase has been split, removal of the transmission and shift drum and forks is a simple task of pulling the assemblies up and out of the crankcase.

Transmission ratios are listed in **Table 1** (end of chapter).

NOTE
If disassembling a used, well run-in engine for the first time by yourself, pay particular attention to any additional shims that may have been added by a previous owner. These may have been added to take up the tolerance of worn components and must be reinstalled in the same position since the shims have developed a wear pattern. If new parts are going to be installed, these shims may be eliminated. This is something you will have to determine upon reassembly.

TRANSMISSION OPERATION

The basic transmission has 6 pairs of constantly meshed gears (**Figure 1**) on the mainshaft (A) and countershaft (B). Each pair of meshed gears gives one gear ratio. In each pair, one of the gears is locked to its shaft and always turns with it. The other gear is not locked to its shaft and can spin freely on it. Next to each free spinning gear is a third gear which is splined to the same shaft, always turning with it. This third gear can slide from side-to-side along the shaft splines. The side of the sliding gear and the free spinning gear have mating "dogs" and "slots." See A, **Figure 2**. When the sliding gear moves up against the free spinning gear, the 2 gears are locked together, locking the free spinning gear to its shaft. Since both meshed mainshaft and countershaft gears are now locked to their shafts, power is transmitted at that gear ratio.

Shift Drum and Forks

Each sliding gear has a deep groove machined around its outside (B, **Figure 2**). The curved shift fork arm rides in this groove, controlling the side-to-side sliding of the gear, and therefore the selection of different gear ratios. Each shift fork (A, **Figure 3**) slides back and forth on a guide shaft, and has a peg that rides in a groove machined in the shift drum (B, **Figure 3**). When the shift linkage rotates the shift drum, the zigzag grooves move the shift forks and sliding gears back and forth.

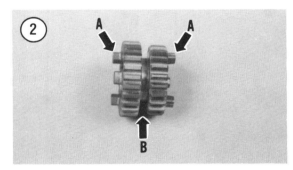

TRANSMISSION TROUBLESHOOTING

Refer to Chapter Two.

TRANSMISSION OVERHAUL

Removal/Installation

Remove and install the transmission and internal shift mechanism as described under *Crankcase Disassembly and Crankcase Assembly* in Chapter Five.

Transmission Service Notes

1. A divided container such as an egg carton (**Figure 4**) can be used to help maintain correct alignment and position of the parts as they are removed from the transmission shafts.

2. The circlips are a tight fit on the transmission shafts. They should all be replaced during reassembly.

3. Circlips will turn and fold over, making removal and installation difficult. To ease replacement, open the circlip with a pair of circlip pliers while at the same time holding the back of the circlip with a pair of pliers and remove it. See **Figure 5**.

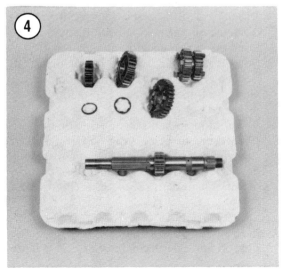

7

Mainshaft
Disassembly/Assembly

A hydraulic press (**Figure 6**) and a bearing splitter (**Figure 7**) will be required to disassemble and reassemble the mainshaft. If you do not have access to a press, have the mainshaft rebuilt by a Yamaha dealer or machine shop.

Refer to **Figure 8** for this procedure.

1. Place the assembled shaft into a large can or plastic bucket and thoroughly clean with solvent and stiff brush. Dry with compressed air or let sit on rags to drip dry.

NOTE
When using a press and bearing splitter to disassemble the mainshaft in Step 2, follow the manufacturer's instructions and guidelines when using their equipment. It is recommended to wear safety glasses when using press equipment.

2. Press off mainshaft second gear as follows:

a. Measure the width of the installed gears on the mainshaft with vernier calipers (**Figure 9**) and measure the clearance between the mainshaft second and fifth gears (**Figure 10**); record each measurement. This information will be used when reassembling the mainshaft.

b. Install a bearing splitter below mainshaft second gear. Then tighten the bearing splitter and install the mainshaft into the press. See **Figure 11**.

c. Press off mainshaft second gear (**Figure 12**). Make sure to place your hand or another support underneath the transmission assembly to catch it as second gear is pressed off.

d. Remove mainshaft second gear (**Figure 13**).

3. Slide off fifth gear (**Figure 14**).

4. Slide off third/fourth combination gear (**Figure 15**).

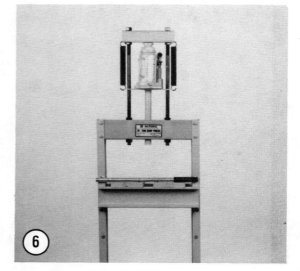

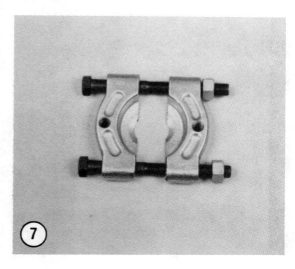

8 — TRANSMISSION

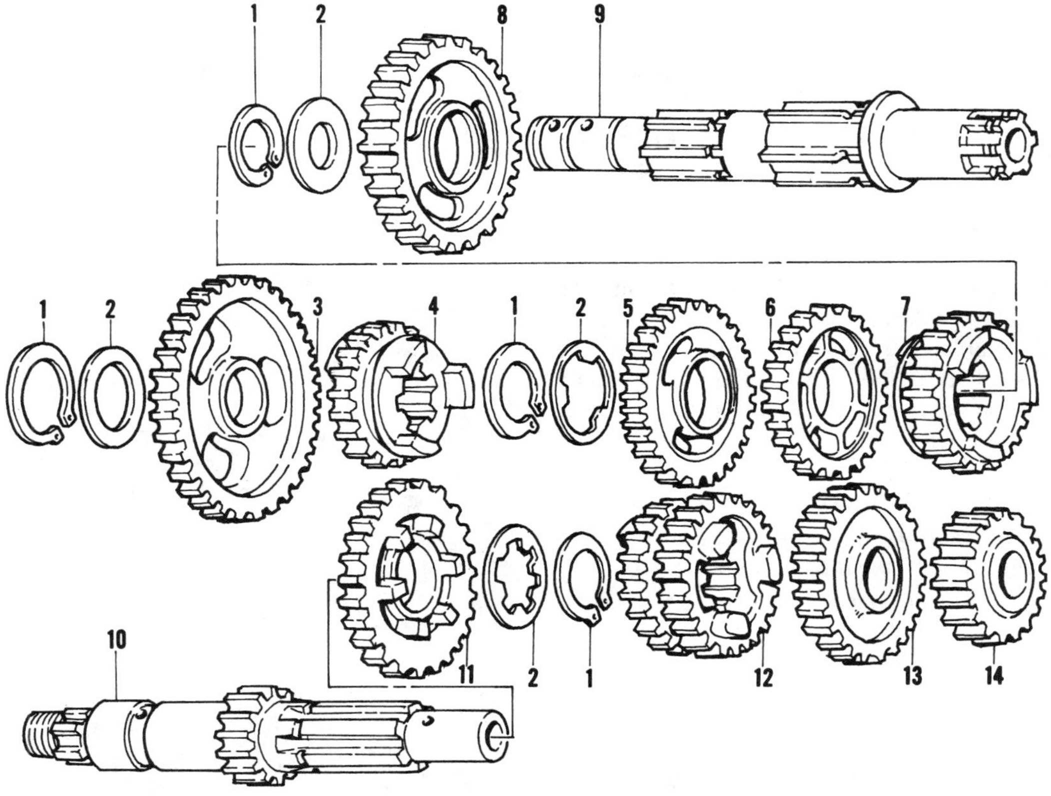

1. Circlip
2. Spacer
3. Countershaft first gear
4. Countershaft sixth gear
5. Countershaft third gear
6. Countershaft fourth gear
7. Countershaft fifth gear
8. Countershaft second gear
9. Countershaft
10. Mainshaft/first gear
11. Mainshaft sixth gear
12. Mainshaft third/fourth gear
13. Mainshaft fifth gear
14. Mainshaft second gear

5. Remove the circlip (**Figure 16**).

6. Remove the splined washer (**Figure 17**).

7. Slide off sixth gear (**Figure 18**).

8. Mainshaft first gear (**Figure 19**) is part of the mainshaft assembly.

9. Inspect the mainshaft parts as described under *Transmission Inspection* in this chapter.

10. Slide on sixth gear so that the flat portion rests against first gear (**Figure 18**).

11. Install the splined washer (**Figure 17**).

12. Install the circlip into the groove next to the splined washer (**Figure 16**).

13. Slide on third/fourth combination gear (**Figure 15**) so that the smaller diameter gear engages with sixth gear.

14. Slide on fifth gear (**Figure 14**) so that the side with the gear dogs faces toward fourth gear.

15. Press second gear (A, **Figure 20**) onto the mainshaft as follows:

  a. Assemble the bearing splitter onto the mainshaft as shown in A, **Figure 21**. Apply a light coat of assembly oil to the inside of second gear.

NOTE

The small shoulder on second gear (B, Figure 20) should face toward fifth gear during assembly.

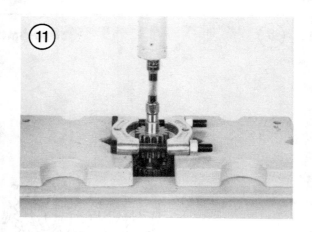

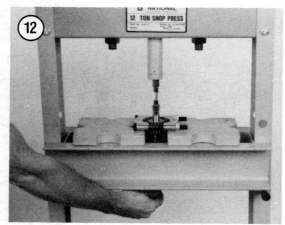

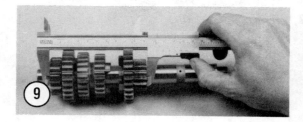

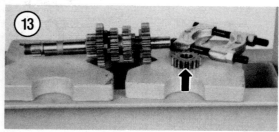

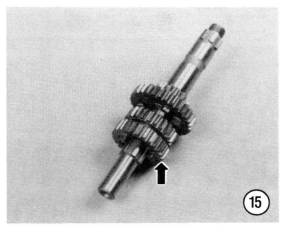

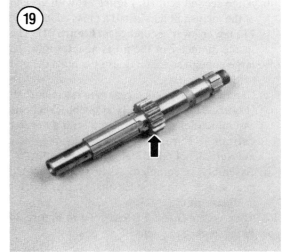

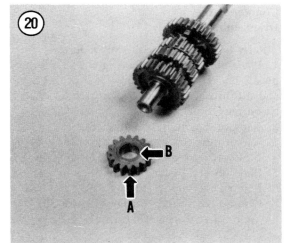

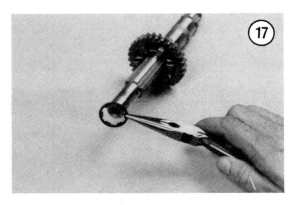

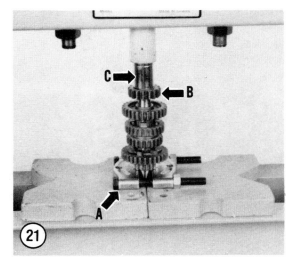

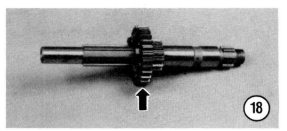

7

b. Align second gear (B, **Figure 21**) with the end of the mainshaft and install a press adapter (C, **Figure 21**) over second gear (**Figure 21**). The inside diameter of the press adapter must be large enough so that it doesn't contact the end of the mainshaft.

c. Carefully press second gear onto the mainshaft (**Figure 22**). Periodically stop and check the assembled length of the gears with a vernier caliper (**Figure 23**). Refer to the measurements taken before disassembly.

d. Assembly is complete when the assembled gear length is the same as that recorded prior to disassembly.

16. After assembly is complete, refer to **Figure 24** for the correct placement of all gears.

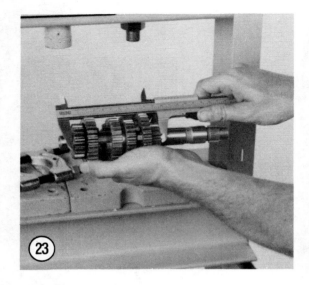

Countershaft
Disassembly/Assembly

Refer to **Figure 8** for this procedure.

1. Place the assembled shaft into a large can or plastic bucket and thoroughly clean with solvent and stiff brush. Dry with compressed air or let it sit on rags to drip dry.
2. Remove the circlip (**Figure 25**).
3. Remove the flat washer (**Figure 26**).
4. Slide off first gear (**Figure 27**).
5. Slide off sixth gear (**Figure 28**).
6. Remove the circlip (**Figure 29**).
7. Remove the splined washer (**Figure 30**).
8. Slide off third gear (**Figure 31**).

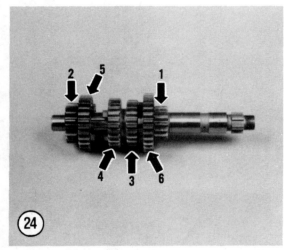

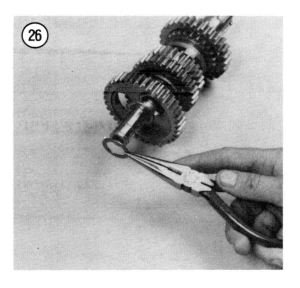

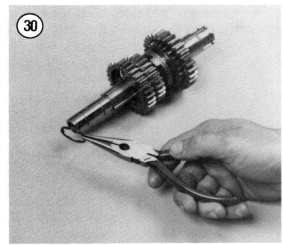

7

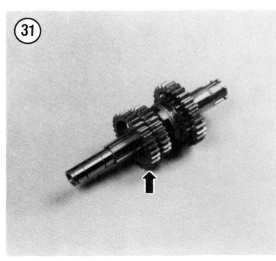

9. Slide off fourth gear (**Figure 32**).

10. Slide off fifth gear (**Figure 33**).

11. Remove the circlip (**Figure 34**).

12. Remove the splined washer (**Figure 35**).

13. Slide off second gear (**Figure 36**).

14. Check the countershaft assembly as described under *Transmission Inspection* in this chapter.

15. Install second gear (**Figure 36**).

16. Install the splined washer (**Figure 35**).

17. Install the circlip (**Figure 34**) in the groove next to the washer.

18. Slide on fifth gear in the direction shown in **Figure 33**.

19. Slide on fourth gear so that the flat side (**Figure 32**) faces away from fifth gear.

20. Install third gear in the direction shown in **Figure 31**.

21. Install the splined washer (**Figure 30**).

22. Install the circlip (**Figure 29**) in the groove next to the washer.

23. Install sixth gear in the direction shown in **Figure 28**.

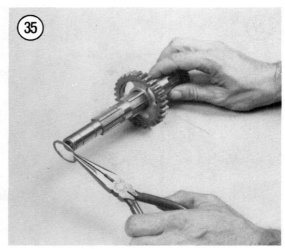

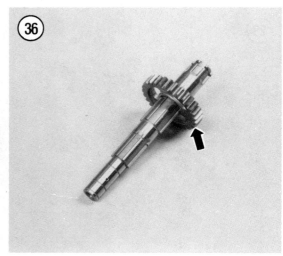

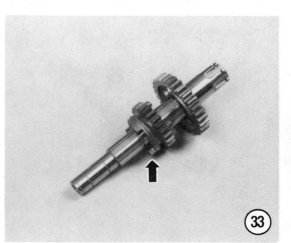

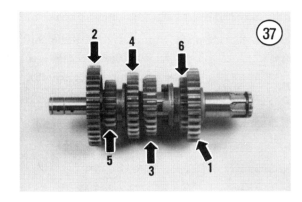

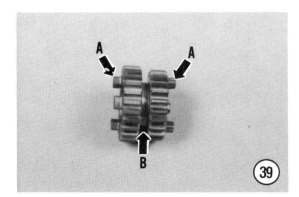

24. Install first gear (**Figure 27**).

25. Install the flat washer (**Figure 26**).

26. Install the circlip in the groove next to the washer (**Figure 25**).

27. After assembly is complete, refer to **Figure 37** for the correct placement of all gears. Make sure all circlips are seated correctly in the countershaft grooves.

NOTE
*After both transmission shafts have been assembled, mesh the 2 assemblies together in the correct position (**Figure 38**). Check that all gears meet correctly. This is your last check prior to installing the assemblies into the crankcase to make sure they are correctly assembled.*

Transmission Inspection

1. Check each gear for excessive wear, burrs, pitting, or chipped or missing teeth.

2. Make sure the lugs (dogs) on the gears are in good condition. See A, **Figure 39**.

3. Check each sliding gear groove (B, **Figure 39**) for wear, cracks or other damage.

4. Check each stationary gear bore (**Figure 40**) for scoring, cracks or other damage.

5. Check each sliding gear shaft groove (**Figure 41**) for scoring, cracks or other damage.

6. Make sure that all gears slide or turn on their respective shafts smoothly. If any gear movement is noisy or rough, replace the gear and/or shaft as required.

NOTE
Defective gears should be replaced, and it is a good idea to replace the mating gear even though it may not show as much wear or damage.

7. Check the mainshaft and countershaft splines (A, **Figure 42**) for wear, cracks or other damage. Also check the mainshaft first gear (B, **Figure 42**). If the gear is damaged, replace the mainshaft assembly.

8. Place each transmission shaft on V-blocks and check runout with a dial indicator (**Figure 43**). If runout exceeds 0.08 mm (0.0031 in.), replace the transmission shaft.

9. Replace all circlips during reassembly. In addition, check the washers for burn marks, scoring or cracks. Replace if necessary.

INTERNAL SHIFT MECHANISM

Removal/Installation

Remove and install the transmission and internal shift mechanism as described under *Crankcase Disassembly and Crankcase Assembly* in Chapter Five.

Shift Fork
Inspection

Refer to **Figure 44** for this procedure.

1. Inspect each shift fork (**Figure 45**) for signs of wear or cracking. Examine the shift forks at the points where they contact the slider gear. This surface should be smooth with no signs of wear or damage. Make sure the forks slide smoothly on their respective shaft (**Figure 44**). Make sure the shaft is not bent. This can be checked by removing the shift forks from the shaft and rolling the shaft on a piece of glass. Any clicking noise detected indicates that the shaft is bent.

2. Check for any arc-shaped wear or burn marks on the shift forks. This indicates that the shift fork has come in contact with the gear. The fork fingers have become excessively worn and the fork must be replaced.

Shift Drum
Disassembly/Inspection/Reassembly

Refer to **Figure 44** for this procedure.

> *NOTE*
> *An impact driver with a T-30 Torx bit* (***Figure 46***) *will be necessary to loosen the shift drum screw in Step 1.*

1. Loosen and remove the Torx screw (**Figure 46**).

2. Lift the side plate (**Figure 47**) off of the shift drum.

3. Remove the 5 short dowel pins (**Figure 48**).

4. Remove the segment (**Figure 49**).

5. Remove the stopper plate guide (**Figure 50**).

6. Remove the long dowel pin (**Figure 51**).

7. Remove the stopper plate (**Figure 52**).

8. Remove the dowel pin (**Figure 53**).

9. Check the grooves in the shift drum (**Figure 54**) for wear or roughness.

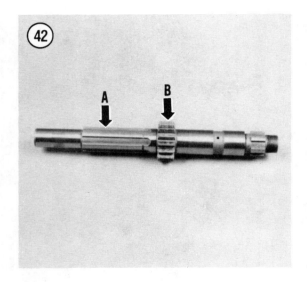

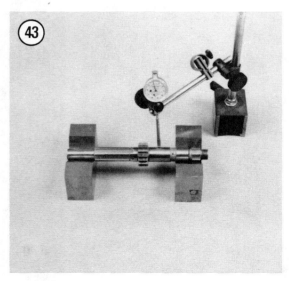

INTERNAL SHIFT MECHANISM

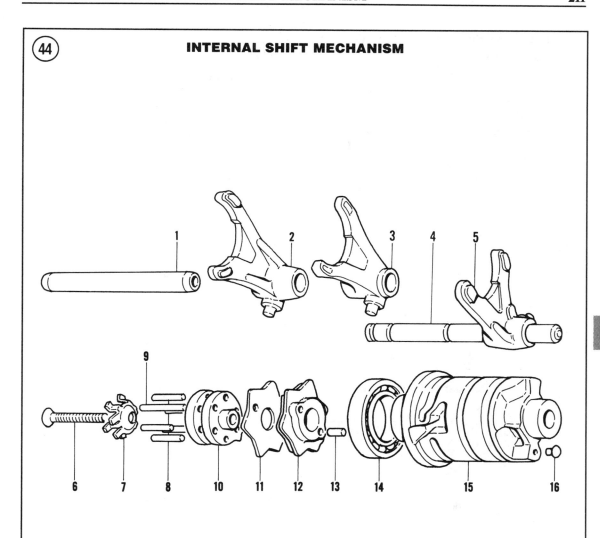

1. Shift fork shaft
2. Shift fork No. 3
3. Shift fork No. 1
4. Shift fork shaft
5. Shift fork No. 2
6. Screw
7. Side plate
8. Pins (5 short)
9. Pin (1 long)
10. Segment
11. Stopper plate guide
12. Stopper plate
13. Pin
14. Bearing
15. Shift drum
16. Neutral point

10. Check the bearing (**Figure 55**) for roughness or damage. If necessary, replace the bearing by pressing it off of the shift drum with a press. Reverse to install the bearing.

11. Oil the bearing with clean engine oil.

12. Install the dowel pin into the end of the shift drum (**Figure 53**).

13. Align the hole in the stopper plate (A, **Figure 56**) with the pin (B, **Figure 56**) and install the stopper plate. See **Figure 52**.

14. Install the long pin (**Figure 51**). Push the pin in until it bottoms.

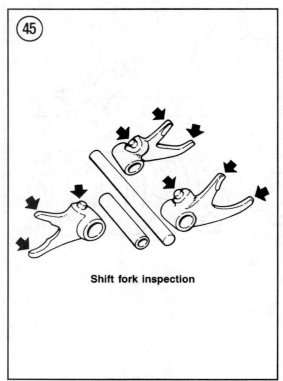

Shift fork inspection

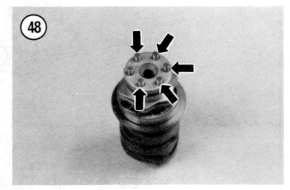

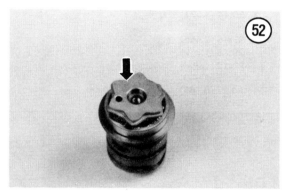

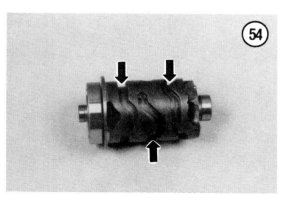

15. Align the hole in the stopper plate guide with the long dowel pin and install the guide (**Figure 50**).

16. Align the through hole in the segment with the long dowel pin and install the segment (**Figure 49**).

17. Install the 5 short dowel pins (**Figure 48**) into the segment.

18. Install side plate (**Figure 47**) so that the U-shaped portion fits around the long dowel pin.

19. Apply Loctite 242 (blue) to the Torx screw threads and install the screw. Tighten the screw securely.

7

Table 1 TRANSMISSION RATIOS

XT350	
Primary reduction ratio	72:23 (3.130)
Secondary reduction ratio	
1985-1995	52:19 (2.736)
1996-on	55:19 (2.894)
Gear ratios	
1st	37:15 (2.466)
2nd	29:16 (1.812)
3rd	30:22 (1.364)
4th	27:25 (1.080)
5th	24:27 (0.889)
6th	22:29 (0759)
TT350	
Primary reduction ratio	70:24 (2.916)
Secondary reduction ratio	50:14 (3.571)
Gear ratios	
1st	37:15 (2.466)
2nd	29:16 (1.812)
3rd	26:19 (1.368)
4th	27:25 (1.080)
5th	24:27 (0.889)
6th	22:29 (0.759)

CHAPTER EIGHT

FUEL, EXHAUST AND EMISSION CONTROL SYSTEMS

The fuel system consists of the fuel tank, shutoff valve, Teikei carburetors and air filter. There are slight differences among the various models and they are noted in the various procedures.

The exhaust system consists of an exhaust pipe assembly and a muffler.

All XT350 models originally sold in California are equipped with an evaporative emission control system.

This chapter includes service procedures for all parts of the fuel, exhaust and emission control systems.

Carburetor specifications are listed in **Table 1** (XT350) and **Table 2** (TT350). **Tables 1-3** are at the end of the chapter.

FUEL/EMISSION CONTROL DECALS (XT350)

A vehicle emission control information decal (A, **Figure 1**) is fixed to the backside of the right-hand side cover. This decal lists all emission control related tune-up information.

On models sold in California, an emission hose routing label (B, **Figure 1**) is fixed to the back of the side cover. Refer to this decal whenever reconnecting one of the emission control hoses.

AIR FILTER

The air filter must be cleaned frequently. Refer to Chapter Three for specific procedures and service intervals.

CARBURETOR SERVICE

Carburetor Identification

Refer to **Table 1** (XT350) or **Table 2** (TT350) for carburetor specifications.

Removal/Installation

1. Place a milk crate or wood block(s) under the engine to support it securely.
2. *XT350*: On California models, disconnect the carbon canister hose at the carburetor (**Figure 2**).
3. Remove the fuel tank as described in this chapter.
4. *TT350*: Remove the rear shock reservoir (**Figure 3**) from the left-hand frame tube and position it out of the way.

> *WARNING*
> *Do not disconnect the pressure hose to the reservoir.*

5. Label the 2 throttle cables at the carburetor (**Figure 4**). Then loosen the nuts and disconnect the throttle cables at the carburetor.

6. Loosen the screws on both clamps on the rubber boots (**Figure 5**). Slide the clamps away from the carburetor.

7. Make sure all overflow and drain tubes are free.

8. Carefully work the carburetor free from the rubber boots and remove it.

9. Stuff clean shop rags into the intake manifolds to prevent dirt and other debris from entering the cylinder head.

10. Take the carburetor to a workbench for disassembly and cleaning.

11. Install by reversing these removal steps. Adjust the throttle cables as described in Chapter Three.

Disassembly/Reassembly

Refer to **Figure 6** (XT350) or **Figure 7** (TT350) for this procedure.

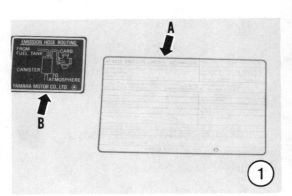

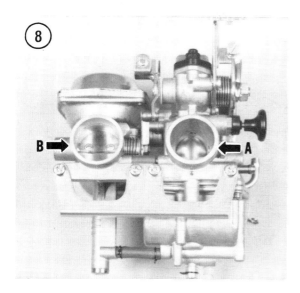

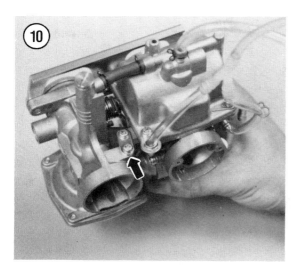

The carburetors assemblies are identified in **Figure 8**:

 a. Primary (A).

 b. Secondary (B).

During the following procedures, the carburetor assemblies will be referred to as either primary or secondary.

1. Remove the fuel line and all drain and overflow tubes.

2. Separate the carburetor assemblies as follows:

NOTE
An impact driver with a Phillips bit (described in Chapter One) will be necessary to loosen the front bracket screws. Attempting to loosen the screws with a Phillips screwdriver may ruin the screw heads.

 a. Remove the screws holding the front bracket to the carburetor assemblies. Remove the front bracket (**Figure 9**).

 b. Remove the screws holding the rear bracket to the carburetor assemblies. Remove the rear bracket (**Figure 10**).

 c. Pull the carburetor assemblies apart (**Figure 11**).

NOTE
Steps 3-7 describe secondary carburetor disassembly.

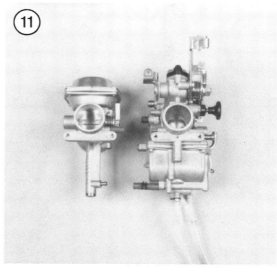

8

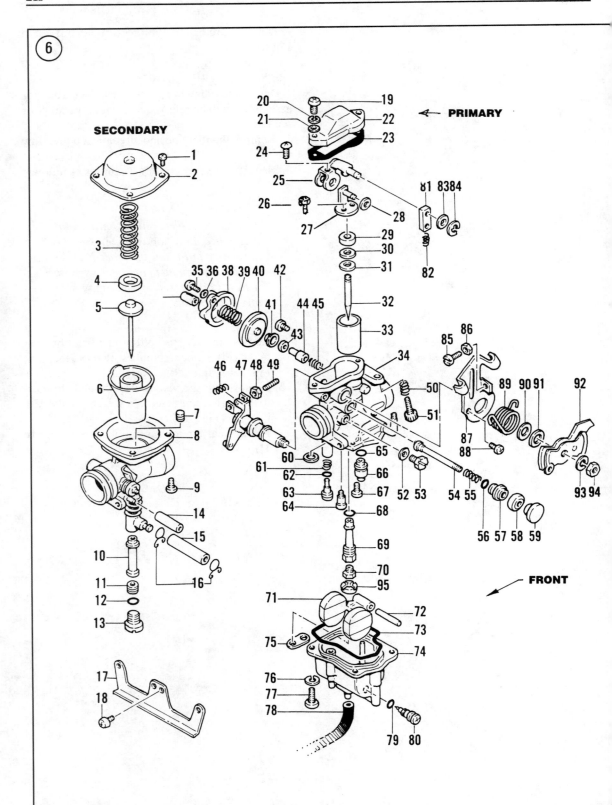

⑥

SECONDARY

PRIMARY

FRONT

CARBURETOR
(XT350)

1. Screw
2. Cover
3. Spring
4. Spring seat
5. Jet needle assembly
6. Vacuum piston
7. Main air jet
8. Secondary carburetor housing
9. Screw
10. Needle jet
11. Main jet
12. O-ring
13. Blind plug
14. Hose
15. Hose
16. Clips
17. Front plate
18. Screw
19. Screw
20. Lockwasher
21. Washer
22. Cover
23. Gasket
24. Screw
25. Bracket
26. Screw
27. Spring seat
28. Washer
29. Seat
30. Clip
31. Clip
32. Jet needle
33. Throttle valve
34. Primary carburetor housing
35. Screw
36. Washer
37. Hose
38. Cover
39. Spring
40. Diaphragm
41. Plunger tip
42. Screw
43. Cap
44. Plunger
45. Spring
46. Spring
47. Throttle lever

48. Locknut
49. Adjust screw
50. Spring
51. Throttle stop screw
52. Washer
53. Bolt
54. Choke rod
55. Spring
56. O-ring
57. Sleeve
58. Seal
59. Knob
60. Gasket
61. Spring
62. Washer
63. Pilot air screw
64. Pilot jet
65. O-ring
66. Needle valve
67. Screw
68. O-ring
69. Needle jet
70. Main jet
71. Floats
72. Float pin
73. O-ring
74. Float bowl
75. Hose guide
76. Lockwasher
77. Screw
78. Hose
79. O-ring
80. Drain screw
81. Block
82. Spring
83. Washer
84. Clip
85. Screw
86. Nut
87. Cable guide
88. Screw
89. Spring
90. Washer
91. Washer
92. Throttle lever
93. Lockwasher
94. Nut

8

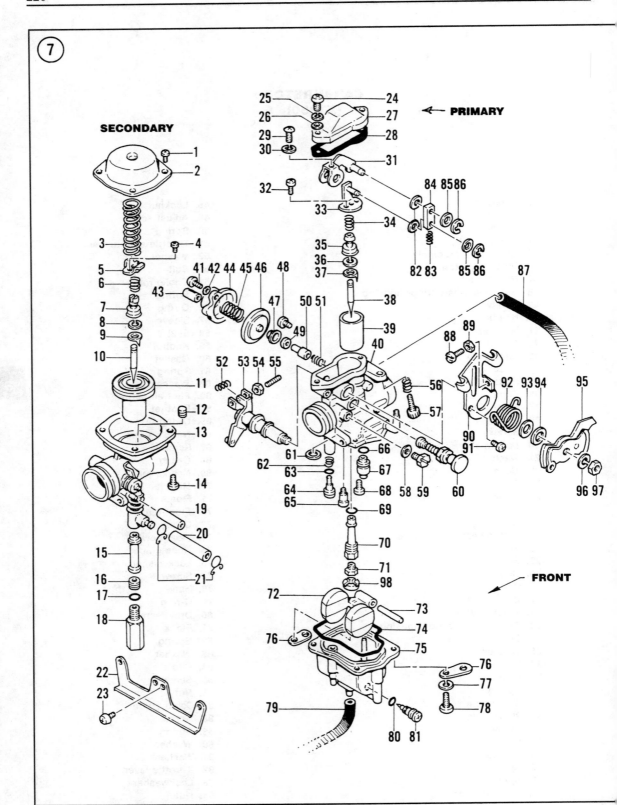

CARBURETOR
(TT350)

1. Screw
2. Cover
3. Spring
4. Screw
5. Spring seat
6. Spring
7. Lock
8. Clip
9. Clip
10. Jet needle
11. Vacuum piston
12. Main air jet
13. Secondary carburetor housing
14. Screw
15. Needle net
16. Main jet
17. O-ring
18. Blind plug
19. Hose
20. Hose
21. Clips
22. Front plate
23. Screw
24. Screw
25. Lockwasher
26. Washer
27. Cover
28. Gasket
29. Screw
30. Lockwasher
31. Bracket
32. Screw
33. Spring seat
34. Spring
35. Lock
36. Clip
37. Clip
38. Jet needle
39. Throttle valve
40. Primary carburetor housing
41. Screw
42. Washer
43. Hose
44. Cover
45. Spring
46. Diaphragm
47. Plunger tip
48. Screw
49. Cap

50. Plunger
51. Spring
52. Spring
53. Throttle lever
54. Locknut
55. Adjust screw
56. Spring
57. Throttle stop screw
58. Washer
59. Bolt
60. Choke
61. Gasket
62. Spring
63. Washer
64. Pilot air screw
65. Pilot jet
66. O-ring
67. Needle valve
68. Screw
69. O-ring
70. Needle jet
71. Main jet
72. Floats
73. Float pin
74. O-ring
75. Float bowl
76. Hose guide
77. Lockwasher
78. Screw
79. Hose
80. O-ring
81. Drain screw
82. Washers
83. Spring
84. Block
85. Washer
86. Clip
87. Hose
88. Screw
89. Nut
90. Cable guide
91. Screw
92. Spring
93. Washer
94. Washer
95. Throttle lever
96. Lockwasher
97. Nut

8

3. Remove the blind plug. See 13, **Figure 6** (XT350) or 18, **Figure 7** (TT350).

4. Remove the main jet (**Figure 12**) and needle jet (**Figure 13**).

5. Remove the cover (**Figure 14**) and spring (**Figure 15**).

6. Remove the diaphragm (**Figure 16**).

7. Remove the screw from inside the slide (**Figure 17**) and separate the slide/jet needle assembly. See **Figure 18**.

NOTE
Steps 8-16 describe primary carburetor disassembly.

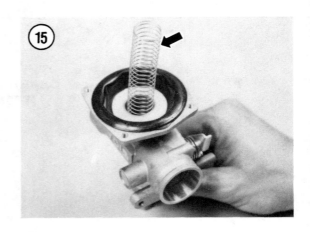

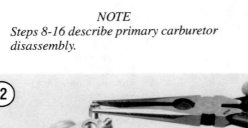

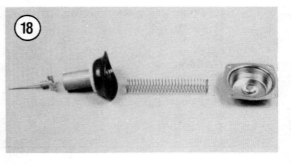

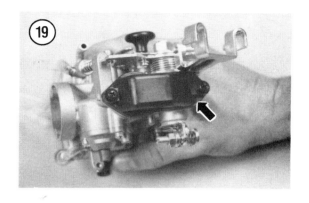

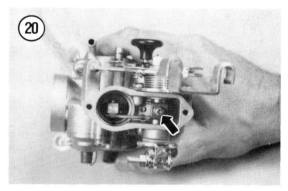

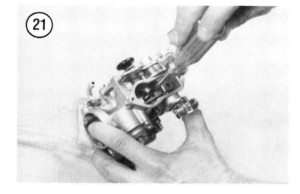

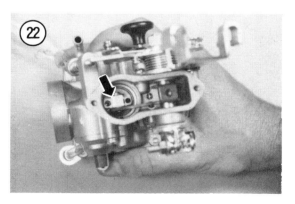

8. Remove the primary throttle valve as follows:

   a. Remove the cap (**Figure 19**).
   b. Remove the connecting arm screw (**Figure 20**).
   c. Remove the screw (**Figure 21**) securing the throttle valve assembly. See **Figure 22**.
   d. Disconnect the throttle shaft (**Figure 23**) and remove the throttle valve (**Figure 24**).

9. Unscrew and remove the choke valve assembly (A, **Figure 25**).

10. Remove the float bowl (B, **Figure 25**).

8

11. Remove the O-ring (**Figure 26**).

12. Remove the float pin (**Figure 27**) and remove the float and fuel valve assembly (**Figure 28**).

13. Remove the screw securing the fuel valve seat (**Figure 29**) and remove the seat (**Figure 30**).

14. Remove the pilot jet (**Figure 31**).

15. Remove the main jet (**Figure 32**).

16. Remove the needle jet (**Figure 33**).

17. Perform the following to remove the coasting enrichener:

    a. Remove the 2 screws and remove the coasting enrichener cover (**Figure 34**).

    b. Remove the spring (**Figure 35**).

    c. Remove the diaphragm (**Figure 36**).

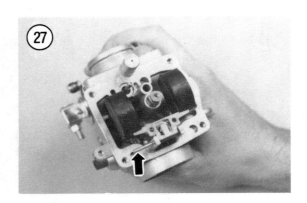

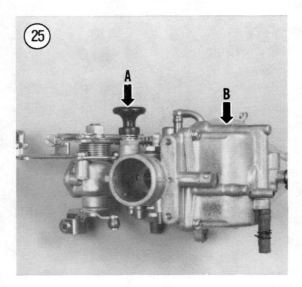

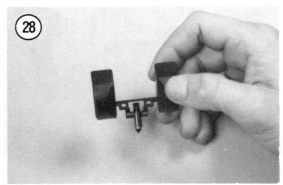

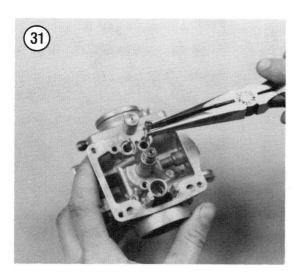

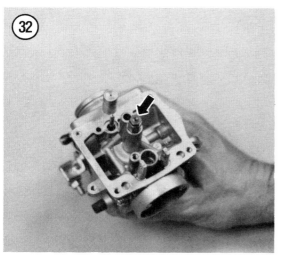

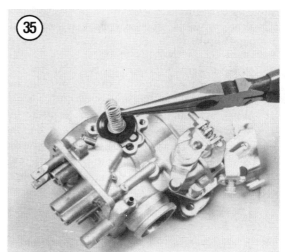

8

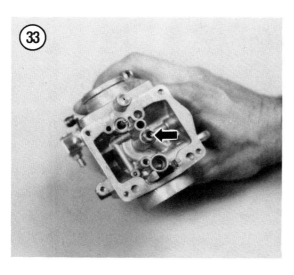

18. On all models, the pilot air screw is located underneath the float bowl in the primary carburetor housing. See 63, **Figure 6** (XT350) or 64, **Figure 7** (TT350). On some models, the pilot air screw is fixed in a blind housing and removal is not recommended as the housing plug must be removed. On other models, the pilot air screw can be removed. If you are going to remove the screw, count the number of turns required to lightly seat the screw, then turn the screw counterclockwise and remove it and the spring.

19. Clean and inspect the carburetor components as described in this chapter.

20. After all parts have been cleaned and dried, reverse these steps to assemble the carburetor. Note the following.

21. When installing the primary carburetor throttle valve, align the slot in the valve with the pin in the valve bore (**Figure 37**).

22. When installing the coasting enrichener diaphragm (**Figure 36**), align the tab on the diaphragm with the recess in the housing.

23. When installing the secondary carburetor diaphragm, align the tab on the diaphragm with the notch in the carburetor housing. See **Figure 38**.

24. When installing the pilot air screw, install the screw until it lightly seats. Then back it out the number of turns recorded during removal. If you did not record the number of turns during removal, refer to the pilot air screw specifications in **Table 1** (XT350) or **Table 2** (TT350).

25. Check the float height and adjust if necessary. Refer to *Float Adjustment* in this chapter.

26. Assemble the carburetor primary and secondary housings (**Figure 39**) as follows:

   a. Align the carburetor housings and connect them at the 3 hose connections. See **Figure 40** and **Figure 41**.

   b. Make sure the roller on the secondary carburetor engages the arm bracket on the primary carburetor (A, **Figure 42**).

   c. Install the front bracket (B, **Figure 42**). Install the front bracket screws finger tight.

   d. Install the rear bracket (A, **Figure 43**) and screws.

   e. Tighten both bracket screws securely.

27. Install all hoses to the fittings on the bottom of the carburetor.

28. Before installing the carburetors onto the bike, perform the *Carburetor Synchronization* procedures described in this chapter.

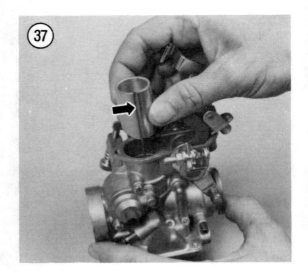
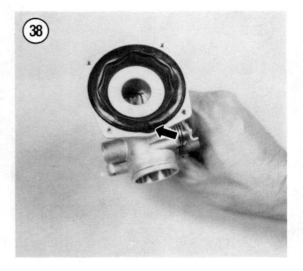
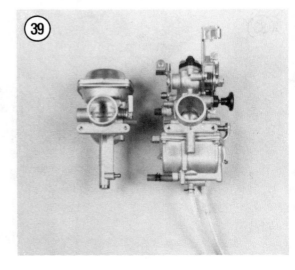

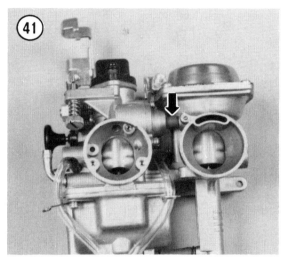

29. After the carburetor has been installed on the bike, adjust the idle speed. Refer to Chapter Three.

Cleaning/Inspection

1. Clean all parts in solvent.

> *CAUTION*
> *Do not soak the carburetor housings in a carburetor cleaner unless the entire carburetor assembly has been disassembled. The cleaner will destroy any rubber O-rings, seals or plastic parts left assembled in the housing. This includes the O-ring installed on the pilot air screw.*

2. Remove all parts from the cleaner and wash thoroughly in soap and water. Rinse with clean water and dry thoroughly.
3. Blow out the jets with compressed air. *Do not* use a piece of wire to clean them as minor gouges in the jet can alter flow rate and upset the fuel/air mixture. If compressed air is not available, use a piece of straw from a broom to clean the jets.
4. Be sure to clean out the float bowl overflow tube from both ends.
5. Inspect the tip of the float valve for wear or damage. Replace the valve and seat as a set.

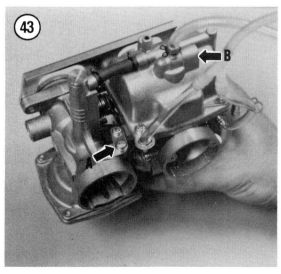

6. O-ring seals (**Figure 44**) tend to become hardened after prolonged use and heat and therefore lose their ability to seal properly. Inspect all O-rings and replace if necessary.

7. Check the floats (**Figure 28**) for leaks. Fill the float bowl with water and try to push the floats down. There should be no signs of bubbles. Replace the floats if they leak.

8. Check the choke valve assembly (**Figure 45**) for wear, scratches or other damage. Replace if necessary.

9. Check the throttle valve (**Figure 46**) for scratches or other damage that would allow it to stick open during engine operation.

10. Check the secondary carburetor diaphragm (**Figure 47**) and the coating enricher diaphragm (**Figure 48**) for tears, splitting or other damage. Replace if necessary.

11. Check the secondary carburetor throttle valve (A, **Figure 49**) operation by operating the throttle valve shaft (B, **Figure 49**). The valve and shaft should turn smoothly. If the shaft is tight or damaged, replace the secondary carburetor assembly as the valve is not available as a replacement item.

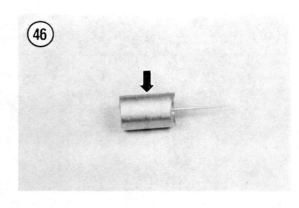

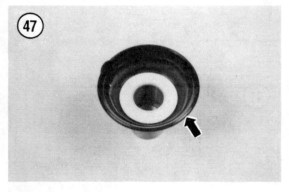

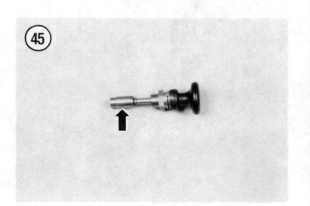

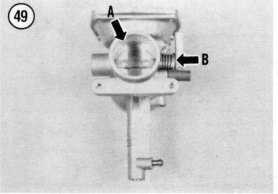

CARBURETOR ADJUSTMENT

Float/Arm Height Adjustment

The fuel level in the primary carburetor float bowl is critical to proper performance. The fuel flow rate from the bowl up to the carburetor bore depends not only on the vacuum in the throttle bore and the size of the jets, but also upon the fuel level. Yamaha gives a specification of actual *fuel level*, measured from the top edge of the float bowl with the carburetor held level (**Figure 50**).

The measurement is more useful than a simple float height measurement because actual fuel level can vary from bike to bike, even when their floats are set at the same height. However, fuel level inspection requires a special fuel gauge tube that screws into the bottom of the carburetor. You can get the proper fitting at your Yamaha dealer (part No. YM-01312). See **Figure 50**.

The fuel level is adjusted by bending the float arm tang.

Fuel Level Inspection

1. Place a jack underneath the engine and raise the engine so that the carburetor is level.
2. Turn the fuel valve OFF
3. Remove the overflow tube from the bottom of the float bowl (**Figure 51**) and install the Yamaha fuel gauge tube (**Figure 50**).
4. Hold the tube up and start the engine. Allow the engine to idle for a few minutes then turn it off.
5. Hold the clear tube against the carburetor body so that the 0 mark on the tube aligns with the carburetor body edge (**Figure 50**). Measure the distance from the fuel level in the tube to the carburetor body edge (**Figure 50**). The correct level is 6.0 ±0.5 mm (0.24 ±0.02 in.).

> *NOTE*
> *Take your readings just after the fuel level has risen to its maximum in the tube. If you raise the tube (and the fuel drops in the tube) you'll probably get a faulty level reading. Try it again, forcing the fuel level to rise against surface tension within the tube.*

6. If the fuel level is incorrect, adjust the float/arm height setting as described in Step 7. Then recheck the fuel level. Readjust if necessary.
7. Perform the following to adjust the float level:
   a. Remove the carburetor as described in this chapter. However, do not disconnect the throttle cables at the carburetor.

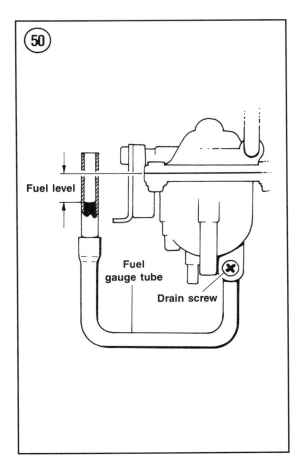

Fuel level

Fuel gauge tube

Drain screw

WARNING
Before removing the carburetor float bowl in sub-step b, place a clean pan underneath the carburetor to catch any gasoline spilling out of the bowl.

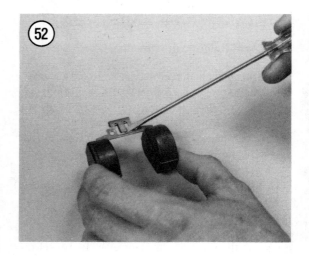

b. Remove the bolts securing the float bowl to the carburetor. Remove the float bowl (B, **Figure 43**).

c. Remove the float pin (**Figure 27**) and remove the float and fuel valve assembly (**Figure 28**).

d. Slip the float pin (**Figure 27**) off of the float arm.

e. Adjust the float by bending the tang with a screwdriver (**Figure 52**).

f. Reverse to install the float assembly. Make sure the O-ring (**Figure 53**) did not fall out. Make sure the O-ring is installed in the groove in the float bowl.

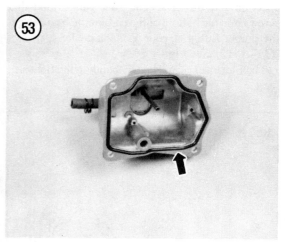

8. After installing the carburetor, reverse Steps 1-6 and recheck the fuel level. Repeat Step 7 as required to adjust the float.

9. When the fuel level is correct, disconnect the Yamaha fuel gauge tube and reconnect the overflow tube (**Figure 51**) to the bottom of the float bowl.

Carburetor Synchronization

1. Remove the carburetors as described in this chapter. However, do not disconnect the throttle cables at the carburetors. Use the throttle grip to open or close the throttle lever in the following steps.

2. *Primary carburetor full-open adjustment*: Perform the following. Refer to **Figure 54**:

a. Rotate the throttle lever to the wide-open position.

b. Measure the throttle valve distance indicated in **Figure 54**. The correct distance is 0-0.1 mm (0-0.04 in.).

c. If necessary, loosen the adjuster locknut and turn the adjuster to position the throttle valve. Tighten the locknut and recheck the adjustment.

d. Release the throttle lever.

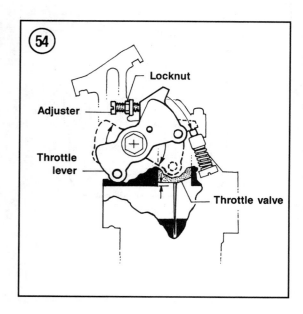

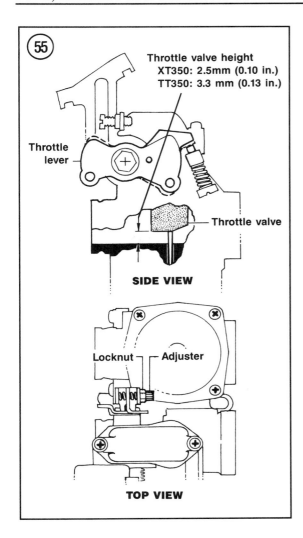

Throttle valve height
XT350: 2.5mm (0.10 in.)
TT350: 3.3 mm (0.13 in.)

Throttle lever

Throttle valve

SIDE VIEW

Locknut — Adjuster

TOP VIEW

3. *Secondary carburetor synchronization*: Perform the following. Refer to **Figure 55**:
   a. Loosen the adjuster locknut.
   b. Raise the primary throttle valve (A, **Figure 56**) to the height distance specified in **Figure 55** for your model.
   c. Then turn the adjuster in or out until the secondary carburetor butterfly valve just begins to open. Tighten the locknut.
   d. Recheck the adjustment.

4. Open the primary throttle valve (A, **Figure 56**) all the way. Then check that the secondary butterfly valve is in a horizontal position (**Figure 57**). If not, repeat Steps 2 and 3.

5. Install the carburetors as described in this chapter.

Needle Jet Adjustment

The position of the needle jet can be adjusted to affect the fuel/air mixture for medium throttle openings.

The top of the carburetor must be removed for this adjustment. It is easier to perform this procedure with the fuel tank removed but it can be accomplished with it in place.

1. Remove either the secondary or primary carburetor cap. If necessary, remove the carburetors as described in this chapter.

NOTE
Prior to removing the top cap, thoroughly clean the area around it so no dirt will fall into the carburetor.

2. Note the position of the clip. Raising the needle (lowering the clip) will enrich the mixture during mid-throttle opening, while lowering it (raising the clip) will lean the mixture.

3. Refer to **Table 1** (XT350) or **Table 2** (TT350) at the end of the chapter for the standard clip position for all models.

4. Installation is the reverse of these steps.

Idle Speed Adjustment

Refer to Chapter Three.

A

B

Pilot Air Screw Adjustment

On all models, the pilot air screw is located underneath the float bowl in the secondary carburetor housing. See 63, **Figure 6** (XT350) or 64, **Figure 7** (TT350). On some models the pilot air screw is fixed in a blind housing and removal is not recommended as the housing plug must be removed. On other models, the pilot screw can be removed. If you are going to remove the screw, count the number of turns required to lightly seat the screw, then turn the screw counterclockwise and remove it and the spring. Refer to *Carburetor Removal/Installation* in this chapter.

High Altitude Adjustment (Main Jet Replacement)

If the bike is going to be ridden for any sustained period of time in high elevations (above 5,000 ft.; 1,500 m), the main jet should be changed to a one-step smaller jet. Never change the jet by more than one size at a time without test riding the bike and running a spark plug test. Refer to *Reading Spark Plugs* in Chapter Three.

The carburetor is set with the standard jet for normal sea level conditions. But if the bike is run at higher altitudes or under heavy load—deep sand or mud—the main jet should be replaced or it will run too rich and carbon up quickly.

> *CAUTION*
> *If the bike has been rejetted for high altitude operation (smaller jet), it must be changed back to the standard main jet if ridden at altitudes below 5,000 ft. (1,500 m). Engine overheating and piston seizure will occur if the engine runs too lean with the smaller jet.*

Refer to **Table 1** (XT350) or **Table 2** (TT350), at the end of this chapter, for standard main jet sizes.

1. Turn the fuel shutoff valve to the OFF position and disconnect the fuel line from the carburetor.
2. Loosen the main jet cover (float bowl plug) and drain out all fuel in the bowl.

> *WARNING*
> *Place a metal container under the cover to catch the fuel that will flow*

out. Do not let it drain out onto the engine or the bike's frame as it presents a real fire danger. **Do not perform this procedure with a hot engine.** *Dispose of the fuel properly; wipe up any that may have spilled on the bike and the floor.*

3. The main jet is directly under the cover. Remove it and replace it with a different one. Remember, change only one jet size at a time.
4. Install the main jet cover; tighten it securely.

FUEL TANK

Removal/Installation

1. Park the bike on its sidestand.
2. Remove the seat.
3. Remove the front air ducts.
4. Turn the fuel shutoff valve to the OFF position (A, **Figure 58**) and remove the fuel line to the carburetor.
5. Remove the bolts securing the fuel tank.
6. *XT350 California models*: Lift the fuel tank slightly and disconnect the hose (B, **Figure 58**) at the roll-over valve mounted underneath the tank.
7. Remove the fuel tank.
8. Install by reversing these removal steps. Check the fuel hose for leaks.

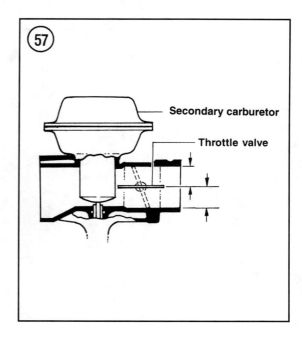

(57)

Secondary carburetor

Throttle valve

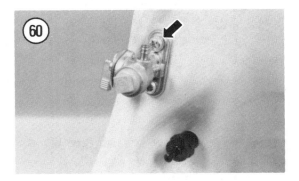

NOTE
*Motorcycle fuel tanks are relatively maintenance free. However, a major cause of fuel tank leakage occurs when the fuel tank is not mounted securely and it vibrates during riding. When installing the tank, make sure that the rubber dampers (**Figure 59**) at the front and rear of the tank are in position and that the tank is mounted securely at the front and back with the proper fasteners.*

FUEL SHUTOFF VALVE

Removal/Installation

1. Remove the fuel tank as described in this chapter.

2. Drain the fuel into a fuel storage container.

3. Remove the bolts holding the fuel shutoff valve (**Figure 60**) to the bottom of the fuel tank. Remove the fuel tank.

4. Remove the screws or nut and disassemble the valve. Clean all parts in solvent with a medium-soft toothbrush, then dry. Check the small O-ring within the valve and the O-ring gasket; replace if they are starting to deteriorate or get hard. Make sure the spring is not broken or getting soft; replace if necessary.

5. Reassemble the valve and install it on the tank. Don't forget the O-ring gasket between the valve and the tank.

6. Pour a small amount of fuel into the tank and check for leaks. Do not install the fuel tank if it leaks.

EXHAUST SYSTEM

Removal/Installation

1. Remove the seat, fuel tank and both side cover/number plates.

2. Park the bike on its sidestand.

3. Loosen the exhaust pipe bolts at the cylinder head.

4. Remove the exhaust pipe to muffler clamp bolt (**Figure 61**). Then remove the front (**Figure 61**) and

8

rear muffler mounting bolts and remove the muffler (**Figure 62**).

5. Remove the exhaust pipe bolts at the cylinder head and remove the exhaust pipe assembly. See **Figure 63** (XT350) or **Figure 64** (TT350).

6. Installation is the reverse of these steps. Note the following.

7. Replace the exhaust pipe gaskets at the cylinder head.

8. Install the exhaust pipe and muffler loosely until the complete exhaust system is installed. Then tighten the bolts starting with the exhaust pipe bolts at the cylinder head and work toward the muffler. See **Table 3** for tightening torques.

Carbon Removal

The spark arrester mounted in the muffler should be cleaned at specified intervals. Refer to Chapter Three for the specified time interval and the complete procedure.

EXHAUST SYSTEM REPAIR

A dent in the exhaust pipe will alter the system's flow characteristics and degrade performance. Minor damage can be easily repaired if you have welding equipment, some simple body tools, and a bodyman's slide hammer.

Small Dents

1. Drill a small hole in the center of the dent. Screw the end of the slide hammer into the hole.

2. Heat the area around the dent evenly with a torch.

3. When the dent is heated to a uniform orange-red color, operate the slide hammer to raise the dent.

4. When the dent is removed, unscrew the slide hammer and weld the drilled hole closed.

Large Dents

Large dents that are not crimped can be removed with heat and a slide hammer as previously described. However, several holes must be drilled along the center of the dent so that it can be pulled out evenly.

If the dent is sharply crimped along the edges, the affected section should be cut out with a

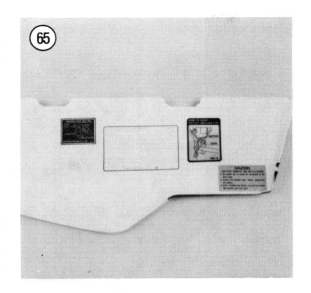

hacksaw, straightened with a body dolly and hammer and welded back into place.

Before cutting the exhaust pipe apart, scribe alignment marks over the area where the cuts will be made to aid correct alignment when the pipe is rewelded.

After the welding is completed, wire brush and clean up all welds. Paint the entire pipe with a high-temperature paint to prevent rusting.

EMISSION CONTROL (XT350 CALIFORNIA MODELS)

All XT350 models originally sold in California are equipped with an evaporative emission control system to reduce the amount of fuel vapors released into the atmosphere. The system consists of a charcoal canister, unvented fuel filler cap, roll-over valve, assorted vacuum lines and a modified carburetor and fuel tank. A schematic of the emission control system is fixed to the back of the left-hand side cover (**Figure 65**).

During engine operation, fuel vapors formed in the fuel tank exit the tank through a roll-over valve and enter the charcoal canister (**Figure 66**) through a connecting hose. The vapors are stored in the charcoal canister until the bike is ridden at a high speed. At which time, the vapors are passed through a hose to the carburetor and mixed and burned with the incoming fresh air. During low-speed engine operation or when the bike is parked, the fuel vapors are stored in the charcoal canister.

The roll-over valve is installed in the bottom of the fuel tank (**Figure 67**). Air and fuel vapor passage through the valve is controlled by an internal weight (**Figure 68**). During normal riding (or when the fuel tank is properly positioned), the weight is at the bottom of the valve. In this position, the breather passage is open to allow the fuel vapors to flow to the charcoal canister where they are stored. If the bike is turned over, the weight moves to block off the passage. In this position, it is impossible for fuel vapors to flow to the charcoal canister. The roll-over valve also prevents fuel from flowing to the carburetor under these conditions, since the fuel filler cap is not vented.

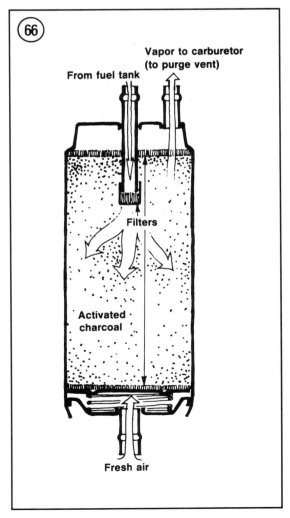

Vapor to carburetor
(to purge vent)

From fuel tank

Filters

Activated charcoal

Fresh air

Service to the emission control system is limited to replacement of damaged parts. No attempt should be made to modify or remove the emission control system.

Parts Replacement

When purchasing replacement parts (carburetor, fuel tank, fuel tank cap, etc.), always make sure the parts are for California emission controlled bikes. Parts sold for non-emission controlled bikes will not work with the emission control system. Order all emission or fuel system related components with your engine serial number.

Charcoal Canister
Removal/Installation

1. Remove the left-hand side cover.
2. Disconnect the canister hose at the carburetor.
3. Disconnect the roll-over valve hose (leading from the fuel tank) at the canister.
4. Remove the bolts holding the canister (**Figure 69**) to the frame. Remove the charcoal canister.

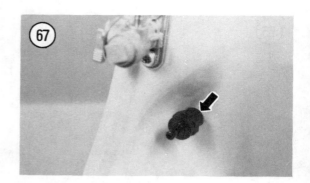

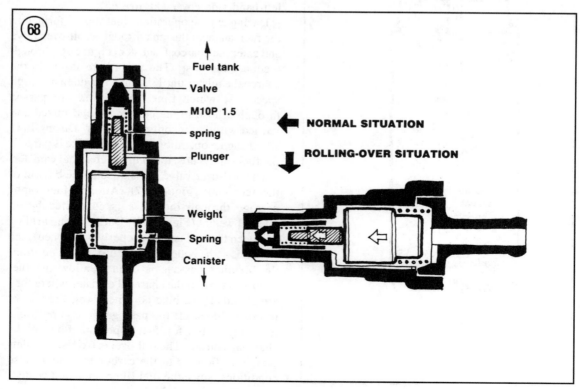

Fuel tank

Valve

M10P 1.5

spring

Plunger

Weight

Spring

Canister

NORMAL SITUATION

ROLLING-OVER SITUATION

5. Installation is the reverse of these steps. Make sure the bottom vent hose is not blocked.

Roll-over Valve
Removal/Installation

1. Remove the fuel tank as described in this chapter.

2. Drain the fuel tank of all gasoline. Store the gasoline in a safety approved gasoline storage canister.

3. Unscrew the roll-over valve (**Figure 67**) from the bottom of the fuel tank.

4. Installation is the reverse of these steps. Check that the fuel tank does not leak.

8

Table 1 CARBURETOR SPECIFICATIONS—XT350

Carburetor type	Y24PV/TEIKEI
I.D. mark	
49-state model	57T00 (1985-1989), 57T01 (1990-1995), 57T03 (1996-on)
California models	56R00 (1985-1989), 56R01 (1990-1995), 56R03 (1996-on)
Fuel level	6 ± 0.5 mm (0.24 ± 0.02 in.)
Float height	Not specified

Part	Primary carb.	Secondary carb.
Main jet	125	106
Main air jet	0.6 (1985-1995), 0.8 (1996-on)	1.4
Jet needle/clip position	5C3C/1-1	4A74/1-1
Pilot jet	42	—
Pilot air jet	1.0	—
Pilot air screw turns out	2.0 ± 1/2	—
Valve seat	2.5	—

Table 2 CARBURETOR SPECIFICATIONS—TT350

Carburetor type	Y24PV/TEIKEI
I.D. mark	1RG-00
Fuel level	6 ± 0.5 mm (0.24 ± 0.02 in.)
Float height	26 ± 2.5 mm (1.02 ± 0.10 in.)

Part	Primary carb.	Secondary carb.
Main jet	122	125
Main air jet	1.0	0.8
Jet needle/clip position	5C9A/3-5	4A70/3-5
Pilot jet	40	—
Pilot air jet	0.8	—
Pilot air screw turns out	2 3/4 ± 1/2	—
Valve seat	2.5	—

Table 3 TIGHTENING TORQUES

Item	N•m	ft.-lb.
Exhaust pipe flange bolt	12	8.7
Muffler clamp flange bolt	20	14
Muffler mount bolt	27	19

CHAPTER NINE

ELECTRICAL SYSTEM

This chapter contains operating principles and service procedures for all electrical and ignition components.

The electrical systems include:

a. Charging system.
b. Ignition system.
c. Lighting system.
d. Switches.

Refer to Chapter Three for routine ignition system maintenance. Electrical system specifications are found in **Tables 1-4** at the end of the chapter.

ELECTRICAL TROUBLESHOOTING

This section describes the basics of electrical troubleshooting, how to use test equipment and the basic test procedures with the various pieces of test equipment.

Electrical troubleshooting can be very time consuming and frustrating without proper knowledge and a suitable plan. Refer to the wiring diagrams at the end of the book and at the individual system diagrams included with the charging system, ignition system and lighting system sections in this chapter. Wiring diagrams will help you determine how the circuit should

work by tracing the current paths from the power source through the circuit components to ground.

As with all troubleshooting procedures, analyze typical symptoms in a systematic procedure. Never assume anything and don't overlook the obvious, such as an electrical connector that has separated. Test the simplest and most obvious cause first and try to make tests at easily accessible points on the bike.

Preliminary Checks and Precautions

Prior to starting any electrical troubleshooting procedure, perform the following:

a. *XT350*: Check the circuit breaker. Reset as described in this chapter.

b. *XT350*: Inspect the battery. Make sure it is fully charged, the electrolyte level is correct and that the battery leads are clean and securely attached to the battery terminals. Refer to *Battery* in Chapter Three.

c. Disconnect each electrical connector in the suspect circuit and check that there are no bent metal pins on the male side of the electrical connector. A bent pin will not connect to its mating receptacle in the female end of the connector, causing an open circuit.

d. Check each female end of the connector. Make sure that the metal connector on the end of each wire is pushed all the way into the plastic connector. If not, carefully push them in with a narrow blade screwdriver.

e. Check all electrical wires where they enter the individual metal connector in both the male and female plastic connector.

f. Make sure all electrical connectors within the connector are clean and free of corrosion. Clean, if necessary, and pack the connectors with a dielectric grease compound.

g. After all is checked out, push the connectors together and make sure they are fully engaged and locked together.

h. Never pull on the electrical wires when disconnecting an electrical connector—pull only on the connector plastic housing.

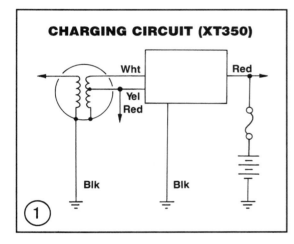

CHARGING CIRCUIT (XT350)

Wht   Red
Yel
Red
Blk   Blk

①

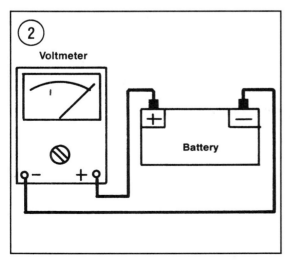

②

Voltmeter

＋   －

Battery

CHARGING SYSTEM
(XT350)

The charging system consists of the battery, alternator and a solid state rectifier/voltage regulator. See **Figure 1**.

The alternator generates an alternating current (AC) which the rectifier converts to direct current (DC). The regulator maintains the voltage to the battery and load (lights, ignition, etc.) at a constant level regardless of variations in engine speed and load. Refer to Chapter Three for battery service.

Charging System Output Test

Whenever the charging system is suspected of trouble, make sure the battery is fully charged before going any further. Clean and test the battery as described in Chapter Three. If the battery is in good condition, test the charging system as follows.

1. Remove the left-hand side cover.

2. Connect a 0-20 DC voltmeter onto the battery terminals as shown in **Figure 2**. The battery is shown in **Figure 3**.

3. Start the engine and operate it at 5,000 rpm. For the charging system to be operating correctly, the voltmeter should read 14-15 volts. If the voltage is less than 14 volts, perform Step 4. If the voltage is more than 15 volts, perform Step 5.

4. If the voltage is less than 14 volts, check the charging coil resistance as described under *Charge Coil Testing* in this chapter.

5. If the voltage is more than 15 volts, check the rectifier/regulator assembly for damaged, loose or dirty connectors. See *Voltage Regulator/Rectifier (XT350)* in this chapter. If the connectors and all wiring are okay, the rectifier/regulator unit is damaged. Replace the rectifier/regulator and retest.

9

③

Charge Coil Testing

It is not necessary to remove the stator assembly to perform the following tests. It is shown removed in the following procedures for clarity.

In order to get accurate resistance measurements, the stator assembly and coil must be warm (approximately 68° F/20° C).

1. Remove the seat and fuel tank.
2. Disconnect the alternator connector (**Figure 4**). The connector contains 4 wires (sky blue, white, black and yellow).
3. Connect an ohmmeter between the white and black wires. Test the connector on the stator coil side (**Figure 5**).

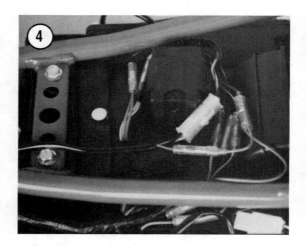

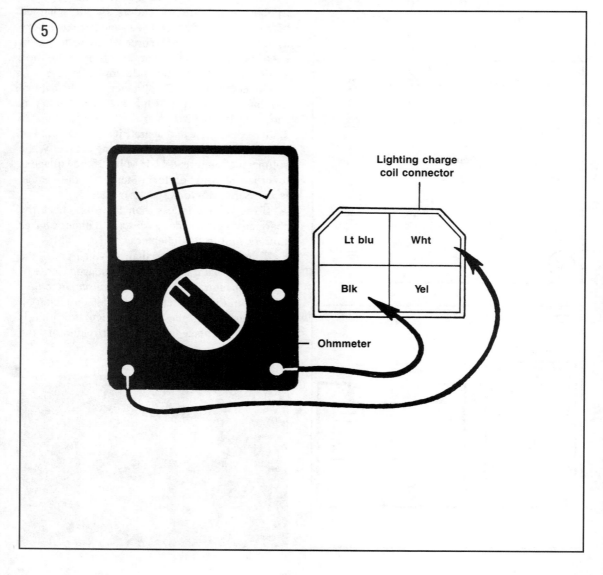

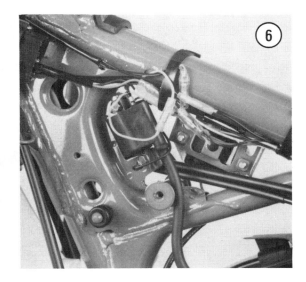

4. If the value is not within the specified range listed in **Table 1**, check the electrical wires to and within the connector. If they are okay, replace the lighting coils as described under *Alternator* in this chapter.

CHARGING SYSTEM
(TT350)

The AC generator charging system performance test is described in the lighting system section of this chapter. Refer to *Lighting System (TT350)* for testing information.

ALTERNATOR

The alternator is a form of electrical generator in which a magnetized field called a rotor revolves within a set of stationary coils called a stator. As the rotor revolves, alternating current is induced into the stator. The current is then rectified to direct current and used to operate the electrical accessories on the motorcycle and to charge the battery (if so equipped). The rotor is a permanent magnet.

Rotor Removal

1. Remove the seat and fuel tank (Chapter Eight).
2. *XT350*: Remove the left-hand side cover and disconnect the negative battery terminal (**Figure 3**).
3. Disconnect the alternator electrical connector. See **Figure 4** (XT350) or **Figure 6** (TT350).
4. Remove the shift lever (**Figure 7**) and remove the left-hand side cover.
5. Use a universal rotor holding tool to secure the magneto and loosen the magneto rotor bolt (**Figure 8**). **Figure 9** shows the rotor used on TT350 models.

6. Remove the bolt and washer.

7. Screw in a flywheel puller until it stops. Use the Yamaha flywheel puller (part No. YM-01189 and adapter YM-01382) or an accessory puller.

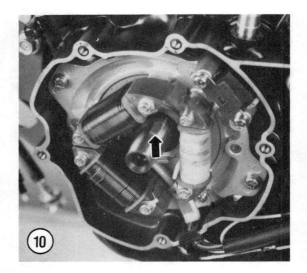

> *CAUTION*
> *Don't try to remove the rotor without a puller; any attempt to do so will ultimately lead to some form of damage to the engine and/or rotor. Aftermarket pullers are available from most motorcycle dealers or mail order houses. If you can't buy or borrow one, have a dealer or service shop remove the rotor.*

8. Hold the puller with a wrench and gradually tighten the center bolt until the rotor disengages from the crankshaft.

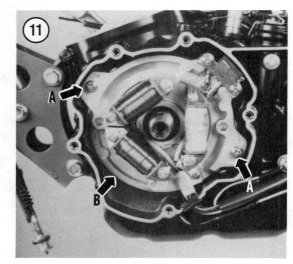

> *NOTE*
> *If the rotor is difficult to remove, strike the puller's center bolt with a hammer a few times. This will usually break it loose.*

> *CAUTION*
> *If normal rotor removal attempts fail, do not force the puller as the threads may be stripped out of the rotor causing expensive damage. Take it to a dealer or service shop and have them remove it.*

9. Remove the rotor and puller.

10. If necessary, remove the Woodruff key (**Figure 10**) from the crankshaft.

11. Check the Woodruff key and the keyway in the rotor for damage.

12. While the rotor is off, check the stator plate screws (A, **Figure 11**) for tightness.

13. Install by reversing these removal steps. Note the following.

> *CAUTION*
> *Carefully inspect the inside of the rotor (**Figure 12**) for small bolts, washers or other metal "trash" that may have been picked up by the magnets. These small metal bits can cause severe*

damage to the magneto stator plate components.

14. Make sure the Woodruff key is in place on the crankshaft (**Figure 10**). Align the keyway in the rotor with the key when installing the rotor.

15. Install the rotor bolt and washer and tighten the bolt to the torque specification in **Table 3**. To keep the rotor from turning, hold it with the same tool used during removal (**Figure 13**).

Stator Assembly Removal/Installation

1. Remove the magneto rotor as described under *Rotor Removal/Installation* in this chapter.

2. Remove the seat and fuel tank (Chapter Eight).

3. Disconnect the electrical wire connectors from the magneto to the CDI unit. See **Figure 4** (XT350) or **Figure 6** (TT350).

4. Remove the wire harness guide (**Figure 14**).

5. Remove the stator plate screws (A, **Figure 11**) and remove the stator plate (B, **Figure 11**). Carefully pull the electrical harness out along with the rubber grommet from the crankcase and any holding clips on the engine.

6. Install by reversing these removal steps. Note the following.

7. Route the electrical wires following the same path noted prior to removal. Make sure to keep them away from the exhaust system.

Coil Replacement

When replacing an individual coil, it will be necessary to heat the wire connection at the bad coil with a soldering iron before disconnecting the wire. When the solder has melted, pull the wire away from the connection. This step will give you enough wire to work with when resoldering. If the wire is cut at the connection, it could cause the wire to fall short at the connection. During reassembly, rosin core solder must be used—never use acid core solder on electrical connections—to reconnect the wire.

Referring to the letter designations in **Figure 15**, the coils are identified as follows:
   a. Pickup coil (A).
   b. Lighting coil No. 1 (B).
   c. Lighting coil No. 2 (C).
   d. Source coil (D).

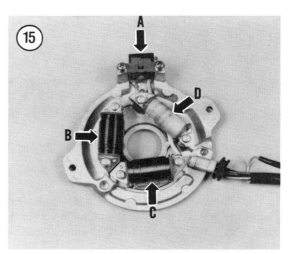

1. Remove the stator assembly as described under *Stator Removal/Installation* in this chapter.
2. Remove the screws securing the coils to the stator plate.
3. Carefully unsolder the wire from the bad coil.
4. Resolder the new coil to the wire.
5. Install by reversing these removal steps.
6. Make sure all electrical connections are tight and free from corrosion. This is absolutely necessary with electronic ignition systems.

VOLTAGE REGULATOR/RECTIFIER (XT350)

Removal/Installation

1. Remove the seat and fuel tank (Chapter Eight).
2. Remove the left-hand side cover and disconnect the battery negative lead (**Figure 3**).
3. Disconnect the electrical connector from the regulator/rectifier and remove the unit (**Figure 16**).
4. Install by reversing these removal steps. Make sure all electrical connections are clean and tight.

Testing

Yamaha does not provide testing information on the voltage regulator/rectifier.

VOLTAGE REGULATOR (TT350)

1. Remove the seat and fuel tank (Chapter Eight).
2. Disconnect the electrical connector from the voltage regulator and remove the unit (**Figure 17**).
3. Install by reversing these removal steps. Make sure all electrical connections are clean and tight.

Testing

Perform the *Troubleshooting* procedures listed under *Lighting System (TT350)* in this chapter. If all test procedure are okay, replace the voltage regulator.

IGNITION SYSTEM (XT350)

The XT350 model is equipped with a capacitor discharge ignition (CDI) system which is a solid-state system that uses no breaker points. Refer to **Figure 18**.

Alternating current from the alternator is rectified to direct current and is used to charge the capacitor. As the piston approaches the firing position, a pulse from the pickup coil is used to trigger the silicone controlled rectifier. The rectifier in turn allows the capacitor to discharge quickly into the primary circuit of the ignition coil, where the voltage is stepped up in the secondary circuit to a value sufficient to fire the spark plug.

An ignition control system is installed on all XT350 models that consists of an ignition control unit, neutral indicator light, neutral switch and a sidestand switch. When the ignition switch and the engine stop switch are ON, the ignition will

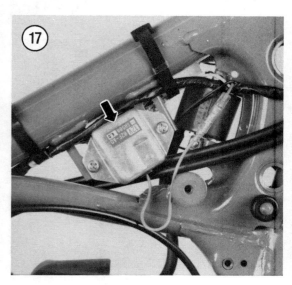

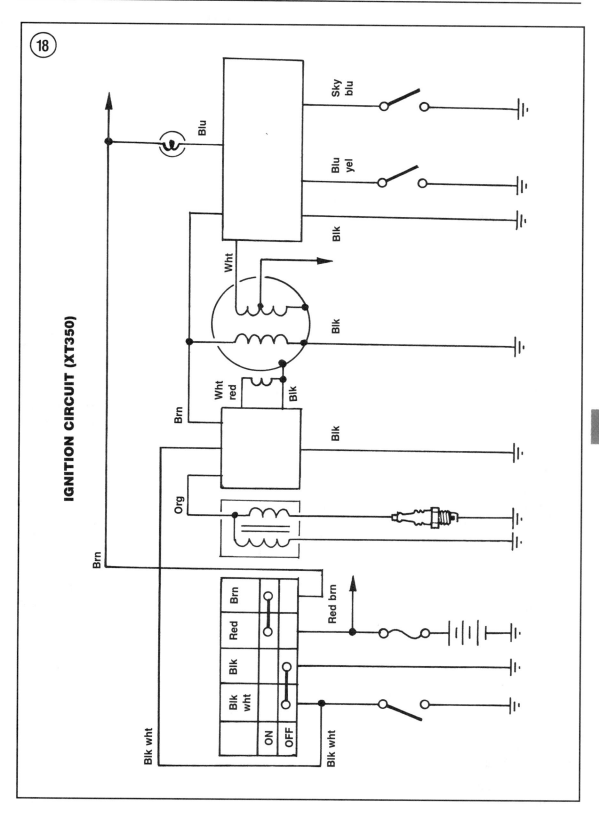

IGNITION CIRCUIT (XT350)

produce a spark for starting only if the following conditions exist:

   a. The sidestand is up (the sidestand switch is ON). The engine will start if the transmission is in gear and the clutch lever is pulled in.

   b. The transmission is in neutral (the neutral switch is ON).

Pre-cautions

Certain measures must be taken to protect the capacitor discharge system. Damage to the semiconductors in the system may occur if the following is not observed.

1. Never connect the battery backwards. If the battery polarity is wrong, damage will occur to the voltage regulator, alternator and ignition unit.

2. Do not disconnect the battery while the engine is running. A voltage surge will occur which will damage the voltage regulator and possibly burn out the lights.

3. Keep all connections between the various units clean and tight. Be sure that the wiring connectors are pushed together firmly.

4. Each solid state unit is mounted on a rubber vibration isolator. Always be sure that the isolators are in place when replacing any units.

Troubleshooting

Problems with the capacitor discharge ignition system are usually limited to the production of a weak spark or no spark at all. Test procedures for troubleshooting the ignition system are found in the chart in **Figure 19**.

Pickup Coil
Removal/Installation

The pickup coil (A, **Figure 15**) is mounted onto the stator plate. Remove the stator plate as described under *Stator Assembly Removal/Installation* in this chapter. If necessary, replace the pickup coil as described under *Alternator* in this chapter.

Source Coil
Removal/Installation

The source coil (D, **Figure 15**) is mounted onto the stator plate. Remove the stator plate as described under *Stator Assembly Removal/Installation* in this chapter. If necessary, replace the source coil as described under *Alternator* in this chapter.

Pickup and Source Coil Testing

It is not necessary to remove the stator plate to perform the following tests.

To get accurate resistance measurements, the stator assembly and coil must be warm (approximately 68° F/20° C).

1. Remove the seat.

2. Disconnect the pickup/source coil connector (**Figure 4**). It has 3 wires (brown, black and white/red). See **Figure 20**.

3A. *Pickup coil resistance check*: Use an ohmmeter set at R × 100 and check resistance between the white/red and black wires. See **Figure 20**. If there is continuity (specified resistance listed in **Table 2**), the coil is good. If there is no continuity or the resistance is much less or more than specified, the coil is bad and must be replaced.

3B. *Source coil resistance check*: Use an ohmmeter set at R × 100 and check resistance between the brown and black wires. See **Figure 20**. If there is continuity (specified resistance listed in **Table 2**) the coil is good. If there is no continuity or the resistance is much less or more than specified, the coil is bad and must be replaced.

4. Reconnect the connector and install the seat.

Ignition Control Unit
Removal/Installation

The ignition control unit is mounted underneath the fuel tank on the right-hand side (**Figure 21**).

1. Remove the seat and fuel tank (Chapter Eight).

2. Disconnect the electrical connector from the ignition control unit and remove it (**Figure 21**).

3. Install by reversing these removal steps. Make sure all electrical connections are clean and tight.

Testing

1. Disconnect the brown wire connector at the ignition control unit (**Figure 21**).

2. Remove the spark plug. Then reconnect the spark plug into the plug cap and lay the plug base against the cylinder head to ground it. Position the spark plug so you can see the electrodes.

(19) IGNITION SYSTEM TROUBLESHOOTING
(XT350)

No Spark or Weak Spark

Remove the spark plug from the cylinder head. Reconnect the spark plug into the plug cap. Lay the spark plug on the cylinder head fins to ground it. Turn the ignition switch ON and the engine stop switch to RUN. Kick the engine over and watch for a spark at the tip of the plug.

If there is no spark, inspect the spark plug as described in Chapter Three. Replace the spark plug and retest.

If there is a spark or a weak spark, proceed to the next step.

Use an ohmmeter and check the ignition coil primary and secondary resistance as described in this chapter.

If the resistance is beyond the specified resistance range, replace ignition coil or spark plug cap.

If the ignition coil resistance is okay, proceed to the next step.

9

Use an ohmmeter and check the main switch, engine stop switch and sidestand switch as described in this chapter. Also check the circuit breaker (this chapter) and the battery (Chapter Three).

If any component tested incorrectly, replace it and retest.

If all components test okay, proceed to the next step.

(continued)

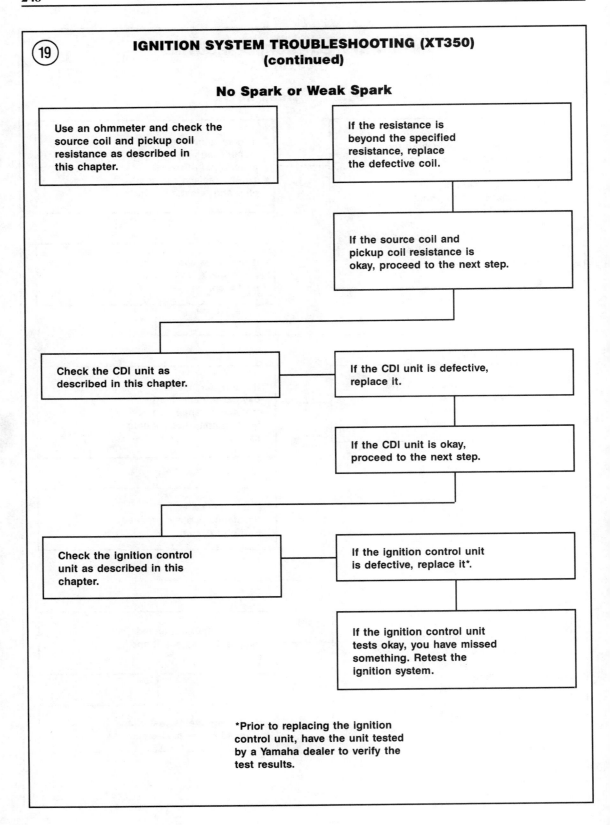

IGNITION SYSTEM TROUBLESHOOTING (XT350)
(continued)

No Spark or Weak Spark

Use an ohmmeter and check the source coil and pickup coil resistance as described in this chapter.

If the resistance is beyond the specified resistance, replace the defective coil.

If the source coil and pickup coil resistance is okay, proceed to the next step.

Check the CDI unit as described in this chapter.

If the CDI unit is defective, replace it.

If the CDI unit is okay, proceed to the next step.

Check the ignition control unit as described in this chapter.

If the ignition control unit is defective, replace it*.

If the ignition control unit tests okay, you have missed something. Retest the ignition system.

*Prior to replacing the ignition control unit, have the unit tested by a Yamaha dealer to verify the test results.

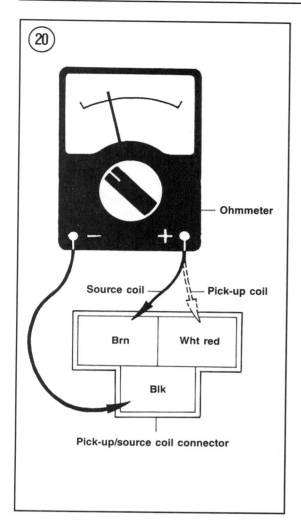

Ohmmeter

Source coil — Pick-up coil

| Brn | Wht red |

Blk

Pick-up/source coil connector

3. Turn the ignition switch and the engine stop switch to ON.

4. Turn the engine over with the kickstarter. A fat blue spark should be evident across the spark plug electrodes.

5. If the spark is good, the ignition control unit is okay.

6. If the spark is not good, check the ignition control unit electrical connectors for dirty or damaged wiring. If these are okay, the ignition control unit is damaged; replace it.

CDI Unit
Removal/Installation

1. Remove the seat.

2. Disconnect the electrical connectors from the CDI unit and remove it. See **Figure 22**.

3. Install by reversing these removal steps. Before connecting the electrical wire connectors at the CDI unit, make sure the connectors are clean of any dirt or moisture.

Testing

The CDI unit should be tested by a Yamaha mechanic familiar with capacitor discharge ignition testing. Improper testing of a good unit can damage it.

9

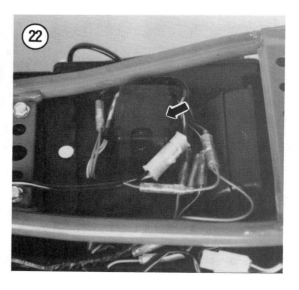

IGNITION SYSTEM
(TT350)

The TT350 model is equipped with a capacitor discharge ignition (CDI) system which is a solid-state system that uses no breaker points. Refer to **Figure 23**.

Alternating current from the alternator is rectified to direct current and is used to charge the capacitor. As the piston approaches the firing position, a pulse from the pickup coil is used to trigger the silicone controlled rectifier. The rectifier in turn allows the capacitor to discharge quickly into the primary circuit of the ignition coil, where the voltage is stepped up in the secondary circuit to a value sufficient to fire the spark plug.

Pre-cautions

Certain measures must be taken to protect the capacitor discharge system. Instantaneous damage to the semiconductors in the system will occur if the following is not observed.
1. Never disconnect any of the electrical connections while the engine is running.
2. Keep all connections between the various units clean and tight. Be sure that the wiring connectors are pushed together firmly to help keep out moisture.
3. Each solid-state unit is mounted on a rubber vibration isolator. Always be sure that the isolators are in place when replacing any units.

Troubleshooting

Problems with the capacitor discharge ignition system are usually limited to the production of a weak spark or no spark at all. Test procedures for troubleshooting the ignition system are found in the chart in **Figure 24**.

Pickup Coil
Removal/Installation

The pickup coil (A, **Figure 15**) is mounted onto the stator plate. Remove the stator plate as described under *Stator Assembly Removal/ Installation* in this chapter. If necessary, replace the pickup coil as described under *Alternator* in this chapter.

Source Coil
Removal/Installation

The source coil (D, **Figure 15**) is mounted onto the stator plate. Remove the stator plate as described under *Stator Assembly Removal/ Installation* in this chapter. If necessary, replace the source coil as described under *Alternator* in this chapter.

Pickup and Source Coil Testing

It is not necessary to remove the stator plate to perform the following tests.

To get accurate resistance measurements, the stator assembly and coil must be warm (68° F/20° C).
1. Remove the seat and fuel tank.
2. Disconnect the pickup/source coil connector (**Figure 6**). It has 3 wires (brown, black and white/red). See **Figure 20**.
3A. *Pickup coil resistance check*: Use an ohmmeter set at R × 100 and check resistance between the white/red and black wires. See **Figure 20**. If there is continuity (specified resistance listed in **Table 2**), the coil is good. If there is no

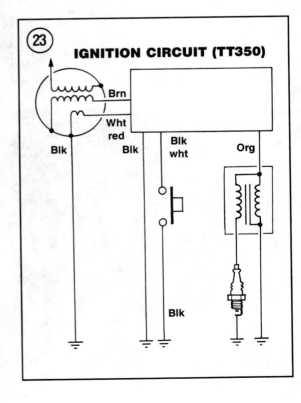

(24)

IGNITION SYSTEM TROUBLESHOOTING
(TT350)

No Spark or Weak Spark

Remove the spark plug from the cylinder head. Reconnect the spark plug into the plug cap. Lay the spark plug on the cylinder head fins to ground it. Make sure the engine stop switch is not depressed. Kick the engine over and watch for a spark at the tip of the plug.

If there is no spark, inspect the spark plug as described in Chapter Three. Replace the plug and retest.

If there is a spark or weak spark, proceed to the next step.

Use an ohmmeter and check the ignition coil primary and secondary resistance as described in this chapter.

If the resistance is beyond the specified resistance range, replace ignition coil or spark plug cap.

If the ignition coil resistance is okay, proceed to the next step.

Replace the engine stop switch if defective.

Use an ohmmeter and check the engine stop switch as described in this chapter.

If the engine stop switch is okay, proceed to the next step.

9

(continued)

continuity or the resistance is much less or more than specified, the coil is bad and must be replaced.

3B. *Source coil resistance check*: Use an ohmmeter set at R × 100 and check resistance between the brown and black wires. See **Figure 20**. If there is continuity (specified resistance listed in **Table 2**), the coil is good. If there is no continuity or the resistance is much less or more than specified, the coil is bad and must be replaced.

4. Reconnect the connector and install the fuel tank and seat.

CDI Unit
Removal/Installation

1. Remove the seat and fuel tank (Chapter Eight).
2. Disconnect the electrical connectors from the CDI unit and remove it. See **Figure 25**.
3. Install by reversing these removal steps. Before connecting the electrical wire connectors at the CDI unit, make sure the connectors are clean of any dirt or moisture.

Testing

The CDI unit should be tested by a Yamaha mechanic familiar with capacitor discharge ignition testing. Improper testing of a good unit can damage it.

IGNITION COIL

Removal/Installation

1. *XT350*: Remove the left-hand side cover and disconnect the battery negative lead from the battery (**Figure 3**).
2. Remove the fuel tank as described in Chapter Eight.
3. Disconnect the spark plug lead and the coil primary electrical wires at the electrical connector.
4. Remove the screws securing the ignition coil and remove the coil from the frame. See **Figure 26** (XT350) or **Figure 27** (TT350).
5. Install by reversing these removal steps. Make sure to correctly connect the primary electrical wires to the coil and the spark plug lead to the spark plug. In addition, make sure the ground wire is attached correctly.

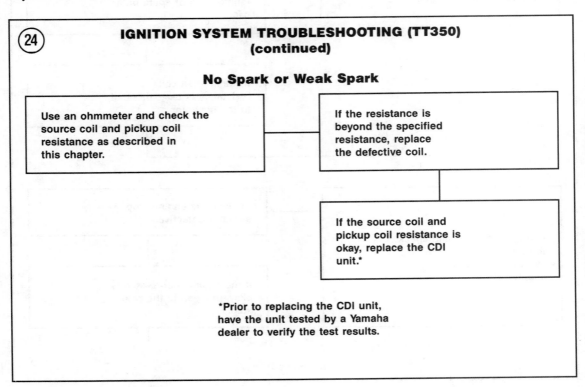

(24) **IGNITION SYSTEM TROUBLESHOOTING (TT350)**
(continued)

No Spark or Weak Spark

Use an ohmmeter and check the source coil and pickup coil resistance as described in this chapter.

If the resistance is beyond the specified resistance, replace the defective coil.

If the source coil and pickup coil resistance is okay, replace the CDI unit.*

*Prior to replacing the CDI unit, have the unit tested by a Yamaha dealer to verify the test results.

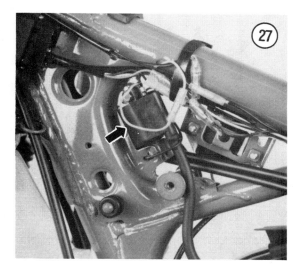

Testing

The ignition coil is a form of transformer which develops the high voltage required to jump the spark plug gap. The only maintenance required is that of keeping the electrical connections clean and tight and occasionally checking to see that the coils are mounted securely.

If the coil condition is doubtful, there are several checks which may be made. Disconnect all ignition coil wires before testing.

NOTE
In order to get accurate resistance measurements, the coil must be warm (approximately 60° F/20° C).

1. Measure the coil primary resistance using an ohmmeter set at R × 1. Measure between the primary terminal (orange wire) and ground (**Figure 28**). Resistance is specified in **Table 2**.
2. Measure the secondary resistance using an ohmmeter set at R × 100. Measure between the secondary lead (spark plug lead) and the orange coil wire (**Figure 28**). Resistance is specified in **Table 2**.
3. Replace the coil if the spark plug lead shows visible damage or if it does not test within the specifications in Step 1 or Step 2.

SPARK PLUG

The spark plug recommended by the factory is usually the most suitable for your machine. If riding conditions are mild, it may be advisable to go to a spark plug one step hotter than normal. Unusually severe riding conditions may require slightly colder plugs. See Chapter Two and Chapter Three for details.

LIGHTING SYSTEM
(XT350)

The lighting system consists of a headlight, taillight, turn signals and indicator bulbs.

Always use the correct wattage bulb. A larger wattage bulb will give a dim light and a smaller wattage bulb will burn out prematurely. **Table 4** lists bulb sizes.

9

Headlight Bulb Replacement

1. Remove the screw securing the headlight cover
(A, **Figure 29**) and remove the cover.
2. Remove the bolts securing the headlight housing
(**Figure 30**) and remove it. Disconnect the
connector at the bulb.
3. Remove the rubber cover (**Figure 31**). Then turn
the bulb holder counterclockwise and remove it.
Remove the bulb from the socket. Replace with a
new bulb.

> *CAUTION*
> *Do not touch the bulb glass with your*
> *fingers because oil on your skin will*
> *transfer to the glass. Any traces of oil*
> *on the quartz halogen bulb will*
> *drastically reduce the life of the bulb.*
> *Clean any traces of oil from the bulb*
> *with a cloth moistened in alcohol or*
> *lacquer thinner.*

4. Install by reversing these removal steps.

Headlight Beam Adjustment

The headlight beam can be set for vertical and
horizontal adjustments.
1. Park the bike on level ground. Block the
kickstand to level the bike.
2. *Horizontal adjustment*: Turn the adjusting
screw (B, **Figure 29**) clockwise to adjust the beam
to the right. Turn the adjusting screw
counterclockwise to adjust the beam to the left.
3. *Vertical adjustment*: Turn the adjusting screw
(C, **Figure 29**) clockwise to raise the beam. Turn
the adjusting screw counterclockwise to lower the
beam.

Taillight Replacement

Remove the screws securing the lens and remove
the lens. See **Figure 32**. Wash the lens with a mild
detergent and wipe dry.

Inspect the lens gasket and replace it if damaged
or deteriorated.

Turn the bulb counterclockwise and remove it.
See **Figure 33**. Reverse to install. When installing
the lens, do not overtighten the screws as the lens
may crack.

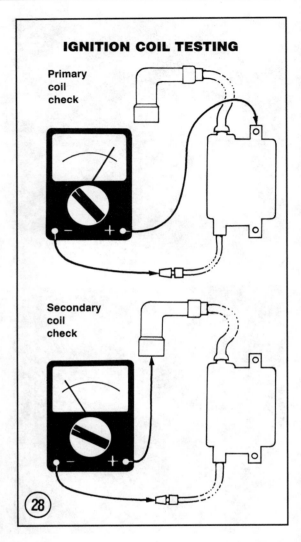

IGNITION COIL TESTING

Primary coil check

Secondary coil check

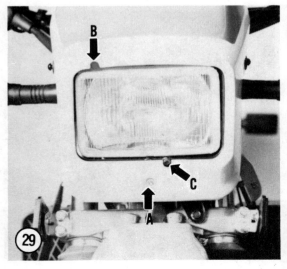

Turn Signal Light Replacement

Remove the screws securing the lens (**Figure 34**) and remove it. Wash out the inside of the lens with a mild detergent. Replace the bulb (**Figure 35**) and install the lens. Do not overtighten the screws as the lens may crack.

Indicator Bulb Replacement

1. Remove the headlight assembly as described under *Headlight Bulb Replacement* in this chapter.
2. Disconnect the speedometer and tachometer cables at the instrument housings (**Figure 36**).
3. Remove the bolts securing the meter housing and remove them from their mounting position.
4. Remove the cotter pin at the bottom of the meter(s) and remove the bottom housings.
5. Remove and replace the bulb(s).
6. Reverse to install.

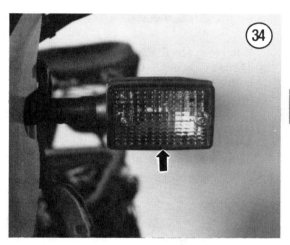

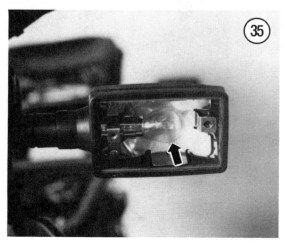

Lighting Voltage Test

If the headlight or high beam indicator lights do not operate correctly, perform the following:

1. Check that the headlight bulb or the high beam indicator bulb is not blown. Refer to *Headlight Bulb Replacement* and *Indicator Bulb Replacement* in this chapter. If the bulbs are okay, leave the headlight housing off and proceed to Step 2.

2. Disconnect the turn signal switch connector. Trace the wire harness from the turn signal switch (**Figure 37**) to the wire junction at the front of the bike.

3. Connect a 0-20 DC voltmeter to the yellow/red terminal on the wire harness connector (**Figure 38**).

4. Start the engine and warm to normal operating temperature.

5. Gradually increase engine speed to approximately 5,000 rpm and note the voltmeter reading. The correct reading is 14-15 volts. Interpret results as follows:

   a. *Voltage correct*: Check the dimmer and ignition switches as described under *Switches* in this chapter.

   b. *Voltage less than 14 volts*: Check the rectifier/regulator assembly for damaged, loose or dirty connectors. See *Voltage Regulator/Rectifier (XT350)* in this chapter. If the connectors and all wiring are okay, the rectifier/regulator unit is damaged. Replace the rectifier/regulator and retest.

   c. *Voltage more than 15 volts*: Perform the *Lighting Coil Resistance Check* in this section.

6. Connect all electrical connectors and install the headlight housing after locating and repairing the electrical problem.

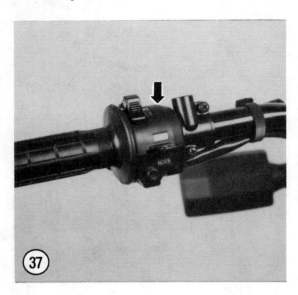

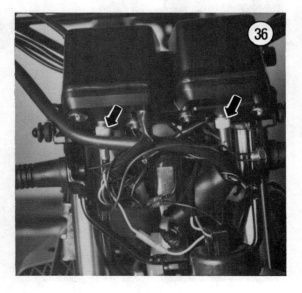

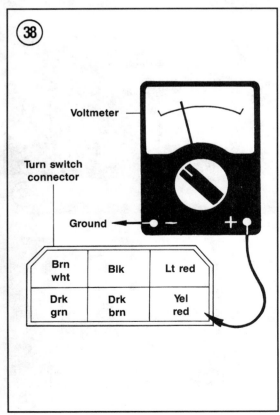

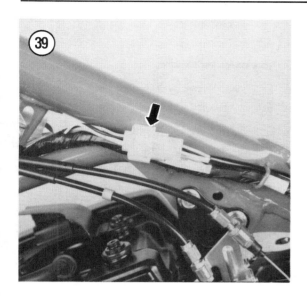

Lighting Coil Resistance Check

1. Remove the seat and fuel tank (Chapter Eight).
2. Disconnect the lighting/charge coil electrical connector (**Figure 39**).
3. Connect an ohmmeter between the yellow and black connector pins (**Figure 40**). Set the ohmmeter on the R × 1 scale. Replace the lighting coil if the reading is not within specifications (**Table 1**). Refer to *Alternator* in this chapter.
4. Remove the ohmmeter and reconnect the electrical connector.
5. Install the fuel tank and seat.

Taillight Troubleshooting

If the taillight does not operate correctly, perform the following voltage test.

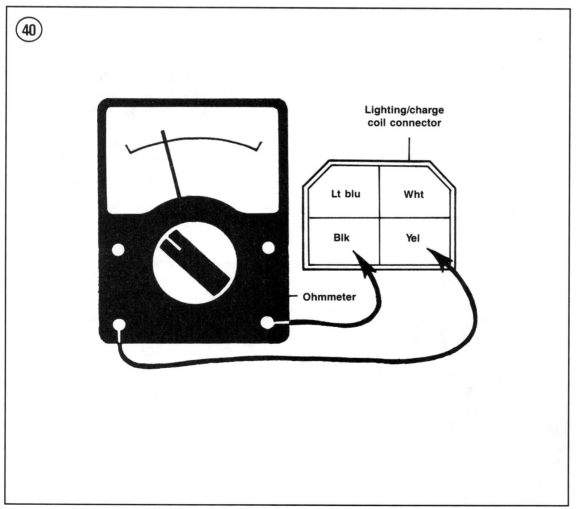

Lighting/charge coil connector

Lt blu | Wht

Blk | Yel

Ohmmeter

9

1. Remove the lens and check the taillight bulb (**Figure 33**). Replace the bulb if blown. If the bulb is okay, reinstall it and perform the following.

2. Remove the left-hand side cover.

3. Disconnect the taillight electrical connector (**Figure 41**).

4. See **Figure 42**. Connect the red voltmeter lead to the brown connector terminal. Connect the black voltmeter lead to a good ground.

5. Turn the ignition switch to ON. The voltmeter should read 12 volts. Turn the ignition switch OFF. Interpret results as follows:

    a. *Voltage correct*: If the bulb is okay, check the wiring from the connector to the bulb socket.

    b. *Less than 12 volts*: Check the ignition switch as described in this chapter. If the switch is okay, check the battery charge as described in Chapter Three.

Flasher Light and Indicator Light Troubleshooting

If the flasher light or its indicator light do not operate correctly, perform the voltage check.

1. Remove the turn signal bulb covers and check the bulb (**Figure 35**). Replace the bulb if blown. Also check that the indicator light bulb in the tachometer housing is not blown. Refer to *Turn Signal Light Replacement* in this section. If the bulbs are okay, leave the headlight housing off and proceed to Step 2.

2. Remove the seat and fuel tank (Chapter Eight).

3. Disconnect the flasher relay connector (A, **Figure 43**) at the relay.

4. See **Figure 44**. Connect the red voltmeter lead to the brown connector terminal. Connect the black voltmeter lead to a good ground.

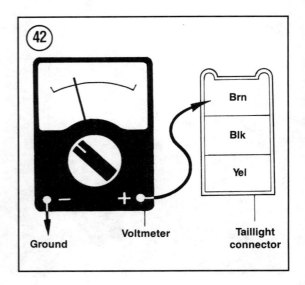

Ground   Voltmeter   Taillight connector

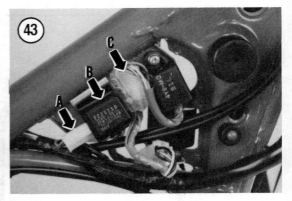

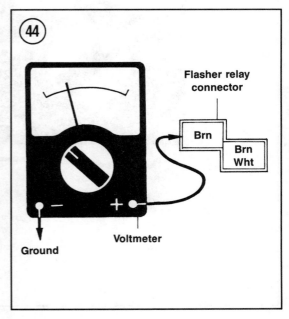

Flasher relay connector

Ground   Voltmeter

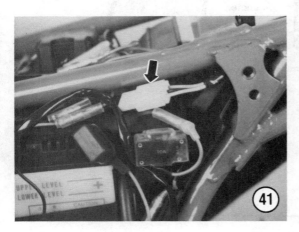

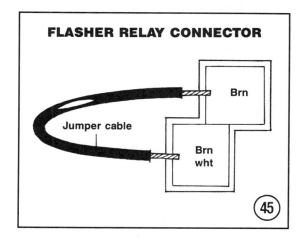

FLASHER RELAY CONNECTOR

Brn

Jumper cable

Brn wht

(45)

(46)

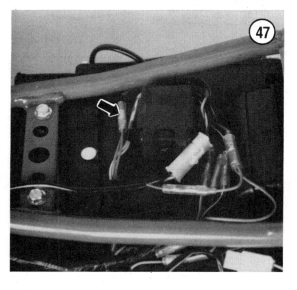

(47)

5. Turn the ignition switch to ON. The voltmeter should read 12 volts. Turn the ignition switch OFF. Interpret results as follows:

    a. *Less than 12 volts*: Check the ignition switch as described in this chapter. If the switch is okay, check the battery charge as described in Chapter Three.

    b. *Voltage correct*: Perform Step 6.

6. If the voltage tested correctly in Step 5, perform the following:

    a. Connect a jumper wire across the brown to brown/white flasher relay connector terminals (**Figure 45**).

    b. Turn the ignition switch to ON. Then turn the turn signal switch on the left-hand handlebar to "L" or "R." The turn signal lights should operate correctly.

    c. If the turn signal operated correctly in sub-step b, check all connections in the flasher and indicator light circuit. If these are okay, replace the flasher relay (B, **Figure 43**). If the turn signal did not operate correctly in sub-step b, replace the turn signal switch as described under *Switches* in this chapter.

Flasher Relay Replacement

1. Remove the fuel tank as described in Chapter Eight.

2. See **Figure 43**. Disconnect the connector (A) at the flasher relay on the right-hand side of the bike. Pull the relay (B) out of its mounting position and replace it.

3. Reverse to install.

Brake Light Troubleshooting

If the brake light does not operate correctly, perform the following.

1. Remove the lens and check the taillight bulb (**Figure 33**). Replace the bulb if blown. If the bulb is okay, reinstall it and perform the following.

2. Remove the seat if you are going to test the rear brake light switch.

3. Disconnect the front (**Figure 46**) or rear (**Figure 47**) brake light switch electrical connectors.

9

4. Connect a jumper cable between the brake light switch connectors. See **Figure 48** (front) or **Figure 49** (rear).

5. Turn the ignition switch to ON and operate the front or rear brake. The front or rear brake light should operate. Interpret results as follows:
   a. *Brake light on*: Check all wiring and connectors in the brake light circuit. If these are okay, replace the brake switch as described under *Switches* in this chapter.
   b. *Brake light off*: Check the ignition switch as described in this chapter. If the switch is okay, check the battery charge as described in Chapter Three.

6. Remove the jumper cable and reconnect the brake light switch connectors.

Neutral Indicator Light Troubleshooting

If the neutral indicator light in the tachometer housing does not come on when the ignition switch is turned to ON and the transmission is in neutral, perform the following voltage test.

1. Check that the neutral indicator light bulb in the tachometer housing is not blown. Refer to *Indicator Bulb Replacement* in this chapter. If the bulb is okay, proceed to Step 2.

2. Remove the fuel tank (Chapter Eight).

3. Disconnect the ignition control unit electrical connector (C, **Figure 43**).

4. See **Figure 50**. Connect the red voltmeter lead to the blue connector terminal. Connect the black voltmeter lead to a good ground.

5. Turn the ignition switch to ON. The voltmeter should read 12 volts. Turn the ignition switch OFF. Interpret results as follows:
   a. *Less than 12 volts*: Check the ignition switch as described in this chapter. If the switch is okay, check the battery charge as described in Chapter Three.
   b. *Voltage correct*: Proceed to Step 6.

6. Connect a jumper wire across the blue to light blue ignition control unit electrical connector (**Figure 51**). Turn the ignition switch to ON and shift the transmission into NEUTRAL. Observe the neutral indicator light. Interpret results as follows:
   a. *Neutral light on*: Replace the ignition control unit as described in this chapter.

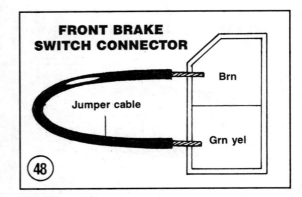

FRONT BRAKE SWITCH CONNECTOR

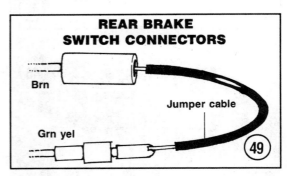

REAR BRAKE SWITCH CONNECTORS

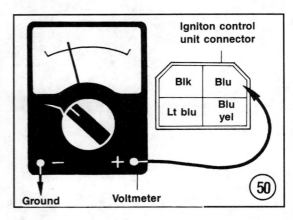

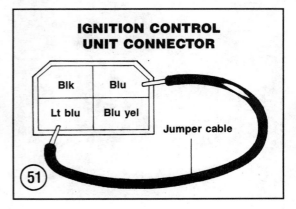

IGNITION CONTROL UNIT CONNECTOR

b. *Neutral light off*: Check all wiring in the neutral light circuit. If the wiring is okay, replace the neutral switch as described under *Switches* in this chapter.

LIGHTING SYSTEM
(TT350)

The TT350 lighting circuit is shown in **Figure 52**. When replacing bulbs, always use the correct wattage bulb. A larger wattage bulb will give a dim light and a small wattage bulb will burn out prematurely. **Table 4** lists bulb sizes.

Troubleshooting

If the headlight or taillight fails to operate properly and you have checked the bulbs and they are okay, follow the procedures listed in the troubleshooting chart in **Figure 53**.

Headlight Bulb Replacement

1. Lift the headlight cover (A, **Figure 54**) up and remove it. Disconnect the connector at the bulb.

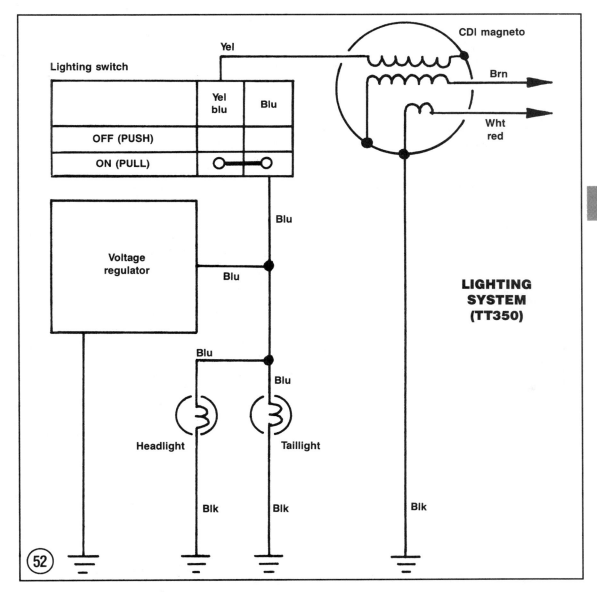

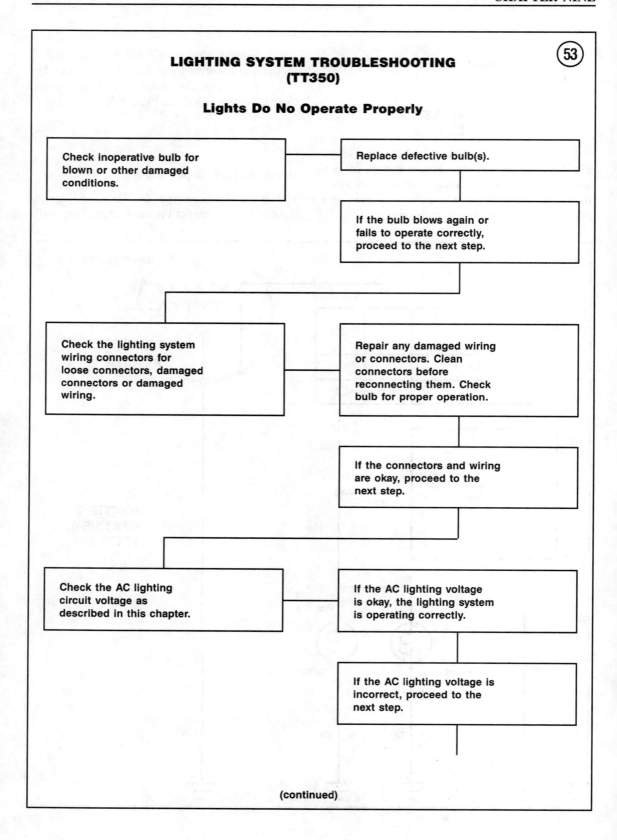

LIGHTING SYSTEM TROUBLESHOOTING
(TT350)

Lights Do No Operate Properly

Check inoperative bulb for blown or other damaged conditions.	Replace defective bulb(s).
	If the bulb blows again or fails to operate correctly, proceed to the next step.
Check the lighting system wiring connectors for loose connectors, damaged connectors or damaged wiring.	Repair any damaged wiring or connectors. Clean connectors before reconnecting them. Check bulb for proper operation.
	If the connectors and wiring are okay, proceed to the next step.
Check the AC lighting circuit voltage as described in this chapter.	If the AC lighting voltage is okay, the lighting system is operating correctly.
	If the AC lighting voltage is incorrect, proceed to the next step.

(continued)

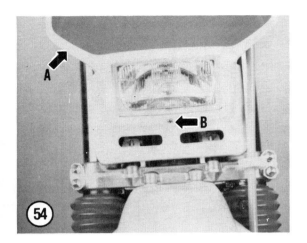

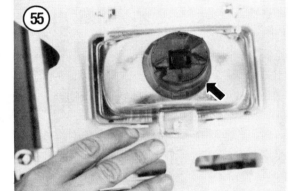

2. Remove the rubber cover (**Figure 55**). Then unhook the bulb holder (**Figure 56**) and remove the bulb. Replace with a new bulb.

CAUTION
Do not touch the bulb glass with your fingers because oil on your skin will transfer to the glass. Any traces of oil on the quartz halogen bulb will drastically reduce the life of the bulb. Clean any traces of oil from the bulb with a cloth moistened in alcohol or lacquer thinner.

3. Install by reversing these removal steps.

Headlight Beam Adjustment

The headlight beam can only be set for vertical adjustment.
1. Park the bike on level ground. Block the kickstand to level the bike.
2. Turn the adjusting screw (B, **Figure 54**) clockwise to raise the beam. Reverse to lower the beam.

LIGHTING SYSTEM TROUBLESHOOTING (TT350)
(continued)

Use an ohmmeter and check the lighting coil resistance as described in this chapter.

If the lighting coil resistance is beyond the specified resistance range, replace the stator assembly.

If the lighting coil resistance is okay, replace the regulator.

Taillight Replacement

Remove the screws securing the lens and remove the lens. See **Figure 57**. Wash the lens with a mild detergent and wipe dry.

Inspect the lens gasket and replace it if damaged or deteriorated.

Turn the bulb counterclockwise and remove it. See **Figure 58**. Reverse to install. When installing the lens, do not overtighten the screws as the lens may crack.

A.C. Lighting Circuit Output Test

1. Remove the headlight housing as described under *Headlight Bulb Replacement* in this section.
2. Connect the red voltmeter lead to the blue headlight connector terminal and the black voltmeter lead to the black headlight connector terminal. See A, **Figure 59**.
3. Switch the voltmeter to the AC20V scale.
4. Start the engine and warm to normal operating temperature.
5. Gradually increase engine speed to 2,500 rpm. At 2,500 rpm, note the voltmeter reading and then turn the engine off. If the voltage is not 11 volts or higher, perform the *Lighting Coil Resistance Check* in this section. If the voltage was 11 volts or higher, the lighting system is operating correctly.

Lighting Coil Resistance Check

1. Remove the seat and fuel tank (Chapter Eight).
2. Disconnect the black and yellow leads at the CDI unit.

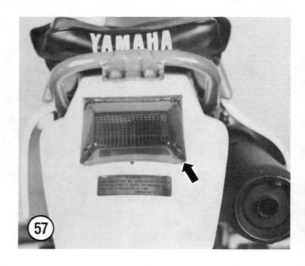

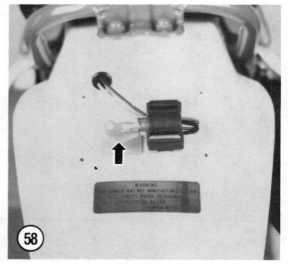

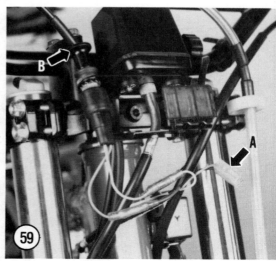

3. Connect an ohmmeter between the yellow and black connector leads. Set the ohmmeter on the R × 1 scale. Replace the lighting coil if the reading is not within specifications (**Table 1**). Refer to *Alternator* in this chapter.

4. Remove the ohmmeter and reconnect the electrical connector.

5. Install the fuel tank and seat.

SWITCHES

Switches can be tested with an ohmmeter (Chapter One) or with a homemade test light

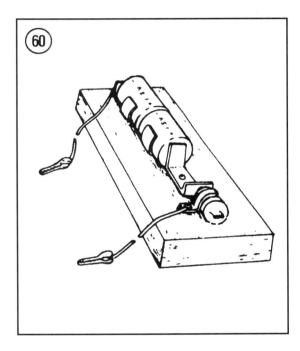

(**Figure 60**). To test a switch, disconnect its electrical connector. Identify its terminals by referring to the continuity diagram in each test procedure. **Figure 61** shows a typical continuity diagram. It tells which terminals should show continuity when the switch is in a given position.

When the switch is in the OFF position, there should be continuity between wire connectors R and E. This is indicated by the line on the continuity diagram. An ohmmeter connected between these wire connectors should indicate no resistance.

When the switch is in the ON position, there should be continuity between wire connectors B, R and E. An ohmmeter connected between these connectors should indicate no resistance.

If the switch doesn't perform correctly, replace it. Refer to the appropriate figure for switch continuity diagrams for your model:

    a. **Figure 62**: XT350 models.

    b. **Figure 63**: TT350 models.

When testing switches, perform the following:

1. *XT350*: Note the following:

    a. First check the circuit breaker as described in this chapter. Reset it if necessary.

    b. Check the battery as described under *Battery* in Chapter Three. Bring the battery to the correct state of charge, if required.

    c. If the switch connectors are not disconnected in the circuit, disconnect the negative cable from the battery.

CAUTION
Do not attempt to start the engine with the battery negative cable disconnected or you will damage the wiring.

    d. When replacing handlebar switch assemblies, make sure the cables are routed correctly so that they are not crimped when the handlebar is turned from side-to-side.

2. When separating 2 connectors, pull on the connector housings and not the wires.

3. After locating a defective circuit, check the connectors to make sure they are clean and properly connected. Check all wires going into a connector housing to make sure each wire is properly positioned and that the wire end is not loose.

SAMPLE SWITCH

SWITCH POSITION	WIRE CONNECTORS		
	B	R	E
OFF		●————●	
ON	●————●	●————●	

SWITCHES (XT350)

MAIN SWITCH

SWITCH POSITION	WIRE COLOR			
	BLK/WHT	BLK	RED	BRN
OFF	●———●			
ON			●———●	

BRAKE SWITCH

BRAKE LEVER OR PEDAL POSITION	WIRE COLOR	
	BRN	GRN/YEL
FREE		
DEPRESS	●———●	

ENGINE STOP SWITCH

SWITCH POSITION	WIRE COLOR	
	BLK/WHT	BLK
OFF	●———●	
RUN		

DIMMER SWITCH

SWITCH POSITION	WIRE COLOR		
	YEL	BLU	GRN
HI	●———●		
LO		●———●	

HORN SWITCH

BUTTON POSITION	WIRE COLOR	
	LT RED	BLK
PUSH	●———●	
OFF		

TURN SWITCH

SWITCH POSITION	WIRE COLOR		
	DRK BRN	BRN/WHT	DRK GRN
L	●———●		
N			
R		●———●	

SIDESTAND SWITCH

SIDESTAND POSITION	WIRE COLOR	
	BLK	BLU/YEL
UP	●———●	
DOWN		

SWITCHES (TT350)

ENGINE STOP SWITCH

SWITCH	WIRE COLOR	
POSITION	BLK WHT	BLK
PUSH	●——————●—	—●

LIGHTING SWITCH

SWITCH	WIRE COLOR	
POSITION	BLU	YEL/RED
OFF (PUSH)		
ON (PULL)	●——————●—	—●

4. To properly connect connectors, push them together until they click into place.

Left Handlebar Switch Replacement (XT350)

1. The left handlebar switch housing (**Figure 64**) is equipped with the following switches:
   a. Dimmer switch.
   b. Turn switch.
   c. Horn button switch.
2. Remove the headlight housing as described under *Headlight Bulb Replacement* under *Lighting System (XT350)* in this chapter.
3. Disconnect the switch connectors (**Figure 65**).
4. Remove the screws holding the switch housings together. Remove the switch (**Figure 64**).
5. Installation is the reverse of these steps.

Engine Stop Switch (XT350)

The engine stop switch is mounted in the right-hand switch housing (**Figure 66**).
1. Remove the headlight housing as described under *Headlight Bulb Replacement* under *Lighting System (XT350)* in this chapter.
2. Disconnect the engine stop switch connectors (**Figure 65**).

9

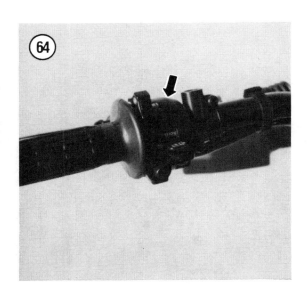

3. Remove the screws holding the switch housings together.

4. Disconnect the throttle cables from the housings. Remove the switch (**Figure 66**).

5. Installation is the reverse of these steps.

6. Adjust the throttle cables as described in Chapter Three.

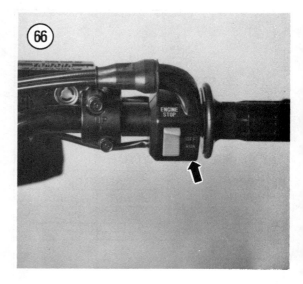

Kill Switch
(TT350)

The kill switch is mounted on the left-hand handlebar (**Figure 67**).

1. Remove the fuel tank as described in Chapter Eight.

2. Disconnect the kill switch connectors at the CDI unit.

3. Remove the screw holding the switch to the handlebar. Remove the switch (**Figure 67**).

4. Reverse to install.

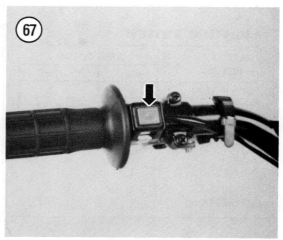

Light Switch
(TT350)

The light switch is mounted beside the speedometer (B, **Figure 59**).

1. Remove the headlight housing as described under *Headlight Bulb Replacement* under *Lighting System (TT350)* in this chapter.

2. Disconnect the electical wires at the light switch (B, **Figure 59**).

3. Remove the switch.

4. Reverse to install.

Ignition switch
(XT350)

The ignition switch (**Figure 68**) is bolted to the upper steering stem between the speedometer and tachometer drive units.

1. Remove the headlight housing as described under *Headlight Bulb Replacement* under *Lighting System (XT350)* in this chapter.

2. Remove the tachometer and speedometer units.

3. Disconnect the ignition switch electrical connectors.

4. Remove the bolts securing the ignition switch to the upper steering stem. Remove the ignition switch.

5. Installation is the reverse of these steps.

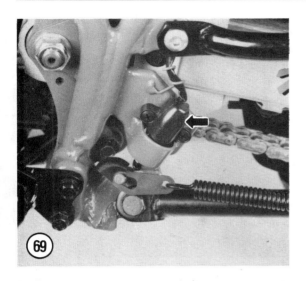

Sidestand Switch
(XT350)

The sidestand switch (**Figure 69**) is mounted on the left-hand side of the bike above the sidestand.
1. Support the bike with a stand other than the sidestand.
2. Remove the seat.
3. Disconnect the sidestand switch electrical connectors underneath the seat.
4. Remove the screws holding the sidestand switch to the frame. Remove the sidestand switch.
5. Installation is the reverse of these steps.

Neutral Switch Replacement
(XT350)

The neutral switch (**Figure 70**) is mounted in the left-hand crankcase near the shift lever. Replace the switch as follows:
1. Remove the shift lever and the left-hand crankcase cover. Lean the right-hand side of the bike against a wall.
2. Place a clean drain pan underneath the neutral switch.
3. Remove the screw and disconnect the wire at the neutral switch.
4. Unscrew the neutral switch (**Figure 70**) and remove it.
5. Reverse to install. Refill the engine oil as required.

9

Front Brake Switch
(XT350)

The front brake switch (**Figure 71**) is mounted on the master cylinder housing.

1. Remove the headlight housing as described under *Headlight Bulb Replacement* under *Lighting System (XT350)* in this chapter.
2. Disconnect the front brake switch electrical connectors (**Figure 65**).
3. Remove the front brake switch (**Figure 71**).
4. Installation is the reverse of these steps.

Rear Brake Switch
(XT350)

The rear brake switch (**Figure 72**) is mounted on the right-hand side of the bike.

1. Remove the seat.
2. Disconnect the rear brake switch electrical connectors underneath the seat.
3. Disconnect the spring at the rear brake switch (**Figure 72**).
4. Loosen the rear brake switch locknut and remove the switch.
5. Installation is the reverse of these steps. Adjust the brake switch as described in Chapter Three.

HORN
(XT350)

Removal/Installation

1. Remove the right-hand engine air scoop.
2. Disconnect the electrical connectors at the horn (**Figure 73**).
3. Remove the bolt securing the horn (**Figure 73**) frame. Remove the horn.
4. Installation is the reverse of these steps.

Testing

If the horn does not sound when the horn button is depressed, perform the following.

1. Check the horn button switch as described under *Switches* in this chapter. If the horn button switch is okay, perform Step 2.
2. Perform a voltage check as follows:
   a. Connect a red voltmeter lead to the brown wire at the horn (**Figure 73**). Connect the black voltmeter lead to a good engine ground.

73

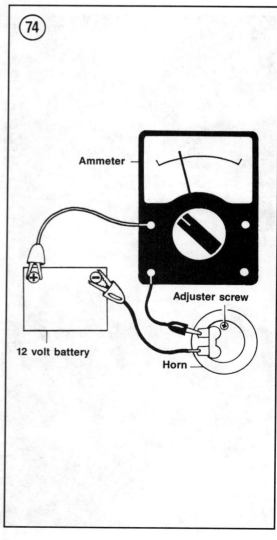

74

Ammeter

Adjuster screw

12 volt battery

Horn

b. Turn the ignition switch to ON. Depress the horn button and read the voltmeter. It should show 12 volts. Turn the ignition switch to OFF.

3. Disconnect the pink and brown wires at the horn (**Figure 73**). Connect an ohmmeter red lead to the horn brown lead. Connect the ohmmeter black lead to the horn pink lead. Set the ohmmeter on the R x 1 scale. It should show a resistance of 1.23-1.25 ohms. If the resistance value is not as specified, replace the horn.

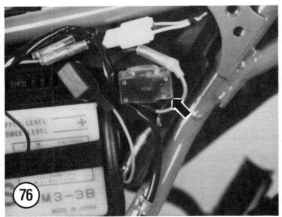

Horn Adjustment

If the horn sound volume has dropped, adjust it as follows.

1. Disconnect the electrical connectors at the horn (**Figure 73**).

2. Connect a battery and an ammeter to the horn, as shown in **Figure 74**. Leave the negative cable from the battery to the horn disconnected until you are ready to adjust the horn.

3. Connect the negative cable from the battery to the horn terminal. When the horn blows, turn the horn adjuster screw until the ammeter reads 2.5 amps.

4. Remove all test leads and equipment and reconnect the horn electrical connectors. Test the horn once again.

CONDENSER
(1986-1995 XT350)

Disconnect the leads at the condenser and remove it (**Figure 75**). Reverse to install.

CIRCUIT BREAKER
(XT350)

A 10 amp circuit breaker is mounted behind the left-hand side cover (**Figure 76**). If a short circuit should occur in the electrical system, the breaker will shut off current. If the circuit breaker shuts the current off, turn off the ignition switch. Then wait 30 seconds and push in the breaker knob. If the circuit breaker shuts off current again, there is a problem in the electrical system. Refer to troubleshooting in Chapter Two and to the procedures listed in this chapter.

WIRING DIAGRAMS

Wiring diagrams for all models are located at the end of this book.

Tables are on the following page.

Table 1 CHARGING SYSTEM TEST SPECIFICATIONS

Item	Specification
Charging system (XT350)	
Type	Flywheel magneto
Battery	12 volts; 3 amp hours
Charging current (1985-1995)	
Day	1.6 A or more @ 3,000 rpm
Night	3.9 A or more @ 3,000 rpm
Charging current (1996-on)	
Day	1.7 A or more @ 3,000 rpm
Night	3.1 A or more @ 8,000 rpm
Charging coil resistance	
Black-to-white connectors	0.41-0.51 ohm*
Lighting coil resistance	
Black-to-yellow connectors	0.29-0.49 ohm*
Charging system (TT350)	
Type	AC magneto
Lighting voltage (minimum)	
1985-1995	6 volts or more @ 2,500 rpm
1996-on	8.7 volts or more @ 1,600 rpm
Charging current (minimum)	
Day	1.2 A or more @ 3,000 rpm
Night	1.0 A or more @ 3,000 rpm
Lighting coil resistance	
Yellow-to-black connectors	0.43-0.53 ohms*

*All tests should be made at an ambient temperature of 68° F (20° C).

Table 2 IGNITION SYSTEM TEST SPECIFICATIONS

Item	Specification
Pickup coil resistance	
Black-to-white/red connectors	199-243 ohms*
Source coil resistance	
Black-to-brown connectors	368-450 ohms*
Ignition coil (1985-1995)	
Primary resistance	0.67-0.91 ohm
Secondary resistance	5.02-6.79 K ohms
Ignition coil (1996-on)	
Primary resistance	0.26-0.36 ohm
Secondary resistance	3.5-4.7 ohms

* All tests should be made at an ambient temperature of 68° F (20° C).

Table 3 TIGHTENING TORQUES

	N•m	ft.-lb.
Rotor bolt	60	43
Crankcase cover screws	7	5.1
Stator plate screws	7	5.1

Table 4 REPLACEMENT BULBS

	TT350	XT350
Headlight	55W (6V)	45W/40W (12V)
Taillight	8W (6V)	—
Taillight/brake light	—	27W/8W (12V)
Flasher light	—	27W (12V)
License plate light	—	8W (12V)
Meter lights	—	3.4W (12V)

FRONT SUSPENSION AND STEERING

This chapter describes repair and maintenance on the front wheel, forks, and steering components.

Front suspension specifications are listed in **Table 1** (XT350) and **Table 2** (TT350). Tightening torques are listed in **Table 3** (XT350) and **Table 4** (TT350). **Tables 1-4** are at the end of the chapter.

Removal/Installation (XT350)

1. Support the motorcycle with the front wheel off the ground.
2. Remove the brake disc cover (**Figure 1**).
3. Disconnect the speedometer cable (A, **Figure 2**) at the front wheel.
4. Remove the front axle nut cotter pin. Then loosen and remove the front axle nut (B, **Figure 2**) and washer (**Figure 3**).
5. Slide the axle out from the right-hand side (**Figure 4**). Don't loose the washer installed on the right-hand side of the axle (**Figure 5**).

> *NOTE*
> *After removing the front wheel in Step 6, insert a piece of wood or hose in the caliper between the brake pads. That*

way, if the brake lever is accidently squeezed, the piston will not be forced out of the brake caliper cylinder. If the brake lever is squeezed and the piston comes out, the caliper might have to be disassembled to reseat the piston and the system will have to be bled.

6. Pull the wheel forward and remove it.
7. Remove the speedometer drive unit (A, **Figure 6**) from the left-hand side of the wheel.

10

8. Remove the spacer and dust cover (**Figure 7**) from the right-hand side of the wheel.

9. Install the axle spacers, washers and axle nut (**Figure 8**) on the axle to prevent their loss when servicing the wheel.

10. To install the front wheel, reverse the removal steps. Note the following:

   a. Clean the axle and axle spacers in solvent and thoroughly dry. Make sure all axle contact surfaces are clean and free of dirt and old grease prior to installation. If these surfaces are not cleaned, the axle may be difficult to remove.

   b. Apply a light coat of grease to the axle, bearings and grease seals.

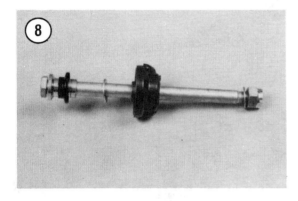

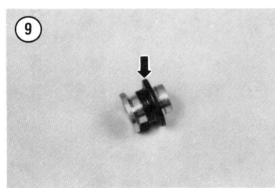

c. Make sure the dust cover is installed on the right-hand axle spacer as shown in **Figure 9**.

d. See **Figure 10**. When installing the speedometer housing, align the tabs in the speedometer housing (A) with the slots in the front hub (B).

e. Carefully insert the disc between the brake pads when installing the wheel.

f. When installing the front wheel, make sure to align the slot in the speedometer drive unit (B, **Figure 6**) with the tab on the left-hand fork tube.

g. Install the axle nut (**Figure 11**). Tighten the axle nut to the torque specification in **Table 3**. Secure the axle nut with a new cotter pin. Bend the end of the cotter pin over to lock it.

h. After the wheel is completely installed, rotate the front wheel and apply the brake. Do this a couple of times to make sure the front wheel and brake are operating correctly.

Removal/Installation (TT350)

1. Support the motorcycle with the front wheel off the ground.

2. Remove the brake disc cover (**Figure 12**).

3. Disconnect the speedometer cable (A, **Figure 13**) at the front wheel.

4. Loosen the front axle holder nuts (B, **Figure 13**).

5. Loosen the axle (C, **Figure 13**). Remove the axle from the right-hand side.

10

NOTE
After removing the front wheel in Step 6, insert a piece of wood or hose in the caliper between the brake pads. That way, if the brake lever is accidently squeezed, the pistons will not be forced out of the brake caliper cylinders. If the brake lever is squeezed and the pistons comes out, the caliper might have to be disassembled to reseat the pistons and the system will have to be bled.

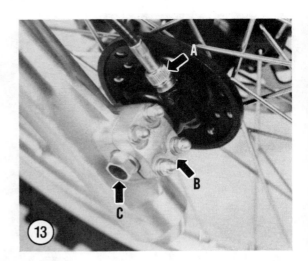

6. Pull the wheel forward and remove it.
7. Remove the spacer and dust cover (**Figure 14**) from the left-hand side.
8. Remove the speedometer drive unit (A, **Figure 15**) from the right-hand side of the wheel.
9. Install the axle spacers, washers and axle nut (**Figure 8**) on the axle to prevent their loss when servicing the wheel.
10. To install the front wheel, reverse the removal steps. Note the following:
   a. Clean the axle and axle spacers in solvent and thoroughly dry. Make sure all axle contact surfaces are clean and free of dirt and old grease prior to installation. If these surfaces are not cleaned, the axle may be difficult to remove.
   b. Apply a light coat of grease to the axle, bearings and grease seals.

c. Make sure the dust cover is installed on the left-hand axle spacer as shown in **Figure 9**.

d. See **Figure 16**. When installing the speedometer housing, align the tabs in the speedometer housing (A) with the slots in the front hub (B).

e. Carefully insert the disc between the brake pads when installing the wheel.

f. When installing the front wheel, make sure to align the slot in the speedometer drive unit (B, **Figure 15**) with the tab on the left-hand fork tube (**Figure 17**).

g. Install the axle (C, **Figure 13**) and tighten it to the torque specification in **Table 4**. Tighten the axle holder nuts to the torque specification in **Table 4**.

h. After the wheel is completely installed, rotate the front wheel and apply the brake. Do this a couple of times to make sure the front wheel and brake are operating correctly.

Inspection

Spokes loosen with use and should be checked periodically. The "tuning fork" method for checking spoke tightness is simple and works well. Tap each spoke with a spoke wrench or the shank of a screwdriver and listen for a tone. A tightened spoke will emit a clear, ringing tone, and a loose spoke will sound flat. All the spokes in a correctly tightened wheel will emit tones of similar pitch but not necessarily the same precise tone.

Bent, stripped or broken spokes should be replaced as soon as they are detected, as they can cause the destruction of an expensive hub. Unscrew the nipple from the spoke and depress the nipple into the rim far enough to free the end of the spoke, taking care not to push the nipple all the way in. Remove the damaged spoke from the hub and use it to match a new spoke of identical length. If necessary, trim the new spoke to match the original and dress the end of the thread with a thread die. Install the new spoke in the hub and screw on the nipple; tighten it until the spoke's tone is similar to the tone of the other spokes in the wheel. Periodically check the new spoke; it will stretch and must be retightened several times before it takes its final set.

Wheel rim runout is the amount of "wobble" a wheel shows as it rotates. You can check runout with the wheels on the bike by simply supporting the wheel off the ground and turning the wheel slowly while you hold a pointer solidly against a fork leg. Just make sure any wobble you observe isn't caused by your own hand.

Off the motorcycle, runout can be checked with the wheel installed on a truing stand (**Figure 18**).

NOTE
A discarded rear swing arm mounted in a vise makes an ideal wheel truing stand.

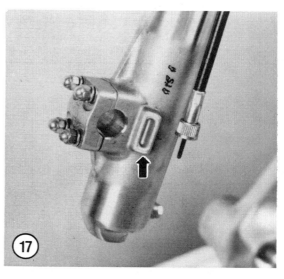

The maximum allowable lateral (side-to-side) and radial (up and down) play is listed in **Table 1** (XT350) and **Table 2** (TT350). Tighten or replace any bent or loose spokes. Always use the correct size spoke wrench (**Figure 19**) or you may damage the spoke nipple.

1. Draw the high point of the rim toward the centerline of the wheel by loosening the spokes in the area of the high point and on the same side as the high point, and tightening the spokes on the side opposite the high point. See **Figure 20**.

2. Rotate the wheel and check runout. Continue adjusting until the runout is within specification. Be patient and thorough, adjusting the position of the rim a little at a time. If you loosen 2 spokes at the high point 1/2 turn, loosen the adjacent spokes 1/4 turn. Tighten the spokes on the opposite side in equivalent amounts.

3. Visually check the front axle surface for cracks, deep scoring or excessive wear. Check axle runout with a set of V-blocks and dial indicator (**Figure 21**). The maximum allowable bend is 0.25 mm (0.01 in.). If you do not have access to the special tools, roll the axle on a flat surface and visually check the runout. Replace a bent axle. Do not attempt to straighten it.

4. Check the speedometer drive assembly (**Figure 22**) for damage.

5. Check the oil seal (**Figure 23**) for signs of wear, cracks or other damage. A damaged oil seal will allow bearing contamination. Replace the oil seal as described under *Front Hub* in this chapter.

6. Turn the inner bearing race (**Figure 24**) by hand and check for any sign of roughness or damage. Replace the bearings (as a set) as described under *Front Hub* in this chapter.

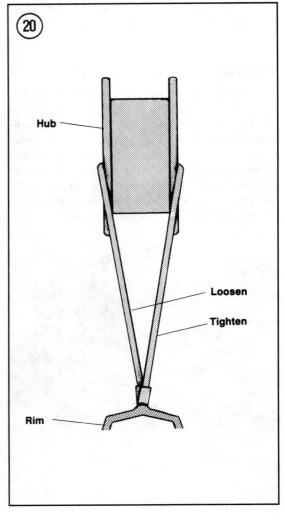

Hub

Loosen

Tighten

Rim

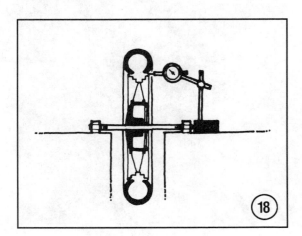

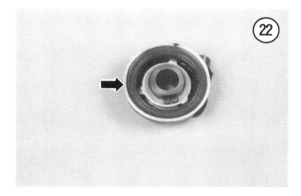

7. Check the front brake disc (**Figure 25**) bolts or nuts for tightness. If loose, tighten the fasteners securely. Check the disc surface for oil residue. Clean with lacquer thinner before reinstalling the front wheel.

FRONT HUB

Refer to **Figure 26** (XT350) or **Figure 27** (TT350) for this procedure.

Disassembly/Reassembly

Do not remove bearings for periodic inspection as bearing removal normally damages the first bearing removed. Turn the inner bearing race (**Figure 24**) by hand and check for any signs of roughness or damage. Replace the bearings as a set.

1. Remove the front wheel as described under *Front Wheel Removal* in this chapter for your model.

2. Remove the oil seal by carefully prying it out of the hub with a long screwdriver. Lift the screwdriver and work it around the seal every few degrees until it pops out of the hub. Prop a piece of wood or rag underneath the screwdriver to prevent from damaging the hub. See **Figure 28**.

3. Remove the left- and right-hand bearings (**Figure 24**) and spacer. To remove them, insert

10

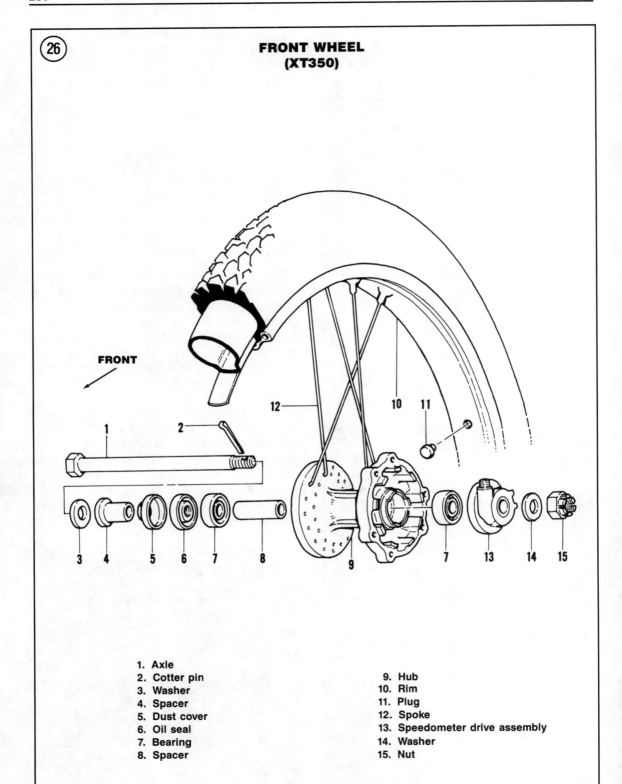

**FRONT WHEEL
(XT350)**

㉖

FRONT

1. Axle
2. Cotter pin
3. Washer
4. Spacer
5. Dust cover
6. Oil seal
7. Bearing
8. Spacer

9. Hub
10. Rim
11. Plug
12. Spoke
13. Speedometer drive assembly
14. Washer
15. Nut

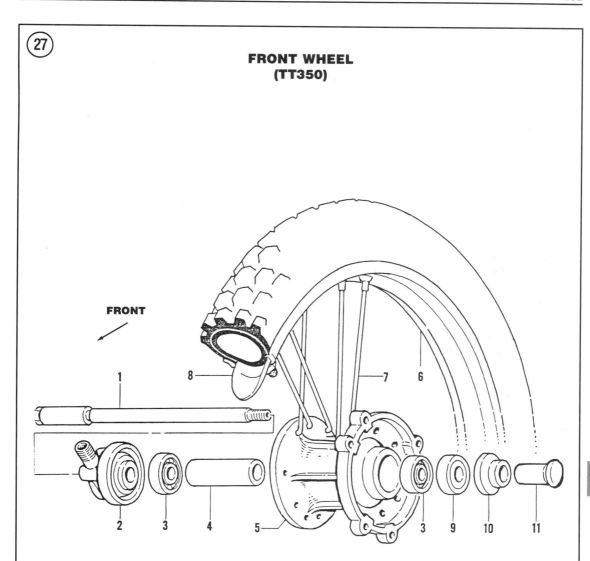

**FRONT WHEEL
(TT350)**

FRONT

10

1. Axle
2. Speedometer drive assembly
3. Bearing
4. Spacer
5. Hub
6. Rim

7. Spoke
8. Rim lock
9. Oil seal
10. Dust cover
11. Spacer

a soft aluminum or brass drift into one side of the hub. Push the distance collar over to one side and place the drift on the inner race of the lower bearing (**Figure 29**). Tap the bearing out of the hub with a hammer, working around the perimeter of the inner race.

4. Remove the middle spacer and tap out the opposite bearing.

5. Thoroughly clean out the inside of the hub with solvent and dry with compressed air or a shop cloth.

NOTE
Fully sealed bearings are available from many good bearing specialty shops. Fully sealed bearings provide better protection from dirt and moisture that may get into the hub.

6. Pack non-sealed bearings with good-quality bearing grease. Work the grease in between the balls thoroughly. Turn the bearing by hand a couple of times to make sure the grease is distributed evenly inside the bearing.

7. Pack the wheel hub and spacer with multipurpose grease.

NOTE
If a bearing has only one sealed side, install the bearing with the sealed side facing out.

CAUTION
*When installing the bearings in the following procedures, tap the bearings squarely into place and tap on the outer race only (**Figure 30**). Use a socket (**Figure 31**) that matches the outer race diameter. Do not tap on the inner race or the bearing will be damaged. Be sure that the bearings are completely seated.*

8. Install one of the bearings.

9. Install the middle spacer. See 8, **Figure 26** (XT350) or 4, **Figure 27** (TT350).

10. Install the opposite bearing.

11. Install a new oil seal. See 6, **Figure 26** (XT350) or 9, **Figure 27** (TT350). Lubricate it with multipurpose grease and tap it squarely into the

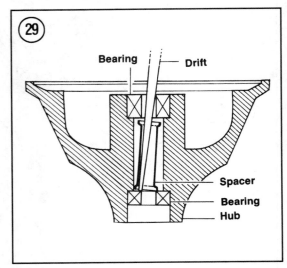

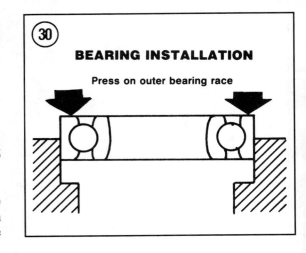

BEARING INSTALLATION

Press on outer bearing race

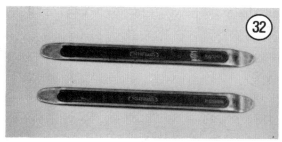

hub with a suitable size socket placed on the outside portion of the seal. Install the oil seal until it is at least flush with the hub.

12. Check the axle spacer dust cover (**Figure 9**) and the speedometer drive unit oil seal (**Figure 22**). Replace the dust cover or oil seal if worn or damaged.

TIRE CHANGING

Removal

Use only quality tire irons without sharp edges (**Figure 32**). If necessary, file the ends of the tire irons to remove rough edges. Do not use screwdrivers or other sharp objects as these tools will probably puncture the tube.

1. Remove the valve cap, nut and core (**Figure 33**) and deflate the tire.
2. Loosen the rim locknuts (**Figure 34**).
3. Press the entire bead on both sides of the tire into the center of the rim.
4. Lubricate the beads with soapy water.
5. Insert the tire iron under the bead next to the valve (**Figure 35**). Force the bead on the opposite side of tire into the center of the rim and pry the bead over the rim with the tire iron.
6. Insert a second tire iron next to the first to hold the bead over the rim. Then work around the tire with the first tire iron, prying the bead over the rim. Be careful not to pinch the inner tube with the tire irons.
7. Remove the valve from the hole in the rim and remove the tube from the tire.

10

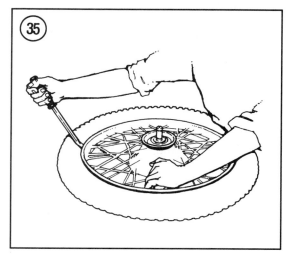

NOTE
Step 8 is required only if it is necessary to completely remove the tire from the rim, such as for tire replacement.

8. Stand the tire upright. Insert the tire iron between the second bead and the side of the rim that the first bead was pried over (**Figure 36**). Force the bead on the opposite side from the tire iron into the center of the rim. Pry the second bead off of the rim, working around as with the first.

Installation

1. Carefully check the tire for any damage, especially inside. On the front tire carefully check the sidewall as it is very vulnerable to damage from rocks.
2. Check that the spoke ends do not protrude through the nipples into the center of the rim to puncture the tube. File off any protruding spoke ends.

NOTE
If you are having trouble with water and dirt entering the wheel, remove and discard the rubber rim band. Then wrap the rim center with 2 separate revolutions of duct tape. Punch holes through the tape at the rim lock and valve stem mounting areas.

3. Install the rim lock if removed.
4. If you are using the rubber rim band, be sure the band is in place with the rough side toward the rim. Align the holes in the band with the holes in the rim.
5. Liberally sprinkle the inside tire casing with baby powder. The powder reduces chafing between the tire and tube and minimizes tube pinching.

NOTE
*Before installing a tire, check the sidewall for a weight identification mark. This is usually a round circle like the one shown in **Figure 37**. When installing the tire, align the weight mark with either the valve stem hole or the rim lock hole in the rim.*

6. If the tire was removed, lubricate one bead with soapy water. Then align the tire with the rim and push the tire onto the rim (**Figure 38**). Work around the tire in both directions (**Figure 39**).
7. Install the core into the tube valve. Put the tube in the tire and insert the valve stem through the hole in the rim. Inflate just enough to round it out. Too much air will make installing it in the tire difficult, and too little will increase the chances of pinching the tube with the tire irons.
8. Lubricate the upper tire bead and rim with soapy water.
9. Press the upper bead into the rim opposite the valve. Pry the bead into the rim on both sides of the initial point with your hands and work around the rim to the valve. If the tire wants to pull up on one side, either use a tire iron or one of your

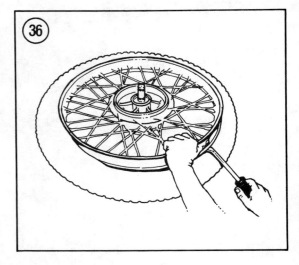

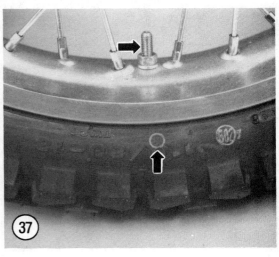

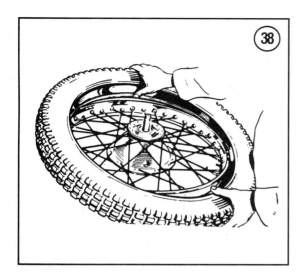

knees to hold the tire in place. The last few inches are usually the toughest to install and is also where most pinched tubes occur. If you can, continue to push the tire into the rim with your hands. Relubricate the bead if necessary. If the tire bead wants to pull out from under the rim, use both of your knees to hold the tire in place. If necessary, use a tire iron for the last few inches (**Figure 40**).

10. Wiggle the valve to be sure the tube is not trapped under the bead. Set the valve squarely in its hole before screwing on the valve nut.

NOTE
*Make sure the valve stem is not cocked in the rim as shown in **Figure 41**.*

11. Check the bead on both sides of the tire for even fit around the rim. Inflate the tire to approximately 25-30 psi to insure the tire bead is seated properly on the rim. If the tire is hard to seat, relubricate both sides of the tire and reinflate.

12. Tighten the rim lock nut securely (**Figure 34**).

13. Bleed the tire back down to between 10 and 14 psi. Never tighten the valve stem nut against the rim. It should always be installed finger-tight, near the valve stem cap rather than flush against the rim (**Figure 33**).

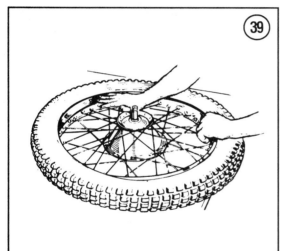

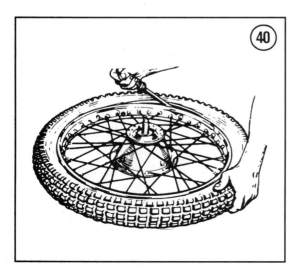

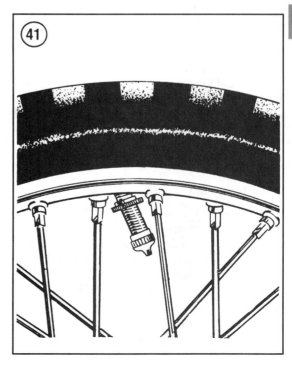

10

TIRE REPAIRS

Every dirt rider eventually experiences trouble with a tire or tube. Repairs and replacement are fairly simple, and every rider should know how to patch a tube.

Patching a motorcycle tube is only a temporary fix, especially on a dirt bike. The tire flexes too much and the patch could rub right off.

> *NOTE*
> *If you do a lot of off-road riding, install a stronger heavy-duty tube. This type of tube lasts longer and is not as easy to puncture.*

Tire Repair Kits

Tire repair kits can be purchased from motorcycle dealers and some auto supply stores. When buying, specify that the kit you want is for motorcycles.

There are 2 types of tire repair kits:
a. Hot patch.
b. Cold patch.

Hot patches are stronger because they actually vulcanize to the tube, becoming part of it. However, they are far too bulky to carry for trail repairs, and the strength is unnecessary for a temporary repair.

Cold patches are not vulcanized to the tube; they are simply glued to it. Though not as strong as hot patches, cold patches are still very durable. Cold patch kits are less bulky than hot and more easily applied while on the road or trail. A cold patch kit contains everything necessary and tucks easily in with your emergency tool kit.

Tube Inspection

1. Remove the tube as described under *Tire Changing* in this chapter.
2. Install the valve core into the valve stem (**Figure 42**) and inflate the tube slightly. Do not overinflate.
3. Immerse the tube in water a section at a time (**Figure 43**). Look carefully for bubbles indicating a hole. Mark each hole and continue checking until you are certain that all holes are discovered and marked. Also make sure that the valve core is not leaking. Tighten it if necessary.

> *NOTE*
> *If you do not have enough water to immerse sections of the tube, try running your hand over the tube slowly and very close to the surface. If your hand is damp, it works even better. If you suspect a hole anywhere, apply some saliva to the area to verify it.*

4. Apply a cold patch using the techniques described under *Cold Patch Repair*, following.
5. Dust the patch area with talcum powder to prevent it from sticking to the tire.
6. Carefully check the inside of the tire casing for small rocks, sand or twigs which may have damaged the tube. If the inside of the tire is split, apply a patch to the area to prevent it from pinching and damaging the tube again.

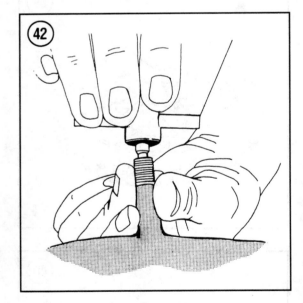

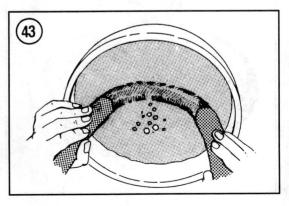

7. Check the inside of the rim. Make sure the rubber rim band is in place, with no spoke ends protruding, which could puncture the tube.

8. Deflate the tube prior to installing in the tire.

Cold Patch Repairs

1. Remove the tube from the tire as previously described.

2. Roughen an area around the hole slightly larger than the patch, using a cap from the tire repair kit or a pocket knife. Do not scrape too vigorously or you may cause additional damage.

3. Apply a small amount of the special cement from the kit to the puncture and spread it evenly with your finger.

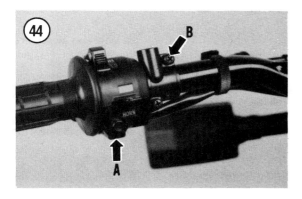

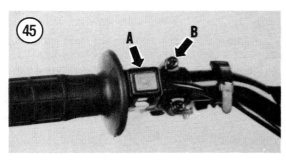

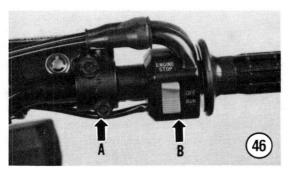

4. Allow the cement to dry until tacky—usually 30 seconds or so is sufficient.

5. Remove the backing from the patch.

> *CAUTION*
> *Do not touch the newly exposed rubber*
> *with your fingers or the patch will not*
> *stick firmly.*

6. Center the patch over the hole. Hold the patch firmly in place for about 30 seconds to allow the cement to set.

7. Dust the patched area with talcum powder to prevent sticking.

8. Install the tube as previously described.

HANDLEBAR

Removal/Installation

1. Remove all electrical cable straps from the handlebar.

2A. *XT350*: Perform the following:
   a. Remove the left-hand switch housing (A, **Figure 44**).
   b. Remove the clutch lever assembly (B, **Figure 44**).

2B. *TT350*: Perform the following:
   a. Remove the kill switch (A, **Figure 45**).
   b. Remove the clutch lever assembly (B, **Figure 45**).

3. Remove the bolts securing the master cylinder to the handlebar and remove the master cylinder. See A, **Figure 46** (XT350) or A, **Figure 47** (TT350). Support the master cylinder so that it does not hang by its hose.

10

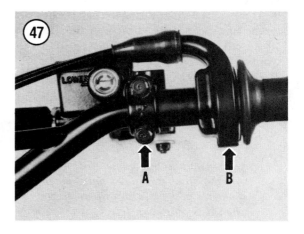

4. Remove the screws holding the throttle assembly to the handlebar. See B, **Figure 46** (XT350) or B, **Figure 47** (TT350). Then separate the throttle assembly halves and disconnect the throttle cables from the twist grip.

NOTE
Carefully lay the throttle assembly and cable over the front fender, or back over the frame, so the cable does not get crimped or damaged.

5. Remove the bolts securing the handlebar holders and remove the holders.
6. Remove the handlebar.
7. Install by reversing these removal steps. Note the following.
8. To maintain a good grip in the handlebar and to prevent them from slipping down, clean the knurled section of the handlebar with solvent. It should be kept rough so it will be held securely by the holders. The holders should also be kept clean and free of any metal that may have been gouged loose by handlebar slippage.
9. Tighten the bolts securing the handlebar to the torque specification listed in **Table 3** or **Table 4**.
10. Install the master cylinder clamp so that the word "UP" faces up.
11. Apply a light coat of light machine oil to the throttle grip area on the handlebar prior to installation.

WARNING
After installation is completed, make sure the brake lever does not come in contact with the throttle grip assembly when it is pulled on fully.

WARNING
Make sure the front brake and clutch operate properly before riding the bike.

STEERING HEAD

The steering head on these models uses tapered roller bearings at the top and bottom pivot positions. Refer to **Figure 48** (XT350) or **Figure 49** (TT350) for this procedure.

Disassembly

1. Remove the front wheel as described in thischapter.
2. Remove the front fender.
3. Remove the headlight assembly as described under *Headlight Bulb Replacement* in Chapter Nine.
4. Remove the handlebar as described in this chapter.
5. Remove the meter assembly.
6A. *XT350*: Loosen but do not remove the steering bolt (1, **Figure 48**).
6B. *TT350*: Remove the steering nut cover (1, **Figure 49**). Then loosen but do not remove the steering nut (2, **Figure 49**).
7. Remove the front forks as described in this chapter.
8. Remove the steering bolt or nut loosened in Step 6.
9. Remove the upper fork bracket (**Figure 50**).
10. Remove the bearing cover (**Figure 51**)

NOTE
After the steering stem adjust nut is removed in Step 11, the steering stem must be held or it will fall to the floor.

11. Remove the steering stem adjust nut (**Figure 51**). Use a large drift and hammer or a spanner wrench and remove the steering stem.
12. Remove the upper bearing from the frame tube.

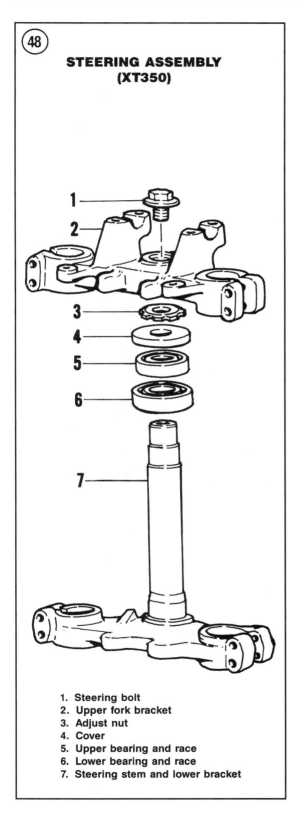

48

STEERING ASSEMBLY
(XT350)

1. Steering bolt
2. Upper fork bracket
3. Adjust nut
4. Cover
5. Upper bearing and race
6. Lower bearing and race
7. Steering stem and lower bracket

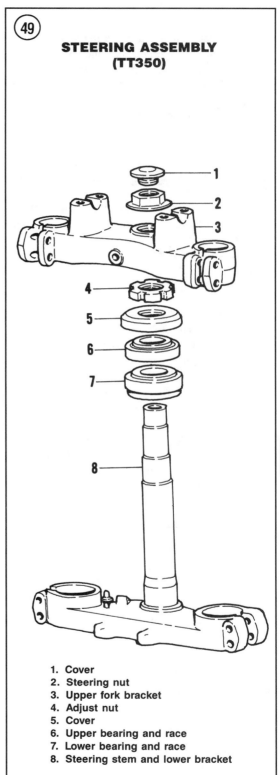

49

STEERING ASSEMBLY
(TT350)

1. Cover
2. Steering nut
3. Upper fork bracket
4. Adjust nut
5. Cover
6. Upper bearing and race
7. Lower bearing and race
8. Steering stem and lower bracket

10

Inspection

1. Clean the bearing races in the steering head, the steering stem races and the tapered roller bearings (**Figure 52**) with solvent.

2. Check the welds around the steering head for cracks and fractures. If any are found, have them repaired by a competent frame shop or welding service.

3. Check the races for pitting or galling and corrosion. If any of these conditions exist, replace the races as described under *Headset Race Replacement* in this chapter.

4. Check the steering nut or bolt, adjust nut and the upper bearing cover for cracks or damage. Replace if necessary.

5. Check the steering stem (**Figure 53**) for cracks and damage.

6. Check the tapered roller bearings (**Figure 52**) for pitting, scratches or discoloration indicating wear or corrosion. If necessary, replace the lower bearing (**Figure 52**) as follows:

   a. Install a bearing puller onto the steering stem and bearing.
   b. Pull the bearing off of the steering stem.
   c. Clean the steering stem thoroughly in solvent.
   d. Slide a new bearing onto the steering stem until it stops.
   e. Align the bearing with the machined portion of the shaft and slide a long hollow pipe over the steering stem until it seats against the inner bearing race. Drive the bearing onto the shaft until it bottoms (**Figure 54**).

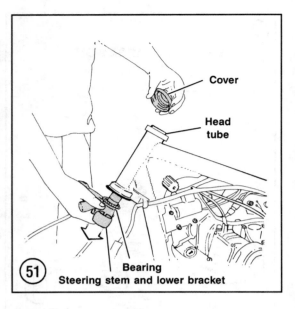

Cover

Head tube

(51) Bearing
Steering stem and lower bracket

(52)

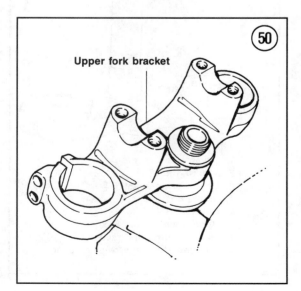

(50)

Upper fork bracket

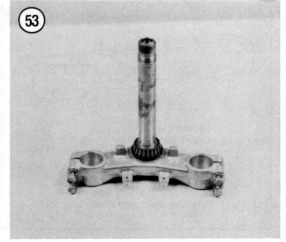

(53)

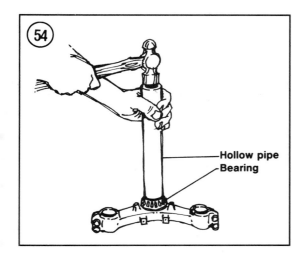

Hollow pipe
Bearing

7. Check the upper and lower fork bracket for cracks or damage, especially where the fork tubes mount.

Headset Race Replacement

To remove an upper or lower headset race, insert a hardwood stick or soft punch into the head tube (**Figure 55**) and carefully tap the race out from the inside. After it is started, tap around the race so that neither the race nor the head tube is damaged.

To install the headset race, tap it in slowly with a block of wood or suitable size socket or piece of pipe (**Figure 56**). Make sure they are squarely seated in the race bores before tapping them in. Tap them in until they are flush with the steering head.

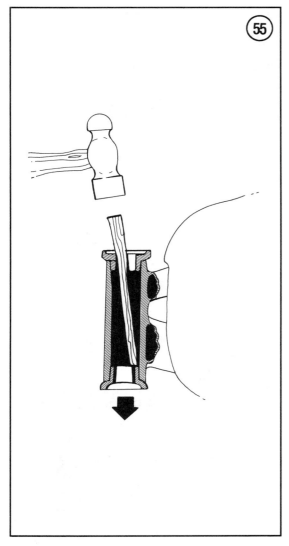

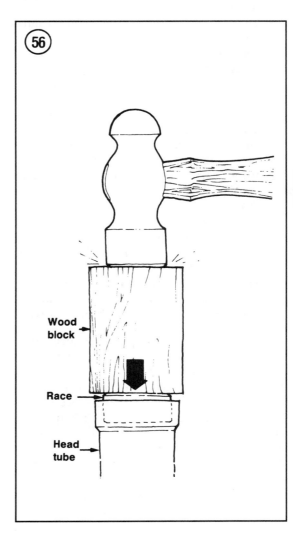

Wood block

Race

Head tube

10

Steering Head Assembly

Refer to **Figure 48** (XT350) or **Figure 49** (TT350) for this procedure.

1. Make sure the steering head and stem races are properly seated.

2. Apply a coat of bearing grease to both tapered roller bearings (**Figure 53**). Carefully work the grease into the rollers.

3. Install the steering stem into the head tube and hold it firmly in place.

4. Install the upper bearing. Push the bearing down to seat it in the race.

5. Install the upper bearing cover (**Figure 51**).

6. Install and tighten the steering stem adjusting nut as follows:

   a. Install the steering stem adjust nut (3, **Figure 48** or 4, **Figure 49**).

   b. The adjust nut should be tightened to an initial torque of 37 N•m (27 ft.-lb.) to seat the bearings. To prevent from overtightening the adjust nut, use the Yamaha ring nut wrench (part No. YU-33975) (**Figure 57**) and a torque wrench. Engage the ring nut wrench with the adjust nut. Attach a torque wrench onto the end of the ring nut wrench so that both wrenches form a right angle (**Figure 58**). Tighten the adjust nut to 37 N•m (27 ft.-lb.). If you do not have the ring nut wrench, tighten the adjust nut with a spanner wrench (**Figure 59**) securely.

   c. Loosen the adjust nut one turn. Then tighten the adjusting nut to approximately 10 N•m (7.2 ft.-lb.). Check the bearing play. The adjusting nut should be just tight enough to remove play, both horizontal and vertical yet loose enough so that the assembly will turn to both lock positions under its own weight after an assist.

7. Install the upper fork bracket (**Figure 50**).

8. Install the steering bolt or washer finger-tight at this time.

9. Slide both fork tubes into position and tighten the lower pinch bolts to the torque specification in **Table 3** (XT350) or **Table 4** (TT350).

10. Tighten the steering stem bolt or nut to the torque specification in **Table 3** or **Table 4**.

11. Tighten the upper fork pinch bolts to the torque specification in **Table 3** or **Table 4**.

12. Continue assembly by reversing Steps 1-5, *Steering Head Disassembly*.

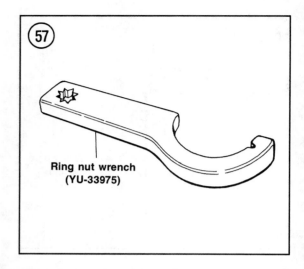

(57)

Ring nut wrench
(YU-33975)

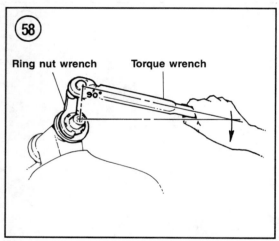

(58)

Ring nut wrench   Torque wrench

90°

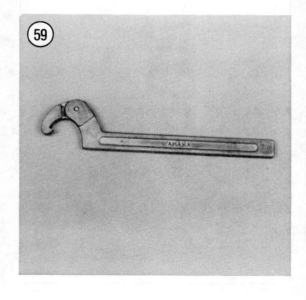

(59)

13. After a few hours of riding the bearings have had a chance to seat; readjust the free play in the steering stem with the steering stem adjusting nut.

Steering Adjustment

1. Raise the front wheel off the ground. Support the motorcycle securely under the engine.
2. Loosen the lower fork tube pinch bolts.
3. Loosen the steering stem bolt or nut.
4. Turn the steering stem adjusting nut with a spanner wrench or punch until you just feel the steering play taken up.
5. Tighten the steering stem bolt or nut to the torque specifications in **Table 3** or **Table 4**.
6. Recheck the steering play.
7. Tighten all bolts and nuts to the torque specifications in **Table 3** (XT350) or **Table 4** (TT350).

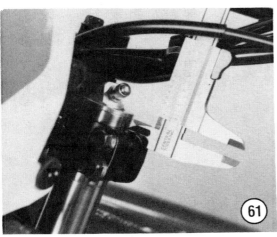

FRONT FORK
(XT350)

The Yamaha front fork is spring-controlled and hydraulically damped. The damping rate is determined by the viscosity (weight) of the oil used, and the spring rate can be altered by varying the amount of oil used by air pressurization of the forks. Before suspecting major trouble with the front fork, drain the fork oil and refill with the proper type and quantity. If you still have trouble, such as poor damping, tendency to bottom out or top out, or leakage around the rubber seals, then follow the service procedures in this section.

To simplify fork service and to prevent the mixing of parts, the legs should be removed, serviced and reinstalled individually.

Each front fork leg consists of the fork tube (inner tube), slider (outer tube), fork spring, damper rod with its damper components and bushings.

If the front fork is going to be removed without disassembly, perform the *Removal* and *Installation* procedure in this chapter. If the front forks require disassembly, refer to *Disassembly* in this chapter.

Removal/Installation

1. Disconnect the front brake hose and the speedometer cable at the left-hand fork tube (**Figure 60**).
2. Remove the front wheel as described in this chapter.

> *NOTE*
> *Insert a piece of wood between the brake pads in place of the disc. That way, if the brake lever is inadvertently squeezed, the piston will not be forced out of the calipers. If it does happen, the calipers might have to be disassembled to reseat the piston. By using the wood, bleeding the brake is not necessary when installing the wheel.*

3. Remove the front brake caliper as described in Chapter Twelve.
4. Measure the distance the fork tube extends above the upper fork bracket (**Figure 61**). Record

10

the measurement so that the fork tubes can be installed to the same height.

5. For 1985-1995 models, remove the air valve cap (A, **Figure 62**) from both fork tubes.

> *WARNING*
> *Protect your eyes and clothing when releasing the front fork air pressure as described in Step 6.*

6. Depress the air valve to release all fork air pressure.

7. Loosen the upper (B, **Figure 62**) and lower fork tube pinch bolts.

8. Twist the upper fork tube and slide the fork tube out of the fork brackets.

9. Repeat for the opposite side.

10. Install by reversing these removal steps. Note the following.

11. Position the fork tube so that the distance from the upper fork bracket to the top of the fork tube is the same as that recorded during disassembly.

12. Make sure the left-hand fork boot clamp is positioned with the cable guide facing to the rear of the bike as shown in **Figure 63**.

13. Tighten the upper and lower fork tube pinch bolts to the torque specification in **Table 3**.

14. Install the front wheel as described in this chapter.

15. Install the front brake caliper as described in Chapter Twelve.

> *WARNING*
> *After installing the front brake caliper, squeeze the front brake lever. If the brake lever feels spongy, bleed the brake as described under **Bleeding the System** in Chapter Twelve.*

> *WARNING*
> *During the next step, never use any type of compressed gas as an explosion may be lethal. Never heat the fork assembly with a torch or place it near an open flame or extreme heat, as this will also result in an explosion.*

16. Make sure the front wheel is off the ground and inflate the forks to within the specifications listed in **Table 1**. Do not use compressed air; use only a small hand-operated air pump.

Disassembly

Refer to **Figure 64** when performing this procedure.

Fork tube disassembly is easier if some of the procedures are performed while the fork tubes are mounted on the bike.

1. Perform Steps 1-4 described under front fork *Removal/Installation*.

2. For 1985-1995 models, remove the air valve cap (A, **Figure 62**) from both fork tubes.

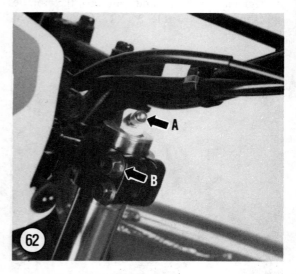

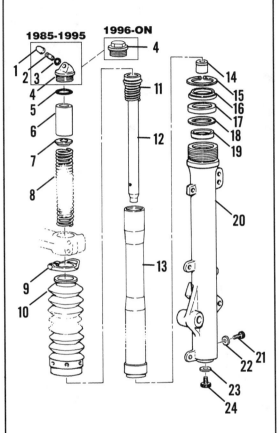

FRONT FORK (XT350)

64

1985-1995   1996-ON

1. Air valve cap
2. Air valve
3. O-ring
4. Fork cap
5. O-ring
6. Spacer
7. Upper spring seat
8. Spring
9. Clamp
10. Fork boot
11. Spring
12. Damper rod
13. Fork tube
14. Oil lock piece
15. Snap ring
16. Dust seal
17. Oil seal
18. Plate washer
19. Guide bushing
20. Slider
21. Drain screw
22. Washer
23. Washer
24. Allen bolt

WARNING
Protect your eyes and clothing when releasing the front fork air pressure as described in Step 3.

3. Depress the air valve to release all fork air pressure.

NOTE
The bottom fork tube Allen bolt is secured with Loctite and is hard to remove. If a heavy duty air powered impact wrench is available, try that first. If necessary, you may be able to keep the damper rod inside from turning with the fork spring, spring seat, spacer and fork cap installed, and at the same time having an assistant compress the fork while you try to loosen the bottom bolt.

If these methods are not successful, you will have to keep the damper rod from turning with a special tool. Yamaha sells a long T-handle (part No. YM-01326) and adapter (part No. YM-33298). You can substitute the long T-handle with a short T-handle and a long 3/8 in. drive extension.

4. Loosen the bottom fork tube Allen bolt as follows:

   a. Insert the axle through the fork tubes as shown in **Figure 65**. This will hold the sliders in position while loosening the Allen bolt.

   b. Loosen but do not remove the fork tube Allen bolt (**Figure 66**).

5. Remove the fork spring assembly as follows:

   a. Loosen the top fork tube pinch bolts (B, **Figure 62**).

   b. Loosen and remove the fork cap (A, **Figure 62**).

   c. Remove the spacer (**Figure 67**).

   d. Remove the spring seat (**Figure 68**).

   e. Remove the fork spring (**Figure 69**).

6. Remove the Allen bolt and gasket from the bottom of the slider (**Figure 66**).

7. Slide the outer fork tube boot away from the slider (**Figure 70**).

10

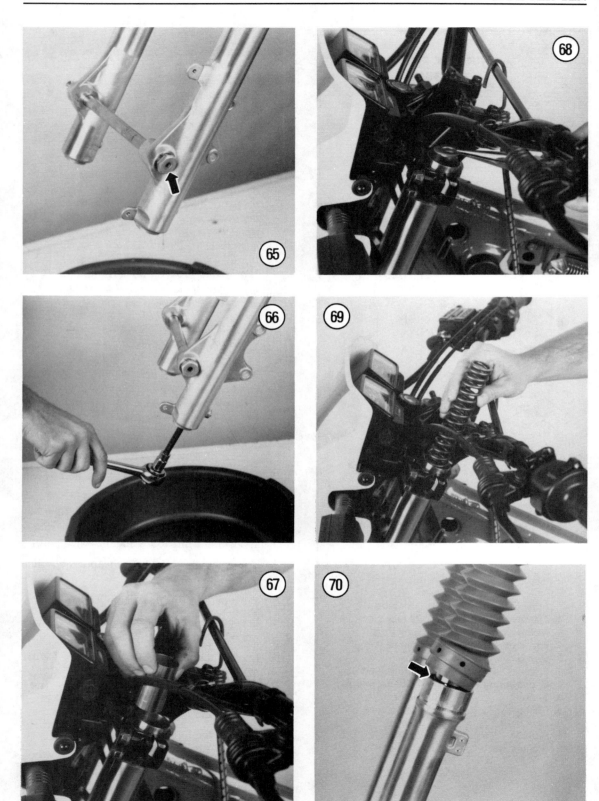

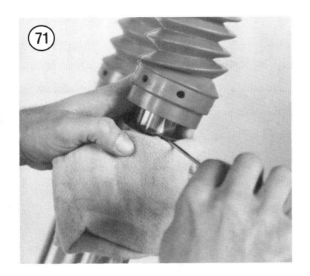

8. Remove the snap ring (**Figure 71**) from the slider.

9. There is an interference fit between the bushing in the fork slider and the bushing on the fork tube. In order to remove the slider from the fork tube, pull hard on the slider using quick in-and-out strokes (**Figure 72**). Doing this will withdraw the dust seal, oil seal, plate washer and guide bushing (**Figure 73**).

10. Remove the oil lock piece from the end of the damper rod (**Figure 74**).

11. Remove the fork tube pinch bolts and remove the fork tube assembly (**Figure 75**).

12. Slide the damper rod and spring out of the fork tube.

13. See **Figure 64**. Slide the following parts off of the fork tube:

   a. Circlip (15).

   b. Dust seal (16).

   c. Oil seal (17).

   d. Plate washer (18).

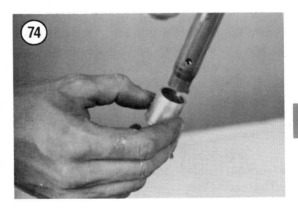

10

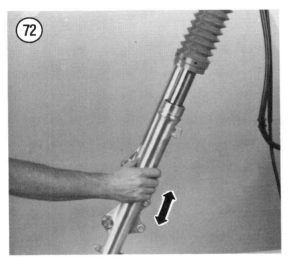

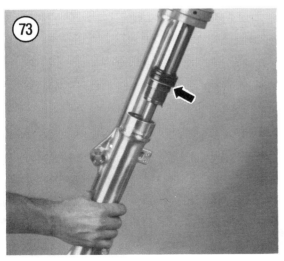

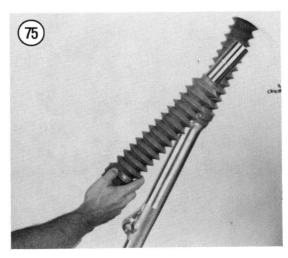

Inspection

1. Thoroughly clean all parts in solvent and completely dry.

2. Check both fork tubes for wear or scratches.

3. Check the fork tube for straightness. If the fork tube is slightly bent, it may be straightened with a hydraulic press. If the fork tube is bent to the point that it has creased or the chrome has flaked, the fork tube must be replaced.

4. Check the oil seal area in the slider (**Figure 76**) for dents or other damage that would allow oil leakage. Check the circlip groove in the slider for cracks or other damage. Replace the slider if necessary.

5. Check the damper rod (**Figure 77**) for straightness by rolling it on a flat surface. Replace the rod if bent or otherwise damaged.

6. Check the damper rod piston ring (**Figure 78**) for damage.

7. Measure the uncompressed length of the stock Yamaha fork springs (**Figure 79**) with a tape measure and compare to specifications in **Table 1**. Replace the fork spring(s) if too short.

8. Replace the fork cap O-ring (**Figure 80**) if deformed or damaged.

9. Check the fork tube Allen bolt washer for damage that would allow oil leakage; replace if necessary.

10. Inspect the fork tube (**Figure 81**) and guide (19, **Figure 64**) bushings. If the Teflon coating is worn off so that the copper base material is showing on approximately 3/4 of the total surface, the bushing must be replaced.

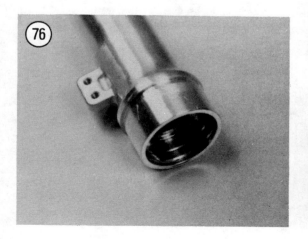

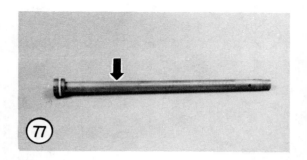

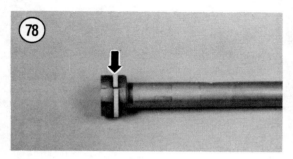

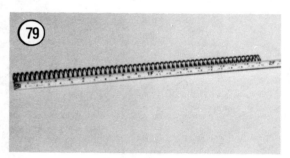

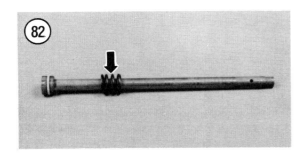

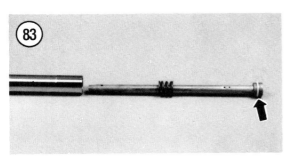

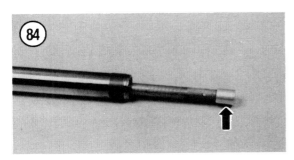

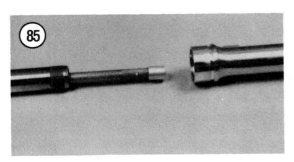

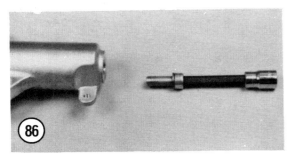

11. Check the oil seal and dust seal for tears or other damage that would allow oil leakage. Replace both seals if necessary.

Assembly

Refer to **Figure 64** for this procedure.

1. Slide the spring (**Figure 82**) onto the damper rod and insert the damper rod and spring into the fork tube. See **Figure 83**.

2. Slide the oil lock piece (**Figure 84**) onto the end of the damper rod.

3. Insert the damper rod/fork tube into the slider (**Figure 85**).

4. Make sure the gasket is on the Allen bolt.

5. Apply Loctite 242 (blue) to the threads on the Allen bolt. Install the Allen bolt (**Figure 86**) and tighten securely.

NOTE
*Use the same tool and procedure as during disassembly to prevent the damper rod from turning when tightening the Allen bolt. **Figure 87** shows the Yamaha tools. **Figure 88** shows how the tool will fit into the end of the damper rod.*

10

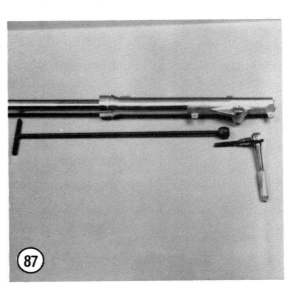

NOTE
See **Figure 89**. *Some type of fork seal driver will be required to install the guide bushing (D), oil seal (B) and dust seal (A). Yamaha sells a fork seal driver set for the XT350; see a dealer for part numbers. The adjustable fork seal driver shown in* **Figure 90** *is made by Suzuki and can be used for all fork tubes. If you do not have a special tool, the guide bushing and oil seals can be installed with a piece of pipe or other piece of tubing that fits over the fork tube. If both ends of the pipe are threaded, wrap one end with duct tape to prevent the threads from damaging the interior of the slider.*

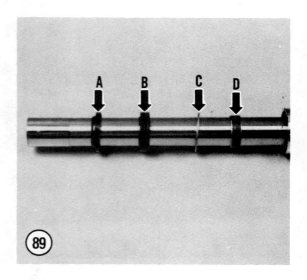

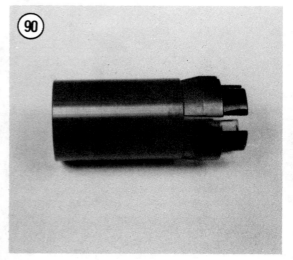

6. Slide the guide bushing (**Figure 91**) over the fork tube. Tap the guide bushing into the slider until it bottoms.

7. Slide the washer (**Figure 92**) down the fork tube until it rests against the bushing. See **Figure 93**.

8. Position the oil seal with the marking facing upward and slide down onto the fork tube (**Figure 94**). Drive the seal into the slider with the fork seal driver. See **Figure 95**. Drive the seal into the slider until it rests against the washer.

9. Slide the dust seal onto the fork tube (**Figure 96**). Drive the seal onto the slider with the fork seal driver (**Figure 97**).

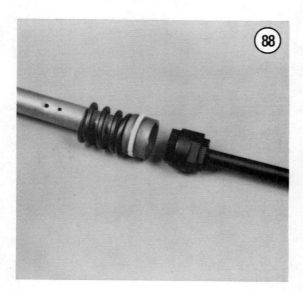

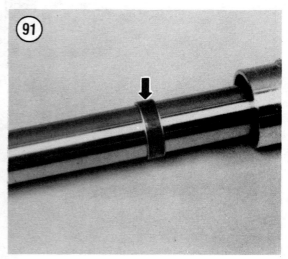

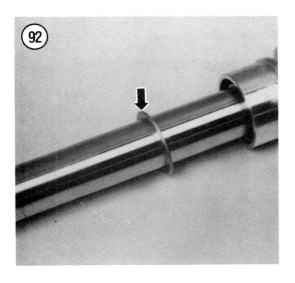

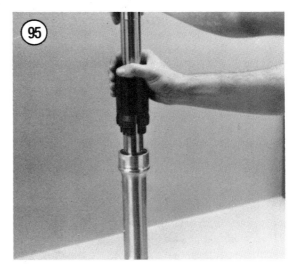

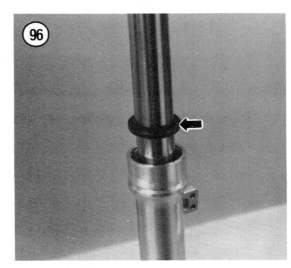

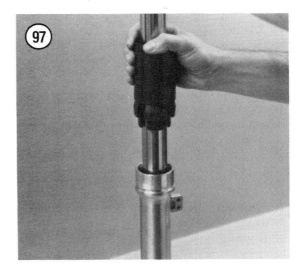

10

NOTE
*Make sure the groove in the slider can be seen above the dust seal (**Figure 98**). If not, the bushing and oil seal will have to be driven farther into the slider.*

10. Slide the snap ring (**Figure 99**) down the fork tube and seat it in the slider groove. Make sure the snap ring is completely seated in the groove.
11. Install the fork boot onto the fork tube.
12. Fill the fork tube with the correct quantity and weight fork oil. See **Table 1**.
13. Install the fork tubes onto the motorcycle as described in this chapter. Reverse Step 5 under *Disassembly* to install the spring assembly. Install the fork spring so that the closer wound coils face toward the top of the fork tube.

FRONT FORKS
(TT350)

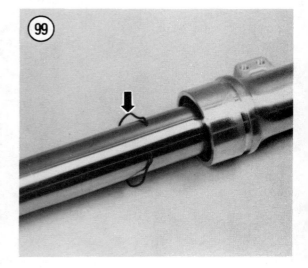

The Yamaha front forks are spring-controlled and hydraulically damped. The damping rate is determined by the viscosity (weight) of the oil used, and the spring rate can be altered by varying the amount of oil used and by air pressurization of the forks. Before suspecting major trouble with the front forks, drain the fork oil and refill with the proper type and quantity. If you still have trouble, such as poor damping, tendency to bottom out or top out, or leakage around the rubber seals, then follow the service procedures in this section.

To simplify fork service and to prevent the mixing of parts, the legs should be removed, serviced and reinstalled individually.

Each front fork leg consists of the fork tube (inner tube), slider (outer tube), fork spring, damper rod with its damper components and bushings.

If the front forks are going to be removed without disassembly, perform the *Removal* and *Installation* procedure in this chapter. If the front forks require disassembly, refer to *Disassembly* in this chapter.

Removal/Installation

1. Disconnect the front brake hose at the left-hand fork tube (**Figure 100**).
2. Disconnect the speedometer cable at the right-hand fork tube (**Figure 101**).

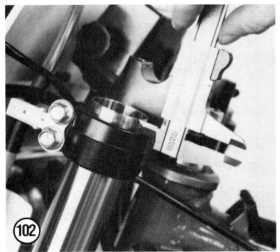

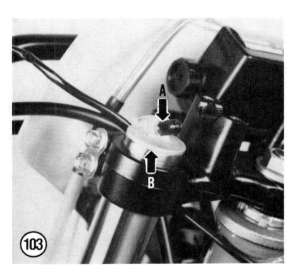

3. Remove the front wheel as described in this chapter.

> *NOTE*
> *Insert a piece of wood between the brake pads in place of the disc. That way, if the brake lever is inadvertently squeezed, the pistons will not be forced out of the caliper. If it does happen, the caliper might have to be disassembled to reseat the pistons. By using the wood, bleeding the brake is not necessary when installing the wheel.*

4. Remove the front brake caliper as described in Chapter Twelve.

5. Measure the distance the fork tube extends above the upper fork bracket (**Figure 102**). Record this measurement so that the fork tubes can be installed to the same height.

6. Remove the air valve cap (A, **Figure 103**) from both fork tubes.

> *WARNING*
> *Protect your eyes and clothing when releasing the front fork air pressure as described in Step 7.*

7. Depress the air valve to release all fork air pressure.

8. Loosen the upper and lower fork tube pinch bolts (**Figure 104**).

10

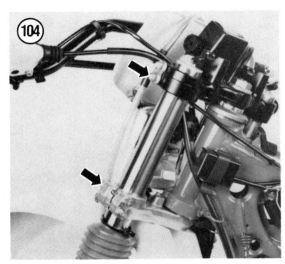

9. Twist the upper fork tube (**Figure 105**) and slide the fork tube out of the steering stem.

10. Repeat for the opposite side.

11. Install by reversing these removal steps. Note the following.

12. Position the fork tube so that the distance from the upper fork bracket to the top of the fork tube is the same as that recorded during disassembly.

13. Tighten the upper and lower fork tube pinch bolts to the torque specification in **Table 4**.

14. Install the front wheel as described in this chapter.

15. Install the front brake caliper as described in Chapter Twelve.

> *WARNING*
> *After installing the front brake caliper, squeeze the front brake lever. If the brake lever feels spongy, bleed the brake as described under **Bleeding the System** in **Chapter Twelve**.*

> *WARNING*
> *During the next step, never use any type of compressed gas as an explosion may be lethal. Never heat the fork assembly with a torch or place it near an open flame or extreme heat, as this will also result in an explosion.*

16. Make sure the front wheel is off the ground and inflate the forks to within the specifications listed in **Table 2**. Do not use compressed air; use only a small hand-operated air pump.

Disassembly

Refer to **Figure 106** when performing this procedure.

Fork tube disassembly is easier if some of the procedures are performed while the fork tubes are mounted on the bike.

1. Perform Steps 1-4 described under front fork *Removal/Installation*.

2. Remove the air valve cap (A, **Figure 103**) from both fork tubes.

> *WARNING*
> *Protect your eyes and clothing when releasing the front fork air pressure as described in Step 3.*

3. Depress the air valve to release all fork air pressure.

> *NOTE*
> *The bottom fork tube Allen bolt is secured with Loctite and is hard to remove. If a heavy duty air powered impact wrench is available, try that first. If necessary, you may be able to keep the damper rod inside from turning with the fork spring, spring seat, spacer and fork cap installed, and at the same time having an assistant compress the fork while you try to loosen the bottom bolt.*
>
> *If these methods are not successful, you will have to keep the damper rod from turning with a special tool. Yamaha sells a long T-handle (part No. YM-01326) and adapter (part No. YM-01300-1). See **Figure 107**. You can substitute the long T-handle with a short T-handle and a long 3/8 in. drive extension.*

4. Loosen the bottom fork tube Allen bolt as follows:

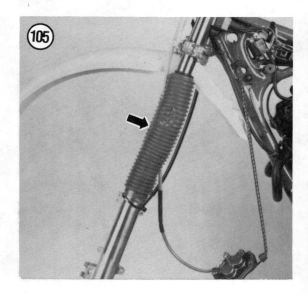

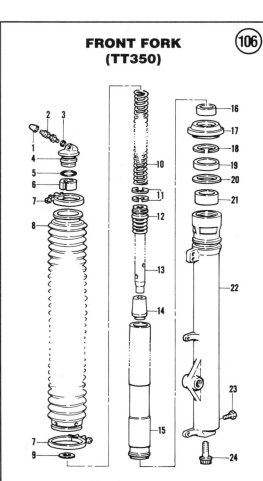

FRONT FORK (TT350) (106)

1. Air valve cap
2. Air valve
3. O-ring
4. Fork cap
5. O-ring
6. Spacer
7. Clamp
8. Fork boot
9. Upper spring seat
10. Fork spring
11. Piston rings
12. Spring
13. Damper rod
14. Oil lock piece
15. Fork tube
16. Guide bushing
17. Dust seal
18. Snap ring
19. Oil sealer
20. Seal spacer
21. Guide bushing
22. Slider
23. Drain screw and washer
24. Allen bolt and washer

a. Insert the axle through the fork tubes as shown in **Figure 108**. This will hold the sliders in position while loosening the Allen bolt.

b. Loosen but do not remove the fork tube Allen bolt (**Figure 109**).

5. Remove the fork spring assembly as follows:

a. Loosen the top fork tube pinch bolts (**Figure 104**).

b. Loosen and remove the fork cap (B, **Figure 103**).

c. Remove the spacer (**Figure 110**).

d. Remove the spring seat (**Figure 111**).

e. Remove the fork spring (**Figure 112**).

6. Remove the Allen bolt and gasket from the bottom of the slider (**Figure 109**).

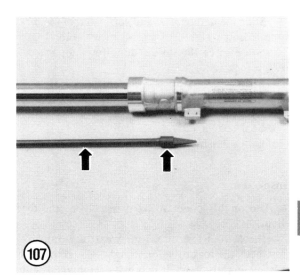

(107)

10

(108)

7. Slide the fork boot away from the slider.

8. Carefully pry the dust seal (**Figure 113**) out of the slider.

9. Remove the snap ring from the groove in the slider (**Figure 114**).

10. There is an interference fit between the bushing in the fork slider and the bushing on the fork tube. In order to remove the slider from the fork tube, pull hard on the slider using quick in-and-out strokes (**Figure 115**). Doing this will withdraw the dust seal, oil seal, plate washer and guide bushing (**Figure 116**).

11. Remove the oil lock piece from the end of the damper rod (**Figure 117**).

12. Remove the fork tube pinch bolts and remove the fork tube assembly.

13. Slide the damper rod and spring out of the fork tube (**Figure 118**).

14. See **Figure 106**. Slide the following parts off of the fork tube:

    a. Dust seal (17).

    b. Snap ring (18).

    c. Oil seal (19).

    d. Seal spacer (20).

    e. Guide bushing (21).

Inspection

1. Thoroughly clean all parts in solvent and dry them.

2. Check both fork tubes for wear or scratches.

3. Check the fork tube for straightness. If the fork tube is slightly bent, it may be straightened with a hydraulic press. If the fork tube is bent to the point that it has creased or the chrome has flaked, the fork tube must be replaced.

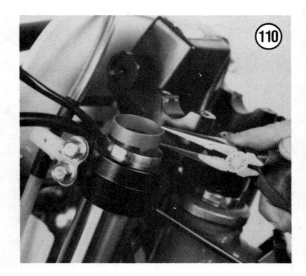

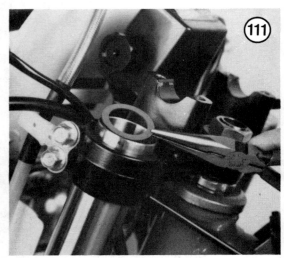

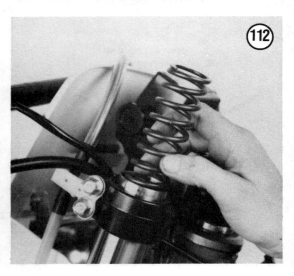

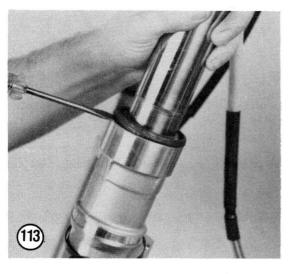

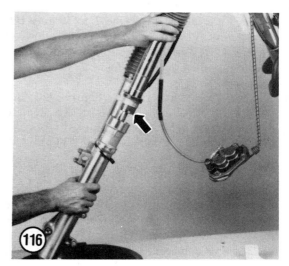

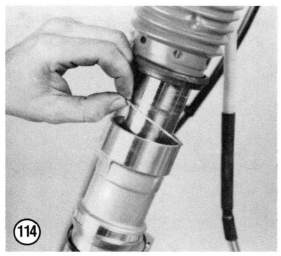

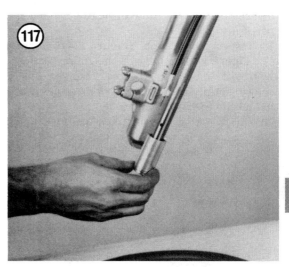

10

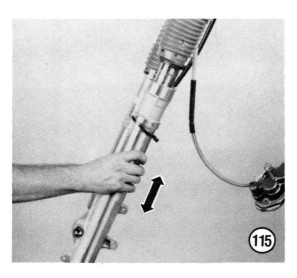

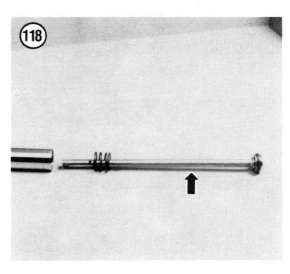

4. Check the oil seal area in the slider (**Figure 119**) for dents or other damage that would allow oil leakage. Check the circlip groove in the slider for cracks or other damage. Replace the slider if necessary.

5. Check the damper rod (**Figure 120**) for straightness by rolling it on a flat surface. Replace the rod if bent or otherwise damaged.

6. Check the damper rod piston rings (**Figure 121**) for damage.

7. Measure the uncompressed length of the stock Yamaha fork springs (**Figure 122**) with a tape measure and compare to specifications in **Table 2**. Replace the fork spring(s) if too short.

8. Replace the fork cap O-ring (**Figure 123**) if deformed or damaged.

9. Check the fork tube Allen bolt washer for damage that would allow oil leakage; replace if necessary.

10. Inspect the fork tube (**Figure 124**) and guide (21, **Figure 106**) bushings. If the Teflon coating is worn off so that the copper base material is showing on approximately 3/4 of the total surface, the bushing must be replaced.

11. Check the oil seal and dust seal for tears or other damage that would allow oil leakage. Replace both seals if necessary.

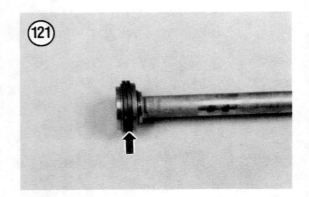

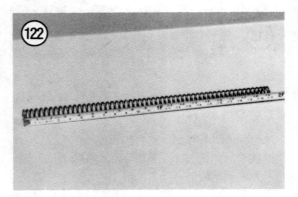

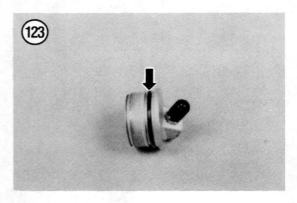

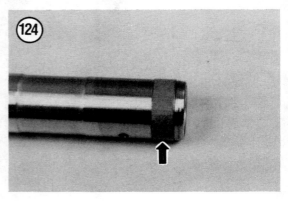

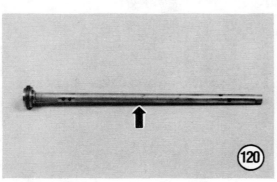

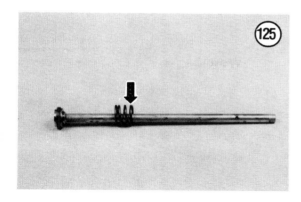

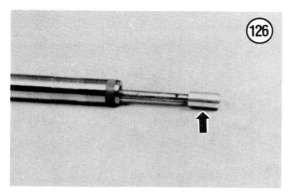

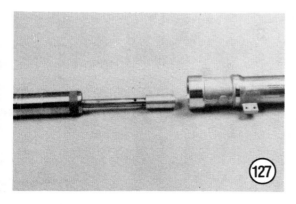

Assembly

Refer to **Figure 106** for this procedure.

1. Slide the spring (**Figure 125**) onto the damper rod and insert the damper rod and spring into the fork tube. See **Figure 118**.

2. Slide the oil lock piece (**Figure 126**) onto the end of the damper rod.

3. Insert the damper rod/fork tube into the slider (**Figure 127**).

4. Make sure the gasket is on the Allen bolt.

5. Apply Loctite 242 (blue) to the threads on the Allen bolt. Install the Allen bolt (**Figure 128**) and tighten securely.

> *NOTE*
> *Use the same tool and procedure as during disassembly to prevent the damper rod from turning when tightening the Allen bolt. **Figure 107** shows the Yamaha tools.*

> *NOTE*
> *See **Figure 129**. Some type of fork seal driver will be required to install the oil seal assembly. Yamaha sells a fork seal driver set for the TT350; see a dealer for part numbers. The adjustable fork seal driver shown in **Figure 130** is made by Suzuki and can be used on all fork tubes. If you do not have a special tool, the guide bushing and oil seals can be installed with a piece of pipe or other piece of tubing that fits over the fork tube. If both ends of the pipe are threaded, wrap one end with duct tape to prevent the threads from damaging the interior of the slider.*

10

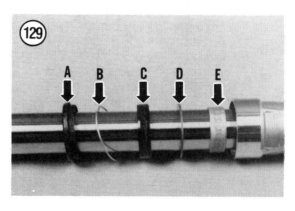

6. Slide the guide bushing (**Figure 131**) over the fork tube. Tap the guide bushing into the slider until it bottoms.

7. Slide the washer (**Figure 132**) down the fork tube until it rests against the bushing.

8. Position the oil seal with the marking facing upward and slide down onto the fork tube (**Figure 133**). Drive the seal into the slider with the fork seal driver. See **Figure 134**. Drive the seal into the slider until it rests against the washer.

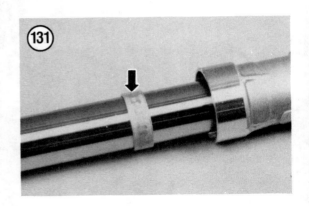

NOTE
Make sure the groove in the slider can be seen above the oil seal. If not, the bushing and oil seal will have to be driven farther into the slider.

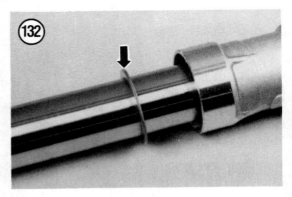

9. Slide the circlip (**Figure 135**) down the fork tube and seat it in the slider groove. Make sure the snap ring is completely seated in the groove. See **Figure 136**.

10. Slide the dust seal onto the fork tube (**Figure 137**). Seat the dust seal into the slider. (**Figure 138**).

11. Fill the fork tube with the correct quantity and weight fork oil. See **Table 2**.

12. Install the fork tubes onto the motorcycle as described in this chapter. Reverse Step 5 under *Disassembly* to install the spring assembly. Install the fork spring so that the closer wound coils face toward the top of the fork tube.

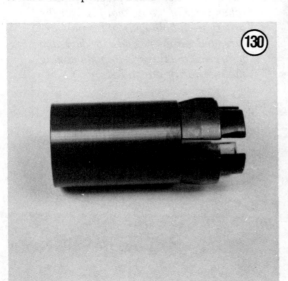

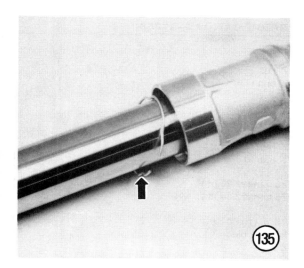

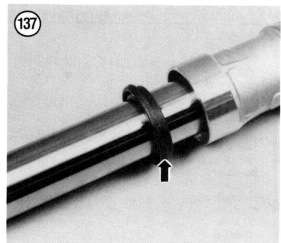

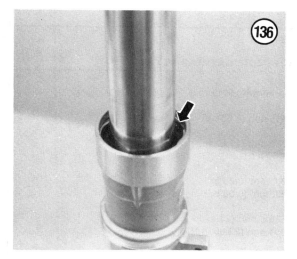

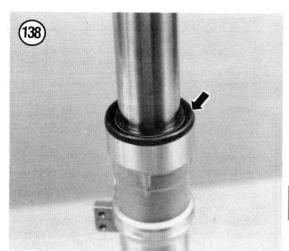

10

Tables are on the following pages.

Table 1 FRONT SUSPENSION SPECIFICATIONS—XT350

Chassis	
Frame type	Diamond
Caster	27° 10'
Trail	107mm (4.60 in.)
Front wheel	
Travel	255 mm (10.0 in.)
Rim size	1.60 × 21
Rim runout	
Radial (up and down)	2.0 mm (0.08 in.)
Lateral (side-to-side)	2.0 mm (0.08 in.)
Front fork spring length	
Standard	580 mm (22.86 in.)
Wear limit	575 mm (22.64 in.)
Front fork oil	
Capacity	319 cc (10.80 oz.)
Oil level	Not specified
Oil grade	10 wt.
Front fork air capacity (1985-1995 only)	
Standard	0 psi (0 kg/cm^2)
Maximum	17 psi (1.2 kg/cm^2)

Table 2 FRONT SUSPENSION SPECIFICATIONS—TT350

Chassis	
Frame type	Semi-double cradle
Caster	27.5°
Trail	115 mm (4.53 in.)
Front wheel	
Travel	280 mm (11.02 in.)
Rim size	1.60 × 21
Rim runout	
Radial (up and down)	2.0 mm (0.08 in.)
Lateral (side-to-side)	2.0 mm (0.08 in.)
Front fork spring length	
Standard	586.9 mm (23.11 in.)
Wear limit	581 mm (22.88 in.)
Front fork oil	
Capacity	533 cc (18.02 oz.)
Oil level	125 mm (4.92 in.)
Oil grade	10 wt
Front fork air capacity	
Standard	0 psi (0 kg/cm^2)
Maximum	17 psi (1.2 kg/cm^2)

Table 3 FRONT SUSPENSION TIGHTENING TORQUES—XT350

	N•m	ft.-lb.
Front axle nut	107	77.4
Handlebar holder	20	14
Front fork pinch bolts	23	17
Steering stem bolt	54	39
Steering adjust nut	*	*
Steering lock	7	5.1
Brake caliper @ front fork bolts	18	13

*See text.

Table 4 FRONT SUSPENSION TIGHTENING TORQUES—TT350

	N·m	ft.-lb.
Front axle nut	58	42
Axle holder nuts	8	5.8
Handlebar holder	23	17
Front fork pinch bolts	23	17
Steering shaft pinch bolts	23	17
Steering adjust nut	*	*
Brake caliper at front fork bolts	18	13
Steering stem nut	85	61
* See text.		

10

CHAPTER ELEVEN

REAR SUSPENSION

This chapter contains repair and replacement procedures for the rear wheel and hub and rear suspension components. Service to the rear suspension consists of periodically checking bolt tightness, replacing swing arm bushings, and checking the condition of the spring/gas shock unit.

Rear suspension specifications are listed in **Table 1**. **Tables 1-6** are found at the end of the chapter.

REAR WHEEL

Removal/Installation
(XT350)

1. Support the bike so that the rear wheel is off of the ground.
2. Unscrew the rear brake adjusting nut completely from the brake rod (**Figure 1**). Withdraw the brake rod from the brake lever and pivot it out of the way. Reinstall the adjusting nut to avoid misplacing it.
3. Remove the axle nut cotter pin. Then loosen and remove the axle nut (A, **Figure 2**).
4. Remove the right-hand chain adjuster (B, **Figure 2**).

5. Push the wheel forward to provide as much chain slack as possible. Then turn the rear wheel and slip the drive chain off of the sprocket.
6. Remove the axle and chain adjuster from the left-hand side. See **Figure 3**.
7. Pull the wheel back as required to disconnect the brake panel from the tab welded to the swing arm and remove the rear wheel.
8. Remove the right-hand axle spacer (**Figure 4**).
9. Remove the left-hand axle spacer (**Figure 5**).

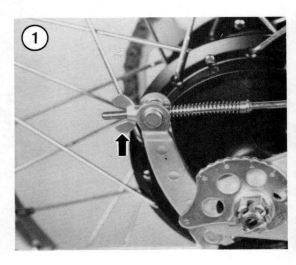

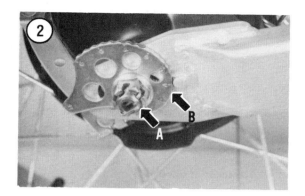

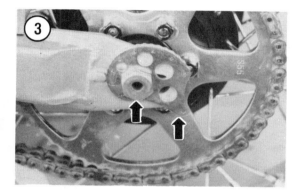

10. Remove the brake panel (A, **Figure 6**) from the right-hand side.

11. If necessary, remove the sprocket coupling as described under *Rear Sprocket Coupling (XT350)* in this chapter.

12. Install by reversing these removal steps. Note the following:

a. Be sure to install the axle spacers. See **Figure 4** (right-hand) and **Figure 5** (left-hand).

b. Make sure to align the groove in the brake panel (B, **Figure 6**) with the tab (**Figure 7**) welded to the swing arm.

c. If the drive chain was disconnected, install the clip on the drive chain master link and install it so that the closed end of the clip is facing the direction of chain travel (**Figure 8**).

d. Install the axle from the left-hand side.

e. Adjust the drive chain as described in Chapter Three.

f. Tighten the axle nut to the torque specification in **Table 2**. Install a new cotter pin.

g. After the wheel is completely installed, rotate it several times to make sure it rotates smoothly. Apply the brakes several times to make sure it operates correctly.

h. Adjust the rear brake as described under *Rear Brake Pedal Adjustment* in Chapter Three.

11

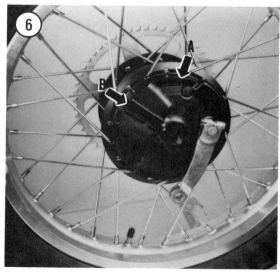

Removal/Installation
(TT350)

1. Support the bike so that the rear wheel is off of the ground.

2. Unscrew the rear brake adjusting nut completely from the brake rod (**Figure 9**). Withdraw the brake rod from the brake lever and pivot it out of the way. Reinstall the adjusting nut to avoid misplacing it.

> *NOTE*
> *The rear wheel can be removed by one of two methods. Refer to Step 3A or Step 3B.*

3A. To remove the rear wheel without removing the axle, perform the following:

   a. Loosen the rear axle nut (A, **Figure 10**).

   b. Push the wheel forward to provide as much chain slack as possible. Then push the drive chain over the side of the swing arm.

   c. Remove the axle bolts from the end of the swing arm (**Figure 11**).

   d. Pull the wheel to the back and remove it from the swing arm.

3B. To remove the rear wheel by removing the rear axle, perform the following:

   a. Loosen and remove the rear axle nut (A, **Figure 10**).

   b. Remove the right-hand chain adjuster (B, **Figure 10**).

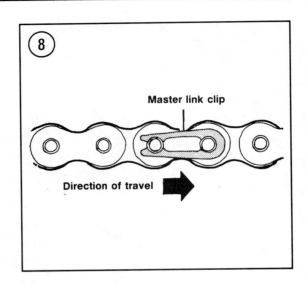

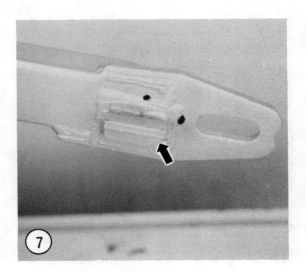

c. Push the wheel forward to provide as much chain slack as possible. Then turn the rear wheel and slip the drive chain off of the sprocket.

d. Remove the axle and chain adjuster from the left-hand side. See **Figure 12**.

e. Pull the wheel back as required to disconnect the brake panel from the tab welded to the swing arm and remove the rear wheel.

f. Remove the axle spacer (**Figure 13**) from the left-hand side.

g. Remove the brake panel (A, **Figure 14**) from the right-hand side.

4. Install by reversing these removal steps. Note the following:

a. Make sure to align the groove in the brake panel (B, **Figure 14**) with the tab (**Figure 7**) welded to the swing arm.

b. If the drive chain was disconnected, install the clip on the drive chain master link and install it so that the closed end of the clip is facing the direction of chain travel (**Figure 8**).

c. Install the axle from the left-hand side.

d. Adjust the drive chain as described in Chapter Three.

e. Tighten the axle nut to the torque specification in **Table 3**.

f. After the wheel is completely installed, rotate it several times to make sure it rotates smoothly. Apply the brake several times to make sure it operates correctly.

g. Adjust the rear brake as described under *Rear Brake Pedal Adjustment* in Chapter Three.

11

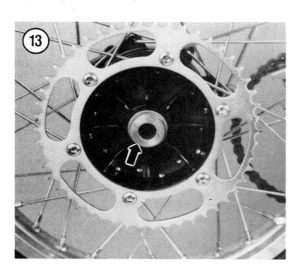

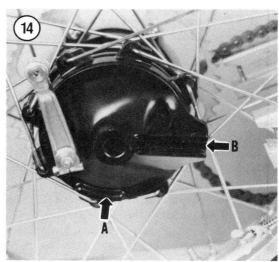

Inspection

Spokes loosen with use and should be checked prior to each race or weekend ride. The "tuning fork" method for checking spoke tightness is simple and works well. Tap each spoke with a spoke wrench or the shank of a screwdriver and listen for a tone. A tightened spoke will emit a clear, ringing tone, and a loose spoke will sound flat. All the spokes in a correctly tightened wheel will emit tones of similar pitch but not necessarily the same precise tone.

Bent, stripped or broken spokes should be replaced as soon as they are detected, as they can cause the destruction of an expensive hub. Unscrew the nipple from the spoke and depress the nipple into the rim far enough to free the end of the spoke, taking care not to push the nipple all the way in. Remove the damaged spoke from the hub and use it to match a new spoke of identical length. If necessary, trim the new spoke to match the original and dress the end of the thread with a thread die. Install the new spoke in the hub and screw on the nipple; tighten it until the spoke's tone is similar to the tone of the other spokes in the wheel. Periodically check the new spoke; it will stretch and must be retightened several times before it takes its final set.

Wheel rim runout is the amount of "wobble" a wheel shows as it rotates. You can check runout with the wheels on the bike by simply supporting the wheel off the ground and turning the wheel slowly while you hold a pointer solidly against a fork leg. Just make sure any wobble you observe isn't caused by your own hand.

Off the motorcycle, runout can be checked with the wheel installed on a truing stand (**Figure 15**).

> *NOTE*
> *A discarded rear swing arm mounted in a vise makes an ideal wheel truing stand.*

The maximum allowable lateral (side-to-side) and radial (up and down) play is listed in **Table 1**. Tighten or replace any bent or loose spokes. Always use the correct size spoke wrench (**Figure 16**) or you may damage the spoke nipple.

1. Draw the high point of the rim toward the centerline of the wheel by loosening the spokes in the area of the high point and on the same side as the high point, and tightening the spokes on the side opposite the high point. See **Figure 17**.

2. Rotate the wheel and check runout. Continue adjusting until the runout is within specification. Be patient and thorough, adjusting the position of the rim a little at a time. If you loosen 2 spokes at the high point 1/2 turn, loosen the adjacent spokes 1/4 turn. Tighten the spokes on the opposite side equivalent amounts.

3. Visually check the rear axle surface for cracks, deep scoring or excessive wear. Check axle runout with a set of V-blocks and dial indicator (**Figure 18**). The maximum allowable bend is 0.25 mm (0.01 in.). If you do not have access to the special tools, roll the axle on a flat surface and visually check the runout. Replace a bent axle. Do not attempt to straighten it.

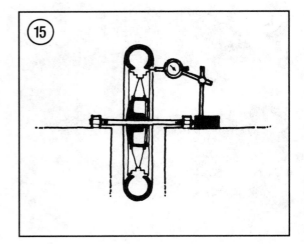

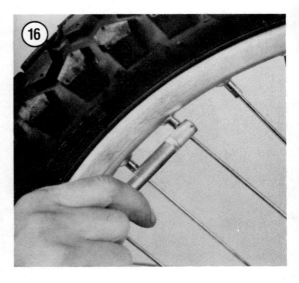

4. Check the rear hub oil seal for wear or damage.
5. Turn the inner bearing race (A, **Figure 19**) by hand and check for any signs of roughness or damage. Replace the bearings (as a set) as described under *Rear Hub* in this chapter.
6. Check the brake drum surface (B, **Figure 19**) for scoring, cracks or other damage. If necessary, refer to Chapter Twelve.

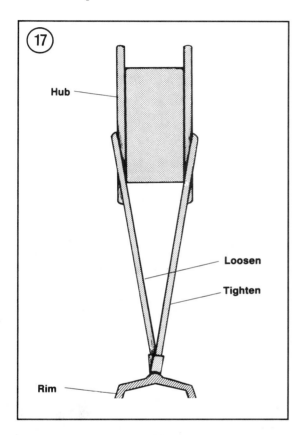

Rear Sprocket Coupling (XT350)

A cushion drive unit is used on XT350 models.
1. Remove the rear wheel as described in this chapter.
2. Pull the rear sprocket coupling (**Figure 20**) out of the rear wheel.
3. Remove the spacer inside the coupling (**Figure 21**).
4. Remove the rubber dampers from the hub (**Figure 22**).
5. Check the rear coupling oil seal for wear or damage.
6. Turn the inner bearing race by hand and check for any signs of roughness or damage. Replace the bearing as described under *Rear Hub* in this chapter.
7. Installation is the reverse of these steps.

11

REAR HUB

Refer to **Figure 23** (XT350) or **Figure 24** (TT350) for this procedure.

Do not remove bearings for periodic inspection as bearing removal normally damages the first bearing removed. Turn the inner bearing race (A, **Figure 19**) by hand and check for any signs of roughness or damage. Replace the bearings as a set.

1. Remove the rear wheel as described under *Rear Wheel Removal/Installation* in this chapter.
2. *XT350*: Remove the rear sprocket coupling as described in this chapter.
3. Remove all axle spacers.
4. Pull the brake panel out of the drum.
5. Remove the oil seal by carefully prying it out of the hub with a long screwdriver. Lift the screwdriver and work it around the seal every few degrees until it pops out of the hub. Prop a piece of wood or rag underneath the screwdriver to prevent from damaging the hub. See **Figure 25**.
6. Remove the left- and right-hand bearings and spacer. To remove them, insert a soft-aluminum or brass drift into one side of the hub. Push the spacer over to one side and place the drift on the inner race of the lower bearing (**Figure 26**). Tap the bearing out of the hub with a hammer, working around the perimeter of the inner race.
7. Remove the middle spacer and tap out the opposite bearing.
8. *XT350*: Remove the bearing from the coupling as follows:
   a. Pry the oil seal out of the coupling (**Figure 25**).
   b. Remove the circlip from the coupling housing (20, **Figure 23**).
   c. Tap the bearing (4, **Figure 20**) out of the coupling.
9. Thoroughly clean out the inside of the hub and coupling with solvent and dry with compressed air or a shop cloth.

NOTE
Fully sealed bearings are available from many good bearing specialty shops. Fully sealed bearings provide better protection from dirt and moisture that may get into the hub.

10. Pack non-sealed bearings with good-quality bearing grease. Work the grease in between the balls thoroughly. Turn the bearing by hand a couple of times to make sure the grease is distributed evenly inside the bearing.
11. Pack the wheel hub and distance collar with multipurpose grease.

NOTE
If a bearing has only one sealed side, install the bearing with the sealed side facing out.

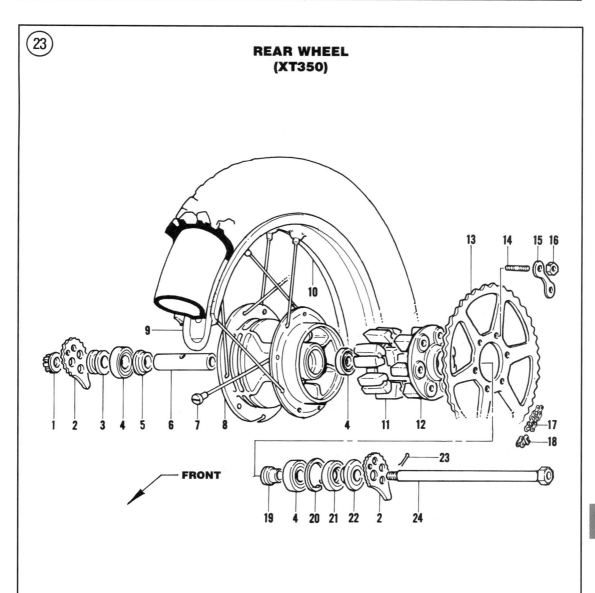

23

REAR WHEEL
(XT350)

1. Axle nut
2. Chain adjuster
3. Spacer
4. Bearing
5. Spacer
6. Spacer
7. Spoke
8. Hub
9. Rim lock
10. Rim
11. Rubber dampers
12. Damper flange
13. Rear sprocket
14. Stud
15. Lockwasher
16. Nut
17. Drive chain
18. Master link
19. Spacer
20. Circlip
21. Oil seal
22. Spacer
23. Cotter pin
24. Axle

FRONT

11

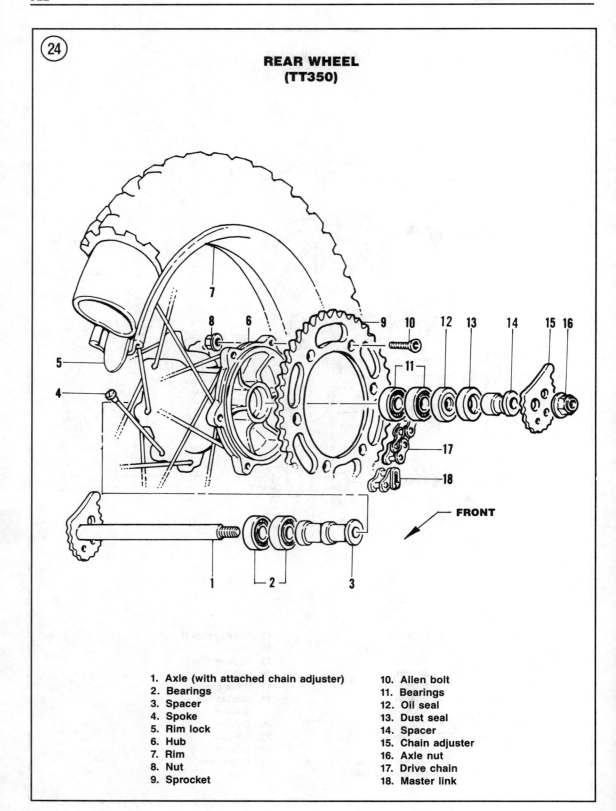

㉔

REAR WHEEL
(TT350)

FRONT

1. Axle (with attached chain adjuster)
2. Bearings
3. Spacer
4. Spoke
5. Rim lock
6. Hub
7. Rim
8. Nut
9. Sprocket
10. Allen bolt
11. Bearings
12. Oil seal
13. Dust seal
14. Spacer
15. Chain adjuster
16. Axle nut
17. Drive chain
18. Master link

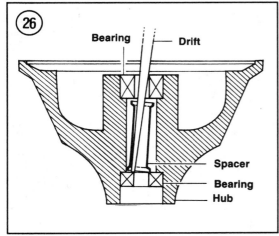

CAUTION
*When installing the bearings in the following procedures, tap the bearings squarely into place and tap on the outer race only (**Figure 27**). Use a socket (**Figure 28**) that matches the outer race diameter. Do not tap on the inner race or the bearing will be damaged. Be sure that the bearings are completely seated.*

12. Install one of the bearings.
13. Install the middle spacer. See 6, **Figure 23** (XT350) or 3, **Figure 24** (TT350).
14. Install the opposite bearing.
15. *TT350*: Install a new oil seal. Lubricate it with multipurpose grease and tap it squarely into the hub with a suitable size socket placed on the outside portion of the seal. Install the oil seal until it is at least flush with the hub.
16. *XT350*: Install the coupling housing bearing. Then install the circlip and a new oil seal (**Figure 29**).

SPROCKETS

This procedure describes service to the front and rear sprockets.

11

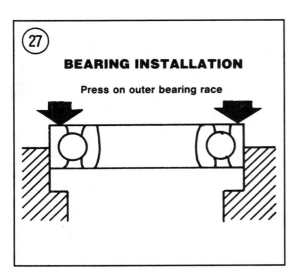

Front Sprocket
Removal/Installation

1. Remove the shift lever and the left-hand side cover. See **Figure 30**.
2. Remove the 2 sprocket lockplate mounting bolts (A, **Figure 31**).
3. Turn the sprocket lockplate (B, **Figure 31**) and slide it off of the countershaft.
4. Slide the drive sprocket (**Figure 32**) off of the countershaft.

> *NOTE*
> *If the drive chain is tight, loosen the rear axle nut and loosen the chain adjusters.*

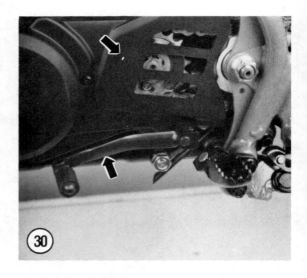

5. Installation is the reverse of these steps. Make sure to align the holes in the lockplate with the holes in the sprocket. Then install the lockplate mounting bolts (A, **Figure 31**) and tighten securely.
6. If the rear wheel axle nut was loosened, adjust the drive chain as described in Chapter Three.

Rear Sprocket
Removal/Installation

Refer to **Figure 23** (XT350) or **Figure 24** (TT350).
1. Remove the rear wheel as described in this chapter.

2A. *XT350*: Pry the lockwasher tabs away from the sprocket nuts. Then loosen and remove the nuts holding the sprocket to the sprocket housing. Remove the sprocket (**Figure 20**).

2B. *TT350*: Loosen the nuts at the back of the sprocket. Then remove the nuts and Allen bolts. Do not loosen the Allen bolts by turning the bolt; this will damage the Allen head. Remove the sprocket (**Figure 33**).

3. Check all of the sprocket fasteners for damage. Replace if necessary. On XT350 models, make sure to replace the lockwashers if the locking tabs are starting to break.

4. Assemble by reversing these disassembly steps. Tighten the bolts to the torque specification in **Table 2** (XT350); bend the lockwasher tabs over the sprocket nuts to lock them. On TT350 models, tighten the nuts securely.

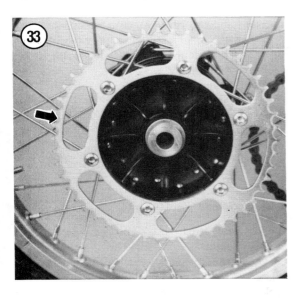

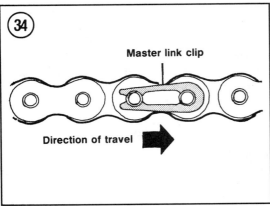

5. Adjust the drive chain as described in Chapter Three.

Inspection

Inspect the sprocket teeth. If they are visibly worn, replace the sprocket.

If the sprocket requires replacement, the drive chain is probably worn also and may need replacement. Refer to *Periodic Lubrication* and *Periodic Maintenance* in Chapter Three.

DRIVE CHAIN

Removal/Installation

1. Place a milk crate or wood block(s) under the frame so the rear wheel is off the ground.

2. Turn the rear wheel and drive chain until the master link is accessible.

3. Remove the master link clip (**Figure 34**) and remove the master link.

4. Slowly rotate the rear wheel and pull the drive chain off the drive sprocket.

5. Install by reversing these removal steps.

6. Install the clip on the master link so that the closed end of the clip is facing the direction of chain travel (**Figure 34**).

Service and Inspection

For service and inspection of the drive chain, refer to *Periodic Lubrication* and *Periodic Maintenance* in Chapter Three.

11

TIRE CHANGING AND TIRE REPAIRS

Refer to Chapter Ten.

MONOCROSS REAR SUSPENSION

All models use a single rear shock absorber/spring unit. The single shock controls swing arm movement through a compound linkage system with bearings at both ends of a vertical connecting rod and a relay arm.

The single shock/spring unit eliminates the requirement for periodic inspection for equal damping and spring tension between dual shocks. However, several suspension bushings carry a great load in the Monocross system and frequent lubrication and wear inspections are necessary to preserve good handling and prevent premature component wear.

MONOCROSS SHOCK ABSORBER

Removal/Installation (XT350)

Refer to **Figure 35** for this procedure.
1. Support the motorcycle with the rear wheel off the ground.
2. Remove the seat and both side covers.
3. Remove the rear shock absorber cover (**Figure 36**).
4. Remove the upper (**Figure 37**) and lower (A, **Figure 38**) pivot bolts.
5. Remove the lower pivot bolt thrust covers (**Figure 39**).
6. Remove the shock absorber (**Figure 40**).
7. Replace the pivot bolt washers and thrust covers (**Figure 41**) if worn or damaged.
8. Check the shock bushings for wear or damage. If necessary, replace them with a press.
9. To install, reverse the removal procedures. Note the following:
   a. Apply a lithium base grease to all pivot bolts.
   b. Tighten the pivot bolts to the torque specification in **Table 2**.

Removal/Installation (TT350)

Refer to **Figure 42** for this procedure.
1. Support the motorcycle with the rear wheel off the ground.
2. Remove the seat and both side covers.
3. Remove the carburetor as described in Chapter Eight.
4. Remove the rear shock absorber cover (A, **Figure 43**).

WARNING
Do not disconnect the reservoir to shock absorber hose when performing Step 5. In addition, do not drop the reservoir and lay it in a position where it could be damaged. The shock and reservoir is under extreme pressure and eye damage could occur from misuse.

5. Remove the shock absorber reservoir (**Figure 44**) from its mount on the left-hand side of the frame.
6. Remove the top and bottom shock (B, **Figure 43**) mounting bolts.
7. Remove the shock absorber.
8. To install, reverse the removal procedures. Note the following:
   a. Apply a lithium base grease to all pivot bolts.
   b. Tighten the pivot bolts to the torque specification in **Table 3**.
   c. Make sure the shock reservoir is properly mounted on the left-hand side of the frame.

Spring Removal

1. Remove the rear shock absorber as described in this chapter.
2. Measure the shock spring length with a tape measure and record the measurement.
3. Using the spanner wrench provided in your bike's tool kit (**Figure 45**), slowly loosen the spring locknut (A, **Figure 46**).
4. Loosen and remove the spring locknut (A, **Figure 46**) and the spring adjuster (B, **Figure 46**).
5. Remove the spring (C, **Figure 46**).
6. Reverse to install the spring. Install the spring to the length measurement recorded in Step 1. Refer to **Table 4** for spring preload length measurements.

Spring Preload Adjustment

1. Remove the rear shock absorber as described in this chapter.
2. Using the spanner wrench provided in your bike's tool kit (**Figure 45**), slowly loosen the spring locknut (A, **Figure 46**).
3. Turn the spring adjuster (B, **Figure 46**) to obtain the desired spring preload within the minimum and maximum limits specified in **Table 4**.
4. Tighten the spring locknut (A, **Figure 46**).
5. Install the shock absorber as described in this chapter.

Rebound Damping Adjustment

1. Rebound damping adjustments are made by turning the rebound adjuster ring at the shock's rear mount bracket. See B, **Figure 38** (XT350) or C, **Figure 43** (TT350). The adjuster on each model

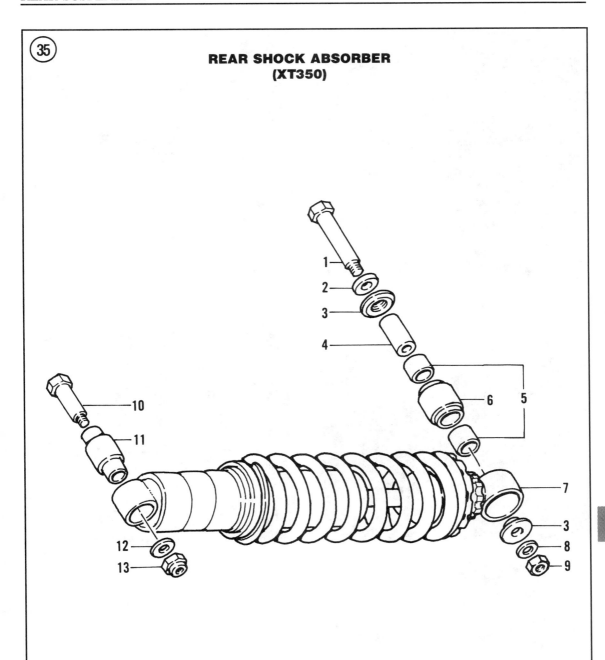

35

REAR SHOCK ABSORBER
(XT350)

1. Pivot bolt
2. Washer
3. Thrust cover
4. Collar
5. Bushings
6. Bushing
7. Shock assembly
8. Washer
9. Nut
10. Pivot bolt
11. Bushing
12. Washer
13. Nut

11

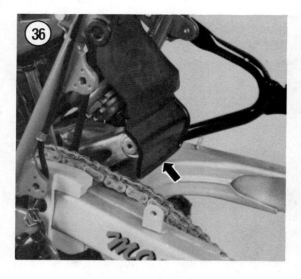

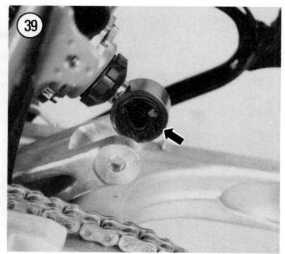

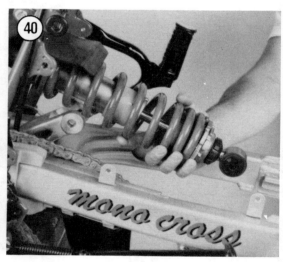

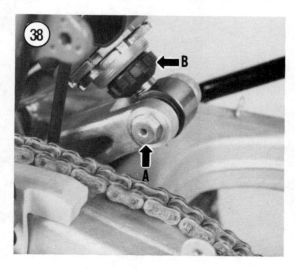

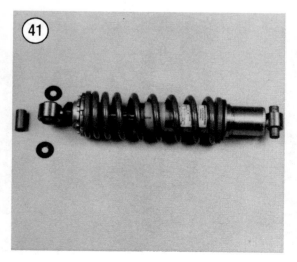

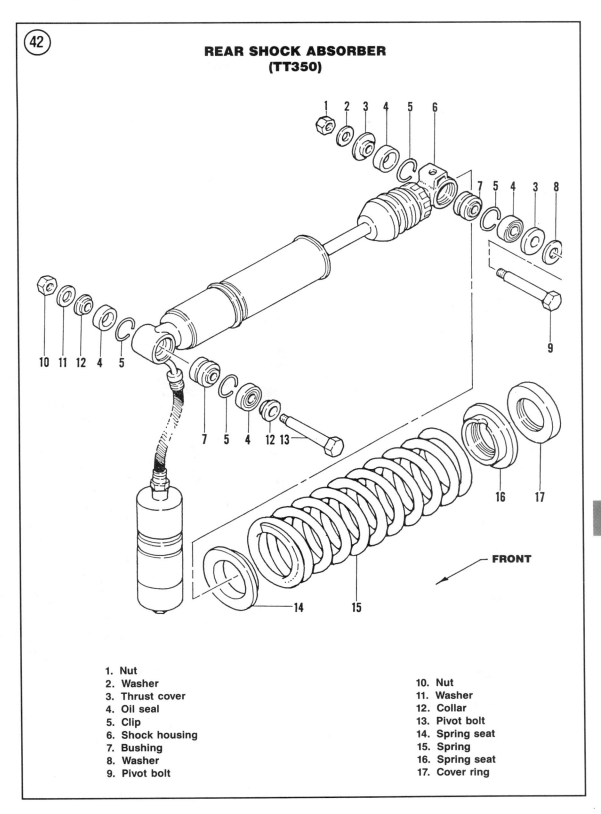

**REAR SHOCK ABSORBER
(TT350)**

1. Nut
2. Washer
3. Thrust cover
4. Oil seal
5. Clip
6. Shock housing
7. Bushing
8. Washer
9. Pivot bolt
10. Nut
11. Washer
12. Collar
13. Pivot bolt
14. Spring seat
15. Spring
16. Spring seat
17. Cover ring

FRONT

11

has a specific number of adjuster positions. See **Table 5** (XT350) or **Table 6** (TT350).

2. To make rebound damping stiffer, turn the adjuster *clockwise* as viewed from the left-hand side of the bike. Turn the adjuster *counterclockwise* to soften rebound damping. Always turn the adjuster ring by hand.

NOTE
When turning the adjuster on XT350 models, make sure it clicks into position. Otherwise the adjuster will automatically be set in the stiffest position.

CAUTION
*Do not turn the adjuster more than the maximum number of adjustments provided. See **Table 5 or Table 6.***

MONOCROSS LINKAGE

The Monocross linkage has a connecting rod mounted on the frame that connects to the relay arm. The relay arm attaches to the swing arm and the rear shock absorber. The bushings at all these joints must be inspected and lubricated according to the maintenance schedule (Chapter Three) and replaced when worn.

NOTE
Grease fittings (zerk fittings) are installed on some models. These can be used to periodically lubricate the bushings. Other models will require disassembly of the linkage for periodic lubrication.

Monocross Linkage
Disassembly/Inspection/Lubrication

Refer to **Figure 47** (XT350) or **Figure 48** (TT350) for this procedure.

1. Support the motorcycle with the rear wheel off the ground.
2. Remove the shock absorber covers. See **Figure 36** (XT350) or A, **Figure 43** (TT350).
3. Remove the pivot bolt connecting the shock absorber to the relay arm. See A, **Figure 38** (XT350) or B, **Figure 43** (TT350).

4. Remove the bolts securing the relay arm to the swing arm and connecting rod. Remove the relay arm.
5. Remove the bolt securing the connecting rod to the frame. Remove the connecting rod.
6. Clean the assembly in solvent and dry thoroughly. Flush the pivot bolts with solvent.
7. Referring to **Figure 47** or **Figure 48**, remove the bearing collars and thrust covers.
8. Inspect the bearings, sleeve bushing and pivot bolts. Replace any bearings that show excessive wear or damage. Bearing replacement requires a press. Refer to *Rear Suspension Bearing Replacement* in this chapter.
9. Lubricate all bearings, bushings and pivot bolts with lithium base wheel bearing grease.

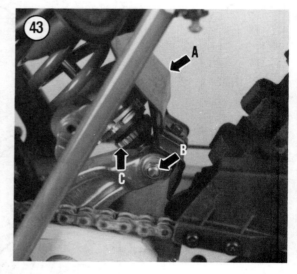

10. To assemble the linkage, reverse the disassembly procedure. Tighten all pivot bolts to the torque specifications in **Table 2** (XT350) or **Table 3** (TT350).

REAR SWING ARM

In time the bearings will wear beyond service limits and must be replaced. The condition of the bearings can greatly affect handling performance and if not replaced they can produce erratic and dangerous handling.

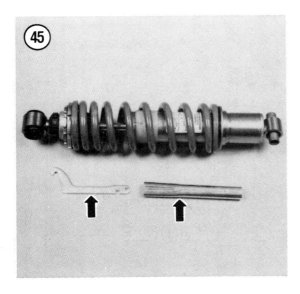

While bearing alignment differs between the 2 models, replacement is the same.

Removal/Installation

Refer to **Figure 49** (XT350) or **Figure 50** (TT350) for this procedure.
1. Remove the seat and both side covers.
2. Remove the rear wheel as described in this chapter.
3. Remove the shock absorber covers. See **Figure 36** (XT350) or A, **Figure 43** (TT350).
4. Remove the pivot bolt connecting the shock absorber to the relay arm. See A, **Figure 38** (XT350) or B, **Figure 43** (TT350).
5. Remove the bolts securing the relay arm to the connecting rod (**Figure 51**).
6. Grasp the swing arm as shown in **Figure 52** and try to rock it back and forth, pulling the top and pushing the bottom, then reversing. If you feel any more than a very slight movement of the swing arm, and the pivot bolt is correctly tightened, the bearings should be replaced.
7. Remove the swing arm pivot nut and bolt (**Figure 53**). If you have to knock the bolt out with a rod, take care not to damage the bearings or the end of the pivot bolt.
8. Remove the swing arm along with any external washers, shims or seals.
9. Inspect the bearings. If necessary, replace them as described in this chapter.
10. Inspect the chain guards and plates for wear or damage. Replace worn parts before the drive chain starts to wear into the swing arm.
11. Clean the old grease from all parts. After the parts have been cleaned and dry, apply a liberal amount of lithium waterproof wheel bearing grease to the bearings, sleeves and pivot shaft.
12. *TT350*: Perform the *Swing Arm Side Clearance Check and Adjustment* as described in this chapter.
13. Installation is the reverse of these steps. Note the following:
   a. Tighten the swing arm pivot shaft nut to the torque specification in **Table 2** (XT350) or **Table 3** (TT350).
   b. Tighten the relay arm pivot bolt to the torque specifications in **Table 2** (XT350) or **Table 3** (TT350).
   c. Adjust the drive chain as described in Chapter Three.

11

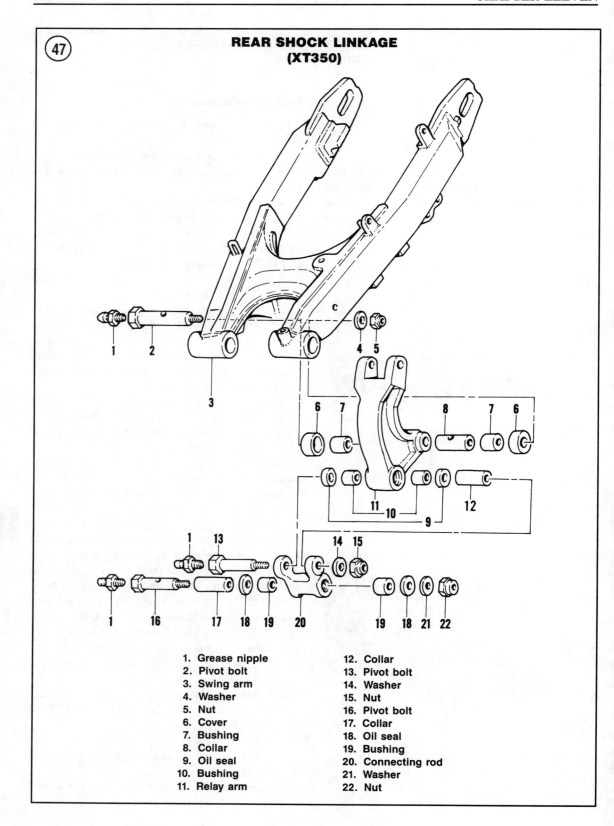

47

REAR SHOCK LINKAGE
(XT350)

1. Grease nipple
2. Pivot bolt
3. Swing arm
4. Washer
5. Nut
6. Cover
7. Bushing
8. Collar
9. Oil seal
10. Bushing
11. Relay arm
12. Collar
13. Pivot bolt
14. Washer
15. Nut
16. Pivot bolt
17. Collar
18. Oil seal
19. Bushing
20. Connecting rod
21. Washer
22. Nut

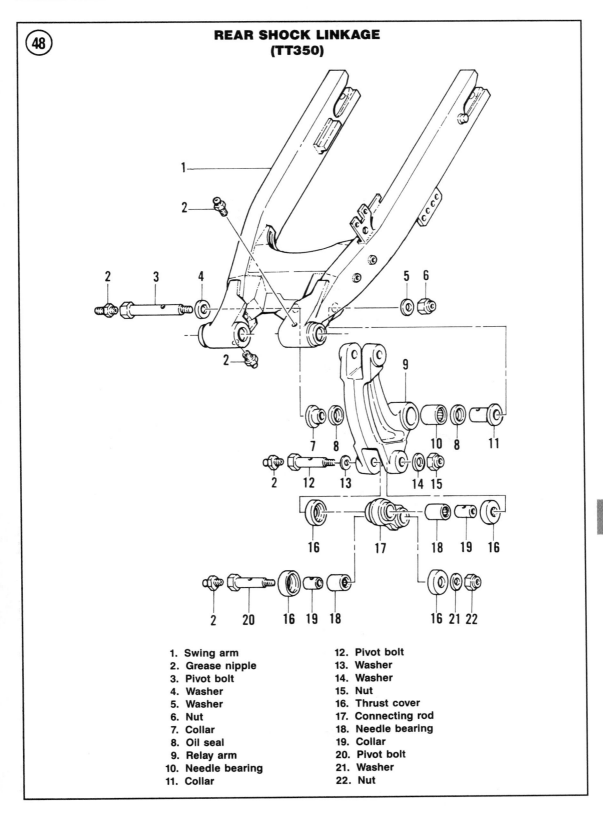

**REAR SHOCK LINKAGE
(TT350)**

1. Swing arm
2. Grease nipple
3. Pivot bolt
4. Washer
5. Washer
6. Nut
7. Collar
8. Oil seal
9. Relay arm
10. Needle bearing
11. Collar
12. Pivot bolt
13. Washer
14. Washer
15. Nut
16. Thrust cover
17. Connecting rod
18. Needle bearing
19. Collar
20. Pivot bolt
21. Washer
22. Nut

11

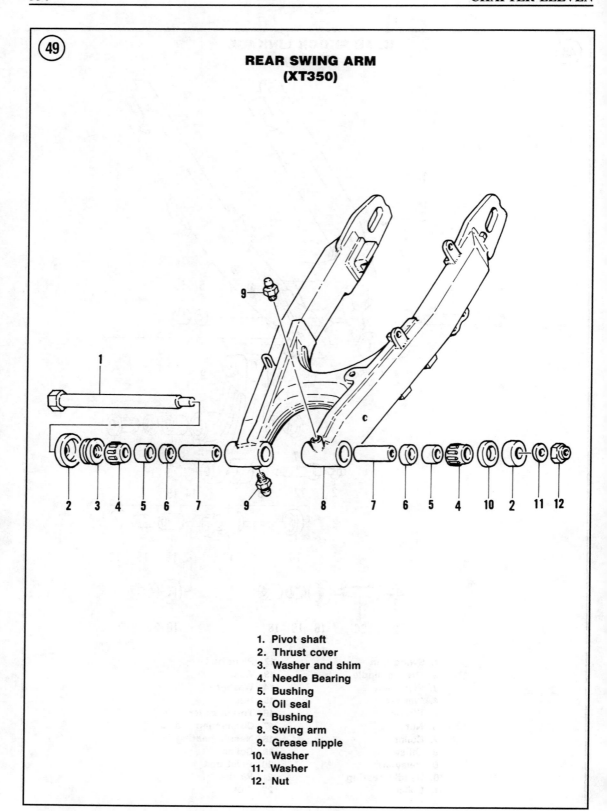

**REAR SWING ARM
(XT350)**

1. Pivot shaft
2. Thrust cover
3. Washer and shim
4. Needle Bearing
5. Bushing
6. Oil seal
7. Bushing
8. Swing arm
9. Grease nipple
10. Washer
11. Washer
12. Nut

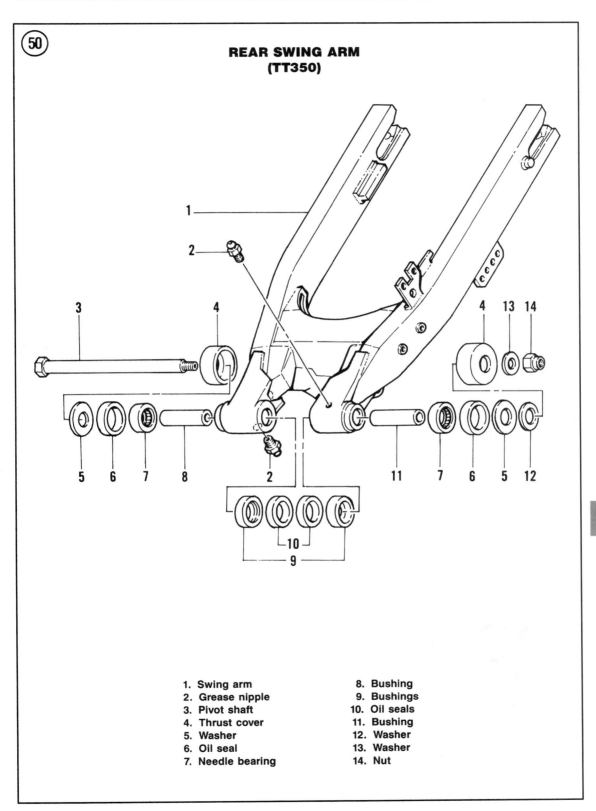

50

REAR SWING ARM
(TT350)

1. Swing arm
2. Grease nipple
3. Pivot shaft
4. Thrust cover
5. Washer
6. Oil seal
7. Needle bearing
8. Bushing
9. Bushings
10. Oil seals
11. Bushing
12. Washer
13. Washer
14. Nut

11

Swing Arm Side Clearance Check and Adjustment (TT350)

This procedure describes how to check and adjust swing arm side clearance. A vernier caliper will be required to check side clearance.

1. Remove the swing arm as described in this chapter.
2. Perform the following:
   a. Measure the width of the engine mount boss (W) with a vernier caliper (**Figure 54**).
   b. Measure the length of bushing A1 (**Figure 55**).
   c. Measure the length of bushing A2 (**Figure 55**).
3. Add the 3 measurements taken in Step 2. Record this measurement.
4. Measure length B in **Figure 55**. Record the measurement
5. Calculate swing arm side clearance by subtracting the recorded measurement in Step 4 from the recorded measurement in Step 3. The correct swing arm side clearance is 0.4-0.7 mm (0.016-0.028 in.).
6. If the side clearance is incorrect, 1 or 2 adjusting shims will be required. Adjusting shims are available in one thickness only: 0.3 mm (0.012 in.).
7. If only one shim is required, install it on the right-hand side. If 2 shims are required, install 1 shim on each side.

REAR SUSPENSION BEARING REPLACEMENT

Refer to **Figure 49** (XT350) or **Figure 50** (TT350) for this procedure.

1. Remove the swing arm as described in this chapter.
2. Secure the swing arm in a vise with soft jaws.

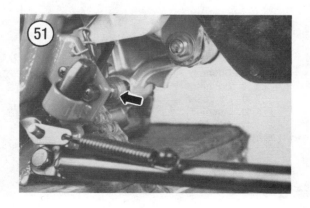

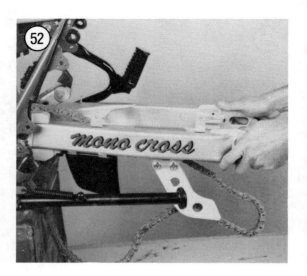

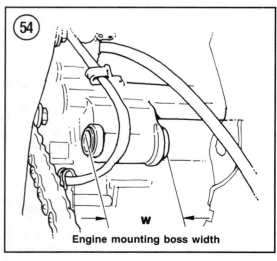

Engine mounting boss width

CAUTION
Do not remove the bearings just for inspection as they are usually damaged during removal.

3. Carefully tap out the bearing. Use a suitable size drift or socket and extension and carefully drive the bearing out from the opposite end.
4. Clean the swing arm thoroughly in solvent. Check the bearing mounting areas for cracks, wear or other damage.

NOTE
A press will be required to accurately and safely install the bearings.

5. Apply a light coat of lithium waterproof wheel bearing grease to all parts before installation.

NOTE
*On TT350 models, install the bearings to the specifications listed in **Figure 56***.

6. Using a press, install the new bearings.
7. After installing the bearings, liberally coat them with lithium waterproof wheel bearing grease.
8. Install the swing arm as described in this chapter.

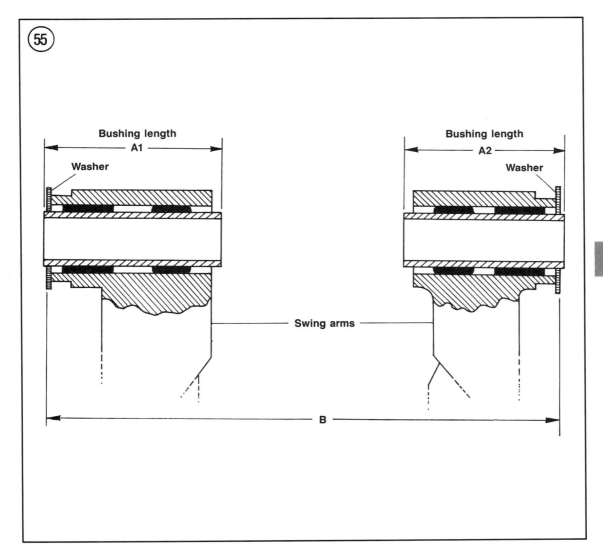

11

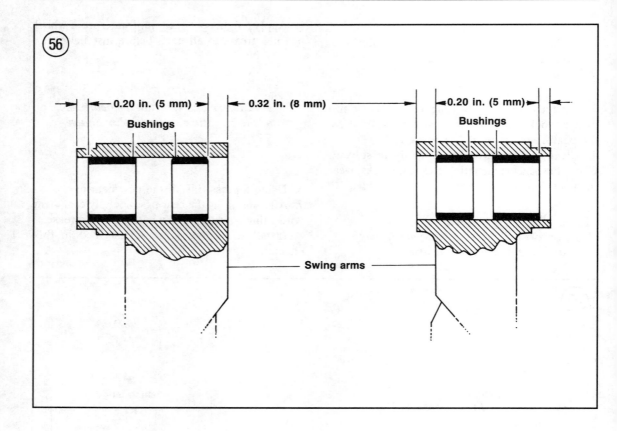

Table 1 REAR SUSPENSION SPECIFICATIONS

Rear wheel	
Travel	
XT350	220 mm (8.7 in.)
TT350	280 mm (11.02 in.)
Rim size	2.15 × 18
Rim runout	
Radial (up and down)	2.0 mm (0.08 in.)
Lateral (side to side)	2.0 mm (0.08 in.)
Swing arm free play limit	
End play	1.0 mm (0.04 in.)
Side play	
XT350	1.0 mm (0.04 in.)
TT350	0.2 mm (0.008 in.)

Table 2 REAR SUSPENSION TIGHTENING TORQUES—XT350

	N·m	ft.-lb.
Rear axle	107	77.4
Swing arm pivot shaft	85	61
Rear shock absorber	32	23
Relay arm		
At swing arm	59	42.7
At connecting rod	32	23
Rear sprocket bolts	30	22

Table 3 REAR SUSPENSION TIGHTENING TORQUES—TT350

	N·m	ft.-lb.
Rear axle	100	72
Swing arm pivot shaft	85	61
Rear shock absorber	32	23
Relay arm		
At swing arm	58	42
At connecting rod	32	23
Frame and connecting rod	58	42
Rear sprocket	*	*
* Not specified by Yamaha.		

Table 4 REAR SHOCK SPRING PRELOAD*

	Standard mm (in.)	Minimum mm (in.)	Maximum mm (in.)
XT350	226 (8.9)	213 (8.4)	234 (9.2)
TT350	247 (9.72)	234.5 (9.23)	257.5 (10.14)
* Turning the spring adjuster 1 complete turn changes the preload by 1 mm (0.04 in.).			

Table 5 REAR SHOCK DAMPING ADJUSTER—XT350

	Soft	Standard	Stiff
Shock position	1	2	3-4-5

Table 6 REAR SHOCK DAMPING ADJUSTER—TT350*

Standard Position Turns out	Minimum position Turns out	Maximum position Turns out
5	30	0
* To increase damping, turn the adjuster clockwise. To decrease damping, turning the adjuster counterclockwise.		

11

CHAPTER TWELVE

BRAKES

All models are equipped with a single disc brake unit on the front and a drum brake on the rear.

Disc brake specifications are listed in **Table 1**. Drum brake specifications are listed in **Table 2**. **Tables 1-3** are at the end of this chapter.

FRONT DISC BRAKE

The front disc brake is actuated by hydraulic fluid and controlled by a hand lever on the master cylinder. As the brake pads wear, the brake fluid level drops in the reservoir and automatically adjusts for wear.

When working on hydraulic brake systems, it is necessary that the work area and all tools be absolutely clean. Any tiny particles of foreign matter and grit in the caliper assembly or master cylinder can damage the components.

Consider the following when servicing the front disc brake.

1. Use only DOT 3/DOT 4 brake fluid from a sealed container (**Figure 1**).

2. Do not allow disc brake fluid to contact any plastic parts or painted surfaces as damage will result.

3. Always keep the master cylinder reservoir and spare cans of brake fluid closed to prevent dust or moisture from entering. This would result in brake fluid contamination and brake problems.

4. Use only disc brake fluid DOT 3/DOT 4 to wash parts. Never clean any internal brake components with solvent or any other petroleum base cleaners.

5. Whenever any component has been removed from the brake system, the system is considered "opened" and must be bled to remove air bubbles. Also, if the brake feels "spongy," this usually means there are air bubbles in the system and it must be bled. For safe brake operation, refer to *Brake Bleeding* in this chapter.

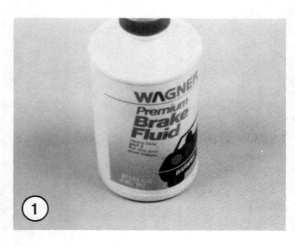

CAUTION
Disc brake components rarely require disassembly, so do not disassemble unless absolutely necessary. Do not use solvents of any kind on the brake system's internal components. Solvents will cause the seals to swell and distort. When disassembling and cleaning brake components (except brake pads) use new brake fluid.

FRONT BRAKE CALIPER
(XT350)

Front Brake Pad Replacement

There is no recommended time interval for changing the friction pads in the front disc brake. Pad wear depends greatly on riding habits and conditions.

To maintain an even brake pressure on the disc, always replace both pads in the caliper at the same time.

Refer to **Figure 2** for this procedure.

1. Place the bike on a stand so the front wheel clears the ground.

2. Remove the brake caliper retaining bolt (**Figure 3**) and pivot the brake caliper up.

3. Remove the inner and outer brake pads (**Figure 4**).

4. Check the condition of the upper and lower pad springs (**Figure 5**). Replace them if cracked or otherwise damaged.

5. Check the brake pad friction surface (**Figure 6**) for oil and dirt contamination. Also check the friction material for cracking or other damage. Replace the brake pads if the surface is contaminated or damaged.

6. Measure the brake pad friction thickness with a vernier caliper or ruler (**Figure 7**). Compare to the specifications in **Table 1**. Replace the brake pads if the friction thickness is too thin.

7. Check the end of the piston assembly in the caliper (**Figure 8**) for signs of fluid leakage or other abnormal conditions. Clean the pad recess with a soft brush. Do not use solvent, wire brush or any hard tool which could damage the cylinder and piston.

8. Carefully remove any rust or corrosion from the disc.

9. When new brake pads are installed in the caliper, the master cylinder brake fluid will rise as the caliper piston is repositioned. Clean the top of the master cylinder of all dirt. Remove the cap (**Figure 9**) and diaphragm from the master cylinder and slowly push the caliper piston (**Figure 8**) into the caliper. Constantly check the reservoir to make sure brake fluid does not overflow. Remove fluid, if necessary, prior to it overflowing. The piston should move freely in the caliper bore. If the piston doesn't move smoothly and there is evidence of it sticking in the caliper, the caliper should be removed and serviced as described in this chapter.

10. Perform the following:

   a. Make sure the upper and lower pad springs (**Figure 5**) are installed onto the caliper bracket.

   b. Align the pad arms with the caliper bracket and install the inner and outer brake pads (**Figure 4**). Install the brake pads so that the round portion on the back of the pad faces toward the *back* of the bike as shown in **Figure 10**. Make sure the friction material faces against the brake disc.

   c. Lower the brake caliper over the brake pads.

   d. Lightly coat the caliper retaining bolt with a lithium base grease.

   e. Install the retaining bolt (**Figure 3**) and tighten to the torque specification in **Table 3**.

11. Spin the front wheel and activate the brake lever as many times as required to refill the cylinder in the caliper and correctly locate the pads.

12. Refill the master cylinder reservoir, if necessary, to maintain the correct brake fluid level. Install the diaphragm and top cover (**Figure 9**).

WARNING
Use brake fluid clearly marked DOT 3/DOT 4 from a sealed container. Other types may vaporize and cause brake failure. Always use the same brand name; do not intermix as many brands are not compatible.

WARNING
Do not ride the motorcycle until you are sure the brake is operating correctly with full hydraulic advantage. If necessary, bleed the brake system as described in this chapter.

12

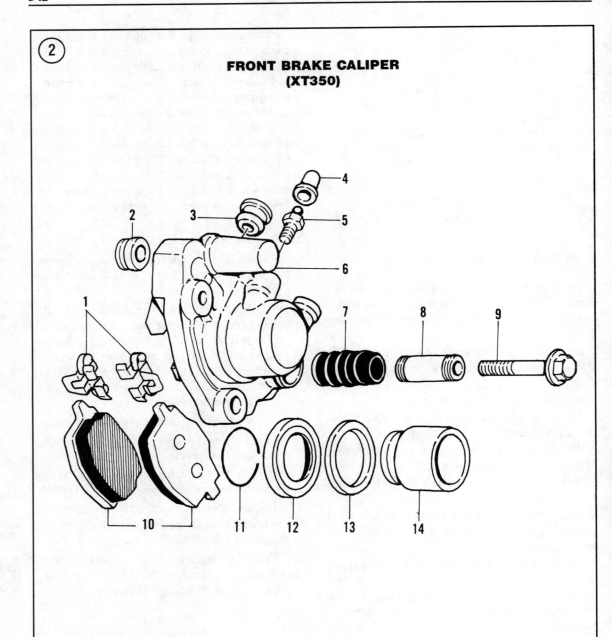

② FRONT BRAKE CALIPER
(XT350)

1. Springs
2. Boot
3. Inspection plug
4. Cap
5. Bleed valve
6. Caliper housing
7. Boot

8. Collar
9. Bolt
10. Brake pads
11. Clip
12. Dust seal
13. Piston seal
14. Piston

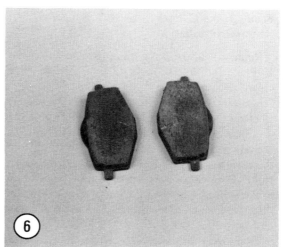

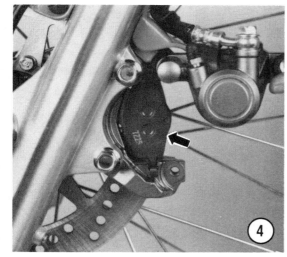

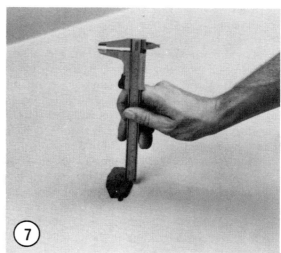

12

Front Brake Caliper
Removal/Installation

Refer to **Figure 2** for this procedure.

1. Place the bike on a stand so the front wheel clears the ground.

2. Loosen the brake caliper banjo bolt (**Figure 11**). Remove the banjo bolt and washers (**Figure 12**).

3. Place the end of the brake hose in a clean container. Operate the front brake lever to drain the master cylinder and brake hose of all brake fluid. Dispose of this brake fluid—never reuse brake fluid. To prevent the entry of moisture and dirt, cap the end of the brake line and tie the loose end up to the forks.

4. Remove the brake pads as described in this chapter.

5. Slide the brake caliper housing (**Figure 13**) off of the mounting bracket.

6. Remove the bolts (A, **Figure 14**) holding the brake caliper mounting bracket to the fork slider. Remove the mounting bracket (B, **Figure 14**).

7. Install by reversing these removal steps. Note the following.

8. See **Figure 14**. Install the mounting bracket (B) and the 2 mounting bolts (A). Tighten the bolts to the torque specification in **Table 3**.

9. Apply a light coat of Lithium base grease to the mounting bracket pivot rod (C, **Figure 14**).

10. Install the brake hose, with a sealing washer on each side of the fitting, onto the caliper (**Figure 12**). Install the banjo bolt (**Figure 11**) and tighten to the torque specification in **Table 3**.

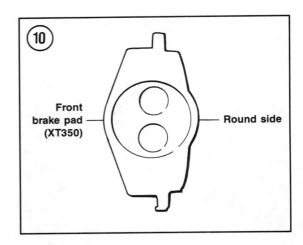

Front brake pad (XT350) — Round side

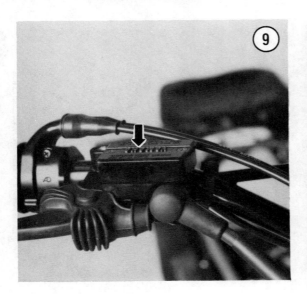

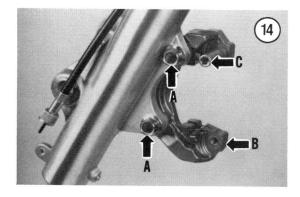

11. Install the brake pads and tighten the caliper bolt as described in this chapter.

12. Bleed the brake as described in this chapter.

> *WARNING*
> *Do not ride the motorcycle until you are sure the brake is operating properly.*

Disassembly/Inspection/Reassembly

Refer to **Figure 2** for this procedure.

1. Carefully pry the clip (**Figure 15**) out of the caliper bore.

2. Cushion the caliper piston with a shop rag. Then apply compressed air (**Figure 16**) through the brake line port to remove the piston (**Figure 17**).

> *WARNING*
> *Cushion the piston with a shop rag. Do not try to cushion the piston with your fingers, as injury could result.*

3. Remove the dust seal (**Figure 18**) from the piston.

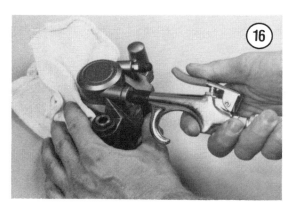

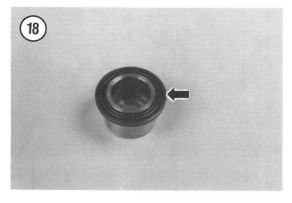

12

4. Remove the piston seal (**Figure 19**) from the piston bore.

5. Check the piston (**Figure 20**) and the piston bore (A, **Figure 21**) for deep scratches or other obvious wear marks. If either part is less than perfect, replace it.

6. Check the caliper housing for damage; replace if required.

7. Remove the bleed screw and check it for wear or damage.

8. Check the banjo bolt threads in the caliper. Check thread condition by screwing the bolt into the caliper.

9. Check the caliper bushings (B, **Figure 21**) for wear or damage; replace the bushings by pulling them out of the caliper. Reverse to install.

10. Check the mounting bracket (A, **Figure 22**) for cracks, breakage or other damage.

11. Check the pad springs (B, **Figure 22**) for cracks or damage. Replace if necessary.

12. Measure the brake pad friction thickness (**Figure 7**) with a vernier caliper or ruler. Compare to the specifications in **Table 1**. Replace the brake pads if the friction material is too thin.

13. Replace the piston (A, **Figure 23**) and dust (B, **Figure 23**) seals. Also check the clip (C, **Figure 23**) for cracks, breakage or other damage; replace if necessary.

14. Clean all parts (**Figure 24**) (except brake pads) with brake fluid.

15. Soak the new piston seal in fresh brake fluid. Coat the inside of the cylinder with fresh brake fluid prior to the assembly of parts.

16. Install the piston seal (A, **Figure 23**) into the second groove in the cylinder bore. See **Figure 19**.

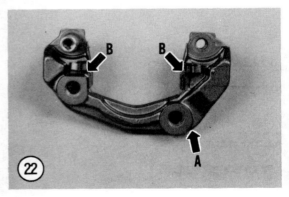

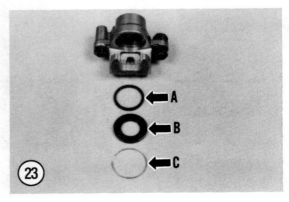

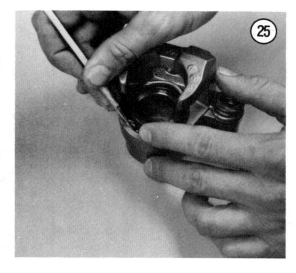

WARNING
Check that the seal fits squarely in the cylinder bore groove. If the seal is not installed properly, the caliper assembly will leak and braking performance will be reduced.

17. Fit the dust seal into the groove on the piston (**Figure 18**).
18. The piston has one open and one closed end (**Figure 18**). Insert the piston into the cylinder so that the open end faces out (**Figure 17**). Push the piston in all the way.
19. Fit the lip of the dust seal into the caliper bore (**Figure 25**). Work carefully so that you don't damage the dust seal. Make sure the seal fits into the caliper bore completely (**Figure 26**).
20. Install the clip (**Figure 15**) into the caliper bore groove. Make sure the clip completely seats in the groove.

FRONT BRAKE CALIPER (TT350)

Front Brake Pad Replacement

There is no recommended time interval for changing the friction pads in the front disc brake. Pad wear depends greatly on riding habits and conditions.

To maintain an even brake pressure on the disc, always replace both pads in the caliper at the same time.

Refer to **Figure 27** for this procedure.
1. Place the bike on a stand so the front wheel clears the ground.
2. Remove the brake caliper bolt (**Figure 28**) and pivot the caliper housing up (**Figure 29**) and away from the brake pads.
3. Remove the brake pads (**Figure 30**).
4. Remove the upper and lower (**Figure 31**) pad springs.
5. Check the condition of the upper and lower pad springs. Replace them if cracked or otherwise damaged. Install new pad springs if new brake pads are being installed.

12

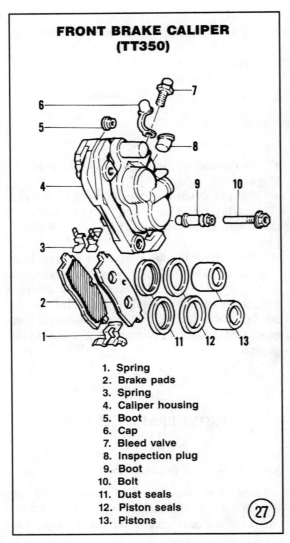

**FRONT BRAKE CALIPER
(TT350)**

1. Spring
2. Brake pads
3. Spring
4. Caliper housing
5. Boot
6. Cap
7. Bleed valve
8. Inspection plug
9. Boot
10. Bolt
11. Dust seals
12. Piston seals
13. Pistons

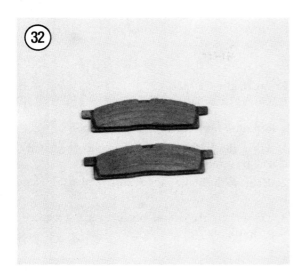

6. Check the brake pad friction surface (**Figure 32**) for oil and dirt contamination. Also check the friction material for cracking or other damage. Replace the brake pads if the surface is contaminated or damaged.

7. Measure the brake pad friction thickness (**Figure 33**) with a vernier caliper or ruler. Compare to the specifications in **Table 1**. Replace the brake pads if the friction thickness is too thin.

8. Check the end of the piston assembly in the caliper for signs of fluid leakage or other abnormal conditions. Clean the pad recess with a soft brush. Do not use solvent, wire brush or any hard tool which could damage the cylinder or piston.

9. Carefully remove any rust or corrosion from the disc.

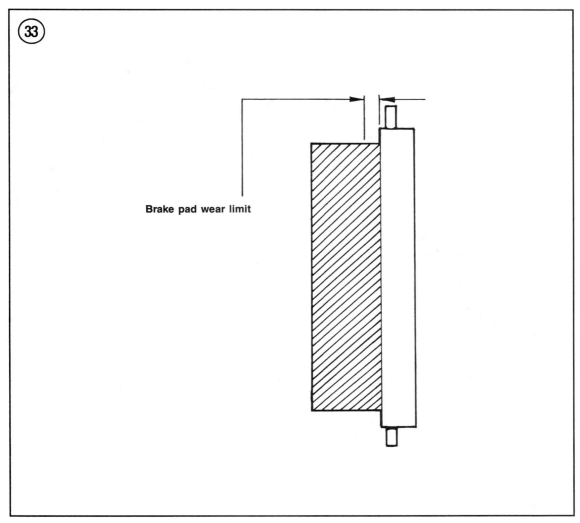

Brake pad wear limit

12

10. When new brake pads are installed in the calipers, the master cylinder brake fluid with rise as the caliper pistons are repositioned. Clean the top of the master cylinder of all dirt. Remove the cap (**Figure 34**) and diaphragm from the master cylinder and slowly push the caliper pistons into the caliper. Constantly check the reservoir to make sure brake fluid does not overflow. Remove fluid, if necessary, prior to it overflowing. The pistons should move freely in the caliper bores. If they don't, and there is evidence of them sticking in the caliper, the caliper should be removed and serviced as described in this chapter.

11. Push the caliper pistons in all the way to allow room for the new pads.

12. Perform the following:

    a. Install the upper and lower pad springs (**Figure 31**) onto the caliper bracket.

    b. Align the pad arms with the caliper bracket and install the inner and outer brake pads (**Figure 30**). Install the brake pads so that the round portion on the back of the pad faces toward the *back* of the bike as shown in **Figure 35**. Make sure the friction material faces against the brake disc.

    c. Lower the bike caliper over the brake pads.

    d. Lightly coat the caliper retaining bolt with a lithium base grease.

    e. Install the retaining bolt (**Figure 28**) and tighten to the torque specification in **Table 3**.

13. Spin the front wheel and activate the brake lever as required to refill the cylinder in the caliper and correctly locate the pads.

14. Refill the master cylinder reservoir, if necessary, to maintain the correct brake fluid level. Install the diaphragm and top cover (**Figure 34**).

> *WARNING*
> *Use brake fluid clearly marked DOT 3/DOT 4 from a sealed container. Other types may vaporize and cause brake failure. Always use the same brand name; do not intermix as may brands are not compatible.*

> *WARNING*
> *Do not ride the motorcycle until you are sure the brake is operating correctly with full hydraulic advantage.*

If necessary, bleed the brake system as described in this chapter.

Front Brake Caliper Removal/Installation

Refer to **Figure 27** for this procedure.

1. Place the bike on a stand so the front wheel clears the ground.

2. Remove the brake pads as described in this chapter.

3. Disconnect the caliper brake hose and washers. See **Figure 36**.

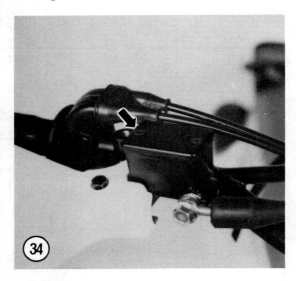

34

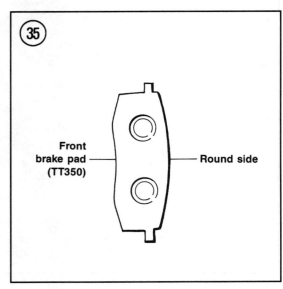

35

Front brake pad (TT350) — Round side

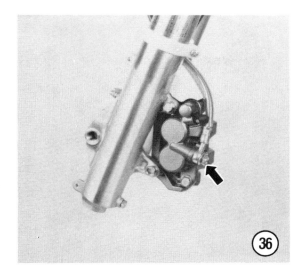

36

37

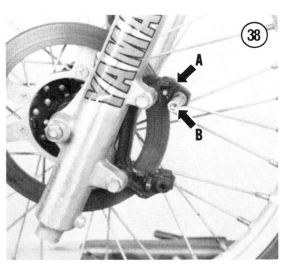

38

A

B

4. Place the end of the brake hose in a clean container. Operate the front brake lever to drain the master cylinder and brake hose of all brake fluid. Dispose of this brake fluid—never reuse brake fluid. To prevent the entry of moisture and dirt, cap the end of the brake line and tie the loose end up to the forks.

5. Pivot the caliper housing counterclockwise (**Figure 37**) and slide it off the caliper bracket.

6. Remove the 2 bracket bolts and remove the bracket (A, **Figure 38**).

7. Install by reversing these removal steps. Note the following.

8. Install the bracket (A, **Figure 38**) and the 2 mounting bolts. Tighten the bolts to the torque specification in **Table 3**.

9. Coat the bracket pivot rod (B, **Figure 38**) with a Lithium base grease.

10. Install the brake hose, with a sealing washer on each side of the fitting, onto the caliper. Install the banjo bolt and tighten to the torque specification in **Table 3**.

11. Install the brake pads and tighten the caliper bolt as described in this chapter.

12. Bleed the brake as described in this chapter.

> *WARNING*
> *Do not ride the motorcycle until you are sure the brake is operating properly.*

Disassembly/Inspection/Reassembly

Refer to **Figure 27** for this procedure.

12

> *NOTE*
> *Keep track of each piston's position. They must be reinstalled in their original cylinder.*

1. Cushion the caliper pistons with a shop rag. Then apply compressed air (**Figure 39**) through the brake line port to remove the pistons (**Figure 40**).

WARNING
Cushion the pistons with a shop rag.
Do not try to cushion the pistons with
your fingers, as injury could result.

2. Remove the dust (**Figure 41**) and piston (**Figure 42**) seals from each piston bore. See **Figure 43**.
3. Check the pistons (**Figure 44**) and piston bores (**Figure 45**) for deep scratches or other obvious wear marks. If either part is less than perfect, replace it. Measure the piston bores with a dial bore gauge and compare the bore diameters to the specification in **Table 1**. Replace the cylinder housing if there is an appreciable difference in bore measurements.
4. Check the caliper housing for damage; replace if needed.
5. Remove the bleed screw (A, **Figure 46**) and check it for wear or damage.
6. Check the banjo bolt threads in the caliper (B, **Figure 46**). Check thread condition by screwing the bolt into the caliper. Repair threads if they are stripped.

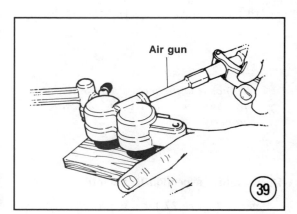

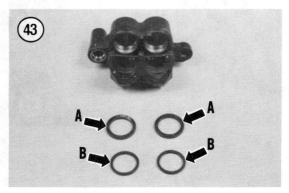

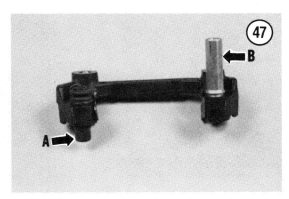

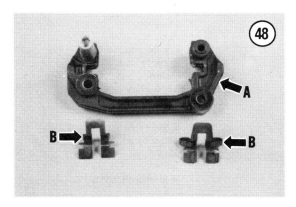

7. Check the bracket bushing (A, **Figure 47**) for wear or damage, replace the bushing if necessary by pulling it out of the bracket. Check the bracket pivot rod (B, **Figure 47**) for cracks scoring or damage, replace the bracket assembly if necessary.

8. Check the threads in the bracket (A, **Figure 48**) for damage. Repair threads if they are stripped.

9. Check the pad springs (B, **Figure 48**) for cracks or damage. Install each spring onto its bracket mounting position and check fit and tightness. Replace the pad springs as a set if any one spring is damaged.

10. Clean all parts (except brake pads) with brake fluid.

11. Soak the new dust seals and piston seals in fresh brake fluid. Coat the inside of the cylinder with fresh brake fluid prior to the assembly of parts.

12. Install a piston seal (A, **Figure 43**) into the second groove in each cylinder bore. See **Figure 42**.

13. Install a dust seal (B, **Figure 43**) into the first groove in each cylinder bore. See **Figure 41**.

> *WARNING*
> *Check that the seals fit squarely in the cylinder bore grooves. If the seals are not installed properly, the caliper assembly will leak and braking performance will be reduced.*

14. The pistons (**Figure 44**) have one open and one closed end. Install the pistons in their respective cylinder so that the open end faces out (**Figure 40**).

15. Coat the bracket pivot rod (B, **Figure 47**) with a lithium base grease.

16. Install the brake caliper assembly as described in this chapter.

FRONT MASTER CYLINDER (XT350)

Removal/Installation

Refer to **Figure 49**.

1. Place the bike on a stand so the front wheel clears the ground.

2. Remove the right-hand mirror.

3. Remove the caliper banjo bolt and washers (**Figure 50**) and disconnect the brake hose at the caliper.

12

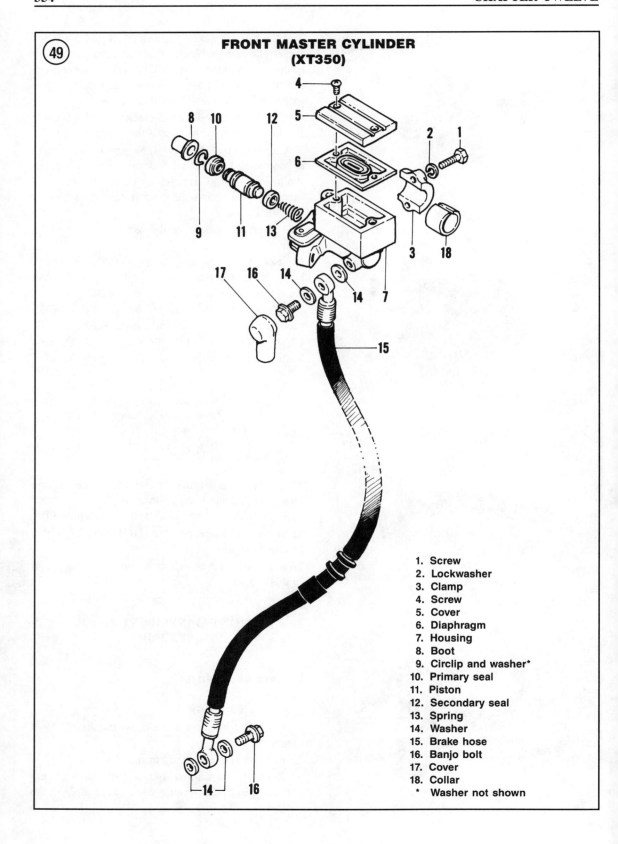

**FRONT MASTER CYLINDER
(XT350)**

1. Screw
2. Lockwasher
3. Clamp
4. Screw
5. Cover
6. Diaphragm
7. Housing
8. Boot
9. Circlip and washer*
10. Primary seal
11. Piston
12. Secondary seal
13. Spring
14. Washer
15. Brake hose
16. Banjo bolt
17. Cover
18. Collar
* Washer not shown

(50)

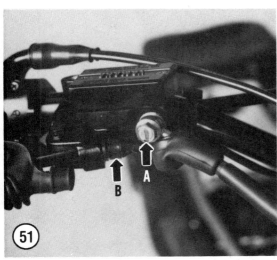

(51)

4. Place the end of the brake hose in a clean container. Operate the front brake lever to drain the master cylinder and brake hose of all brake fluid. Dispose of this brake fluid—never reuse brake fluid. To prevent the entry of moisture and dirt, cap the end of the brake line and tie the loose end up to the forks.

5. Loosen the brake hose banjo bolt (A, **Figure 51**) at the master cylinder. Remove the bolt and washers.

6. Disconnect the brake switch wire connector (B, **Figure 51**) at the master cylinder housing.

7. Remove the bolts (A, **Figure 52**) holding the master cylinder to the handlebar. Remove the master cylinder (B, **Figure 52**).

NOTE
Wrap the end of the brake hose in a plastic bag to prevent brake fluid from dripping onto other parts.

8. Installation is the reverse of these steps. Note the following.

9. Mount the master cylinder housing (B, **Figure 52**) onto the handlebar assembly. Install the handlebar clamp so that the arrow faces UP.

10. Remove the end of the brake hose from the plastic bag (discard the bag).

11. Install the brake hose, with a sealing washer on each side of the fitting, onto the master cylinder housing. Install the banjo bolt (A, **Figure 51**) and tighten to the torque specification in **Table 3**.

12. Install the brake hose, with a sealing washer on each side of the fitting, onto the caliper. Install the banjo bolt and tighten to the torque specification in **Table 3**.

13. Reconnect the front brake switch wire at the master cylinder (B, **Figure 51**).

14. Refill the master cylinder and bleed the brake as described in this chapter.

WARNING
Do not ride the bike until the front brake is working properly.

Disassembly

Refer to **Figure 49** for this procedure.

1. Remove the master cylinder as described in this chapter.

12

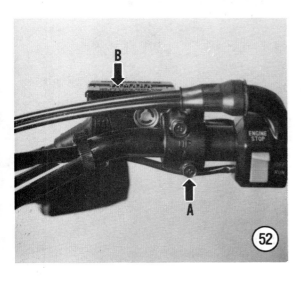

(52)

2. Remove the screws securing the reservoir cap and diaphragm. Pour out the remaining brake fluid and discard it. *Never* reuse brake fluid.

3. Remove the brake lever nut and pivot bolt (A, **Figure 53**) and remove the brake lever (B, **Figure 53**).

4. Remove the spring (**Figure 54**).

5. Remove the rubber boot (**Figure 55**) from the area where the hand lever actuates the internal piston.

6. Remove the piston circlip with circlip pliers (**Figure 56**).

CAUTION
Do not remove the primary or secondary cup from the piston, when removing the piston assembly in Step 7. Removing the cups from the piston will damage them.

7. Remove the piston assembly and washer (**Figure 57**).

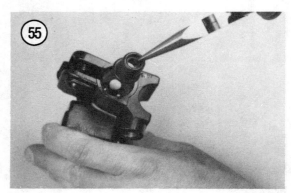

Inspection

1. Clean all parts (**Figure 58**) in fresh brake fluid. Place the master cylinder components on a clean lint-free cloth when performing the following inspection procedures.

2. Check the end of the piston (**Figure 59**) for wear caused by the hand lever. Replace the entire piston assembly if any portion of it requires replacement.

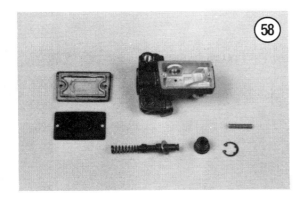

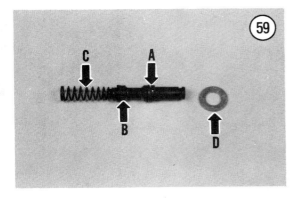

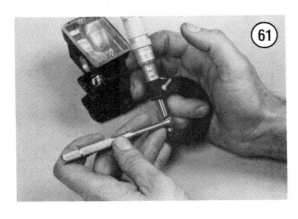

3. See **Figure 59**. Check the primary (A) and secondary (B) cups (on the piston) for damage, softness or swollen conditions. Replace the piston assembly if any cup is damaged.

4. Check the spring (C, **Figure 59**) for cracks or other damage; replace if necessary.

5. Check the washer (D, **Figure 59**) for cracks, bending or other damage. Replace if necessary.

6. Measure the cylinder bore with a small hole gauge (**Figure 60**). Then measure the gauge with a micrometer (**Figure 61**) to determine the master cylinder bore diameter. Replace the master cylinder if the bore exceeds the specifications given in **Table 1**.

7. Make sure the passages (**Figure 62**) in the bottom of the brake fluid reservoir are clear. Check the reservoir cap and diaphragm (**Figure 63**) for damage and deterioration. Replace if necessary.

8. Inspect the threads (**Figure 64**) in the master cylinder body where the brake hose banjo bolt screws in. Repair the threads if stripped or damaged.

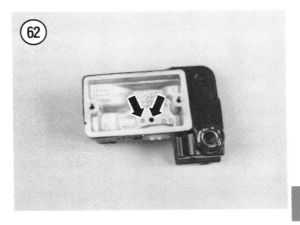

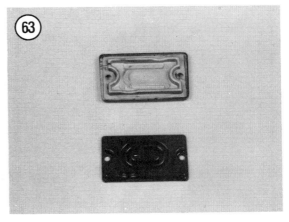

12

9. Check the circlip groove in the master cylinder bore (**Figure 65**) for cracks, breakage or other damage. Replace the master cylinder if the groove is damaged in any way.

10. Inspect the pivot hole (A, **Figure 66**) in the hand lever. If worn, replace the hand lever.

11. Check the brake lever pivot bolt (B, **Figure 66**) for excessive wear or thread damage; replace the bolt if necessary.

Assembly

1. Soak the new piston cups in fresh brake fluid for approximately 15 minutes to make them pliable. Coat the inside of the cylinder with fresh brake fluid prior to assembling the parts.

> *CAUTION*
> *When installing the piston assembly, do not allow the cups to turn inside out as they will be damaged and allow brake fluid to leak within the cylinder bore.*

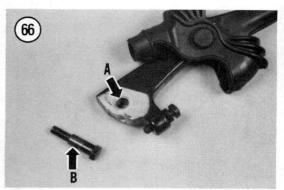

2. Install the spring onto the end of the piston as shown in (C, **Figure 59**). The small end of the spring should fit onto the piston.

3. Install the washer onto the end of the piston and insert the piston assembly (**Figure 57**) into the master cylinder bore.

4. Push the piston (**Figure 67**) into the master cylinder and install the circlip (**Figure 56**) into the master cylinder groove. Make sure the circlip is seated completely in the groove (**Figure 68**).

5. Install the rubber boot (**Figure 55**). Make sure the boot seats completely in the master cylinder (**Figure 69**).

6. Install the spring (**Figure 54**) into the master cylinder.

7. Install the brake lever (B, **Figure 53**) onto the master cylinder. Then install the pivot bolt (A, **Figure 53**) through the brake lever and secure it with the nut.

8. Install the diaphragm and cover. Do not tighten the cover screws at this time as fluid will have to be added later.

FRONT MASTER CYLINDER (TT350)

Removal/Installation

Refer to **Figure 70**.

1. Place the bike on a stand so the front wheel clears the ground.

2. Remove the caliper banjo bolt and washers (**Figure 71**) and disconnect the brake hose at the caliper.

3. Place the end of the brake hose in a clean container. Operate the front brake lever to drain the master cylinder and brake hose of all brake fluid. Dispose of this brake fluid—never reuse brake fluid. To prevent the entry of moisture and dirt, cap the end of the brake line and tie the loose end up to the forks.

4. Loosen the brake hose banjo bolt (**Figure 72**) at the master cylinder. Remove the bolt and washers.

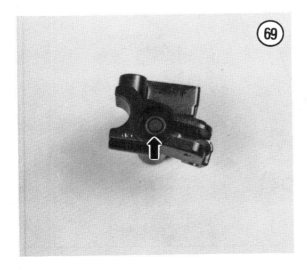

5. Remove the bolts (A, **Figure 73**) holding the master cylinder to the handlebar. Remove the master cylinder (B, **Figure 73**).

NOTE
Wrap the end of the brake hose in a plastic bag to prevent brake fluid from dripping onto other parts.

6. Installation is the reverse of these steps. Note the following.

7. Mount the master cylinder housing (B, **Figure 73**) onto the handlebar assembly. Install the handlebar clamp so that the arrow faces UP.

8. Remove the end of the brake hose from the plastic bag (discard the bag).

9. Install the brake hose, with a sealing washer on each side of the fitting, onto the master cylinder housing. Install the banjo bolt (**Figure 72**) and tighten to the torque specification in **Table 3**.

10. Install the brake hose, with a sealing washer on each side of the fitting, onto the caliper. Install the banjo bolt and tighten to the torque specification in **Table 3**.

11. Refill the master cylinder and bleed the brake as described in this chapter.

WARNING
Do not ride the bike until the front brake is working properly.

Disassembly

Refer to **Figure 70** for this procedure.

1. Remove the master cylinder as described in this chapter.

2. Remove the screws securing the reservoir cap and diaphragm. Pour out the remaining brake fluid and discard it. *Never* reuse brake fluid.

3. Remove the brake lever nut and pivot bolt (A, **Figure 74**) and remove the brake lever (B, **Figure 74**).

4. Remove the spring (**Figure 75**).

5. Remove the rubber boot (**Figure 76**) from the area where the hand lever actuates the internal piston.

6. Remove the piston circlip with circlip pliers (**Figure 77**).

12

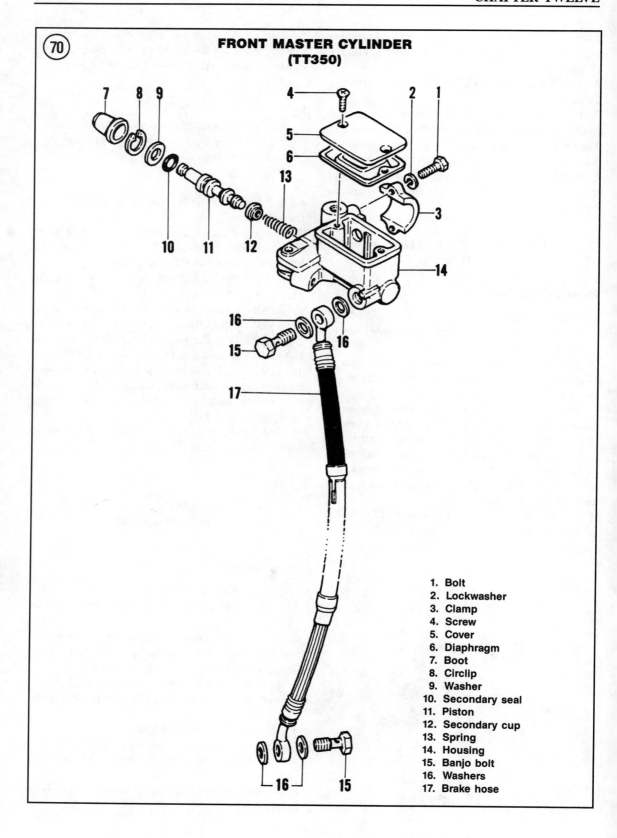

**FRONT MASTER CYLINDER
(TT350)**

1. Bolt
2. Lockwasher
3. Clamp
4. Screw
5. Cover
6. Diaphragm
7. Boot
8. Circlip
9. Washer
10. Secondary seal
11. Piston
12. Secondary cup
13. Spring
14. Housing
15. Banjo bolt
16. Washers
17. Brake hose

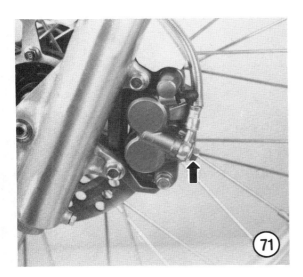

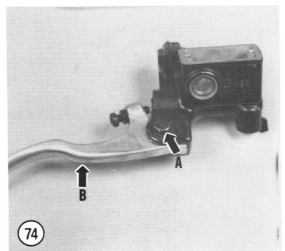

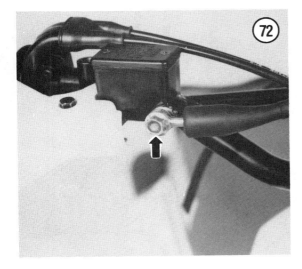

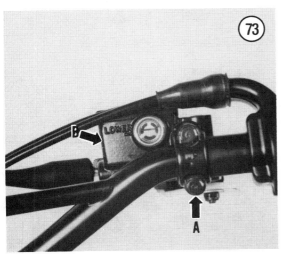

CAUTION
Do not remove the primary or second-ary cup from the piston when moving the piston assembly in Step 7. Re-moving the cups from the piston will damage them.

7. Remove the piston assembly and washer (**Figure 78**).

Inspection

1. Clean all parts (**Figure 70**) in fresh brake fluid. Place the master cylinder components on a clean lint-free cloth when performing the following inspection procedures.

2. Check the end of the piston (**Figure 79**) for wear caused by the hand lever. Replace the entire piston assembly if any portion of it requires replacement.

3. See **Figure 79**. Check the primary (A) and secondary (B) cups (on the piston) for damage, softness or swollen conditions. Replace the piston assembly if any cup is damaged.

4. Check the spring (C, **Figure 79**) for cracks or other damage; replace if necessary.

5. Check the washer (D, **Figure 79**) for cracks, bending or other damage. Replace if necessary.

6. Measure the cylinder bore with a small hole gauge (**Figure 80**). Then measure the gauge with a micrometer (**Figure 81**) to determine the master cylinder bore diameter Replace the master cylinder if the bore exceeds the specifications given in **Table 1**.

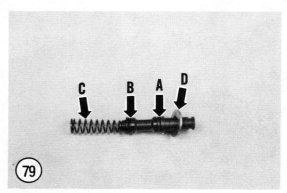

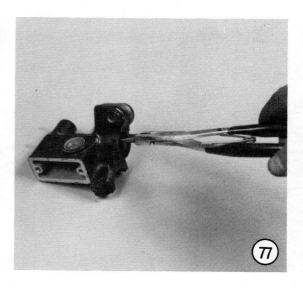

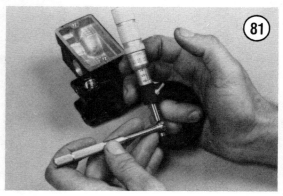

7. Make sure the passages (**Figure 82**) in the bottom of the brake fluid reservoir are clear. Check the reservoir cap and diaphragm (**Figure 83**) for damage and deterioration. Replace if necessary.
8. Inspect the threads (**Figure 84**) in the master cylinder body where the brake hose banjo bolt screws in. Repair the threads if damaged.
9. Check the circlip groove in the master cylinder bore for cracks, breakage or other damage. Replace the master cylinder if the groove is damaged in any way.
10. Inspect the pivot hole (**Figure 85**) in the hand lever. If worn, replace the hand lever.
11. Check the brake lever pivot bolt for excessive wear or thread damage; replace the bolt if necessary.

Assembly

1. Soak the new piston cups in fresh brake fluid for approximately 15 minutes to make them pliable. Coat the inside of the cylinder with fresh brake fluid prior to assembling the parts.

> *CAUTION*
> *When installing the piston assembly, do not allow the cups to turn inside out as they will be damaged and allow brake fluid to leak within the cylinder bore.*

2. Install the spring onto the end of the piston as shown in C, **Figure 79**. The small end of the spring should fit onto the piston.
3. Install the washer (D, **Figure 79**) onto the end of the piston and insert the piston assembly (**Figure 78**) into the master cylinder bore.

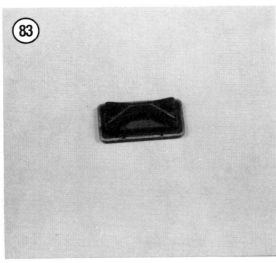

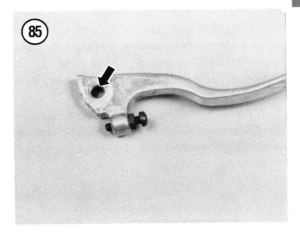

12

4. Push the piston into the master cylinder and install the circlip (**Figure 77**) into the master cylinder groove. Make sure the circlip is seated completely in the groove.

5. Install the rubber boot (**Figure 76**). Make sure the boot seats completely in the master cylinder (**Figure 86**).

6. Install the spring (**Figure 75**) into the master cylinder.

7. Install the brake lever (B, **Figure 74**) onto the master cylinder. Then install the pivot bolt (A, **Figure 74**) through the brake lever and secure it with the nut.

8. Install the diaphragm and cover. Do not tighten the cover screws at this time as fluid will have to be added later.

FRONT BRAKE HOSE REPLACEMENT

The brake hose should be replaced every 4 years or whenever it shows signs of wear or damage.

1. Place a container under the brake line at the caliper. Remove the banjo bolt and sealing washers at the caliper assembly (**Figure 71**).

2. Place the end of the brake hose in a clean container. Operate the front brake lever to drain the master cylinder and brake hose of all brake fluid. Dispose of this brake fluid–never reuse brake fluid.

3. Remove the banjo bolt and sealing washers at the master cylinder.

4. Disconnect the brake hose at the front fork. See **Figure 87** (XT350) or **Figure 88** (TT350).

5. Install a new brake hose in the reverse order of removal. Install new sealing washers and banjo bolts if necessary.

6. Tighten the banjo bolts to the torque specification listed in **Table 3**.

7. Refill the master cylinder with fresh brake fluid clearly marked DOT 3/DOT 4. Bleed the brake as described in this chapter.

WARNING
Do not ride the motorcycle until you are sure that the front brake is operating correctly.

(89)

FRONT BRAKE DISC

Inspection

It is not necessary to remove the disc from the wheel to inspect it. Small marks on the disc are not important, but radial scratches deep enough to snag a fingernail reduce braking effectiveness and increase brake pad wear. If these grooves are found, the disc should be resurfaced or replaced.

1. Measure the thickness around the disc at several locations with a vernier caliper or a micrometer (**Figure 89**). The disc must be replaced if the thickness at any point meets or exceeds the wear limit specified in **Table 1**.

2. Clean the disc of any rust or corrosion and wipe clean with lacquer thinner. Never use an oil based solvent that may leave an oil residue on the disc.

Removal/Installation

1. Remove the front wheel as described in Chapter Ten.

> *NOTE*
> *Place a piece of wood in the caliper in place of the disc. This way, if the brake lever is inadvertently squeezed, the piston(s) will not be forced out of the cylinder. If this does happen, the caliper might have to be disassembled to reseat the piston(s) and the system will have to be bled. By using the wood, bleeding is not necessary when installing the wheel.*

(90)

2. Remove the screws securing the disc to the wheel. See **Figure 90**.

3. Install by reversing these removal steps. Note the following.

4. Install the disc onto the front hub so that the holes drilled in the disc face in the direction as shown in **Figure 91**.

5. Tighten the screws securely.

BRAKE BLEEDING

This procedure is necessary only when the brakes feel spongy, there is a leak in the hydraulic system, a component has been replaced or the brake fluid has been replaced.

12

(91)

1. Flip off the dust cap from the brake bleeder valve
(**Figure 92**).

2. Connect a length of clear tubing to the bleeder
valve on the caliper (**Figure 93**). Place the other end
of the tube into a clean container. Fill the container
with enough fresh brake fluid to keep the end sub-
merged. The tube should be long enough so that a
loop can be made higher than the bleeder valve to
prevent air from being drawn into the caliper during
bleeding.

> *CAUTION*
> *Cover the front wheel, fender and fuel*
> *tank with a heavy cloth or plastic tarp*
> *to protect it from the accidental spill-*
> *ing of brake fluid. Wash any spilled*
> *brake fluid off of any surface immedi-*
> *ately, as it will destroy the finish. Use*
> *soapy water and rinse completely.*

3. Clean the top of the mater cylinder of all dirt and
foreign matter. Remove the cap and diaphragm. Fill
the reservoir to about 10 mm (3/8 in.) from the top.
Insert the diaphragm to prevent the entry of dirt and
moisture.

> *WARNING*
> *Use brake fluid clearly marked DOT*
> *3/DOT 4 only. Others may vaporize*
> *and cause brake failure. Always use*
> *the same brand name; do not intermix*
> *the brake fluids, as many brands are*
> *not compatible.*

4. Slowly apply the brake lever several times.
Hold the lever in the applied position and open
the bleeder valve about ½ turn (**Figure 93**). Allow the lever to travel to its limit. When this
limit is reached, tighten the bleeder valve. As the
brake fluid enters the system, the level will drop
in the master cylinder reservoir. Maintain the
level at about 10 mm (3/8 in.) from the top of the
reservoir to prevent air from being drawn into
the system.

5. Continue to pump the lever and fill the reservoir
until the fluid emerging from the hose is completely
free of air bubbles. If you are replacing the fluid,
continue until the fluid emerging from the hose is
clear.

> *NOTE*
> *If bleeding is difficult, it may be nec-*
> *essary to allow the fluid to stabilize*
> *for a few hours. Repeat the bleeding*
> *procedure when the tiny bubbles in*
> *the system settle out.*

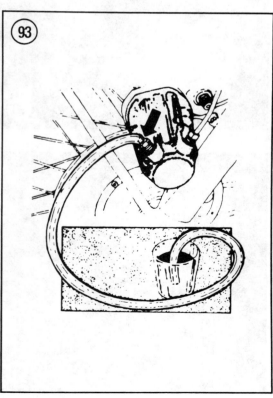

6. Hold the lever in the applied position and tighten the bleeder valve. Remove the bleeder tube and install the bleeder valve dust cap (**Figure 92**).

7. If necessary, add fluid to correct the level in the master cylinder reservoir. It must be above the level line.

8. Install the cap and tighten the screws.

9. Test the feel of the brake lever. It should feel firm and should offer the same resistance each time it's operated. If it feels spongy, it is likely that air is still in the system and it must be bled again. When all air has been bled from the system and the brake fluid level is correct in the reservoir, double-check for leaks.

> *WARNING*
> *Before riding the motorcycle, make certain that the front brake is working correctly by operating the lever several times. Then make the test ride a slow one at first to make sure the brake is working correctly.*

REAR DRUM BRAKE

Figure 94 illustrates the major components of a typical drum brake assembly. Activating the rear brake pedal pulls the rod which in turn rotates the camshaft. This forces the brake shoes out into contact with the brake drum.

Pedal free play must be maintained to minimize brake drag and premature brake wear, and maximize braking effectiveness. Refer to *Rear Brake Pedal Adjustment* in Chapter Three for complete adjustment procedures.

Glaze buildup on the brake shoes reduces braking effectiveness. The brake shoes should be removed and cleaned regularly to assure maximum brake shoe contact.

Disassembly

Refer to **Figure 95** (XT350) or **Figure 96** (TT350) when performing this procedure.

1. Remove the rear wheel as described in Chapter Eleven.

2. Pull the brake panel (**Figure 97**) out of the wheel.

12

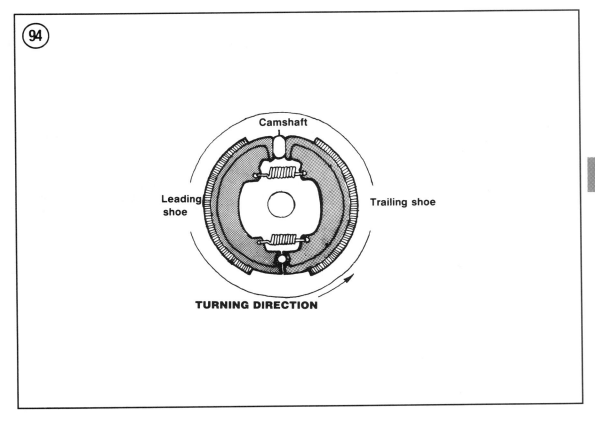

94

Camshaft

Leading shoe

Trailing shoe

TURNING DIRECTION

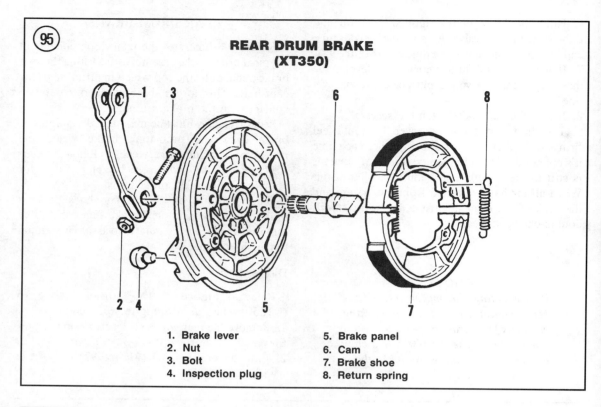

**REAR DRUM BRAKE
(XT350)**

1. Brake lever
2. Nut
3. Bolt
4. Inspection plug
5. Brake panel
6. Cam
7. Brake shoe
8. Return spring

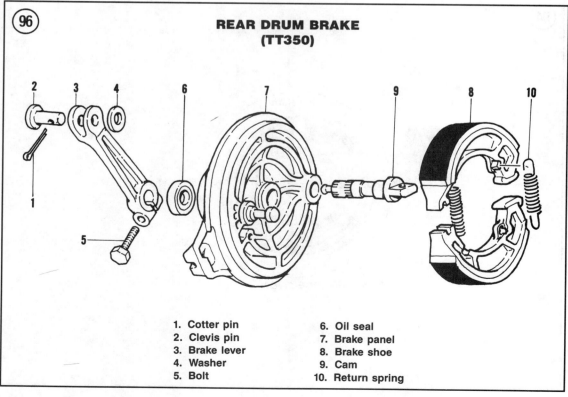

**REAR DRUM BRAKE
(TT350)**

1. Cotter pin
2. Clevis pin
3. Brake lever
4. Washer
5. Bolt
6. Oil seal
7. Brake panel
8. Brake shoe
9. Cam
10. Return spring

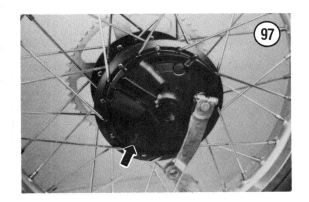

3. Remove the brake shoe assembly, including the return springs, from the brake panel. Pull both brake shoes from the panel (**Figure 99**).

4. Remove the return springs and separate the shoes (**Figure 100**).

5. Mark the position of the brake lever (A, **Figure 101**) as it is installed on the camshaft so it can be reinstalled in the same position.

6. Remove the bolt and nut (B, **Figure 101**) securing the brake lever to the cam. Remove the lever (A, **Figure 101**) and camshaft (A, **Figure 102**).

Inspection

1. Thoroughly clean and dry all parts except the linings.

2. Check the contact surface of the brake drum (A, **Figure 103**) for scoring. If there are deep grooves or the drum surface is severely damaged, the hub will have to be replaced. This type of wear can be avoided to a great extent if the brakes are disassembled and thoroughly cleaned after the bike has been ridden in mud or deep sand.

12

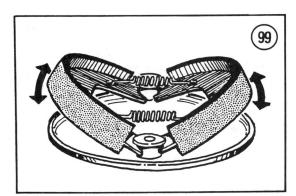

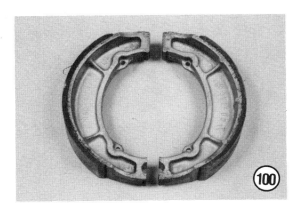

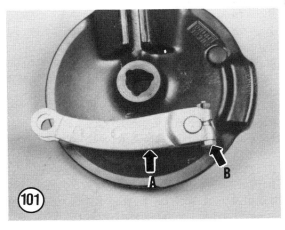

NOTE
If oil or grease is on the drum surface, clean it off with a clean rag soaked in lacquer thinner—do not use any solvent that may leave an oily residue.

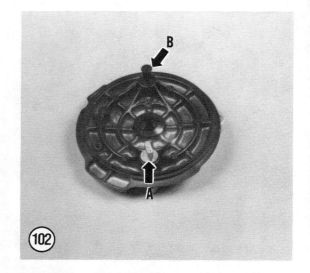

3. Check the sealed bearing (B, **Figure 103**) on the brake drum side for damage that would allow grease to enter the brake drum and contaminate the drum and brake shoes. Replace the bearing as described in Chapter Eleven.

4. Use vernier calipers (**Figure 104**) and check the inside diameter of the drum for out-of-round or excessive wear. Refer to **Table 2** for brake specifications.

5. Inspect the linings (**Figure 100**) for imbedded foreign material. Normal glaze buildup can be removed with a course grade sandpaper. Check for traces of oil or grease. If the linings are contaminated, they must be replaced.

6. Measure the brake lining thickness with a vernier caliper as shown in **Figure 105**. Replace the linings if worn to the wear limits in **Table 2**.

NOTE
Do not include the thickness of the aluminum shoe when measuring lining thickness.

7. Measure the length of the brake shoe spring with a vernier caliper as shown in **Figure 106**. Replace the springs if they exceed the wear limit specifications in **Table 2**. If the brake shoe springs are stretched, they will not fully retract the brake shoes from the drum, resulting in a power-robbing drag on the drums and premature wear of the linings.

8. Inspect the cam lobe and the pivot pin area on the shaft for wear and corrosion. Minor roughness can be removed with fine emery cloth.

9. Check the pivot pin on the brake panel (B, **Figure 102**) for cracks or damage.

10. Check the brake camshaft pinch bolt for thread strippage. Replace the bolt if necessary.

11. *TT350:* Replace the brake panel oil seal if damaged. Pry the seal out with a screwdriver. Install a new seal by driving it into the panel squarely with a suitable size socket.

Assembly

Refer to **Figure 95** (XT350) or **Figure 96** (TT350).

1. Grease the shaft, cam, and pivot post with a light coat of wheel bearing grease. Avoid getting any grease on the brake plate where the linings come in contact with it.

2. Insert the cam into the brake panel (A, **Figure 102**).

3. Install the brake lever (A, **Figure 101**) onto the brake cam. Make sure to align the 2 marks made during disassembly.

4. Hold the brake shoes in a V-formation with the return springs attached (**Figure 99**) and snap them in place on the brake panel. Make sure they are firmly seated on it (**Figure 98**).

5. Install the brake panel assembly into the brake drum. See **Figure 97**.

6. Install the rear wheel as described in Chapter Eleven.

7. Adjust the rear brake as described in Chapter Three.

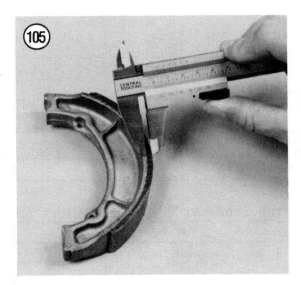

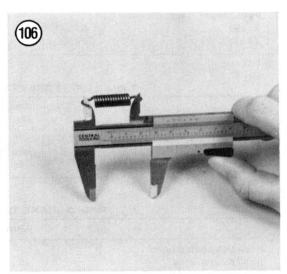

Tables are on the following page.

12

Table 1 DISC BRAKE SERVICE SPECIFICATIONS

Item	Specifications mm (in.)	Wear limit mm (in.)
Brake disc		
Outside diameter		
XT350	245 (9.65)	—
TT350	230 (9.06)	—
Thickness		
XT350	3.5 (0.14)	3.0 (0.12)
TT350	3.0 (0.12)	2.5 (0.10)
Brake pad thickness		
XT350	6.0 (0.24)	0.8 (0.03)
TT350	4.0 (0.16)	0.8 (0.03)
Master cylinder inside		
diameter	11.0 (0.4)	—
Brake caliper inside diameter		
XT350	34.9 (1.37)	—
TT350	26.99 (1.06)	—

Table 2 DRUM BRAKE SERVICE SPECIFICATIONS

Item	Specifications mm (in.)	Wear limit mm (in.)
Brake drum inside diameter	130 (5.12)	131 (5.16)
Brake lining thickness	4 (0.16)	2 (0.08)
Brake shoe spring free length	36.5 (1.44)	—

Table 3 BRAKE TIGHTENING TORQUES

	N•m	ft.-lb.
Brake hose banjo bolts	27	19
Brake caliper bolts	18	13
Brake caliper mounting bracket bolts		
XT350	35	25
TT350	30	22

INDEX

13

WIRING DIAGRAMS

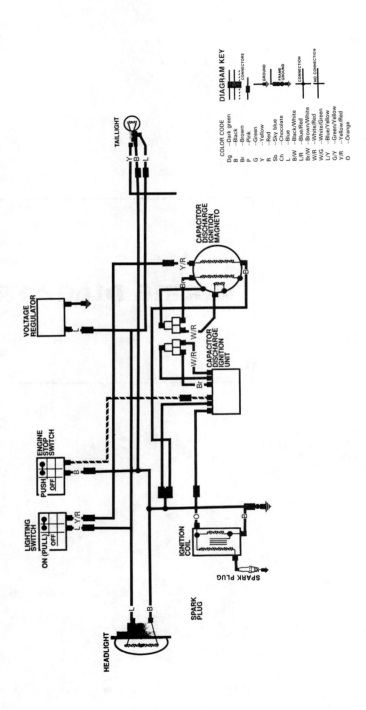

1986-1987 TT350

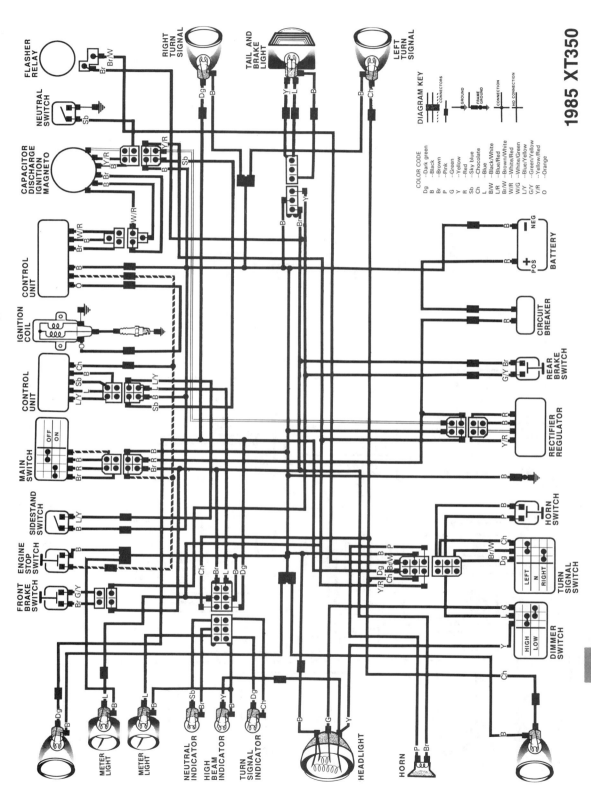

1985 XT350

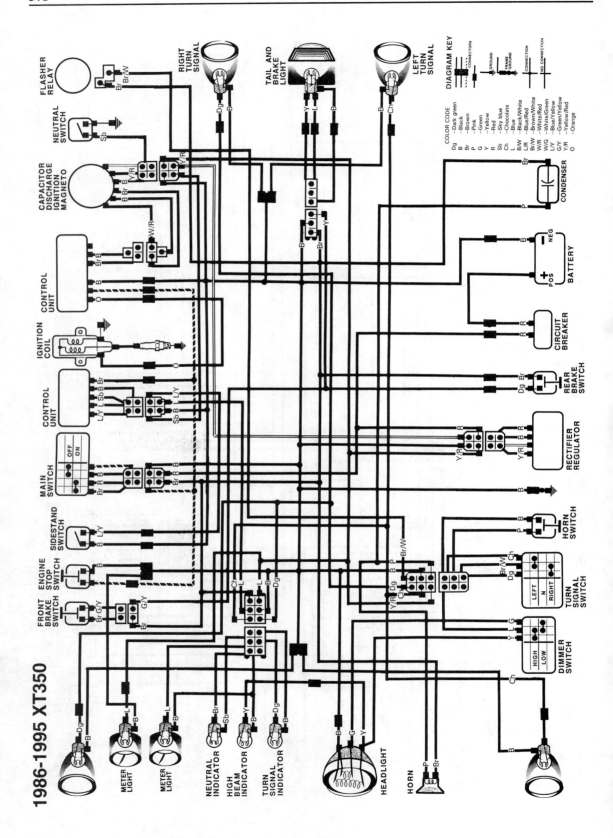

1986-1995 XT350

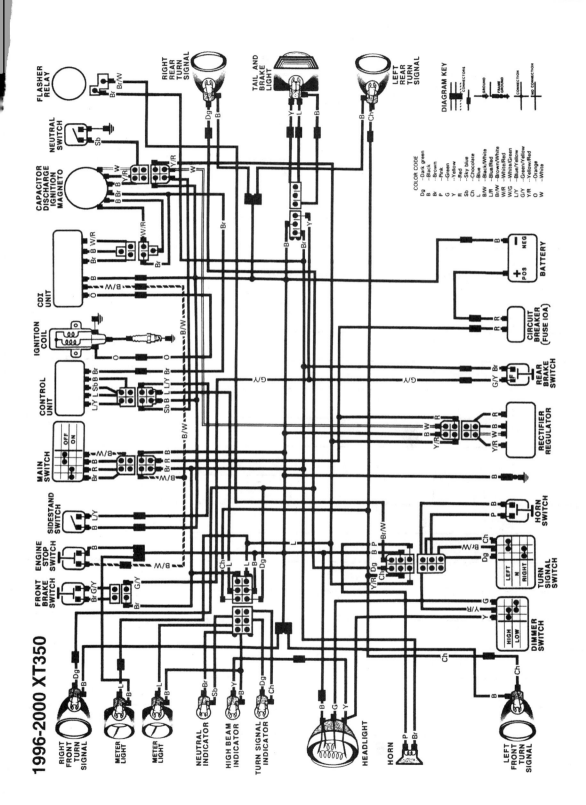

1996-2000 XT350

MAINTENANCE LOG

Date	Miles	Type of Service